Jean Negulesco

ALSO BY MICHELANGELO CAPUA

Anatole Litvak: The Life and Films (2015)
Janet Leigh: A Biography (2013)
William Holden: A Biography (2010)
Deborah Kerr: A Biography (2010)
Yul Brynner: A Biography (2006)
Vivien Leigh: A Biography (2003)
Montgomery Clift: A Biography (2002)

AND FROM MCFARLAND

Jean Negulesco
The Life and Films

MICHELANGELO CAPUA

McFarland & Company, Inc., Publishers
Jefferson, North Carolina

LIBRARY OF CONGRESS CATALOGUING-IN-PUBLICATION DATA

Names: Capua, Michelangelo, 1966– author.
Title: Jean Negulesco : the life and films / Michelangelo Capua.
Description: Jefferson, North Carolina : McFarland & Company, Inc., Publishers, 2017 | Includes bibliographical references and index.
Identifiers: LCCN 2017027989 | ISBN 9781476666532 (softcover : acid free paper) ∞
Subjects: LCSH: Negulesco, Jean. | Motion picture producers and directors—United States—Biography.
Classification: LCC PN1998.3.N3845 C37 2017 | DDC 791.4302/33092 [B] —dc23
LC record available at https://lccn.loc.gov/2017027989

BRITISH LIBRARY CATALOGUING DATA ARE AVAILABLE

**ISBN (print) 978-1-4766-6653-2
ISBN (ebook) 978-1-4766-2752-6**

© 2017 Michelangelo Capua. All rights reserved

No part of this book may be reproduced or transmitted in any form or by any means, electronic or mechanical, including photocopying or recording, or by any information storage and retrieval system, without permission in writing from the publisher.

Front cover: Director Jean Negulesco, circa mid–1940s (Photofest)

Printed in the United States of America

*McFarland & Company, Inc., Publishers
Box 611, Jefferson, North Carolina 28640
www.mcfarlandpub.com*

To my beloved parents
Alberto and Marisa

Table of Contents

Preface   1

1. A Background in Art   3
2. Welcome to America!   11
3. The King of the Shorts   25
4. The Warner Years   39
5. The Zanuck Touch   53
6. Consistency   67
7. In Glorious CinemaScope!   82
8. La Loren   93
9. His Best of Everything   110
10. Twilight   124

Filmography   133

Chapter Notes   219
Bibliography   225
Index   227

Preface

While researching my book on Anatole Litvak, I was struck by several uncanny similarities between Litvak and Jean Negulesco. Both were expatriate Eastern European Academy Award nominees who entered Hollywood working first for Warner Bros. and later for 20th Century–Fox. Both were womanizers who eventually married models and moved back to Europe at the end of their career. And they have never received the appreciation they deserve. They have been either forgotten or dismissed by the critics, and subsequently have been two of the most underrated Hollywood directors in history. Strangely, Negulesco and Litvak belong to a sort of a limbo classification of filmmakers that were not considered "great" (whatever that means), but at the same time never defined as B directors. I was still very surprised to discover how little has been written on either of them. Negulesco's autobiography was often accused of being inaccurate and full of embellished anecdotes, not really sticking to the facts. His persistent justification for his inaccuracies: "My memory fails, I overlooked some details. I wrote what happened to me, what I think happened to me and what happened without my knowledge. I mean the facts that I don't remember but I'm sure I've been part of them."

Once I completed a book on Litvak, Negulesco seemed an obvious subject for my next book.

Often Jean Negulesco has been dismissed by critics as a "women's director" or as "the prince of melodrama" (Douglas Sirk probably being the king), associating him with only sappy, sentimental stories. After watching his body of work, I had an entirely different opinion. I saw a sensitive, skilled man who created a certain style of filming with an slick look that showed elements of class and tenderness. I realized that he was instead a director *tout court*. His curriculum included more than 50 shorts of various subjects along with documentaries, film noir, comedy, action, musical and of course melodrama. Over the past years, *The Mask of Dimitrios* (1944), *Humoresque* (1948), *Johnny Belinda* (1948), *Road House* (1948), *How to Marry a Millionaire* (1953) and *Daddy Long Legs* (1955) have become classics, even though many do not know they were made by the same director.

The Romanian-born Negulesco was more than a competent filmmaker. He was witty and sophisticated, had refined taste and was a talented painter. His love for the arts led him to live in several European cities before he came to America—first Washington, D.C., and then New York. He eventually arrived in Hollywood, where he was hired to work as a freelance sketcher on the sets of a couple of films, and later as an assistant director. The first film on which he was credited as a solo director, *Singapore Woman*

(1941), was a flop. Three years later, *The Mask of Dimitrios,* was warmly received by the critics, and the public allowed him to start a career that spanned over three decades.

People in the industry were impressed by his kindness and generosity, especially his actors whom he allowed complete freedom in expressing their craft. Negulesco often helped them with his sure touch and sense of detail. His main goal was to tell a good story and, when possible, demonstrate his sense of humor. How his stars accomplished this goal was irrelevant to him as long as it showed up on the screen. And like Alfred Hitchcock, who would "sign" his films appearing as an extra, Negulesco signed with his artwork. In most of his films, there's at least one of his paintings or sketches included in the set dressing.

Undeniably, Jean Negulesco belongs to the Golden Age of Hollywood directors who transformed the American cinema. He was certainly not the greatest or the most individual of directors, but was definitely the first real master of CinemaScope, managing to make some unforgettable films.

In writing this book, I have benefited from the help of many individuals and institutions and from the assistance and support of friends. I would like to thank Yaakov Perry, Beatrice Nadalutti and the helpful staff of the British Film Institute Library in London, in particular Anastasia Kerameos and Sarah Currant, for their kind help; the staff of the Performing Art Library at Lincoln Center in New York; Christine Kruger from the Margaret Herrick Library of the Academy of Motion Picture Arts and Sciences in Beverly Hills; Madame Annick Verron from Bibliothèque du Cinéma François Truffaut in Paris; the staff of the Frick Art Reference Library—The Frick Collection in New York; the staff of the Museum of Modern Art Library in Manhattan; the staff of the British Library Humanities Reading Room in London; Biblioteca Renzo Renzi-Cineteca di Bologna; Biblioteca Nazionale di Napoli; Dollie R. Banner from Jerry Ohlinger's Movie Materials in New York; and Malcolm Abbey, an old friend of Jean Negulesco.

I'd also like to thank Alain Garel and François Guerif for their kind permission to quote from their article, "Jean Negulesco: Une Histoire d'Amour," which first appeared in *La Revue du Cinéma* in March 1990.

My deepest gratitude goes to my editor and friend Stuart Williams. Without his help and kind generosity, completing this book would have been impossible.

1
A Background in Art

"If you are too skillful, your work becomes gloomy, boring, dull. Difficult situations challenge you and you do better things."—Jean Negulesco

At the dawn of the twentieth century, Craiova was a flourishing, vibrant city in Oltania, a historical province in Romania. Situated between the Danube, the Southern Carpathians and the Olt river, the city was attractive to aristocratic intellectuals and populated by affluent bourgeoisie. Wealthy businessman Georghe Negulescu—"Ghiţă"—was one of them. He was the owner of Calat, one of Craiova's most elegant hotels, and of several other buildings in the city center, including the Court House. His business was not limited to real estate, but also included fisheries of the Danube, with the exclusivity of trading on both Romanian and Bulgarian riverbanks.

In spite of his wealth, Ghiţă's life seemed somehow incomplete. His marriage to former teacher Elena Hirliceanu—"thin and delicate like a leaf," as Jean later described his mother—was "cursed" by having four pretty daughters, Georgeta, Aneta, Virginia and Gabriela. Finally, on February 29, 1900, the streak was broken when the entire street heard the Negulescu girls scream from number 10, "It's a boy. It's a boy!" Elena had given birth to a healthy baby named Ian (after famous Romanian playwright Ion Luca Caragiale). A three-day celebration was held at the Negulescus with friends and relatives visiting to wish Ghiţă and Elena happiness and success with their newborn.

The history of his name, first and last, bears some explanation. On some documents his name is spelled Ioan or Jan. He often went by the nickname Iancu. He changed his first name to Jean when he moved to Paris beause it sounded more French. Later when he moved to the South of France he changed his last name from Negulescu to Negulesco, signing his artwork as Jean Negulesco, a name he kept for the rest of his life and used on documents when becoming an American citizen.

In the six years following his birth, another boy, George, and two more daughters, Athena and Sabina, were welcomed into the Negulescu family. In their large house, surrounded by a garden and a large courtyard and furnished with rugs, paintings and silver, the eight children grew up with all the comforts, surrounded by an attentive staff of servants, free to play. Every Sunday and holidays they accompanied Elena to the church, where she sat on a high chair inscribed with her name and they would pray together during the mass.

At age five, Iancu was an outgoing child with a head full of curly black hair. His parents and siblings would tease him, calling him Ianculeţ after his curly hair. Ghiţă began to spend more quality time with his son. On many afternoons, he took him to the Bazilescu Brewery, where moving images were shown on a bare wall. They also strolled together in one of Craiova's gardens.

Ghiță wanted little Iancu to follow in his footsteps as a businessman or, better yet, a respected politician. But from an early age, Iancu showed an interest in the arts. At 12, he proved to be a talented sketcher, impressing his siblings with an amazing sketchbook full of drawings inspired by a duel from a silent swashbuckler film he recently watched at an open air cinema in the Minerva Gardens. Some of his schoolteachers had already predicted Iancu's promising artistic career, encouraging him to participate in a national drawing contest. He won first place. His parents enrolled him at Carol I National College, the most prestigious high school in Craiova. Many years later, Negulesco recounted:

> I began to paint during World War I. At that time, my father wanted me to be a violinist. He was very rich.... He wanted that his child would play the violin. But my fingers were too big. My teacher used to say, "He's not good for the violin, he is more suitable for a violoncello." Our province, Oltania, was occupied by the Germans and we left as refugees to the Northern part of Romania, and I lost my violin. At the time the easiest and cheapest things to buy were pencils and sheets of paper. Therefore, I began to sketch. It's for this reason that all my life I've always said that talent is a result of work. We are born with a capacity to learn something faster or to struggle. Yet if you are too skillful, your work becomes gloomy, boring, dull. Difficult situations challenge you and you do better things...[1]

In another interview given the same year, Negulesco said, "When I was 14 I knew already my vocation: politics are for the politicians, business trading left me indifferent since I could not understand its mechanisms and I did not like to study.... For this reason, at an early age, I decided to leave my paternal house and go to Vienna because I wanted to be a painter. But World War I forced me to return home."[2]

When the Great War broke out, Germans invaded the southern part of Romania. Economic uncertainty threatened the country's stability and Ghiță was forced to move his wife and children to Iași, the new capital of Romania. It was located in the northeastern region of Moldavia, away from the military front. Like all Romanians, the Negulescus faced a period of great hardship, but still Ghiță tried to give to his children the best possible upbringing. Upon their arrival in Iași, Iancu was asked to join the local hospital branch as a Boy Scout. After a short training period, he was assigned to assist the Red Cross, serving in trains that carried wounded soldiers from the front to the local hospitals.

While in Iași, Iancu attended a concert given by the great composer and violinist George Enescu, who was touring the country entertaining war refugees, orphans and widows. Mesmerized by the virtuoso music, Iancu sketched the silhouette of the maestro. The sketch was displayed in the window of a local bookstore, sparking curiosity among the admiring passersby. A few days later, it was sold to Enescu. Ian was ecstatic: Not only had he received recognition for his art, he'd also earned his first income. Sketching and painting suddenly became his passion.

When the worst was over, the family returned to Craiova. Ghiță had to face reality and accept Iancu as an artist. He arranged for a small workshop near his home after his son swore that he would resume his studies, which had been interrupted by the war. Iancu kept his promise and received a baccalaureate diploma with honors. There was a small exhibition of his artwork in Craiova; he was later awarded with a scholarship that allowed him to attend the National School of Fine Arts in Bucharest. Regardless of his son's artistic achievement, Ghiță continued to hope that his son would make art a hobby

1. A Background in Art

Jean Negulesco showing his parents' portraits.

and eventually carry on the family business. But, to his father's chagrin, Iancu proved to be very resolute about moving to Bucharest. A factor that influenced Iancu's choice to accept the scholarship: a Bucharest girl, two years his senior, with whom he had fallen in love. It was not a coincidence when he rented a small apartment in the same building where his girlfriend and her mother lived. He spent all his time in their company when he was not busy attending classes at the art institute.

There are at least three different accounts of what happened to Iancu during his time in Budapest. In his autobiography, he revealed that he quickly abandoned his studies, mesmerized by the bohemian lifestyle of his girlfriend and her mother. Both of them artists, they taught him "to reproduce in pastel colors the official portraits of King Ferdinand and Queen Marie and sold them to public offices for a good price. So I forgot my studies at the academy; and a life of kings and queens, love and commercial artistic pursuits, opened for me."[3] When his father heard the news, he immediately traveled to Bucharest with a plan in mind to rescue Iancu from that alternative lifestyle. After impressing the two ladies with some flowers and charming talk, Ghiță took Iancu to lunch in one of Bucharest's fine restaurants. During the meal, he complimented his son for his girlfriend ("She is right for you—lovable, productive…") and also made him believe that the kind of life Iancu had chosen for himself was the only life a young talented man *should* have. He also mentioned casually, "a possibility you might be interested in, a remarkable chance to pursue your passion in the arts." Ghiță said that he had a friend, a ship captain who owed him a favor and money, ready to sail the next day from Constanția on the Black Sea to Naples, Italy, with stops in Istanbul and Athens. The seaman had given him a free ticket, which Ghiță was willing to present to Iancu, as it was an amazing opportunity for him to visit the great Italian art cities. Then from there he could reach Paris, where Ghiță's brother Costea had emigrated. The idea of being in Paris, the dream of all the artists, along with visiting all those interesting places, museums, art galleries and monuments which he only knew from books, was enough to convince Iancu to accept his father's offer. He immediately returned home, packed, said goodbye to his astonished girlfriend and ran to take the first train to the Black Sea where he boarded the ship.[4] In an interview published in 1986, Jean Negulesco reminisced about that episode of his life:

> I left for Paris around 1917 thanks to my father. He was an intelligent man, who thought I was too young to get married and have a quiet life; I had to first discover the world…. So I went on an amazing journey to reach the French capital; by boat through Bosporus, Turkey, Greece, Italy, Naples, Rome, Florence and finally Paris! What young man with a remarkable fondness for art would not be tempted by such a trip?[5]

Romanian film critic and University Professor Manuela Cernat reported the second account about Iancu's life in Bucharest. Cernat wrote a profile of Negulesco that included an interview with his youngest sister Sabina Negulescu-Florian. This more detailed account about Iancu's activities at the National School of Fine Arts seemed to present him in a different light as a hard-working student, eager to improve his skills, far from the bohemian life he described in his autobiography. In school, thanks to Prof. George Demetrescu Mirea, Iancu learned to work hard. Artist Constin Petrescu introduced him to the art of portrait and the technique of fresco painting. A huge influence in his artistic education was eminent painter Ipolit Strâmbu, who taught Iancu the simplicity of the details and the architectural vision in a painting—characteristics which he applied to his work as filmmaker years later.

During his Bucharest studies, Negulesco also had his first experiences in the theater. When the Little Theatre of Bucharest produced *Nyu* by the famous Romanian dramatist Dinov, Iancu was chosen to design the decor and costumes.

His first experience as playwright was not too successful, as he remembered years later: "I am the author of the biggest theatrical flop in Bucharest. I wrote and directed a piece, which had 18 acts. During the first three, you could only see the shadows of the actors on stage. Only my father stayed through to the end…."[6]

At the National School of Fine Arts, Iancu befriended the president of the student political union, Horia Igiroşanu, a sculptor turned film writer-director. Igiroşanu was swept up in a political scandal connected to a student strike against the regime. Iancu avoided having his name in the police records for subversive political action because, on the day of a police raid, he was in bed with the flu. From that point on, he avoided political activism. When Ghiţă was informed of his son's dangerous political involvement, he was so outraged that he thought immediately sending Iancu to Paris was the best way to keep him out of trouble.[7] This seems a more plausible explanation than the romance-driven one given by Negulesco in his memoir and in other interviews.

In an interview from the early 1990s, Jean gave a third version about that trip to France: "At 19 I was able to organize my first exhibition in Budapest [sic] with the paintings I have done while I was in the army. It was a great success and the earnings from the works I sold allowed me to visit Greece and Italy, two countries of great inspiration for artists. The next destination was, obviously, Paris: which was the center of the latest trends in the art world."[8] No matter which story is closest to the truth, they all end with Iancu sailing from Romania across the Mediterranean Sea.

After visiting Italy, Ian arrived in Paris at the end of 1918. His uncle Costea rented a tiny room for him on Rue de Rivoli and in, the days that followed, introduced Iancu to all the best spots in town. One night Costea treated him to dinner at Chez Maxim, the most renowned restaurant in Paris. It was the last time Iancu saw his uncle, who disappeared without leaving any trace. Although Iancu was left alone in Paris without knowing a word of French, he did not despair. "I began to try to understand song lyrics: it helps a lot when you have a date with your first shop girl."[9]

His first task was to enroll himself in a good art school: the Académie Julian, an illustrious institution that prepared students not only for the exams at the prestigious École des Beaux-Arts, but offered independent training in the arts. It was then Iancu decided to use the French equivalent of his first name, Jean. He later changed his last from Negulescu to Negulesco when he moved to Juan-les-Pins.

In Paris he moved into a bigger space, located on the top floor of a very old five-story building in Rue de Seine, not too far from the Louvre, where a high concentration of art galleries and antique dealers were scattered around. Jean also used this space as a studio. He always remembered his Parisian period with great nostalgia:

> I was lucky enough to experience "the movement" of that golden age in the French capital where you cross paths with the Dadaists, Georges Duhamel, Diaghilev and his Russian Ballets and Cocteau. At that time my best friend was Brâncuşi. We both came from the same region of Romania and in Paris we became closer. He was a keen observer. We'd frequently take long strolls along the Seine; one day he noticed a piece of wood curiously shaped by the wind and the rain. He picked it up and showed it to a museum that took it in! So many people had walked by that piece of wood but nobody had noticed it…. What counts is having quality, a sharp eye. At that time I used to say that I was a student of Brâncuşi; actually I was keeping his workshop in order and running the daily errands![10]

Constantin Brâncuşi, 24 years Jean's senior, was a sculptor-painter-photographer making his career in France. He became a pioneer of modernism and one of the most influential sculptors of the 20th century. Jean and Constantin often went to Chez Chartier, a small brasserie in Boulevard Saint Michel in the Latin quarter, to wash dishes in exchange for dinner made from the daily leftovers. (Brâncuşi's first bust exhibited at the Salon D'Automne was the head of the owner of Chez Chartier.) At Brâncuşi's atelier, Jean had the opportunity to meet Amedeo Modigliani. He recalled years later:

> I lived in the shadow of extraordinary people such as Tristan Tzara—another Romanian—Modigliani, Ionesco.... We all had very little money, but would always meet for endless conversations at La Grande Chaumiére or Chez Mere Rosalie in Rue Campagne-Première. Mother Rosalie was an Italian peasant, who loved painters. She would feed us often with an amazing bean soup, pasta and bread accompanied by a little glass of red wine. We would pay with drawings done at the table; she had hanged on the top of the counter this famous sentence: *Today it's free. Will pay tomorrow.* Therefore we got it right and we never paid.... We often met there Kiki, Foujita, Riesling, Matisse, Picasso or Utrillo. Modigliani spoke very loud like all the respectable Italians but with an extremely musical voice. He'd show up reciting verses from D'Annunzio or Dante. He was very handsome—one of the sexiest men I've ever met. Once he entered into the restaurant and I heard him saying:
> MODIGLIANI: What do you have to eat?
> ROSALIE: What have brought with you to pay your meal?
> MODIGLIANI: My presence!
> ROSALIE: It's not enough.
> MODIGLIANI: My talent...
> ROSALIE: I don't know your talent.
> MODIGLIANI: Don't move!
> A pencil appeared out of his pocket and he sketched on the wall a portrait of Rosalie while saying: "Madam, yesterday you were a simple woman, today you are a goddess." Rosalie took a look at the drawing and said: "Okay, you won your meal."[11]

Every day after his classes at the Académie Julian, Jean went to La Rotonde or to Le Dôme, two very popular cafés among artists in Montparnasse.

> There, we often met two bearded men who played chess in a corner. They were Lenin and Trotsky. But I did not know much about them, because like everyone else I only cared about one thing: myself. Those were the years when we thought: What's the use to imitate a painter like Michelangelo, when his works were only mistakes to a delirious nth degree. I will create something, a painting or a book like no one in the world has ever known before. Funny was that we never did anything, we would get drunk and have fun regardless of the people around us. Then, later on, I read the book ... *The Wine of Genius* (*The Life of Maurice Utrillo*). A small volume about life in Montparnasse and the change from Montparnasse to Montmartre and the return of Montparnasse. It was thanks to this book that I found out that those two bearded men who played chess in a corner at *La Rotonde* were Trotsky and Lenin.... [H]istory was happening around us, while we remained on the side.[12]

A demanding teacher, Pierre Laurents never seemed satisfied with Jean's art. Jean said, "At the beginning I was copying the great masters, then I looked for *the reason* in nature, and Paris appealed to me for that amazing buzz of young spirits."[13]

His teacher's dissatisfaction prompted Jean to attend extra evening courses both at the Académie de la Grande Chaumière and at the Académie Colarossi to improve his skills in sketching nude models. Still the master was not pleased. At the end of the first year, one of his paintings, representing in very pale colors the romantic tale of Daphnis and Chloe, was selected by the director of the Académie Julian as the best piece of the week and hung on the wall of the atelier. But Laurents was not impressed, dismissing Jean's work as utterly boring. "Negulesco, you have lost all interest in the adventure Art offers," he reportedly said to his pupil.[14] He ordered Jean, from that moment on, to draw with his left hand using the hardest pen. The struggle quickly became a victory that made Jean a convincing artist. That challenge, as he admitted, helped him reach that "deadly combination" of ability and boredom he had always despised. Jean's gratitude and admiration for Pierre Laurents lasted a lifetime.

Suddenly, the monthly check from Ghiță stopped arriving. The news had reached his parents in Romania that he was living a Parisian life as a full-time bohemian artist, not attending any school of economics or trade. In the subsequent weeks, Jean learned what it really meant to be a starving painter. He unsuccessfully tried to present a large painting, representing a scene on a crowded and smoky dance floor of a Parisian nightclub, to the *Salon des Indépendants*, a venue for unknown artists. After he had spent all his savings to complete it, he was now broke, with three months' rent to pay and no coal or wood to burn to heat his freezing studio. Every night he had to go to bed fully clothed and keep washing dishes and scrubbing the floor at Chez Chartier to have a warm meal. Every day there was the challenge of hunger in what he would later ironically call "the lean years."

In 1922 Jean went back to Craiova for a short holiday with high hopes of persuading Ghiță to support his art, but his father's position was firm. Even Elena's efforts to convince her husband to support their son were unsuccessful. A disappointed Jean returned to France, carrying with him some pocket money his mother secretly gave him. There was another full year of living in dire straits, working odd jobs. Then Jean, encouraged by Brâncuși and his teachers, felt confident enough to return once again to Romania where he was able to organize his first solo exhibition.

On Sunday, December 30, 1924, the *Vernissage* opened in Bucharest, at the prestigious Romaniam Athenaeum, a landmark in the heart of the capital city. The show ran for one month but the critics panned it. *Rampa*, one of the most respected local cultural magazines of the time, in an unsigned article reported, "Mr. D. [sic] Negulescu undoubtedly has much talent [but] the paintings—for my taste—are too sentimental in design.... [P]aintings are not paintings because they have no color..."[15]

Ghiță felt so embarrassed by the negative reviews that he barred Jean from the house, ordering him to sleep in a hotel. Support from his father to continue his artistic education was now completely out of the question. Since there was no work to be found, Jean traveled back to Paris.

In the early months of 1924, Jean contracted mild pulmonary tuberculosis. The doctors ordered him to move to the sunny French Riviera, following the example of many artists who had chosen to work in a more favorable climate where life was much cheaper than in the capital. Irish film director Rex Ingram bought one of his nudes exhibited at the *Salon d'Automne* for the incredible sum of 3000 francs, and now Jean could afford to move to the South of France. He rented two rooms in a fisherman's cottage nearby the port in Cagnes-sur-Mer, a small village just outside Nice, famous as the final retreat of the French impressionist painter Pierre-August Renoir. "I would work during the day together with a group of friends but without selling any paintings. I had to survive! After buying a tuxedo we were hired as professional dancers inviting on the dance floor the female customers of the Hotel Negresco. We earned 50 francs per night excluding tips."[16]

Negulesco joked that people often asked him if he was related to the Hotel Negresco, Nice's most prestigious hotel, since it sounded like Negulesco. He enjoyed leaving an aura of mystery around that connection.

Jean was a professional dancer-gigolo in a luxurious hotel but there were rules, including strictly no dates with the female clients. It did not take long for Jean to break the rule and began dating a young American girl. This soon cost him his job. "Many years later, while I was shooting *A Certain Smile*, we had a suite reserved at the Negresco. There I met again the manager, Mr. Louis, and he recalled my time there as a gigolo. He looked at me and said: 'Mr. Negulesco, I congratulate you for not having changed!' I replied stunned, 'What? I make films, I am famous...' He explained then, 'Yes, but you are still a gigolo, you still entertain since it's the production that pays for your rooms! Bravo, to your intelligence and your luck!'"[17]

Years later, Negulesco explained in an interview that, after buying his work, Rex Ingram had become his friend, asking him to play in the film *The Four Horsemen of the Apocalypse* (1921) he was shooting in Nice. But according to Ingram's biographies, the picture was shot in Hollywood and the director did not work at the Victorine studios in Nice before 1925. Once again the thin line between real vs. fantasy was blurred.

On March 4, 1926, at the city hall of Nice, Jean married 32-year-old Winifred Hayers Havlicek, a wealthy American widow (or, according to other sources, divorcée) and mother of a little girl named Suzanne. Negulesco never discussed his first marriage publicly and only casually mentioned in his autobiography. A few details emerged in 1930 when a little scandal involving the couple was reported by the American newspapers: Shortly after the wedding, the Negulescos moved to Juan-les-Pins, a small village near Cannes. Jean spent much of his time painting the sunny marine landscape and sketching portraits of famous and less famous people including the American dancer Isadora Duncan and the English author and poet Richard Le Galliene. In preparation of an upcoming solo show at the Galerie Campagne Première in Montparnasse, Jean was now starting to sign his work Jean Negulesco. The exhibition was a hit, receiving rave reviews. *L'Art Moderne* enthusiastically remarked, "Mr. Negulesco's colors are vibrant, luminous, sometimes a bit bright but they are so perfectly tuned that we can see in them another artist, Negulesco, the musician." The art critic Teriade of the prestigious *Cahiers d'Art* wrote, "[L]ike his fellow country man the sculptor Brancussi [sic], he had preferred to be ahead and not to be satisfied with what he already has. It's the best way to believe in himself."

2

Welcome to America!

"Quit painting!"—Élie Faure to Jean Negulesco

Jean's overnight success, combined with Winifred's encouragement, convinced him to leave Paris for America. The passenger manifests show that the Negulescos traveled separately. Winifred and her daughter Suzanne boarded on the ocean liner S.S. *Suffren* at Cherbourg, arriving to New York on March 29, 1927. Jean travelled two weeks later from Le Havre aboard the ocean liner S.S. *Rochambeau*, disembarking in New York on April 15, 1927.

The apartment Winifred rented at 3 Washington Square North in the heart of Greenwich Village was large enough to include Jean's workshop. In preparation of her husband's arrival, she announced to the press that a famous Romanian painter who had officially completed a portrait of Princess Marie of Romania was arriving after the extraordinary success of his last exhibition in Paris. There are two press photographs taken in Jean's New York studio. One, dated May 6, 1927, shows Jean standing next to stepdaughter Suzanne, putting finishing touches on her portrait. The second, dated June 25, 1927, shows Jean shaking hands with the American painter Rockwell Kent with Winifred sitting by his side. A few articles about Jean, calling him the "court painter of the wandering queen, Marie of Romania," appeared in several newspapers across the country. Jean had in fact made a portrait of Princess Marie of Edinburgh, more commonly known as Marie of Romania. "The court painter" was the angle used to promote himself as an artist. The exaggerated story was fabricated for the media to give Jean an aura of royalty.

Jean's first assignment in his new environs was to paint the most typical American children. With this in mind, he wandered the sidewalks of the East Side where he finally found a group of children playing in the street.

He touched one little girl on the arm. "Votre mere?" he asked. "Paint moi you pose?"

The child shrieked, for the mixture of French and English was quite beyond her understanding. She didn't have the teeniest little idea that the Rumanian court painter was addressing her and asking her to pose for him. So she rather naturally conceived the idea that she was face to face with one of the kidnapers against whom she had been warned. The other children began to shriek and the circle broke up. All ran. But the artist, being nimble, ran too. He chased his little girl around a block, past crazy push carts, into a long, lean dark entry, and finally up a flight of stairs, where a large, indignant woman suddenly faced the artist bristling. In another flash, half a dozen angry East Siders panted up those stairs and stood jabbering. Other fists waved, and blows might have been struck, but just then the strange young man broke into a outpour of dulcet, Romanian words.

The mother changed from frowns to smiles. "But yes! I will let my little girl pose for the great queen," said she. For she was a Rumanian woman herself.

Since that day the artist visited children's hospitals, schools, the mall in Central Park where nurses bring their youngsters, all places where children gather, to find nine other "pure American types," as he called them. And, hunting his types, he has formed his idea of why American children look so differently from European children.

"Over there," says Negulesco, "we crush our youngsters with too many centuries. Their childhood cannot cope with the weight of tradition they are born to. Our children are polite—and stifled. Your children are impudent and self-expressing. Don't worry about their monkey-shines. Thank the good Lord for them. In Europe a child may never have used the telephone. In France we have few radios and little other household machinery. But here your children are what I call—'civilized mechanique'—that is, the machinery which surrounds them has made them keener, cleverer, more alert than a European child can ever be."

Already, in addition to his first little Rumanian-American, Mr. Negulesco has painted the young son of Rockwell Kent, the distinguished American artist. That boy he calls his "radio child—sharp-eyed, quick at the uptake."

[Jean's stepdaughter Suzanne], a little red-haired girl, he calls "Young Imp." She's a type of young, feminine, American self-expression.

So it goes, though the list has only half been chosen. In addition, this rather native painter has been accorded permission to paint "the avenue" high up....[1]

The above story ended by revealing that Jean had been chosen as the official artist for the American Child Welfare Week, and he had promised to paint the healthiest child chosen by the social workers.

Life in New York was not as dreamy as Jean expected. Even though he was able to drive his first car and have a studio in an isolated section of the Catskills in upstate New York, he was not happy. He was far from fluent in English and he had to rely on Winifred for everything, including economic support. And they were beginning to have significant differences.

In May 1927, Jean's first American art show of paintings and drawings opened at the Anderson Galleries on Park Avenue. Richard Le Gallienne wrote a short preface to the flyleaf released on this occasion. As the art critic Walter Shaw cited in a flattering article published before the opening, "To English and American lovers of art, the pleasure of knowing the pictures of Jean Negulesco; and to this young Rumanian genius the success he deserves! There is in these pictures an imagination which has the power of carrying external realities to the utmost limit of underlying form ... and withal this high adventurer of the palette owns to no more years of age than 26 and comes—how rightly—to the land of youth for recognition."[2]

The exhibition was very well received. The owner of the space bought two nudes which he resold in an auction held at the Anderson Galleries the following February.

On November 5, 1927, Jean's second exhibition opened at the Wayne Gallery in Manhattan. *The New York Times* reported the news in the art section, mentioning Jean's successful earlier shows in Paris and "in London" [sic].[3] This time many subjects were on display, from landscapes of the Riviera and Morocco, to portraits of Richard Le Galliene and French stage actress Marguerite Jamois. Still life and nudes in pen and pencil were also included along with a series of caricatures of celebrities including Charlie Chaplin, Ruth Draper and Isadora Duncan.

Jean's marriage with Winifred was on the rocks due to significant differences. He threw himself into his work, giving art classes and even making picture frames.

On April 12, 1928, with the help of George S. Hellman, president of the New Gallery on Madison Avenue, Jean showed 16 oil paintings and some drawings. A small catalogue included an updated introduction by Le Gallienne and a few words of appreciation by art collector and critic Duncan Phillips and artist Rockwell Kent. The latter wrote,

> The work of Jean Negulesco is distinguished to a rare degree by the high quality of precision, the precision of a mind conscious of its own intention, and of a nature clearly sensitive to those most subtle human values which it grasps. And that the beauty of his work appears so early and fluently achieved reveals the artist's spirit to be simply and directly responsive to what in life is beautiful.[4]

The New Gallery exhibition became the talk of the town after receiving strong reviews from the local press. *The New York Times* wrote, "The precise bounding line, elastic in defining a human form, severe in denoting an architectural element, is in this work the imprimatur of an artistic personality."[5]

And according to art critic Margaret Breuning,

> Though Negulesco is essentially a liner artist, he does not negate the third dimension, but following Cézanne employs his acute line to terminate simplified places that build up.
>
> This is the third opportunity I have had to see the work of this gifted young artist. At each exhibit the impression of the power and individuality of this painter's work is increased. He appears more and more able to express his sensitive vision of the world about him in a highly individual use of color, arabesque of pattern, incisive, sinuous line. There is something fresh and vigorous about all his paintings. In the landscapes one feels that he has translated the beauty of natural forms in the terms of his art so rapidly that the first delight in their color and contour still lives in them.[6]

Ten months later, the show traveled to Washington, D.C., opening on February 4 at the Yorke Gallery. Fifty-three of Jean's works (including some Venetian landscapes painted during a short trip to Italy) were exhibited for two weeks under the patronage of the Romanian Minister, who organized a large reception party. Seven paintings were sold on the opening night, four to Duncan Phillips, one to Mrs. Archibald and another to an unknown buyer. *The Washington Post* described the event as "one of the most significant exhibitions that has come to Washington for a long time. It puts us in touch with some of the best work that is being produced today. While Negulesco is certainly modern, he is sane and vital, thoroughly himself and expressive of his nation. These paintings along with these in the Memorial Gallery, go a long way to giving us a real cosmopolitan outlook, or rather in look, on art."[7]

For the exhibition catalogue, Jean wrote "Notes of a Painter," nine observations about his idea of what art is. They provide insight into his personality as an artist:

> The first and the most important condition of art is LOVE. Between the creator and the subject, this sentiment must absolutely and continually exist: without this, the production of art is the result of a formula.
>
> Very often I am asked: "Are you a modern or classic?"—Mon Dieu! I am a painter, that's all. Cubism, impressionism, expressionism and all the other terms of art are formulas absolutely unnecessary, the refugee for those who cannot be themselves.
>
> The most difficult attitude of the artist is to be sincere, to be himself. Usually one works in the shadow of the others.
>
> The great error is to look for an explication of the production of art: You like it, or you do not. That's all!
>
> For me the drawing of a child is always the best lesson: painted only for his simple joy, without ambition, without motive, and between him and the drawing nothing exists of the baggage acquired in schools, museums, and books. This is the greatest lesson. Have you noticed that children never sign their work? The drawing of a child is complete: the signature is not necessary.
>
> Color does not exist in a drawing: a drawing is pure line, emotion of the arabesque, equilibrium

of contours. A drawing has nothing in common with a painting, and a portrait drawn must be completely different from the same portrait painted.

Painting must live by itself: Literature, music and other expression of art cannot help you to like it.

The real portrait must be a profound caricature.

The subject is of no importance in the production of art, it is only an old habit.

By the time the exhibition opened, Jean had made Washington his permanent home, establishing a school for art beginners and children at his studio in the Wardman Park Hotel. Showing kids a new way to see beauty in everyday things was a new challenge that gave him immense pleasure. It also allowed him to express his art with a new point of view. His biggest fan, Duncan Phillips, offered him the opportunity to become the director of the Duncan Phillips Collection, an art museum founded by Phillips and his wife in 1921 as the Phillips Memorial Gallery. Jean proudly told his family in several letters that he was also invited by two academies of art to give master classes.[8]

Requests for portraits by the wealthy and famous started to pour in. So while his financial situation improved, his marriage collapsed. Soon began a bitter, complex and sad legal battle which would last ten years.

In April 1929, Jean was asked by the Western Association of Art Museums to exhibit his work as a foreign, emergent painter of the year in different West Coast venues. His work would be presented along with that of Rockwell Kent. He traveled west by car, leaving Winifred in Washington. According to Jean, his wife forged his signature on an order permitting her to remove valuable furniture from a local warehouse and to withdraw money from his bank account. Precious objects, including Romanian and African art, cases of liquor received as a gift from his students and diplomats, over 150 paintings and more than 300 drawings, works prepared for a future exhibition, all disappeared. On his return, Jean sued Winifred, who was arrested on a forgery charge. She was released on $2000 bail but an arraignment was held before a U.S. commissioner. The charge was subsequently dismissed. Winifred's version was that she had spent $50,000 in cash and securities to bring Jean to America and establish his art reputation and that she had "furnished him with pocket money and clothing so that he might present a good appearance and entertain persons who would aid him in obtaining recognition of his ability as an artist, for exhibition of his paintings and for advertising and publicity in an endeavor to build up his reputation as an artist."[9]

She added that she spent more than $7000 to set up a cabin, as Jean's retreat studio, in the Catskills. By April 1929 she had exhausted her resources. Therefore, the things she had taken from the storage belonged to her. Furthermore, she claimed that Jean had run off that following August with another woman, Hannah Jorgensen, surreptitiously taking some of Winifred's wardrobe for the other woman. According to Winifred, the couple took a three-month trip by car to California and while on the road they posed as husband and wife. Winifred also accused Jean of treating her with coldness, being neglectful, and indulging in love affairs with several different women while they lived in Washington. In 1932 when Winifred filed a separate suit against Jean, she exhibited in court letters from women in which they stated that they were in love with Jean and referred to their rendezvous.

In the spring of 1930, Jean left Washington for good and moved to California. According to a statement made by Winifred during the divorce arraignment, she traveled to Los Angeles to seek support and reconciliation with Jean, but had no success.

During the three-month journey to California by car across America, Jean was inspired to paint different landscapes. These new paintings were ready just in time when, in May 1930, the Braxton Galleries agreed to show his works in a space at Hollywood's Roosevelt Hotel. The two-week exhibition gave Negulesco great visibility and the best introduction in Hollywood an artist could have in those days. He met the Hollywood in-crowd. Celebrities, executives and producers commissioned portraits for themselves or their family members. Once again, money began to pour in. But soon Jean got bored.

> One of my biggest faults as a painter is that it comes too easy. No matter what technique I used (drawing, painting, etc.), no matter what genre (still life, landscape, portrait), no matter how hard, it was never a problem for me. I did it quickly, probably too well, but I did not have any pleasure from what I was doing because I was doing it too easily. All my life, everything I have done, it has been like a hobby. And I had enough of this hobby.... I was in Hollywood when this great Frenchman, Mr. Élie Faure just arrived to the United States to give a series of lectures on art and cinema. When he stopped in Los Angeles, I was chosen to help him, as an escort and as his translator. We became friends. At the beginning, he detested the Californian cuisine.... Therefore, when we finished a formal dinner, I used to take him to a Viennese bistro where he would have sauerkraut and beer. I introduced him to some film stars I knew because I made their own portraits (or their husbands' or their wives' or their children's). I took him to the premiere of *City Lights* (1931) where he met Chaplin. He was so happy! That same night he told me, "But you really know everybody here! What films have you made?—I have something to confess, I'm not into films, I am a painter." There was a silence—a bit embarrassing. A man, who I admired, who I was fond of, when I told him what I was doing he was not interested in it, especially since he was about to finish a long and beautiful article on Soutine [Chaïm Soutine, a Russian expressionist painter]. After a moment he told me, "Listen Jean, it's possible that you are a great painter, it's possible that you are a genius. I see that you have a spirit of an adventurer, that you are thirsty of knowledge, of discovery. Why don't you put aside the brush for a while? Maybe one day you'd take it back? You have a foot inside the studios. You are friend with the studios' biggest names. They will help you. This is the art of the future. This is the art that uses all the other arts: dance, music, literature, etc. Look here at the beer, it's lifeless but if you point a camera here, the scene will have a certain rhythm, you walk with it and inanimate objects become alive and the beer starts to dance. (I've never forgot that. Every time I had a scene too static with a long conversation, I'd slowly move the camera from right to left, from left to right. It would create a rhythm in a scene, which otherwise would be dead.) I was so happy that someone who I admired had told me: "Quit painting." That night I put aside the brush. It took me 13 years to make my first film. But that period of my life had been amazing.[10]

That conversation with Faure was eye-opening for Jean, who now felt ready to work into film. A few years later, when Jean was starting to co-direct his first pictures in Hollywood, Faure sent him *Introduction à la mystique du cinéma*, an essay he had just written and dedicated to Jean. Jean tried unsuccessfully to have it published in English.

Two exhibitions (one in January 1931 at the Honolulu Academy of Arts, the other at the Art Institute of Seattle) earned Jean $19,000. He invested it in the production of *Three and a Day,* lavishing a good deal of enthusiasm upon the project. "I loved films—hungrily, with no reserve, passionately—and I loved filmmaking, not only for the enjoyment of the finished product, but all its phases, from the conception of an idea to the film in the theaters." He wrote a script about the day in the life of three characters: a painter, a dancer and a farmer. He cast Russian-born actors Mischa Auer as the artist, Katya Sergava as the ballet dancer and athlete John Rox as the farmer.

Except for one location at San Pedro, the picture, planned as a two-reel feature, was shot in Jean's Hollywood studio apartment in the fall of 1931. The news that the young Romanian portrait painter was producing and directing his first picture was reported in major industry magazines. *Variety* described it as " a two-reel symbolic silent ... with a musical score to come,"[11] while *Film Daily* characterized it as a "dramatic subject."[12]

Jean hired French cameraman Paul Ivano, who later became an established cinematographer.

In spite of his technical ignorance, Negulesco stubbornly wanted to shoot the picture his way. "I wanted to make something different, unconventional." He explained years later: "When someone would point out that I was wrong about something I would reply that that was my money and my film."[13]

Fourteen reels (other sources indicate 21) were shot. Once *Three and a Day* was completed, Jean employed an out-of-work editor, who during a long weekend, while Jean was away on a holiday, was unable to put together what he (the editor) later called "a fucking mess." He suggested Jean burn the film. The director asked for help from Gunther von Frisch, who confirmed that it was impossible to match any two sequences.

Fourteen years later, Jean admitted in his first *New York Times* interview,

> That picture should have been entitled *How Not to Make a Movie*. It was full of artistic shots and camera angles that had no real place in the picture. When the time came to put the film together, [von Frisch and I] couldn't make head or tail. We never did fit the various scenes together. That was the best lesson in picture-making I ever had. Every mistake cost me money and I remembered it.[14]

The negative of *Three and a Day* was left in the vault of a Hollywood storage company and disposed of a year later for non-payment of storage fees. Making the film left Jean so broke that he had to pay the laundry service with a $1.50 bad check.[15]

But something good came out of it. His friend Mischa Auer introduced him to Paramount director Frank Tuttle. The filmmaker knew Jean's artistic background and asked him if he was interested in sketching the opening of *This Is the Night*, a musical that he was about to direct. The scene was set in Paris and Jean recreated the city streets, calling upon all his memories of life in the French capital. Benjamin Glazer, the producer of the picture, was so impressed by Jean's sketches that he hired Jean for $50 a week as a technical adviser.

Jean's clever suggestions for the settings and camera angles earned him a job at Paramount. In 1932, he was a production assistant on *The Phantom President* and *A Bedtime Story*, both directed by Norman Taurog, and Tuttle's *The Big Broadcast*. About those days, Negulesco recalled that producer Benjamin Glazer:

> took me as his assistant, and I was an assistant producer for the production of his pictures. You are a kind of a messenger boy between the director and the publicity people. But I was so much interested in the actual making of a picture that I was always spending all my time on the sets, in the cutting room, in the music department, wanting to learn everything about making a film. Not as much interested in telling a story as in making a film, visually telling a story, and let the words come out of the situation, which should be carried visually.[16]

When Paramount's *Alice in Wonderland* (1933) was in pre-production, Jean was chosen to draw several animated cartoon sequences. Paramount originally planned a combination of live action and animated production, possibly in color. But that idea was dropped and the film was shot without any animated characters.

Jean's next assignment was to sketch a rape scene for the film *The Story of Temple Drake*, based on William Faulkner's novel *Sanctuary*. Glazer was concerned with how to shoot the violent sequence without being censored. Jean carefully read the script and sketched his own conception of that notorious scene, which was set in an old barn. He drafted a special group of black and white drawings, suggesting how the cameras should shoot the scene through the rapist's legs as he approached his woman (Miriam Hopkins) lying in the corncrib. Jean used a sketch technique playing with shadows and light, which would be enhanced by the black and white photography.

On the day of the shooting, he was on the set to supervise. Director Stephen Roberts carefully shot the sequence following all the details as illustrated in Jean's drawings. After the final take, the entire crew applauded, Hopkins hugged and kissed him. Jean had succeeded. The scene was okayed by the censor. Suddenly Jean became the industry "rape expert." "It took me years to live down that title, which I got on that film," he later revealed.[17]

After the film was completed, William Faulkner's literary agent, Ben Wasson, also a friend of Jean, organized a dinner when the author was in Hollywood. After the meal, Jean showed Faulkner a portfolio of his drawings. "Exactly what I had in mind," said Faulkner after carefully studying the pictures. Negulesco gave him the album. Since Faulkner had not seen *The Story of Temple Drake*, Negulesco asked him to come to Paramount for a screening. Faulkner and Jean went to see it. Afterwards, Faulkner said, "Tell Negulesco I thank him for helping make the story into a moving picture I'm not ashamed of."[18] *The Story of Temple Drake* gave a great boost to Negulesco's career.

Glazer, who was about to produce a version of Ernest Hemingway's *A Farewell to Arms*, asked Jean to storyboard all the battle sequences, including the big retreat from Caporetto. The result was so impressive that the director of the film, Frank Borzage, made Jean second unit director of all the crowd and battle scenes. Borzage had established a solid reputation in Hollywood by winning Oscars for *Seventh Heaven* (1927) and *Bad Girl* (1931). On the *Farewell to Arms* set, Borzage immediately noticed Jean's amazing skill in finding the right camera angles, probably due to the painter's pictorial sense. In fact, Jean was often asked by the various movies' cinematographers or directors to help them camera-wise. He carefully observed how Borzage worked and tried to complement his direction. The filmmaker did not believe in giving excessive direction. He relied on the intuitions of his actors and gave them the freedom to improvise, a method Negulesco would later apply in directing his stars.

Four hundred extras gathered at the Paramount Ranch where the outdoor scenes were shot in five nights, filming under water jets and the light of 300 spotlights. For the famous scene of the retreat of Caporetto, Jean erected a miniature mountain where incessant rain causes an avalanche, all created by the special effects department. According to Borzage's biographer, that sequence was "too long, stylistically jarring, and threatened to throw the film off balance"; he cut it to five minutes, reducing Jean's contribution to a modest "mosaic predominated by chaos and light."

Jean and Borzage got along on the set, but Jean described the filmmaker as "a strange man. He'd have a scene with, say, three hundred extras, and all he'd be interested in was the way water would drip from a leaf and the way you'd see Gary Cooper passing by through this dripping water in the big retreat of Caporetto."[19] Borzage also had the bizarre habit of asking his own brother Lew, working as an uncredited assistant director, to play the violin before filming a scene between Cooper and Hayes to get the two stars in the right mood.[20]

Borzage ended the film like the novel, with Catherine dying while giving birth to the lieutenant's stillborn child. Not satisfied with it, Paramount wanted a happy ending in order to get a more favorable reaction from women. Since Borzage was already working on his next project, the task fell to the second unit director. At the end of November 1932, just a month before the picture opened nationwide, Jean shot the second, less bleak ending in only two days. It was his first time directing major Hollywood stars like Cooper and Hayes. In spite of a great fear of another failure, Jean did a fine job. Hemingway was very annoyed with Paramount's ending. At the time of the release, the author told the press that he never intended a happy ending, which the film made for the American audience. In other countries, the movie had Borzage's original ending. *A Farewell to Arms* was Oscar-nominated for Best Picture, Art Direction, Cinematography and Sound Recording; the latter two were winners.

According to a February 1933 *Hollywood Reporter*, "Jean Negulesco, assistant to associate producer Benjamin Glazer at Paramount, has had option picked up on his term ticket."[21] For the next three years, Jean earned his Paramount salary working for Glazer. He was an uncredited production assistant on director Rouben Mamoulian's *The Songs of Songs* (1933) and Norman Taurog's *The Way to Love* (1933). He was technical advisor on *Enter Madame!* (1935), a film set in the opera world, starring Cary Grant and Elissa Landi. According to *Stage magazine,* Jean admirably directed the glorious *Easter Hymn* scene from *Cavalleria Rusticana* in the film. He also supervised four other opera scenes in the film from *Tosca* and *Il Trovatore,* backed by the Los Angeles Opera Company.

"As Negulesco showed it," *Stage* magazine reported, "the scene was broken up into a dozen significant bits, photographed from a score of angles...."[22] The amazing experience of directing part of an opera inside a film, even as a second unit director, gave Jean the confidence and desire to make a full-length picture. He proposed directing the first grand opera in motion pictures, Mascagni's *Cavalleria Rusticana*, and additionally designing all its sets and costumes. Paramount executives showed interest in the idea, announcing the upcoming production to the press. Eventually the project was shelved after being considered an investment too costly and risky in the hands of an inexperienced director. Nonetheless, two years later, the media announced that Jean would direct the picture, this time titled *Chivalry*, starring Mary Ellis and Mexican tenor José Mojica. Once again, this time for unknown reasons, the project was dropped.

The Man Who Broke His Heart, a poetical story about Christ on a fishing wharf, suffered a similar fate. It was announced that Negulesco would replace the film's director, Stephen Roberts. Jean strove to assemble the perfect cast (considering John Lodge as the lead), but the picture was never made.

If the name Jean Negulesco was not appearing yet in the film credits, it was definitely becoming familiar in the gossip columns. Jean loved the company of beautiful women, especially young starlets. His cosmopolitan background and his thick accent was a sort of magnet for the ladies. His first reported conquest was starlet Sidney Fox, who had made her screen debut beside with Bette Davis in *Bad Sister* (1931). In 1932 several articles announced that the couple would wed after Jean's divorce. In reality, Winifred and Jean were nowhere near reaching any agreement. For Jean, his marital status was the perfect excuse to avoid rushing into a second marriage.

On the set of *Enter Madame!* Jean met Elissa Landi, an Italian-born actress who was about to divorce her husband. During their short but intense liaison, Landi introduced him to screenwriter Eric Knight, who later became the internationally renowned author of *Lassie Come Home* (1943). The two became occasional tennis partners. According to two letters written by Knight in 1935 to his friend, British documentary filmmaker Paul Rotha, Jean was contracted to make six shorts films for an English company with a guarantee of $10,000 each. Four of the films were written by Knight:

> I have written two scenarios (both really very good) for possible independent production by Negulesco, who has backing for production but can find no outlet for distribution. They are three- or four-reel shorts. Negulesco is a Rumanian ... the boy who did the cutting at the beginning of Frank Tuttle's *This Is the Night*, and all the retreat scenes in *Farewell to Arms*. Most of the latter were cut out for purposes of Mussolini-cajoling by Paramount. Italian armies mustn't retreat in the pictures. They can only do that in real wars.[23]

In the second letter, written a month later, Knight said,

> I have done two short scripts for Negulesco.... I have written one comedy ... sort of a modern *Sorcerer's Apprentice*. And I've done a social comedy based on a broken-down actor's troupe and a fake stage-money $100 bill, which starts the town in prosperity by passing from hand to hand and finishing back with the actor. However, I do not like the set-up much, as Negulesco has very poor ideas and wants a love angle in the $100 bill plot. But it is a chance to get independent production.[24]

One of those scenarios, titled *Lesson in Love* and marked as UNPRODUCED, is in the Paul Kohler Agency records at the Margaret Herrick Library in Beverly Hills. On its cover, it reads "Jean Negulesco and Stephen M. Avery from an outline by Stephen Avery and Eric Knight."

As Knight mentioned in his letters, all the projects remained unrealized, most likely because Jean was unable to find proper distribution. This did not discourage him from writing scripts, a sideline he had started to enjoy. Jean's script *New Orleans*, written at the end of 1934 and described as a romance of New Orleans, was bought by Universal in October 1935. The studio announced it in the summer of 1937, first as *New Orleans* and later as *To-Night We Live*. It never went into production.

In February 1934, two days before Jean's thirty-fourth birthday, *Variety* announced, "George [*sic*] Negulesco and Harlan Thompson will co-direct Paramount's *Kiss and Make-Up* formerly *Cosmetics*. Cary Grant is the only cast name to date."

Kiss and Make-Up started production in April; the film marked the first time that Paramount gave Cary Grant lead billing and a story focused on his character. Jean had already worked with Grant in *This Is the Night* and *Enter Madame!* (the latter was shot before *Kiss and Make-Up* but released later). Set in Paris and on the Riviera, the picture dealt with a romantic beauty doctor (Grant) whose operation on Genevieve Tobin not only makes her a fascinating and cold beauty, but also captivates his heart. Once it was completed, the film was previewed in early June 1934. Because of the audience's negative reaction, it was put back into production for retakes and added scenes. It was still panned by reviewers. Only *The Hollywood Reporter* praised Jean's work: "The new directing team of Harlan Thompson and Jean Negulesco did exceptionally well."[25]

The comedy did not do much for Grant, a rising star, but for Jean *Kiss and Make-Up* was a great accomplishment since his name, as associate director, was included for the first time in the opening credits of a motion picture. Future movie star Ann Sheridan was an extra in the movie; six years later, she and Jean dated briefly before he introduced her to his close friend and colleague Anatole Litvak. They had a long and tempestuous affair.

In the spring of 1935, Jean lost his job at Paramount, which was on the verge of bankruptcy. The studio dropped 30 writers from its contract list, bringing down the total to around 50. In addition, three directors, including Jean, did not have their contract renewed. He joined the Schulber-Jaffe Agency. (Sam Jaffe had been Jean's sponsor at Paramount.)

Ernst Lubitsch was now Paramount's production manager, becoming the only major Hollywood director to run a large studio. He had trouble delegating authority, which was a problem when he was overseeing 60 different films. He was fired after a year on the job. Jean remembered his good friend Lubitsch telling him, "It's a pity those people at Paramount cannot see what a talented director you could be, and gave chances to other people instead of you." Jean also recalled, "When Lubitsch became head of the studio, I was sure that this was going to be my great chance. Well, three months later my option was dropped—not only that, but Lubitsch lost his job. So it took about a year and a half of starving and tryings, going back to painting for a while to make ends meet."[26]

According to *Variety*, in October 1935 Jean joined the Warner Brothers special effects department.[27] This led to his working as a second unit director on the lavish production *Captain Blood* starring Errol Flynn and Olivia de Havilland, and directed by Michael Curtiz. Jean was placed in charge of directing complicated battle sequences filmed on location in Laguna Beach by cinematographer Byron Haskin. One scene involved one of the largest technical crews ever been assembled for a film, with the participation of more than 2,500 extras. Since Jean had proved his ability on *A Farewell to Arms,* the producers trusted his directorial skills.

"Curtiz took care of Flynn and de Havilland, while I was shooting the action scenes," Jean explained years later. "It was a very important experience as a filmmaker. I was the only one able to direct the horses, the extras. There were also a few retakes. When a shot scene appears not to be good enough in the editing room, the director is not always available to reshoot it: you have then to rely on the second unit director."[28]

While at Warners, Jean was asked to help revise the final script of *Hearts Divided*, a historical drama set in Napoleonic France. Casey Robinson started the screenplay in September 1934. After ten days of shooting, producer William R. Hearst ordered the script rewritten by James K. McGuinness and Charles Lederer. Jean provided "Negulesco's touch" to the story, but too many cooks had spoiled the broth, and *Hearts Divided,* directed by Frank Borzage, was still doomed.

In the spring of 1936, Jean was associate director on *Crash Donovan*. Universal hired him as a freelancer to work with William Nigh. Together they took over from director Edward Laemmle. Jean directed the car racing sequences and the retakes, while Nigh handled the dramatic scenes. Years later Jean explained how hard it was to share a film with another director:

"You cannot direct as a pair, especially when you are young. Each has his own idea about the film, his own dreams."[29]

A fast-moving drama, *Crash Donovan* concerned the adventures of a former stunt motorcycle rider (Jack Holt) who joins the California Highway Patrol after a friend is

Jean Negulesco in 1934 at Warner Bros. studios.

shot. The reviews were generally positive but the film did not do much for Jean's career. While he was working on *Crash Donovan,* gossip columnists spread some new rumors:

> Lovely little Luise Rainer came to Hollywood nursing a ghost romance supposedly. She was still true to a sweetheart who was killed in a tragic accident a year or so ago. But now a friendship that they'll have you believe is more than platonic has sprung up between the tiny Viennese charmer and Jean Negulesco, the artist. They're about all the time. Jean must like them small and dark. He used to be the head man with Sidney Fox, you'll remember.[30]

Jean described Rainer as a woman with "an unusual beauty and a brilliant mind."[31] But the fling lasted only a few weeks; Jean was soon spotted in the company of new beautiful ladies.

From 1936 until 1940 Jean turned into a full-time writer, collaborating on several films for different studios. His first screenplay to be turned into a film was Warners' *Expensive Husbands.* It was based on an original story by Kyrill de Shishmareff; Lillie Hayward and Jay Brennan shared screenplay credits with Jean. Originally titled *She Hired an Husband,* the script was completed in June 1936 and went into production the following year. After the amazing success of Columbia's *It Happened One Night* (1934), light comedies were in demand. The 60-minute low-budget production was directed by Bobby Connolly. Many critics found the story too slim ("strictly lightweight" according to *Variety*). It dealt with a young film star, visiting Europe, who marries an impoverished Austrian prince to impress her friends and public back home. *Expensive Husbands* opened at the end of November 1937 but disappeared from screens a few days after its release.

Almost simultaneous with *Expensive Husbands'* release, *Fight for Your Lady* opened nationwide. Jean and Isabel Leighton co-authored the original story. Reviews were positive toward this comedy, whose story seemed to have all the required elements of a funny slapstick farce. The most flattering words came from *Variety*: "*Fight for Your Lady* is the type of picture that will click with any kind of audience. [It's] one of the snappiest comedies of the season. It hasn't a boring moment."[32]

In March 1937, Jean signed a contract as a writer with Metro-Goldwyn-Mayer. He recalled that he wrote an original story for Laurel and Hardy, "which was the worst flop they ever had, because it was literally the idea of a blasé Chevalier story, but Laurel and Hardy had to play it. I think it was called *Swiss Miss*, but after it came out they called it *Swiss Cheese*. They were right."[33]

Jean wrote *Swiss Miss* in collaboration with Charles Rogers. It was planned as a musical comedy and was purchased by producer Hal Roach, who had made a deal for four films with Stan Laurel Productions. Roach presented his comic stars with an undeveloped story idea outlined by Jean and Rogers, called *Swiss Cheese*. "What I was trying to do," Roach recalled, "is to make musicals where a second plot carried on, so that Laurel and Hardy didn't have to be on all the time. And Laurel because he did not understand those kind of things, was not very cooperative in making those kind of films." Laurel later said of the storyline, "I thought it lacked very much. Hal Roach and I differed a great deal on story ideas and gags and … we didn't get along too well on that picture; disagreed very much. When Roach told the other writers to write this or that, they wrote it that way, although they disagreed with the way it was being handled. And they were all for my version of it, but just couldn't sell it to Roach."[34]

Although the story was very weak, Roach decided not to intervene. The reviews were mixed, with many considering *Swiss Miss* predictable. A couple of gags were universally acclaimed.

In August 1939, almost a year after the picture's release, writer Isabella Knotter filed a plagiarism suit for injunction, accounting and damages against Loew's Inc., MGM and Hal Roach Studios. The plaintiff claimed to have submitted her story *So Zwei Pechvogel* (*Two Down and Outs*) to Hal Roach Studios in July 1937 and she alleged that it was infringed upon in two of Roach's films, *Way Out West* (1937) and *Swiss Miss*. Knotter's manuscript had been returned in August 1937 with a notation stating that it was unread. It is unknown whether Negulesco, the credited writer of the original story, was involved in the lawsuit.

Before *Swiss Miss* began filming, Hal Roach, who released his films through MGM, proposed to Jean he move to Rome to write for Italian cinema. Roach had just conceived a joint business venture with Vittorio Mussolini, son of fascist Italian dictator Benito Mussolini, to form a production company called R.A.M. (Roach and Mussolini). This proposed business alliance with Mussolini caused MGM to intervene and force Roach to pay his way out of the venture. This embarrassment, coupled with the underperformance of many of Roach's new features, led to the end of Roach's relationship with MGM. Jean turned down the offer, uninterested in working for a dictator in a country at war.

That same year, Jean sold Warner Bros. *Too Much of Everything*, a story co-written with Wally Klein. It was released the following year as *The Beloved Brat* in North America and as *Girls on Probation* in England. Although Jean Negulesco and Wally Klein are the names printed on the original script as the authors, the on-screen credits list Negulesco as the sole author of the original story and Lawrence Kimble as the only screenwriter without mentioning Wally Klein's name. The script detailed the life of a problem child who gets "too much of everything" except love and understanding from her wealthy parents. The young family lawyer understands her and at his insistence, she is sent to a school presided over by a competent principal. After many disappointments, the schoolmaster finally gets the girl to see the error of her ways and changes her into a model pupil. Fifteen-year-old Bonita Granville was cast in the role of the brat along and former silent film star Dolores Costello played the principal. Director Arthur Lubin was borrowed from Universal to direct.

On November 29, 1937, the Hollywood press reported:

> Binnie Barnes, film actress, and Jean Negulesco, scenario writer, said today they would be married as soon as Negulesco is divorced by his present wife. Negulesco met Miss Barnes' train yesterday when she returned from three months of film work in London. She was divorced recently from Samuel Joseph, book dealer.

Jean and English actress Barnes had been dating for a few months when the engagement news appeared in print all over the country. When Winifred Negulesco learned about her estranged husband's intention of marrying another woman, she made Jean defendant to a divorce action, demanding $350 a month alimony and $5000 in attorney fees. Winifred asserted that Jean was earning $2000 a month in addition to pay for work as a portrait painter. She claimed that in 1933 she was induced to enter into a property settlement she considered unfair to her. Under it, Jean agreed to pay $5000 at the rate of $125 a month. She now asked that the agreement be set aside and that she be awarded alimony for $350 a month.

Jean had started an action against her nearly four years earlier with a complaint in which he alleged that Winifred had carried on an affair in 1931 in New York with Franklin J. Swigart and posed as his wife. He also charged desertion and mental cruelty. Winifred then filed a counter-complaint asking for separate maintenance, but the suit was not prosecuted. Now she changed her plea from separate maintenance to divorce.

Finally, with the approach of the holiday season, the couple began to settle their differences. A property agreement was arranged out of court, and Winifred dropped the allegation relative to Jean deserting her during a three-month trip with Hannah Jorgensen, as she had claimed in 1929 in her previous lawsuit against Jean.

At last, as a welcome Christmas gift, on December 24, 1938, the bitter divorce litigation was put to an end after Winifred appeared before Judge Carl A. Stutsman, who granted a divorce on the grounds of desertion. She told the court that Jean frequently threatened to desert her. "I am going" was all he said at the time they separated, according to her testimony. Jean failed to appear in court to oppose the charge and Winifred was granted the decree. It was an agreeable conclusion to the long, stormy divorce litigation. But by the time the divorce became effective, Jean's relationship with Binnie Barnes was already over.

Jean's often extravagant Hollywood lifestyle was supported by the sale of his art (mostly portraits and caricatures of celebrities) and by the money from his writing. He was always trying to dream up new ideas for a script or a story. After reading a fascinating article about a gambler in South America, he got the inspiration for a story: *Rio*. Once he completed it, his agent Sam Jaffe sold it to Universal for $10,000—an extraordinary amount for a relatively unknown writer.

The studios were looking for a second vehicle for French actress Danielle Darrieux after the success of her first American film *The Rage of Paris* (1938) and *Rio* seemed the perfect story. The plot had a South American background centering in Rio de Janeiro, although part of the story took place around Paris. It concerned a swindler, escaped from a French penal colony. After learning that his wife has taken a lover, he attempts to kill the man.

Darrieux turned down the part due to previous commitments, so Universal lowered the production budget replacing the French star with Norwegian-American starlet Sigrid Gurie, who played opposite Basil Rathbone and Robert Cummings. *Rio* got above average reviews, and some of them mentioned Jean.

With the $9000 received from the sale of *Rio* (ten percent went to Jaffe's agency) Jean decided to travel to Mexico with his agent Sam Jaffe and his wife Mildred. He later described the trip as "three of the best months in my life: a special model on every corner, singing color, mañana and siesta. I was drunk with excitement."[35] In Mexico he made almost 600 drawings that were all sold upon his return.

In the summer of 1939, Jean was invited to the wedding of Joan Fontaine and Brian Aherne. He boarded a small plane at Los Angeles Airport for Monterey, California, along with actor Alan Napier and sportsman Tim Durant. At the resort, Jean shared his lodge with the groom, who was a close friend. On the night of the pre-wedding dinner-dance, Jean had the unpleasant task of telephoning Fontaine in her room to tell her that Aherne had cold feet and wanted to cancel the wedding.

"Jean, in his Romanian accent, said no, Brian wouldn't talk to me, he was too agitated," the actress remembered. "Having no parents with whom to discuss this shattering development ... I could only say to Jean that I would be at the church at noon and Brian could take it from there. If he wanted to divorce me the next day, he could, but I did not know how to stop the preparation Mother had set in motion."[36] Jean and Aherne's best man Buddy Leighton spent the entire night talking to Aherne, who was persuaded to show up at the church on the following day.

On February 29, 1940, Jean celebrated his 40th birthday with a lavish party. The press joked about the fact that he was actually ten years old, having been born on February 29 in a leap year, 1900. Many readers replied to the articles, pointing out that there was no February 29 in 1900. The readers were correct: In all the countries using the Gregorian calendar, there was no leap year in 1900. But Jean was born in Romania, which did not adopt the Gregorian calendar until 1919. Jean usually celebrated his birthday on February 26, a day that many thought *was* his birthday.

3

The King of the Shorts

"Each film for sure is a new adventure."—Jean Negulesco

Negulesco's second unit work at Paramount and Universal, along with his ability as a writer, impressed Warner Brothers' short subjects producer Gordon Hollingshead. When Warners took over First National Pictures, Hollingshead became unit manager. He came up with the idea for *Give Me Liberty* (1936), which broke all attendance records for a short subject and elevated Hollingshead to the number one position as producer in charge of all Warner shorts.

In the spring of 1940, Hollingshead hired Jean to direct the Technicolor two-reel short *The Flag of Humanity*, which dealt with the foundation of the American Red Cross. Although Jean collaborated through all drafts of the script, Charles L. Tedford received sole screenwriter credit. A biography of Clara Barton, *Flag of Humanity* showed her service in the Civil War and the Franco-Prussian War and her many attempts, ultimately successful, to gain recognition of an American Red Cross from the U.S. government. Nana Bryant starred as Barton and John Hamilton was President Garfield. To promote the short, Warners received full cooperation from the American Red Cross, for the first time in its history helping to publicize a commercial product. The short was released in October 1940, concurrent with the annual Red Cross Drive.

Jean's second short, *Alice in Movieland*, was released earlier even though it was filmed after *Flag*. Based on a story by Ed Sullivan, it dealt with a young girl (Joan Leslie) who, after winning a local beauty contest, is off to Hollywood to try to become a star. She falls asleep on a train and dreams of entering a studio, encountering the predictable events until she reaches the Dream Factory. Leslie recalled *Alice in Movieland* as "a delightful story."[1] Ronald Reagan, Jane Wyman and Alexis Smith made cameo appearances as stars dining in a nightclub. For both shorts, Jean received flattering reviews. The industry magazine *Showmen's Trade Review* described his direction as "praiseworthy" and "capable."

In the late spring of that year, Jean replaced his friend, director Anatole Litvak, for the final four days of shooting *City for Conquest*, starring James Cagney and Ann Sheridan. Litvak had suffered an eye injury due to an infection and felt reassured when he heard that Jean had assumed the direction.

Jean's next shorts were in the *Melody Masters Series*, showcasing the talents of famous American big bands of 1940: *Joe Reichman and His Orchestra, Jan Garber and His Orchestra, Henry Busse and His Orchestra* and *Skinnay Ennis and His Orchestra*. These one-reelers were produced under the supervision of Gordon Hollingshead at Warners in Burbank.

From 1940 until 1944, Jean directed a total of 54 shorts, four of which received Academy Award nominations: *The Gay Parisian* (1941), *The United States Marine Band* (1942), *Women at War* (1943) and *Cavalcade of Dance* (1943). Jean's short *A Ship Is Born* (1942) was Oscar-nominated for Best Documentary. The credit line "Directed by Jean Negulesco" became synonymous with high quality in short subject entertainment.

The two shorts that attracted the most attention were made in 1942. *The Gay Parisian* (*Gaîté Parisienne*) and *Spanish Fiesta* (*Capriccio Español*), both featuring Léonide Massine's Ballet Russe de Monte Carlo, were made as part of the *Technicolor Specials* series. In the summer of 1941, Russian choreographer Massine and the Monte Carlo Ballet came to California to perform at the Hollywood Bowl. They also agreed to appear in two Warners shorts. All the major members of the company were screen-tested. With her crooked nose, Alexandra Danilova, the ballet *étoile*, did not test well. Jean replaced her with Milada Vladova. The ballerina hesitated to accept the role so closely associated with the legendary Danilova, but Jean told Vladova that Danilova was neither young enough nor photogenic enough.

When he explained his reasons to Danilova, she replied, "My *nose* does not dance," and ran out of the room in tears.[2] Jean said,

> [T]he difficulty was that usually a dancer, a first ballerina, is not the most beautiful photographically speaking, so the greatest drama was to convince the first ballerina that she should play just in corners and we would like to take a little young chorus girl to play the small part. With the Russian, their drama is pretty strong so we had to use more than diplomacy. I had two or three times chances of being killed, but I survived. So did the shorts.[3]

The atmosphere on the set was tense after Daniolova was invited to teach her role to the younger and prettier colleague. *Film Daily* described Jean's direction as "perfect."[4] Warners offered Frederic Franklin (who appeared in both shorts) a seven-year contract, which he turned down.

Jean enjoyed the experience tremendously, especially since he got involved in the artistic side of the production. "We designed our own very interesting sets, like in *Capriccio Español,* we tried to copy some of the sets of Goya. Massine was a great help on that. [For *Gaîté Parisienne*] we tried to make sets according to Offenbach's *Parisienne*. We got an old Degas and a little Lautrec in it."[5] Jean attributed most of the shorts' success to Ernest Haller, the extraordinary cinematographer of *Gone with the Wind* (1939). Away from the set, Jean started a brief romance with Tamara Touvanova, who was cast as a gypsy fortuneteller in *Capriccio Español*.

Jean's short *The Dog in the Orchard* (1941) was a thrilling adaptation of a suspenseful mystery by Mary Roberts Rinehart. *At the Stroke of Twelve* (1941) was based on a short story by Damon Runyon, which Warner had already adapted into *Midnight Alibi* (1934). Once again critics raved about Negulesco's work. *The Film Daily* called it "crisp and sure."

Hollingshead became responsible for national defense films being made by Warner in cooperation with the U.S. government, and Jean was assigned to direct various military shorts including the Oscar-nominated *A Ship Is Born* about the built of a Victory ship. The documentary *Food and Magic* (1943), made for the U.S. Office of War Information, was about the importance of food and the war effort. With *The Spirit of Annapolis* and *The Spirit of West Point*, both shot on location in 1942, Jean gave a patriotic glimpse into the training routine at two of the country's most prestigious military academies.

3. The King of the Shorts 27

The bulk of Negulesco's shorts were musical features concerned with popular bands or dancers. With the help of noted cameramen George Barnes and Charles Rosher, Jean did incredible things (shooting in mirrors or with bizarre angles) in his shorts on Leo Reisman, Ozzie Nelson, Richard Himber and Henry Busse. Unknown young actors were usually cast to play in those one- or two-reel productions, which would typically require no more that two full days of work. In an interview with a French magazine in the early 1990s, Jean said, "I shot between 60 and 70 shorts.... Making shorts [is] the best school for a filmmaker, because you have to imagine everything. You have no set, no money, no actors. If you have an orchestra that plays a song, how would you shoot it in a way that is interesting for the audience?"[6]

Jean Negulesco directs the short *Richard Himer and His Orchestra* (1934).

Jack Warner decided to find new directors who could bring a fresh approach to low-budget subjects. Jean was promoted as a full feature director. *Variety* in September 1940 noted, "[Negulesco's] first full-length chore will be in the Bryan Foy unit, assignment still undecided."[7]

Warner told Jean that he could direct a full-length film if he found a story whose rights belonged to Warner, on the condition that its budget did not exceed a half-million dollars. Jean chose one of his favorite books, *The Maltese Falcon*, based on the Dashiell Hammett novel, which had been previously filmed twice before by Warner Bros. In 1931, Roy Del Ruth directed *The Maltese Falcon* starring Bebe Daniels and Ricardo Cortez, and in 1936 William Dieterle made an adaptation entitled *Satan Met a Lady* starring Bette Davis and Warren William. According to Jean, both versions performed poorly at the box office because their screenwriters added their own ideas to the story and introduced new, unnecessary scenes. Jean was ready to make a faithful adaptation of the novel. After Warner gave his blessing, Jean worked for four months on the script. Just when it was about to go into pre-production, Jean was sent to the East Coast to shoot an Army short. (According to Jean's autobiography, it was *Women at War*, but the actual production dates do not match. Furthermore, the short was shot in Iowa and not on the East Coast.) On his return, the studio notified him that *The Maltese Falcon* had been reassigned to John Huston. Warner had promised Huston that he could direct any film of his choice if his (Huston's) *High Sierra* (1941) proved to be a hit, and it was.

Bryan Foy gave Jean the chance to direct his first feature-length production for Warners. Jean was assigned to *Hard Luck Dame,* a remake of Warners' Bette Davis starrer

Dangerous (1935). Before its May 1941 release as *Singapore Woman*, the picture went through several titles—from *Hard Luck Dame* to *Jinx Woman*, then *Singapore* and *Woman from Singapore*. Jean rarely talked about that disappointing experience but one occasion when he explained:

> *Singapore Woman* was, like *Kiss and Make-Up,* a collaboration with another director. The producer, with whom I enjoyed a lot going out with women, told me: "You can do it, we are going to make a good movie with two young ones." So I read the original script. It was a good story that Bette Davis had already done winning also an Oscar. "It will be perfect," he added. "It would have Clark Gable and Norma Shearer—I would try to get them for you. Work on this perspective." So I started working with another writer on adapting the script with Gable and Shearer in mind. On the eve of the shooting, "I'm deeply sorry but we couldn't get them, but you can have David Bruce and Brenda Marshall!" Another director came to help me because the producer feared that I wouldn't be able to complete the film, which was probably true, since I was not ready yet.[8]

As often is the case with Jean's statements, the actual facts were skewed. There is no indication that either Gable nor Shearer were ever considered for the leads, but Ida Lupino was attached to the project in its early stage. Jeffrey Lynn was cast as the male protagonist, but he was suspended from the Warners payroll following his refusal to accept this role. Lynn wanted to do a picture at another studio and had been balking at the type of parts he had been getting at Warner, so they replaced him with David Bruce. Alexis Smith, star of several major Hollywood movies in the 1940s, would play the tiny role of a secretary.

David Bruce, Brenda Marshall and Gilbert Emery in *Singapore Woman* (1941).

3. The King of the Shorts

Singapore Woman was the story of the romance between a rubber planter and a woman who believes herself jinxed. Apparently one of the reasons that the studio decided to make the film was the availability of the rubber plantation set used in Bette Davis' melodrama *The Letter* (1940). Principal photography started on January 20, 1941, after Jean refused to start the picture, as at that time it was still entitled *Jinx Woman* and set to start production on Friday the thirteenth. His aversion to the thirteenth start date was because he had made 12 successful shorts and Warner insisted that he make another one. He refused and they threatened to replace him. Reluctantly he started his thirteenth short *Hal Kemp and His Orchestra* and the bandleader was killed in a car accident the day after the picture was finished. Being very superstitious, he did not want to take another chance and the film production was postponed to the following Monday.

Jean asked the casting office for the most cosmopolitan crowd of extras possible for a Singapore cafe sequence. His request was fulfilled: According to technical advisor Louis Vincenot, 34 different nationalities were cast for that scene. The star of *Singapore Woman*, Brenda Marshall, was at the peak of her career after appearing in Errol Flynn's *The Sea Hawk* (1940). Marshall was engaged to rising star William Holden, who often visited her on the set.

It is unclear why Jean was fired in the middle of the production. The picture was completed by the associate producer Harlan Thompson, Jean's co-director on *Kiss and Make-Up*. Negulesco received full credit as the sole film director.

Singapore Woman was regarded by critics as a dull, trite B movie, "melodramatic to the point of narrowly escaping absurdity," wrote *The Hollywood Reporter*. "Negulesco's artistic pretensions are labored, and the histrionics he inspires, empty."[9]

In the summer of 1941, Benjamin Glazer, now a Universal producer, asked Jean to work as a second unit director on the B spy thriller *Paris Calling*. Although Jean was very busy shooting Warners shorts, he could not refuse the favor to Glazer who had been the first one to believe in him. He was then assigned to direct all the picture's road scenes, which involved military troops and car chases.

On January 22, 1943, Jean became a naturalized American citizen. For the next two years he kept directing Warners shorts. His name was also attached to several projects which for various reasons went unrealized. They included an adaptation of Puccini's opera *La Bohème* and *I Hear America Singing*, a two-reel short based on Walt Whitman's best-known poems.

Away from the set, Jean was leading the life of a playboy who lived extravagantly, spoke a multitude of languages and was as charismatic as he was brilliant. Elegantly dressed, he would go out every night to the best restaurants and nightclubs in town, always in the company of beautiful women. He had a reputation as a great ladies' man. From 1941 to 1943, Jean was romantically linked to a number of beautiful ladies including Patricia Morison, Ann Sheridan, Laetitia Fairbanks (the niece of Douglas Fairbanks and Mary Pickford), Frances Farmer, Carole Landis, Marguerite Chapman, Leslie Brooks and Sherry Shadburne.

Negulesco has told two different stories about what led him into the making of his first solo, full-length film, *The Mask of Dimitrios*. In his autobiography he wrote that in April 1942 he was a guest at a farewell party, for John Huston, who had just joined the U.S. Army Signal Corps and had to report in Washington for active duty on the following day. While playing gin rummy with Jean, Huston apologized about "stealing" *The Maltese Falcon* from him. The director claimed that he had not been aware until then that Jean had worked on that script for four months before being pulled off the assignment. Jean said he had no hard feelings and complimented Huston on the magnificent film he had made. Huston told him that Warner Bros. owned the screen rights of *A Coffin for Dimitrios,* a novel he had found as interesting as *The Maltese Falcon* and he advised Jean to show it to producer Henry Blanke before proposing it to Jack Warner. Jean thanked the director for the tip, bought the book the next day and fell under its spell. (The book was originally published in England in 1939, and became a bestseller.)

In the other account, there was a gin rummy tournament at Anatole Litvak's; Jean maintains that Litvak told him about *A Coffin for Dimitrios,* an amazing book written by Eric Ambler. "When you read it," Litvak said, "you'll be as eager to do it as you were with *The Maltese Falcon*."[10]

It is irrelevant which of the two stories is true: Jean loved the book and through his new agent, Frank Orsatti, pitched the idea of making a film to Jack Warner, who was not impressed but did not dismiss it either. For three nights in a row, with the help of Blanke, Jean pasted up the individual pages of the book, improvising a script to show Warner.

Blanke had been the production supervisor of *Jezebel* (1938) and *The Maltese Falcon.* He was confident that Jean, an artist and an expert on antiques, could successfully bring the novel to the screen. Finally Jack Warner assigned *A Coffin for Dimitrios* to Jean. Right at the start, the movie title was changed to *The Mask of Dimitrios*. In the novel, an Englishman, traveling in Turkey, begins to trace the history of a petty crook and murderer, Dimitrios. Even though Dimitrios is dead, suddenly he seems to live again. The trail

Sydney Greenstreet and Peter Lorre in *The Mask of Dimitrios* (1944).

winds through the Balkans to Paris. The Englishman discovers he is not the only one obsessed with the life and death of Dimitrios.

Screenwriter Frank Gruber adapted the novel for the screen. Jean made sure that the script preserved the qualities that Eric Ambler had given it: mood, suspense, intrigue and the spirit of adventure. Jean came up with the idea to pair two of the studio's most popular character actors, Peter Lorre and Sydney Greenstreet, as the obsessive searchers for Dimitrios. As the mysterious villain Dimitrios Makropoulos, Zachary Scott was cast by Jack Warner, who had put him under contract after seeing him on Broadway in *Those Endearing Young Charms*. Jean explained,

> There were no stars in the picture, only character actors. This is the reason why its cost did not reach $340,000. We had to be imaginative recycling some things from other sets. For instance, the scene in the subway was not in the script, but I saw a set design from a Bette Davis film. I said: "Let's shoot a suspenseful scene. We will attach it after the sequence in the movie theater because after combining them still we won't see the man yet."[11]

In spite of its Eastern European emphasis, the entire film was shot at Warners. The research for the scenes set in various exotic countries involved an intensive study of costumes, dialects, backgrounds and the history of the time (from 1922 to 1938). When the time came to screen test the actors, Lorre and Greenstreet almost sabotaged the entire project. They clowned their way through most of the test while Jean said nothing. "I saw the rushes," Blanke said the next morning. "They are terrible, I want to tell you something, Jean. This is your first chance to make a picture. But if the first day's rushes are as bad as the test I've just seen, you won't be doing the film."[12] The following day the pair stopped monkeying around, allowing the picture to proceed smoothly. Because of Peter Lorre's thick accent, his character, the British writer Charles Latimer, was transformed into the Dutch mystery author Cornelius Leyden.

On November 22, 1943, the three stars were called in to discuss the *Dimitrios* script. Jean had planned to impress his cast with a speech he had written and rehearsed in front of a mirror the night before. On his arrival on the set, he asked assistant director Jack Sullivan to find a high chair on which he could sit in order to be above the three actors. Once the trio was around him, he clearly explained the importance of the first scene to be shot, giving very precise instructions and how to follow through with them. At the end of his speech he waited for applause but nobody moved inside Stage 11, where the studio's carpenters had built a huge sprawling nightclub. Suddenly Lorre stood up and exclaimed, "Fuck you!" Everybody on the set broke into laughter. Jean was petrified but he later understood that he had learned his first lesson. Never tell professionals what to do. They know how already and how to execute it. In the following days, the wardrobe fittings were completed and in early December cameras were ready to roll. Jean recalled his directorial debut as a sole director:

> I was very happy I had done all those shorts and gone to all the departments and I knew what a film was made of, and I knew what to ask. The most important thing for a director is—as with a symphony conductor—even if he doesn't play the violin himself, he knows the violin and knows what to ask of his instruments, how to get the effect. I found out that it has been so helpful to me, because I went through all those problems, that when I get between two and three hundred technical questions every day, at least I know how to answer. You can make an immediate decision, in as much as the element is of very great importance in the making of a picture. Sometimes the losing of half an hour of indecision may mean the difference between loss and gain on the picture-making.[13]

Jean often allowed Lorre freedom to improvise. Jean would later describe him as one the most talented men he has ever worked with, maintaining that the entire picture was held together by his amazing performance. A fractured bone in Jean's foot did not stop him from finishing *The Mask of Dimitrios* $100,000 under the forecasted budget. The film wrapped on January 27, 1944.

It premiered in June at Hollywood's Pantages Theater, where Jean arrived escorting Anita Colby. The couple dined and danced together at the after party at Ciro's. Walter Winchell reported: "The reason that Jean Negulesco looks so beautiful is his right arm decoration, Anita Colby, star and Powers model." *Dimitrios* opened nationwide in July. Despite receiving mixed reviews, it proved to be a hit, earning Warner Bros. almost $2 million. "This is Jean Negulesco's most effective directorial effort to date, notable for its creation of mood and suspense," *The Hollywood Reporter* noted.[14]

For many years to come *The Mask of Dimitrios* was Jean's favorite film:

> The reason is that I had the luxury of being innocent, the pride of being inexperienced. You don't try to make a better film of the previous one, everything is new. You don't think of the budget or the audience, you just think to make a film. It's the first time in your life that you are like God. That's why I love *Dimitrios*. Each film for sure is a new adventure, but I never found that same original enthusiasm again.[15]

While filming *Dimitrios*, Jean dated Veronica Lake, the beautiful blonde star, who was very popular in her film noir roles. Lake often had lunch with Jean at the Warner Brothers cafeteria and then would spend the whole afternoon on his set, watching him direct. "I was always faithful to Jean Negulesco, the director, during the time we dated," Lake wrote in her autobiography. "Jean was the one who told people at one of my kitchen parties that he was embarrassed whenever I looked at him. "I always think my fly is open when Ronni [Lake's nickname] looks at me," he told everyone. "I don't think it really bothered him, though."[16]

Jean was so smitten by Lake that he gave her a $5,000 diamond-and ruby-studded wristwatch as a gift. But the three-month love story was over in March when he was spotted, first in the company of Marianne O'Brien and later with the dancer Ann Miller.

Five weeks after wrapping *The Mask of Dimitrios*, Jean was back behind the camera directing *The Conspirators*. A year earlier, Jack Warner had announced that his studio had bought the screen rights to Frederic Prokosch's novel of the same title and that a film adaptation would re-unite male members of the cast of *Casablanca* (1942), one of the studio's biggest successes. According to an early press release, Humphrey Bogart, Paul Henreid, Sydney Greenstreet, Helmut Dantine and George Coulouris were all supposed to be included in the cast but because many of them were involved in other productions, only Henreid and Greenstreet (and later, Peter Lorre) were able to join it. In the female lead, Warner cast Ann Sheridan, but due to a previous commitment she had to be replaced. The studio tried to borrow Joan Fontaine from producer David Selznick, but he refused. Finally, Hedy Lamarr was borrowed from MGM; she was swapping her for John Garfield, who had to make two films for her one. In the final screenplay there were no significant American characters, which probably explains Warner's choice of a cast consisting of foreign-born actors.

The making of *The Conspirators*, whose title was changed briefly to *Give Me This Woman* (and then back again), was very troubled. Hal B. Wallis, producer of *Dark Victory* (1939) and *Casablanca*, was assigned to the picture. Wallis chose Jean to direct it after watching *The Mask of Dimitrios*. Production had just started when Wallis clashed with

3. The King of the Shorts   33

Victor Francen and Hedy Lamarr in *The Conspirators* (1944).

Jack Warner over Warner's acceptance of the Best Picture Oscar for *Casablanca*. Wallis was fired and replaced by Jack Chertok. Suddenly the script was changed along with the location and the story pace. Now it was only loosely based on the novel.

War-time Lisbon was the setting for this espionage thriller which concerned the clash between a member of the Dutch resistance movement, played by Paul Henreid, and some Nazi spies. He eventually falls in love with Irene (Hedy Lamarr). The woman is secretly a member of an Allied spy ring, whose leader Sydney Greenstreet helps fugitives escape from the Nazi-held countries and sabotages Nazi war factories, railroads, troop concentrations and airfields. Editor Rudi Fehr joked, "It was a mishmash of leftovers from *Casablanca* and *Passage to Marseille*, so we re-titled it *The Constipators*, starring Headache Lamarr and Paul Hemorrhoid."[17]

In her autobiography Lamarr devoted very little space to *The Conspirators*, revealing that she agreed to star in it so as not to make the mistake she had made in refusing *Casablanca*, because of the its plot's complexity. During filming, Lamarr discovered she was pregnant.[18] She was given a two-day rest, but on the morning of the second day she received a call from the studio that she was needed for a scene. When she arrived for work, they completely covered her with a blanket and shot the scene. Jean explained to some reporters on the set, "Even when Hedy Lamarr is covered up she can be felt in a scene."[19]

Working with Lamarr was a real nightmare for Jean. Among many specific requests included in her contract with Warner Bros., Lamarr made sure that her portable dressing room from MGM was moved to the Burbank set. According to Henreid, Lamarr was quite insecure and needed to be coached with her acting technique. She often slowed the shooting, as she required extensive rehearsals along with a lot of rest.

"A pain in the ass, a drag," as Jean remembered her:

> She, the great star, did not want to be directed by someone who had only made one film. The co-producer, who was in love with her, had to convince her. I really suffered a lot making that picture. She was that type of actress that would say, "Why do I have to stay here to take off my coat?"
> "But darling, because you arrive at a big party at the embassy in Lisbon, you put away your big coat and behind you there is a staircase that climbs up, people who pass by, this gives movement."
> "I've been to embassies. I've never stopped in front of some stairway."
> "Where do you want to stand then?"
> "I don't know. You tell me. You are the director."
> She'd call the producer, who asked me, "Why do you argue with her?"
> "I do not argue with her, I just asked her to stay here but she doesn't want to."
> Then we'd go to eat…. We had so many nuisances like this. Paul Henreid was gentle though.[20]

One day, Jean asked Lamarr to express flustered embarrassment in a scene. But the actress couldn't do it. After several vain attempts, Jean had an idea: He pretended to stop filming while Henreid approached his co-star and whispered something in her ear in their native Viennese dialect. Lamarr genuinely blushed, and it was caught by the camera. At Jean's suggestion, Henreid had whispered, "My dear! That light behind you! … You are practically nude!"[21]

Peter Lorre was the only one who enjoyed shooting that picture. Once before shooting a scene, he made a joke with Greenstreet about Lamarr being flat-chested and wearing a low-cut dress. Peter screamed, "Hey Sydney, you're the only person on the set with a pair of tits."

According to Lorre, production was held up for two hours while Greenstreet and Lamarr chased him around the set, fitting one reviewer's description of the actors as a "Pekingese and a great Dane out for a romp." Lorre said that Jack Warner fined him $10,000 for the delay.[22]

Warner invested in the construction of elaborate sets for the film. Art director Anton Grot outdid himself recreating the narrow streets of Lisbon, the fishing village of Cascais and the luxurious Estoril casino. The picture, a sumptuous production with an implausible plot, earned decent money at the box office. Nonetheless the reviewers didn't buy it and *The Conspirators* was widely panned. *The Hollywood Reporter,* a fan of *The Mask of Dimitrios,* had only harsh words for Jean's new work: "[A] dated inept direction which tries desperately to be arty and succeeds only in being irritating."[23]

Paul Henreid later blamed Jean for the finished product: "[H]is accent was atrocious and his command of English even worse."[24] The author of *The Conspirators,* Frederic Prokosch (whose first name was misspelled in the film credits as Fredric), watched the film and described his reaction in a letter appearing in *The New Republic*: "All I felt when I rose to go was weariness, intense boredom and a certain amazement. Weariness and boredom after the preposterous rubbish I had been observing; amazement also at the mentality which can concoct such nonsense with a straight face; amazement also at the mentality which is willing to pay to see such tedious stuff."[25]

"It's a film I try to forget," was Jean's comment on that picture many years later.

In June 1944, *Life* magazine dedicated two pages to Negulesco in the art section. "Director-Artist," the article on his artistic background and his experience as a new filmmaker, was accompanied by six photographs of him sketching the faces of the stars who had acted in his film including Hedy Lamarr, Peter Lorre, Jack Carson and Paul Henreid.[26] Jean was very proud of that article, which gave him visibility beyond the Hollywood film magazines, not only as a reputable artist but as an emergent director.

In July, a short *Variety* article announced that *Nobody Lives Forever* was Jean's next assignment. Warner Bros. had reportedly paid $20,000 for the rights to a W.R. Burnett's story "I Wasn't Born Yesterday," later made into a full novel. Burnett, the author of the crime novels *Little Caesar* and *High Sierra,* had written the story with Humphrey Bogart in mind. Ann Sheridan and Bogart were in fact to star in the film, with Robert Lord as director, but after Bogart turned it down, the project was shelved for four years and reassigned to Jean. It would feature John Garfield, Geraldine Fitzgerald, George Couloris, Walter Brennar and Faye Emerson. *Nobody Lives Forever* was the first of Garfield's three collaborations with Negulesco.

In this melodrama combining gangsterism with romance, con man Garfield returns from the war to discover that his girlfriend has stolen his money and left him for another man. He heads out to California where he swindles a rich widow out of her wealth. Because of Jean's great passion for realism, art directors meticulously recreated Manhattan streets on the back lot along with a beach oil field. A pier, derricks and 300,000 gallons of water were used to double as the Pacific Ocean.

Working with Garfield and Geraldine Fitzgerald was very pleasurable compared to the miserable experience Jean had with Hedy Lamarr on *The Conspirators.* The only moment of tension arose when Fitzgerald had to be slapped in the face by George Couloris in a dramatic scene. The slap was so realistic that the Irish actress came out of the take badly shaken. "I was afraid I was going to walk right out of the scene and slug somebody," she confessed.

"Who? Couloris?" asked Jean. "No, you," said Geraldine. "You are the one who wrote that slap in the script." Negulesco smiled and said, "Everything happens to us Romanians."[27]

Between takes, Jean did drawings or caricatures of the male members of the cast. Geraldine begged him to do one of her but Jean refused, saying, "The worst mistake a caricaturist can make is to draw a woman. I made a caricature of just one woman in my whole life. That was my wife. When I finished she looked at it a long time, and then said, 'Do I really look like that?' I said, 'Yes.' I'm still paying alimony!"[28]

Warner Bros. organ-

John Garfield and Jean Negulesco on the set of *Nobody Lives Forever* (1946).

ized Garfield's schedule in order for him to act in two films at the same time. In the morning he played Al Schmid on the set of *Pride of the Marines* opposite Eleanor Parker, and in the afternoon as Nick Blake under Jean's direction. Jean's hand was filmed as the ghostly one that creeps into one scene to fire a gun.

Nobody Lives Forever premiered in New York in October 1946, after being shelved by Warner for almost two years. Reviewers dismissed it as just another melodramatic gangster film. But Jean created an effective noir atmosphere that was recognized by some of the critics.

In September 1944, during the promotion of *Nobody Lives Forever,* an article about Jean's reputation as a Casanova written by Erskine Johnson, a popular Hollywood gossip columnist, appeared in the *New York World Telegram* and was syndicated nationwide. According to the article, "Wolf Picks Ten Best Wolves," "[W]hen the lights go on along the nightclub strip, Negulesco is a bon vivant, master of the continental charm, gourmet extraordinaire, and companion of such glamour ladies [as] Veronica Lake and Anita Colby." Jean responded,

> The genuine wolf is a personality of charm and the ideal companion for the beautiful lady. He is definitely not a heel.... Sometimes I get very disturbed about this matter—not for myself, you understand—because something that really requires a great deal of brains and talent is turned and twisted into a very unfortunate understanding. I suppose the principal explanation of it is that there are a lot of fellows around Hollywood who would love to be wolves, but simply cannot seem to make the grade. Now for example there are a certain group of brothers in Hollywood who are rather persistent with the young ladies, but they persist in the old Continental hand-kissing routine, which became old hat about the time of the bustle. That's the sort of thing that gives a wolf a bad name.[29]

He then lists the dos and don'ts of a true "wolf," and the piece closes with Jean's list of the ten best "wolves" in Hollywood including producers, actors and other celebrities. The article prompted several letters of complaint from women who did not appreciate its mocking spirit.

Since his permanent move to the U.S., Jean had always kept in touch with his family in Romania, corresponding mostly with his younger sister Sabina, who had married Jean's childhood friend Vasile. Yet with the outbreak of World War II, Jean started to receive very limited news from his family, due to the unstable political situation in Romania. He was happy to learn from a Russian dispatch that his brother-in-law Raliu Goirman, married to his sister Georgeta, had been reinstated as the police chief of Bucharest. At that time with the state of war all over the world, a trip to Europe was impossible for Jean, who had to rely only on his sisters' rare letters, often delivered after long delays.

Production on his new film, *Three Strangers,* began on January 10, 1945. It was based on the 49-page original story "Three Men and a Girl," written by John Huston in 1937, when he was writing but not yet directing films. Originally Huston pitched the script to Angus MacPhail, head of the Gaumont-British story department. The executive told him that the story was perfect material for Alfred Hitchcock, who had liked it also. But the heads of the studio, the Balcon brothers, were less enthusiastic about it and turned it down. Then the story was bought by Warner Bros., which commissioned Huston to write a script based on it. He was hired at $500 a week, later raised to $750 when the studio decided to option it. With the help of screenwriter Howard Koach and British author John Collier, Huston completed his assignment. He envisioned directing the picture with Humphrey Bogart, Sydney Greenstreet and Mary Astor in the leads, but when he went off to war the project ended up with Jean, who wanted Peter Lorre instead of Bogart.

Peter Lorre, Geraldine Fitzgerald and Sydney Greenstreet in a publicity shot for *Three Strangers* (1946).

Jack Warner found Negulesco's casting idea crazy but, knowing how tight the budget was, he agreed. For the role of Arbutny, Lionel Atwill, Donald Crisp, Ian Hunter and Claude Rains were considered; for Crystal, Miriam Hopkins and Kay Francis; and for West, Errol Flynn, David Niven, Leslie Howard, Douglas Fairbanks, Jr., and Robert Montgomery. Warner executives found the idea of re-teaming Peter Lorre and Sydney Greenstreet the most sensible and economical choice and gave a green light to the production. Geraldine Fitzgerald was cast in the role of Crystal. *Three Strangers* was the story of three oddly matched people (each a criminal in his or her own way) who make a pact on the eve of the Chinese New Year before the statue of an ancient goddess of fortune, destiny, life and death: Kwan-Yin. The trio agrees to share the winnings of a sweepstake ticket, no matter what is going to happen to them.

All the members of the cast worked in perfect harmony. Fitzgerald had warm memories of working with Lorre and Greenstreet. She confirmed that Lorre had an outgoing personality off the set and spoke of his erudition and generosity in helping her, particularly in difficult scenes. She also recalled Greenstreet's gluttony and how he devoured with gusto a delicious dinner specially prepared by Jean, who was an excellent cook.[30]

There was an awkward moment when Lorre plopped his tired body on a bed on the set next to co-star Joan Lorring, who was lying on it. The actress mistook his meaning and slapped him. She immediately felt embarrassed for her overreaction and apologized to Lorre, who acted very cool without getting angry.[31]

According to a Lorre biographer, Jean often clashed with producer Wolfgang Reinhardt on Lorre's interpretation of his character. Those arguments created a few interruptions that slowed the production, which was completed in six weeks, eight days behind schedule and nearly $50,000 over the $440,000 budget.[32]

Three Strangers did not have any weight as a box office attraction but it received a warm critical reception. Some reviewers described it as "an experimental drama," acknowledging Jean's skillful job in interweaving the three characters' separate stories into a convincing cohesive one.

4

The Warner Years

"Kid, we did it again! We got 12 nominations. Next time we'll get 13."—Jack Warner to Jean Negulesco

Jerry Wald was an established Hollywood writer-producer with a background as a journalist. For his film *Mildred Pierce* (1945), Joan Crawford received an Academy Award, and its success made him one of Warners' hottest producers. A passionate and energetic personality, Wald was one of the very few who could stand up to Jack Warner. In 1945, Jean started a professional relationship with Wald that resulted in three of the most important films in Negulesco's career: *Humoresque*, *Johnny Belinda* and *The Best of Everything*.

In 1942, playwright Clifford Odets was hired by Warner to write a script loosely based on George Gershwin's life. The author delivered a 900-page script, but its massive length scared off the producer. Odets promised to shorten it, but the executive producers involved in the project advised Warner to go with a new, different script. Jerry Wald showed the screenplay to Jean who loved it, calling it "a real act of love," and admitted that even though nobody would ever produce it, it would have made a superb picture.

Wald asked Barney Glazer to prepare a treatment of a script based on *Humoresque*, a Fannie Hurst story published by *Cosmopolitan* in 1919 and made into a silent film by Frank Borzage in 1920, but also using fictional material from the original Odets script. Wald warned Glazer not to take any material from the Odets screenplay that pertained to the life of Gershwin, since under Warner's contract with the Gershwin estate, the studio had the right to make only one picture (which was already in production as *Rhapsody in Blue*). The final draft of the script became a collaboration between Odets and Zachary Gold who were instructed, in anticipation of what audiences' tastes and reactions would be, to transform the Jewish background of the immigrant family with a prodigy violinist son into something vaguely Italian, keeping the original name Boray. The result bore a resemblance to Odets' play *Golden Boy* that was made into a 1939 film starring Barbara Stanwyck and William Holden where the poor ghetto boy becomes a boxing champion.

After considering John Dall, a new face at Warners, John Garfield was cast as the virtuoso Paul Boray and Ruth Nelson cast as his pushy mother. Pianist-composer Oscar Levant was hired to play Sid Jeffers, Boray's friend and mentor. Levant wrote in his memoir that Wald "drew upon my personal experiences as a concert artist to authenticate the role of the violinist played by John Garfield."[1]

Several actresses were considered for the minor but relevant role of Helen Wright, the bored Park Avenue nymphomaniac, alcoholic, patron of the arts, who sponsors the Lower East Side boy Paul Boray. Eleanor Parker was Wald's first choice after considering Bette Davis and Barbara Stanwyck. Eventually Joan Crawford got the part after campaigning for days with Wald, who hated the idea of using her in a supporting role. But Garfield gave his blessings and the cast was completed. Crawford admired Garfield as a serious actor and wanted to work with him. Her part was eventually beefed up and she received top billing above Garfield, who was the film's true star.

According to a *Los Angeles Times* article, Crawford invited Jean to lunch to give her input regarding her character. When the two met, they discussed everything but the character of Helen Wright. "I can't tell an actor about a character," Negulesco explained. "Actors know more about that than directors do. It's their life work. So instead of telling Joan, I went home and did something I do know how to do. I took canvas and paints and painted a picture of the rich, discontented woman whose money and social power could buy a career for a great violinist but not love and happiness for herself."[2]

When Crawford unwrapped the painting, she was ecstatic and almost in tears. She thanked Jean for the amazing gift, which gave her the perfect insight to her character. In Negulesco's version of this story, a panicky Crawford telephoned Wald complaining that the director was not giving her any insight about her character. The producer con-

Jean Negulesco celebrates his 46th birthday with the *Humoresque* (1946) crew and the cast (Paul Cavanagh, Joan Crawford and John Garfield are pictured).

vinced Jean to talk to Crawford, but he decided to make a portrait that proved to be more effective than a thousands words.

After Crawford's wardrobe (exclusively designed by Adrian) had been tested and Garfield had finished practicing the violin for two weeks, shooting started on the morning of December 17, 1945. The biggest challenge in *Humoresque* was making Garfield look like a violinist. He had learned how to bow and properly finger a violin, but did not actually know how to play it. Jean suggested putting a mask of Garfield on a real violinist and shoot the violinist in a long shot, but the rubber mask was too thick and restricted the musician's breathing and movement. Makeup artist Perc Westmore suggested using a violinist who physically resembled Garfield, and photographing him in semi-darkness, but again the result proved unsatisfactory. Finally, two professional violinists were used. One knelt underneath Garfield (who was shot only above the waist) and the other behind Garfield, inserting his hands through holes fashioned in the elbows of Garfield's coat, allowing the real fiddler's hands to finger the violin. The violins used in all the musical shots were eighteenth century Stradivari, Guadagnini and Guarnerius instruments. The Strad was insured for $30,000.

The final result was staggering with Garfield looking like a real professional, while Isaac Stern's violin was, in fact, playing the music. Fans were so impressed by Garfield's performance that in later years he was often asked to play the violin on publicity tours. After directing Garfield in *Nobody Lives Forever*, Jean felt closer to the actor who, under his guidance, began painting landscapes.

On the set, Crawford and Garfield got along well even though when they were first introduced, John pinched Joan's breast. Initially enraged, she later admired his boldness and told him so. Crawford and Oscar Levant had a brawl after he vulgarly commented on her furious knitting between takes and rehearsals, asking her, "Do you knit when you fuck?" After that, the two stopped talking to each other for several days.

Years later, Joan reminisced about *Humoresque*:

> John Garfield, who really was a brilliant young actor, did a fine job. He was so much the young, struggling musician I think the audience felt he really played the violin himself. Negulesco directed it with feeling, the right sort of feeling. And most of the time I thought I was doing well. But when I finally saw it, not just the rushes or the unedited film, but the final print, it reminded me of *Rain*, and I cringed. I overacted and over-reacted in so many scenes. I don't know. I should have done better.[3]

According to Bob Thomas, Joan was temperamental on the set. "When she didn't get the key light she wanted in close-ups, she suddenly developed a headache. She would not appear for work during her menstrual period, reasoning that she didn't photograph as well."[4] Crawford did not mind wearing glasses because they drew attention to her facial features. Since she wanted to appear genuinely near-sighted, she asked Negulesco if she could wear a real pair instead of prop glasses. "I wore glasses and couldn't see through them, which made it look good because I squinted all through it looking at Johnny Garfield—and boy, you don't have to squint to look at that guy. He was *sensational*!"[5] By wearing those rimless glasses, Joan caused quite a fashion trend in Hollywood.

Despite some minor disagreements with Crawford, Jean had a good relationship with her. "She didn't improvise in *Humoresque*," he said years later. "She is a very effective actress and so much a star that her acting spills over into her private life."[6] He recalled that one evening at Jerry Wald's Beverly Hills home, the diva appeared with a real diamond placed on her forehead above the left eye. Jean, too curious to remain silent, asked her why she was wearing such a thing. "Johnny [Crawford's nickname for Negulesco], don't you see? Nobody has noticed the bags under my eyes!"[7]

Filming had its tense moments, however. On one occasion Jean asked Oscar Levant to reflect deep concern in a dramatic scene. After several takes, the director was still dissatisfied and told the actor to picture his children very sick. Levant got so mad that he almost punched Jean in the face.[8]

Robert Blake, who portrayed Paul Boray as a child in a flashback, wrote in his autobiography that it was difficult to rehearse with Jean, "who had an accent that would give a multi-language interpreter fits, I couldn't understand at least half of the time."[9] Jean made it clear to Blake that he should not look into the camera, but just in one direction. After many rehearsals, Blake still felt unsure and confused by the presence of so many crew members around him. Finally Garfield took Jean off to the side and asked for some time alone with the child. The star reassured the kid, telling him not to worry about the crew and coached him through the entire scene as Jean filmed it. Blake was grateful for Garfield's help, but did not like Jean's directing: "He wasn't terribly sensitive.... He was more of an interpreter. He knew where to put the camera and he knew where to put the actors and he knew what he wanted, but he never really knew how to get it."[10]

The final dramatic scene of Helen Wright taking her life by walking into the ocean was shot at Malibu Beach. Its filming was stopped for a long time by a whale that insisted on being in the picture. No one from the crew knew how to shoo away a whale, so everyone had to wait quietly until it decided for itself to continue on its way.[11]

The production of *Humoresque* lasted almost four months, sometimes with three units shooting simultaneously. Jean headed the first unit while James Leicester worked on special effects and Roy Davidson on location at Laguna Beach. During production, Jean had his 46th birthday. The crew gave a small party on the set.

Humoresque, released on Christmas 1946, became one of the top-grossing pictures of the 1946–47 season. One cinema in Mexico played it without interruption for three years. The reviews were mostly favorable. Some critics were enthusiastic in their praise for Jean. According to *The Hollywood Reporter*, "The faults of Negulesco's work are far outnumbered by its many virtues."[12] *Film Daily* reported that Negulesco's direction "skillfully maintains proper tones and highlights"[13]

Jean remembered that after *Humoresque*, he was often defined as a director who favored style over substance. As he once explained, "I have occasionally been criticized for some of the fancy dissolves I used in it—the blind-roll dissolving into the piano keyboard, the soda-water dripping from the siphon and dissolving into a wave, etc. This was a period in which I was trying to be 'clever' and when such arty effects were all the rage. Later they become so over-indulged that people looking at them today exclaim, 'My God, that's so banal!'"[14]

The following year, the Academy of Motion Picture Arts and Sciences snubbed *Humoresque*, giving it only one nomination (for Best Music).

On July 21, 1946 Negulesco, "the most eligible bachelor director" in Hollywood, married 28-year-old Ruth Edwin "Dusty" Anderson. Dusty was born in Toledo, Ohio, on December 17, 1918. Her mother was a former opera singer of Cherokee origin, who gave up singing to marry Dusty's Swedish father. As a child, Dusty was offered a contract to appear in the *Our Gang* comedy series, but her parents turned thumbs-down. At DeVilbiss High School in Toledo, she became president of the dramatic association and played the queen in *The Husband's Queen* and Joan in *Joan of Arc*. Later she enrolled for special training at the Museum of Art of Toledo, continuing her studies for six years. With diploma in hand, she then studied at the University of Toledo and modeled part-time for local artists and photographers. After winning a $400 jackpot on Bank Night at a movie theater in her home town, she decided to head for New York. In the Big Apple she started a career as a commercial photographer's model, getting a contract with Conover Cosmetic. Owner Harry Conover renamed her Dusty after making her a Conover cover girl. In 1941, Dusty met New York newspaperman Charles Mathieu, whom she married a few months later. In April 1943, while her husband was overseas with the U.S. Marines Corps, Dusty and 15 other models were cast in the Columbia film *Cover Girl* (1944) starring Rita Hayworth. The beautiful girls traveled from New York to Hollywood in a special car, chaperoned by Anita Colby, the film's press agent. Dusty revealed to Hollywood columnist Sheilah Graham that Columbia boss Harry Cohn "decided on a publicity stunt and also on our protection. He knew the Hollywood wolves would be howling around the door, so he decided to make us inaccessible. He rented a large house that had been the annex to Marion Davies' house in Beverly Hills."

Life in Hollywood for those gorgeous girls was not as golden as expected. In New York, the models earned about $1000 a week. But in Hollywood, Cohn, with the excuse he was launching their careers in the film industry, paid them just $100 a week, out of which they paid their $25-a-week rent.

"After a month," Dusty told Graham, "we became angry. Not so much at the salary, but at the confinement. Eight of us decided to leave the house and find a place that would be more congenial. We were in Hollywood and we wanted to have some fun." They rented two bigger villas at the Garden of Allah complex. They were surprised to find that Cohn did not overreact, as they had expected. The models were supposed to stay six weeks for the film, but the job lasted six months."[15]

While staying at the Garden of Allah, Dusty met comedian Charlie Butterworth and the two started dating on and off until his death in a car accident in June 1946.

Dusty landed an exclusive contract with Columbia and appeared in *A Thousand and One Nights* (1945). In February 1945, two months after her husband returned from the war with malaria, she filed for divorce.

Colby told Jean that, among all the beauties she was chaperoning, Dusty was the one who had an X factor. A few days later, at an auction at the Aimes Art Galleries in Beverly Hills, Jean was in the company of Paulette Goddard when he noticed in the crowd "a tall shapely beauty, wearing a black hood, a black turtle-neck sweater, and black leather slacks. A tasteful blue turquoise Navajo necklace was dangling between her lovelies."[16] That gorgeous brunette was Dusty, who was introduced to Jean by publicist Dorothy Campbell, Anderson's escort at the event. The model gave her name before returning her attention to the auction and bidding on an antique mirror. Suddenly, a bidding war began between Jean and Dusty. Negulesco won the mirror, which he planned to give as a gift to the model. When he looked for her to invite her to dinner, she was already gone.

Jean got her telephone number and asked her out. Dusty declined, explaining that she was divorcing her husband and was instructed by her attorney to keep a low profile to avoid legal consequences. Her husband had reportedly blackened her eye after a violent domestic altercation. A few weeks later, Dusty called Jean to accept his invitation. From that night on, the two were inseparable. Jean tried to borrow his girlfriend from Columbia to play a role in his next picture, but Cohn refused. The tyrannical boss, who often invaded the private life of the stars working for him, did not approve of Dusty's love interest and warned her repeatedly about Jean's playboy reputation, and even accused him of being bisexual. Dusty was devastated and ready to leave. But when she discovered she was pregnant, Jean was able to convince her to marry him. Dusty's divorce became final in June and on July 21, 1946, she and Jean tied the knot in an informal wedding ceremony officiated by the Rev. James K. Stewart, in the back garden of the West Los Angeles home of director Howard Hawks. Pianist Jose Iturbi gave the bride away. Dusty's attendants were Slim Keith (Hawks' wife), Joan Perry (Harry Cohn's wife) and Dorothy Campbell. Howard Hawks was Jean's best man. The wedding was followed by a reception at the couple's recently purchased home on North Camden Drive in Beverly Hills.

A wedding party photo, published nationwide, depicted Jean, Dusty and Jose Iturbi, with Iturbi kissing the bride. This awkward photo brought an interesting response from Dusty's aunts in Niagara Falls: "We saw your husband in a picture last night," they wrote, "and are very glad you married such a talented pianist."

Some newspapers reporting the happy event revealed that on the same day as the wedding, Jean's stepdaughter Suzanne (from his marriage with Winifred) had delivered a baby, making him a step-grandfather.

The newlyweds enjoyed a brief honeymoon at Laguna Beach and delayed their extended honeymoon trip to Europe until the following year because Jean could not get away from Warner Bros.

To prevent paying an idle actress, Ida Lupino, who was under contract but momentarily without any planned work, Warner Bros. dusted off from its vault of properties *Deep Valley*. It was originally announced in 1942 as a picture starring Humphrey Bogart, John Garfield and Ann Sheridan. In July 1943, producer Alex Gottlieb and director Delmer Daves were attached to the project, this time starring John Garfield and John Ridgely. Finally, in 1945, a new cast was selected including Ida Lupino, Dane Clark and Wayne Morris. Jean was chosen to direct. The Salka Viertel–Stephen Morehouse Avery script, based on a novel by Dan Totheroh, was almost completed when Warners decided to hire William Faulkner to write some additional dialogue. However, none of the future Nobel Prize novelist's lines were used.

When the picture was about to go into production, the studio workers went on strike: first the set decorators, who demanded higher wages and a recognition as a separate union, followed by carpenters, painters and script readers. The studio's entrance was picketed daily. Jean was instructed to shoot the picture on location. On September 23, 1946, during a severe heat wave, cameras started rolling at Surfboard Point in the Palos Verdes Estates on the California coast.

Dusty and Jean Negulesco at the premiere of *Night and Day* (1946).

Deep Valley was the story of Libby Saul, a shy parent-dominated farm girl who shelters a young convict in her father's barn after his escape from a chain gang. She sympathizes with the criminal and falls in love with him. He is discovered by a posse and gunned down, dying in Libby's arms.

In mid–October the cast and crew of 85 (later expanded to 99) moved to Bartlett's Lake near Big Bear Lake, California and stayed at the Paramount Lodge. The scenes to be shot were set in the summer, but the temperatures often reached freezing. Plastic flowers were used to match the previous summer footage. Jean was able to make creative use of the natural mountain location, working for the first time for an entire shooting without the restriction of limited studio lot space.

In the early days of the production, Dane Clark showed a slight nervousness when playing opposite Ida Lupino, who was at the height of her career. "It isn't lack of confidence," the actor explained to Jean, who had noticed the actor's awkwardness. "It's just that a man is bound to be a bit jittery when he moves into the big time circuit." After a couple of weeks of shooting, Clark relaxed to the point where he could rib Lupino right back when she accused him of taking life too seriously. In the end, Lupino was satisfied with his co-star's work—especially in the love scenes they had together, which she admitted Clark played "with terrific abandon!"

During the one-month stay in the mountain resort, Lupino, like many of the crew, caught a bad cold. In addition, while running barefoot, she injured her toe and developed an infection. But she insisted finishing the picture, delivering a powerful performance. "She is a bundle of talent," said Jean about his star. "It even comes out from the end of her hair."[17]

Jean Negulesco, Dane Clark and Ida Lupino on the set of *Deep Valley* (1947).

Deep Valley wrapped 40 days behind schedule on January 27, 1947. As customary at Warners, just before the picture was previewed, all the crew members including Jean, the writers and the producers dined with Jack Warner in the studio's executive dining room. Later they were all taken to one of Warners' movie theaters on the periphery of Los Angeles County. The preview was a success and Warner expressed his satisfaction to the entire crew. Many critics dismissed the picture as a somber, romantic melodrama, and it was not a very successful product.

After making four films in a row, Jean was assigned to direct Errol Flynn, Warners' most bankable male star, in *Adventures of Don Juan.* Originally the picture was slated for production in early 1945, according to Warner Bros. interoffice memos. Raoul Walsh was first chosen to direct the film, which was postponed for various reasons, including the lengthy industry strike that also affected the making of *Deep Valley.* By the time the production was set to start, Flynn had fallen out with Walsh and Michael Curtiz, with whom he had made highly successful pictures. Jean was then attached to the project. He collaborated with the screenwriter, expressing his interest in showing a more human side of Don Juan. Don Juan was no longer seen as a predator of women but more a victim of them. Jean expressed his ideas in a lengthy May 6, 1947, memo to Jerry Wald:

> Following our conversation yesterday regarding the story outline of *Don Juan*, I believe you understand how important it is for us to realize that there come moments in the show business when the tide of the public taste has changed its direction. As much as you are talking about things which you should give to the public, or should give as an Errol Flynn starring vehicle, and about trying to run away from formulas which have been proven flops, I believe maybe we should look at what makes box office today with the public. For that reasons we should approach maybe a little more unusual manner our story. I am giving you a few little general ideas about our story.
>
> I am against *Don Juan* being called home because he has been an ambassador of bad will. That brings up the point I worried about in the first script—Don Juan (and Errol Flynn, our star) appears then in the light of an unnecessarily quarrelsome fellow, which I think is just as bad as having him a deliberate seducer of women and broker of homes. It would seem to me advisable that he appears not so much as a chippy chaser as a chivalrous fellow who cannot refuse a pretty woman or an ugly one or a good old man like Don Juan or a dwarf asks him for help. What gets him involved in love affairs and duels is his physical attraction, his legend, which knocks the pretty girls for a loop, even when he is not trying to court them.... He is not doing anything, or he thinks he isn't, to attract all the attention he gets. Of course, once Don Juan has started to help out some pretty woman who is not being treated right by her rascally lover or husband, ends up in a clinch with her, he is much too courteous a fellow, and he is ardent too, to go away without a kiss or two. But that is unfortunately where he always gets into a conflict with some other man who can be expected to see Don Juan has gotten into the boudoir in chivalrous answer to the woman's call, and that the romance is really the woman's fault rather than that of good old, kind-hearted and terribly magnetic Don Juan. It is not that he takes the women away from other guys. It is rather that the women leave the other guys.... The plot idea of a man in search of love, and when he meets it, it is unobtainable, is still the right line of our story. Do not dismiss lightly, dear Jerry, the short, clever scene of Don Juan making love in different countries with women answering him in their native language and Don Juan talking the language of love...[18]

When Flynn read the first draft, he immediately dismissed it. The star was not interested in the psychological side of his character. He only wanted to maintain his screen image as the romantic swashbuckler-hero. None of Jean's ideas was used except the suggestion of casting Swedish actress Viveca Lindfors as the queen. After weeks of arguing, Jack Warner summoned Jean into his office and told him that Flynn did not want him as director. Since the actor was Warners' biggest box office asset, Warner was obliged. Jean was fired and replaced with Vincent Sherman.

Warner suggested that Negulesco see Jerry Wald and choose one of the scripts the producer had optioned. Wald showed Jean three stories. He picked one called *Johnny Belinda*, intrigued by the name Belinda, which was the brand of the cigars he had just begun to smoke. After reading it, he sent a memo to Wald saying, "I'd love to do it."

Elmer Harris wrote *Johnny Belinda* as a play. He first tried to sell the story to MGM but the studio passed on it, questioning the commercial value of a film with a non-speaking main character. A rape scene was also central to the story, and would be subject to strict censorship. In 1941, Harris sold the story to a theatrical producer, and the play ran on Broadway for 321 performances with Helen Craig as Johnny Belinda. Despite good reviews, it was not a hit. In 1946 the story landed on Wald's desk. Fascinated by it, the producer convinced Jack Warner and Steve Trilling to purchase it. He saw the elements of a commercially salable story with strong box office potential.

"Why nobody has purchased this property before this is somewhat beyond my powers of comprehensions," Wald wrote in a memo to Trilling.[19] He reminded Trilling that Paramount and RKO had already made successful pictures about a hearing- or speech-impaired woman: *And Now Tomorrow* (1944) starring Loretta Young and *The Spiral Staircase* (1946) with Dorothy McGuire. *Johnny Belinda* would become the first film whose main female protagonist had both disabilities.

Warner was finally convinced and bought the rights for $50.000. Wald read several script drafts but none seemed to comply with the rules of the Production Code. In December 1946, Irmgard von Cube and Allen Vincent completed a dramatic screenplay that was passed by the censors.

Johnny Belinda was the melodramatic story of a deaf mute girl who leads a lonely existence in a Nova Scotia fishing village in. Living with her stern fisherman father and a kind aunt, she is befriended by a young new-in-town doctor who teaches her sign language and lip reading. When Belinda becomes a victim of a brutal rape by a local bully, the doctor steps in to help.

Delmer Daves was Wald's first choice to direct the picture but the filmmaker was unavailable. Jean, unexpectedly free from *Adventures of Don Juan*, seemed the right second choice. By the summer of 1947, the cast had not yet been chosen. Jean and Wald were determined to find the right actors, but no one seemed appropriate, especially in the lead.

For the role of the doctor, Wald considered Ronald Colman and Robert Donat, while Jean thought of Brian Aherne, but they both favored Marlon Brando, who had been screen-tested in New York City after his extraordinary success on Broadway in Tennessee Williams' *A Streetcar Named Desire*. Jack Warner complained that Brando did not talk but mumbled, and advised them to cast Lew Ayres, who had successfully played Dr. Kildare in a popular series of ten MGM films. "I would have loved to be the man who discovered Brando," admitted Jean on a TV program in the 1980s.

Ayres read the script and felt strongly about the material. "That role was different," commented the actor. "The [film] had some content to it that I think was new and refreshing at the time."[20] After a successful screen test, Ayres was signed to play the doctor. But the search for the leading lady was still on. Bette Davis, Eleanor Parker and Teresa Wright were all considered for the role of Belinda, but for some reason they were each dismissed. In an interview with a French magazine in the 1980s, Jean revealed that Viveca Lindfors was actually the first choice for the female lead but, since she did not speak English fluently, was dropped. Wald, who had seen Jane Wyman in *The Yearling* (1946), thought she might be the right one. Wyman had been under contract with Warner Bros. since 1936 appearing in almost 40 films, mostly in secondary roles. In 1945 she had proved her acting ability in Billy Wilder's *The Lost Weekend,* receiving flattering reviews. In 1947 she got an Oscar nomination for *The Yearling*, which was the incentive for Jack Warner and Wald to cast her in *Johnny Belinda*, with Jean's blessing. Wyman was then going through a rough time. Her marriage to Ronald Reagan was on the rocks. He had become more and more involved with politics, focusing on his position as president of the Screen Actors Guild and dedicating less of his time to his acting career. After Wyman prematurely gave birth to a daughter who died, the marriage was a shambles. Wyman fell into a deep depression; her work helped in her recovery. She said in an interview,

> *Johnny Belinda* came to me out of the blue. I had completed *The Yearling* and was on tenterhooks awaiting public opinion.... Jerry Wald telephoned in the midst of my anxiety to say that he had caught a rough cut of the picture, admired it, and wanted to suggest a property for my next vehicle. He spoke of *Belinda*. Here was another opportunity for characterization: I read it, loved it, and Jerry rushed to Jack Warner to buy it for me. Jack shared mine and Jerry's enthusiasm. He realized that here was something entirely different, the like of which had never been seen before in motion pictures.[21]

When Warner gave the go-ahead signal, Wyman plunged into the task of creating Belinda, but an illness prevented her from starting the picture on the original scheduled date. As soon she recovered, the actress began intense preparations, reading the script night and day and memorizing everybody's lines, since her character had none. Elizabeth Gessner, paid $35 a day, was Wyman's technical advisor, teaching her sign language and lip reading. Gessner also found a young Mexican girl, who had been born deaf, to serve as Wyman's model for her emotions. The girl regularly visited the star's home and the studio where several tests of her were made in 16mm and 35mm for Wyman to study. The actress spent hours in the company of the young girl watching her every move and reaction. Lew Ayres also learned sign language for his role, although he had picked up some basic signs when he lived in a boarding house and befriended his neighbor Lon Chaney's parents, who were both deaf.

Weeks of tests followed, but Wald was dissatisfied and distressed. He required additional makeup and wardrobe tests for Wyman, writing in a memo to the studio production manager T.C. Wright, "If this film is to have any honesty at all, Belinda and her family should look like farmers and not like fugitives from Hollywood."[22] So Wyman started to study hair styles, thumbing magazines showing photographs of the rustic Nova Scotians to see what her character would wear. Finally, she cut her hair in a bowl cut. This horrified Jack Warner, who ordered Negulesco to have Wyman wear makeup, like a real star. The director ignored his boss' request.

Wald decided to have the entire film shot on location on the Pacific Coast at Fort Bragg and Mendocino, far from studio interference. Everyone worked in perfect harmony. Jean allowed his actors to work out their scenes themselves, giving them leeway. Jean and Wyman developed a special bond on the set. "I feel so fortunate to have had Jean as my director," Wyman said years later. "This man is not only a very sensitive director but an accomplished artist in every sense of the word, and a good friend and a loving husband to Dusty—an artist in her own right."[23] Jean suggested that Wyman wear plastic, wax and cotton in her ears to block out all sound and conversation throughout shooting, to gain

4. The Warner Years

Jane Wyman and Jean Negulesco on the set of *Johnny Belinda* (1948).

the necessary reactions of a deaf woman. The director and the star started to communicate in a sign language of their own so he could direct her when she had her ears plugged. The cast and the crew developed their own set of signals in order to communicate with her. As a result, Wyman completely altered the timing of her acting to where she was always one beat late, never squarely on cue. So whenever she walked into a scene, she began with her left foot instead of her right and used her left hand to get over the feeling of unsureness.

Co-starring in the picture were Charles Bickfors and Agnes Moorehead, who played Belinda's father and aunt. Moorehead and Jean formed a strong professional friendship. This was the first of three films Moorehead made under Jean's direction. Stephen McNally was the only actor in the picture who had appeared in the original theatrical production. On Broadway, McNally played the role of the doctor, while in the film he played the rapist.

Wyman remarked in several interviews, "*Johnny Belinda* represents ensemble effort. No matter how many screen veterans were there among us, we decided on a policy of mass approval—that is, for the actors. It put all of us on our mettle."[24] Moorehead added that Negulesco "was so delighted he just let us go ahead with the criticisms and suggestions. Now we're all eager, the five of us, to do a second film."[25]

"I never had such passionate cooperation from the crew, cast and the executives," Jean commented many years later. "It was like everybody's favorite child."[26] On another occasion, he said, "One thousand and three hundred shots were photographed.... Jane Wyman appeared only in one hundred and eighty, one seventh in total, nevertheless when people remember that picture they only remember Jane Wyman because the entire action revolved around her. But I took many more shots of Agnes Moorhead, Charles Bickford, Lew Ayres and the local people, but nobody remembers them, all the sequences referred to Jane Wyman. That's because the value of things is relative."[27]

One of the main problems of filming *Johnny Belinda* on location was the fact that it was impossible to view the rushes, as was always done at the end of each day's shooting in the studio. Another problem was the difficulty of matching the quality of the studio footage to that of the scenes shot on location. Cinematographer Ted McCord had the hard task of imagining how each scene would have been lighted in the actual location, and matching his lightning set-up accordingly. "We bent over backwards to make all lightning to coincide with natural sources," he revealed in an interview.

A few weeks into the shooting Jack Warner saw the rushes and started to complain that Jean was indulging in too many foggy landscapes and local nature shots, which Jean claimed he needed for his final scene. The settings were so ruggedly beautiful that McCord and his operator Ellsworth Fredericks had to constantly tone it down so that it wouldn't "steal the scene" from the actors. "It was a great experience working with director Jean Negulesco," McCord observed. "An artist, he has an uncommon camera sense possessed by very few directors. He is also one of the most 'fluid' directors I've worked with. By that, I mean he has no set pattern for approaching a scene. He's always receptive to suggestions and ready to try new ideas of camera approach."[28]

Warner allegedly said to Wald, "The way [Negulesco] fusses over this damned picture. You'd think he had another *Gone with the Wind* on his hands. For Christ's sake, it's only about a deaf mute who gets raped, knocked up, and later kills the rapist. I've heard enough of that 'art' shit from Bette Davis. I don't mind if the picture has some class, but I want to sell it, goddamn it."[29]

As Jean remember it, "They actually took the camera away from me at one point."[30] Warner threatened to replace Jean if he did not see real scenes being shot. Wald fought back, indicating that if Jean was fired, he would quit.

Wald's main concern was how Jean would shoot the rape scene. Negulesco, whose first job in the industry was to sketch the rape sequence in *The Story of Temple Drake*, felt very confident of success with this picture. The rape was entirely suggested through a clever use of light and shadow, followed by a shot of the desolate seacoast before finally dissolving on Wyman's desperate and grim face.

Off the set, Jean, inspired by the incredible landscape, encouraged Wyman, Ayres and Moorehead to try their hand at painting. Negulesco made beautiful portraits of his cast members, who were excited to learn his technique. Wyman became an accomplished and recognized painter and she always credited Jean with being the man who initiated her into the art.

Production was completed in late 1947. When the editing process was over, veteran composer Max Steiner wrote a score that added to the picture's drama. Wald and Jean were enthusiastic about the final cut; Jack Warner watched it and hated it. "We invented talking pictures," he bitterly commented, "and you two make a picture about a deaf and dumb girl. Only one thing can save it: put some narration over her close-ups to tell the public what she is thinking." Wald and Jean balked, so Warner did not pursue the idea.[31]

Jack Warner's brother Harry saw it in a screening room at the Warner Bros. office in New York and was impressed. None of the studio's executives believed in the picture, considering it grim and morbid. Upon distribution, the advertising campaign did not mention the word "deaf" or "sign language." Instead the publicity department promoted the picture as a rape movie.

All the picture's performances were strong and unanimously praised by the critics, who also admired Jean's subtle and tasteful direction. *Film Daily* wrote, "Negulesco's direction as the stamp of a genius."[32] *The Hollywood Reporter* added, "Jean Negulesco's direction combines dramatic emphasis and pace with the required sensitivity. His artistry, and that of Jane Wyman..., gives the picture some rare moments which linger long in the memory."[33]

Johnny Belinda became Warner's highest-grossing film in 1948: over $4,000,000. "When 12 Oscar nominations were announced for *Belinda*, Jack Warner called Jean to congratulate him. 'Kid, we did it again! We got 12 nominations. Next time we'll get 13!" Jean was very surprised by that phone call since Warner had fired him a few months earlier, as soon as the film was completed. Warner did not even allow Jean to do his own editing. Negulesco's answer was, "I have news for you, J.L. There are only 12 nominations in every picture." "We'll invent one extra. And we will get it," replied Warner.[34]

Agnes Moorehead and her portrait (made by Negulesco) on the set of *Johnny Belinda* (1948).

Jean declared years later that one reason *Belinda* was his favorite film was "the personal satisfaction of being fired at the end of the picture, then being called long distance the day of the nomination by the same man who fired me."

Jean received his first and only nomination but Oscar night was a big disappointment for the *Johnny Belinda* nominees. Jane Wyman was the only winner as Best Actress. Very moved but excited, she delivered the evening's shortest acceptance speech: "I accept this very gratefully for keeping my mouth shut for once. I think I'll do it again."[35]

After the ceremony, Jack Warner hosted a party at the Mocambo, a trendy nightclub, where he publicly praised himself as a great producer of quality films and Jean and Wald for their work.

The end of the year brought a sad event to the Negulescos. After five months of pregnancy, Dusty lost her baby, who she had planned to name Belinda. The miscarriage made her very ill. They later tried once again and once more she was denied a living child. Doctors advised her that it would have been too risky for her to try again. It was devastating news but the couple was able to cope, making their marriage stronger than ever.

The sudden death of director Ernst Lubitsch was a great shock for Jean, a huge admirer of his work and an intimate friend. Years earlier, they had bonded when the German director called Negulesco asking him for help with one of his mistresses. "Like a sailor," Jean told Lubitsch's biographer Scott Eyman, Lubitsch "had an official mistress in every port." Lubitsch was very worried about the overlapping presence of two of his lovers, one about to visit from New York and a second one from Vienna already in town. "You have to come to dinner, make love to the New York mistress," implored Lubitsch. Jean arrived at the restaurant and with his *savoir faire* was able to flirt with the woman. Suddenly, he felt a kick under the table. Surprised, Jean looked up to see Lubitsch leaning over, whispering, "Not so much."[36]

After Lubitsch's death, his secretary Steffie Trundle became Jean's private assistant until 1950 when she died at age 58.

5

The Zanuck Touch

> If you made a mistake, Darryl Zanuck wouldn't hold you responsible. He'd say: "Don't try to be a hero."—Jean Negulesco

After being fired for making Warners' most successful film of 1948, Jean felt betrayed and discouraged. His agent Frank Orsatti had just died, so he signed with the Charles K. Feldman agency. With no job offers, he borrowed Brian Ahern's bungalow in Palm Springs and started to paint again, away from the Hollywood scene. An unexpected call came from 20th Century–Fox's production chief Darryl Francis Zanuck. As Jean recalled that difficult period of his life:

> After Warner gave me the sack, I was very sad and I thought of going back to painting and quit making films. I told myself: "I know how to paint. I am not a director. There are people who do not understand anything." But Charlie Feldman, my agent, made me part of a package—with Ida Lupino and Edward Chodorov—that he sold to Mr. Zanuck. My first meeting with him was very amusing. When I was told that Mr. Zanuck wanted to see me, I was not jumping for joy with the idea of going back to what I liked the most, even if I made up my mind to quit directing. At the first meeting, he said: "I've watched a film of yours that I liked a lot: *Deep Valley*." My first impression was good. After he gave me the screenplay of *Road House*. He said: "There are three excellent directors who have turned this script down. The reason why they refused to film it, is that they haven't seen its value. Only you and I can see the quality of this story."[1]

Jean took home the script *The Dark Love* (later retitled *Road House*), read it, liked it and agreed to direct it. He explained that the story was based on an old formula used in several Warner pictures. "It's very simple: When a pretty girl walks by, all the lights have to be pointed on her breasts, and when someone throws a hat on the floor, you start a fight—it's a formula just like any other. It's well constructed: It starts good, it develops right and it ends well. What's most important is that it is well made and that the actors are good."[2]

Charles Feldman, who bore a striking resemblance to Clark Gable, was a shrewd agent and businessman. He had bought *Dark Love*, written by Margaret Gruen and Oscar Saul, for $20,000 as a vehicle for Ida Lupino and resold the rights to Fox with the agreement that the actress would play the lead. The deal was made for $130,000 with Lupino being paid $95,000. Edward Chodorov was asked to write the script in only four weeks.

Zanuck was so eager to start the film that he took care of the casting choices, hiring Cornel Wilde for the role of Jefty and Richard Widmark for Pete, after considering Charles Bickford and Lee J. Cobb for the former and Victor Mature for the latter. Chodorov recalled,

> I've only had the time to write two-thirds of the screenplay when Zanuck called me one day saying, "I have under contract Lupino, Widmark, Cornel Wilde and Celeste Holm. We have three weeks to shoot the film with those actors. Can you make it?" It was like a *tour de force,* a technical struggle, because when the shooting was about to start, I hadn't finished yet, so I had to write day by day the new scenes. It was I that suggested that Ida Lupino sang. They wanted her to be dubbed by a classic singer....[3]

Jean, David Hertz and Serge Bertensson got involved in Chodorov's daily writing, having input on the development of the story, although their names did not appear in the credits. In recent years, Celeste Holm claimed that the picture was the only one she never wanted to make and did so only because she had been on suspension and was going broke.

Jefty Robins (Widmark), owner of a road house, becomes obsessively jealous when his singer Lily Stevens (Lupino) falls in love with Pete Morgan (Wilde), the road house manager. Jefty frames Pete on a robbery charge and then has him released into his custody. To show his control over them, Jefty takes the couple along on a trip to his hunting lodge, where he is knocked unconscious during his drunken attack on Morgan. The lovers try to escape and in pursuing them, Jefty is killed by Lily.

Production started at the end of March, and according to some articles from the time of the shooting, Dusty was included in the cast. Perhaps she was cut from the final print of the film since she doesn't appear in the picture nor in the credits. Apparently a good love scene between Wilde and Dusty was rehearsed many times as Jean was always dissatisfied with its outcome. At one point he walked over to Wilde who was standing next to Dusty and said, "Here, let me show you what I want you to do," taking his wife in an embrace. "You hold her like this, see, as if you meant it, and you speak the lines."

Cornel Wilde, Ida Lupino and Richard Widmark in a *Road House* (1948) publicity shot.

Wilde was visibly embarrassed. "You don't have to explain how, but remember that I'm working under a handicap. Whenever I look at the camera and see you glaring at me, I become self-conscious. I'll bet it would be the same way if you were doing the scene with my wife and I was watching." The awkward episode was forgotten that same night when the Negulescos invited the Wildes for dinner. The Wildes saw their hosts' home and Dusty was asked the next day to decorate their new house.[4] After reading the script, Wilde realized he would need instructions in both boxing and judo: the boxing for two fistfights with Widmark and the judo to effectively handle a wrestler for a rough brawl in the road house.

On the set, there was amazing chemistry between Jean and Ida Lupino. Jean always remembered her generosity: "All the suggestions she used to give on the set were all beneficial for the story and not for her role."[5]

A few years later, Lupino became one of the only female directors in Hollywood. In the picture, the actress had a total of 20 wardrobe changes, and performed with her husky, sensual voice the bluesy numbers "Again," "There'll Be Some Changes Made," "The Right Kind" and "One for My Baby," which became an instant radio hit. Since Lupino refused to use a double, she had black and blue bruises as the result of a 300-pound ex-wrestler picking her up in a tavern scene and shoving her around while she fought off spectators who attempted to interfere. Next she tripped and twisted an ankle. A few days later she pulled the tendons in her neck and dislocated a vertebra when she was knocked down during a fight sequence with Wilde and Widmark. A week before the film was finished, she lost her voice screaming at Widwark and couldn't speak for three days. In spite of all her physical efforts, the actress stated, "This is exactly the kind of picture I've wanted to do for a long time. It has everything I've looked for the last year—hard-hitting drama, action, suspense and a love story with a completely new twist. If such a story hadn't come along, I'd still be at home reading scripts."[6]

After the first two weeks, Fox had the shooting schedule rearranged to allow Richard Widmark to finish in time to be available for his next picture.

When *Road House* opened in November 1948, it was a box office success. Reviewers almost unanimously applauded the performances, but expressed some doubts about the melodramatic story and its rhythm. The picture has now attained the status of a classic film noir with many critics remarking about Jean's great sense of style, the superb script and the characters' emotional and physical isolation. *Road House* was Negulesco's only film noir.

Jean Negulesco in a publicity shot from the late '40s.

Jean had been signed with 20th Century–Fox for a one-picture commitment, but the unforeseen success of *Road House* had Zanuck offering him a seven-year contract. The original agreement was a salary of $3000 a week with an optional raise up to $15,000 by the end of the seventh year. Jean's agent advised him not to accept a salary that could have quickly reached more than $7000 a week, because it would make Jean a director that would be too expensive for many producers and be passed by. Instead, Feldman negotiated a contract with one salary and no options that would give Jean a steady, robust income, and the opportunity of a large selection of films. Jean later recounted,

> Fox was very different to work for from Warner. It was not as tight or as strict. It was much more liberal. If they liked what you were doing, there was no limit to your budget, no restrictions on your way of shooting, on your casting or anything. Whereas Jack Warner was a difficult man to enthuse—he told you what to do and how to do it—Darryl Zanuck was a man who, if you could spark a little enthusiasm in him, would get twice as enthusiastic as you were. Not only that, if you made a mistake, he wouldn't hold you responsible. He'd say, "Don't try to be a hero."[7]

Jean's first feature under the Fox contract was *Britannia Mews*, a Victorian melodrama set in the 1870s, based on a Margery Sharp novel. On May 17, 1948, Jean landed in England to start research for the picture. (The studio had not yet decided whether the film would be made in the U.S. or in England.) Accompanying Jean were Dusty, on her first trip to Europe, and producer William Pearlberg's assistant, Freddie Fox. The trip brought the trio to England, France, Italy and Belgium. Finally, Zanuck agreed to shoot on location for a greater atmosphere of authenticity, making the film one of the first Fox productions made overseas after the war.

On the set of *The Forbidden Street* (1949): an unidentified man, Dusty Negulesco, Maureen O'Hara, an unidentified woman and Jean Negulesco.

Jean received the script with a warning note from Fox's executives: "The story that you are going to read is not as good as the novel. But do not worry, someone of ours is coming to England, a first rate writer will write everything again there."

"I am still waiting," the director joked years later. "We shot the picture the way it was."[8]

Maureen O'Hara and Dana Andrews played the leads surrounded by top drawer supporting performers from the London stage, including Dame Sybil Thorndyke, A. E. Matthews and Fay Compton. Before the arrival of the two major stars, Jean filmed a lot around London landmarks. There was a reception for Andrews at the Shepperton Studios outside London, where the interiors were to be shot. The actor was enormously popular after his film *The Best Years of Our Lives* (1946), which had been continuously shown in the country for 18 months. Andrews was cast as two distinct, unrelated characters, a drunken, struggling British artist and a sympathetic American lawyer. Both are romantically involved at different times with Adelaide Culver (O'Hara), a resident of the infamous slum Britannia Mews. Normally two different actors would have been engaged for these parts, but struck by the neat halfway division of labor imposed by the death of the first character, Fox decided to take a chance and asked Andrews to undertake both personalities. The star accepted the challenge and for one of his roles managed a believable British accent. But he was very upset when he discovered at the film's premiere that he had been dubbed by an unknown British actor.

In her memoir, O'Hara described *Britannia Mews* as one of the least memorable films of her career. She claimed that the only reason to watch it was her co-star Andrews, who did a fine job in his dual role, and Sybil's performance that stole the picture.[9] Thorndyke's makeup took three weeks to devise, as Jean wanted it to be grotesque but not a caricature of "the sow," the terror of the mews. The cosmetic illusion took two hours to apply every day, but the result was so good that critics praised her amazing transformation.

Jean maintained that he played Cupid for O'Hara (a claim never confirmed by the Irish actress) by arranging for her to date his friend Charlie Blair, a handsome pilot who was running a private, independent airline. The two fell in love and eventually married. "Maureen can do everything, anything," Jean declared, defining her "a juicy beauty."[10]

Before the picture was completed, Fox changed its title twice, first to *Affairs of Adelaide*, then *Impulse*. Fox decided to release the picture in two versions: *Britannia Mews*, cut in England by Richard Best for the European market, and *The Forbidden Street*, cut in Hollywood for North American audiences. Three minutes were censored from the U.S. version to avoid the suggestion that "The Blazer," a minor character, might be a prostitute.

Britannia Mews was a flop in both countries. Jean called it "a disaster": "The critics murdered us. I sent a note to Darryl assuming all the blame. 'I liked the story, accepted the cast, enjoyed making the picture.' I promised that somehow I would make up for it." Zanuck assumed his share of responsibility in the failed project, ending his note with "Try not to do it again."[11]

Since it was Dusty's first trip overseas, Jean decided to take her to Paris. Besides showing her all the Parisian points of interest, Jean was eager to introduce her to all the most important art galleries. In their first expedition, they were accompanied by Academy Award–winning screenwriter, and later best-selling author, Sidney Sheldon, who was also an art collector. The trio visited the Galerie Drouant—David in the fashionable Rue du Faubourg Saint-Honoré. Jean asked the owner, Emanuel David, to show them a canvas by the unknown painter Bernard Buffet. Jean was intrigued by the painting, *The Absinthe Drinker,* and asked to see other Buffet works. In an attic above the gallery there were 21 paintings by new artists. Jean examined them all carefully and then asked the price for all of them, including any others David could get in the next few days before he returned to London. Jean bargained the price, making a firm offer of 210,000 francs. David was perplexed. Those paintings were worth three times what Jean was offering. In selling them at that price, he was afraid of devaluating the market price of the artist. He finally accepted, thinking that if Jean showed them off in Hollywood, it would be nice publicity for Buffet and therefore for his gallery. Before his departure from Paris, David was able to arrange a meeting between Jean and 20-year-old Buffet. Negulesco's first impression of the artist was that he was staring at one of the artist's characters. "He looked as if he stepped down from one of his paintings. He was tall, lean with a nervous face, a long aquiline nose, gaunt cheeks, stooped shoulders. Trying to smile but not knowing how, what he gave is was a forced grimace…. He smoked incessantly…. He was wise, but still pompous, an angry French man."[12] In spite of Jean's first impression, he and Buffet became friends, even collaborating on a project in the early 1960s.

Back home, Jean gave some of the paintings as a gift to friends in his Hollywood clique and was able to use some of them as set dressing in some of his films. In the following years he developed a sort of obsession with the artist, claiming to have owned more than 150 Buffet paintings at one point, becoming the artist's #1 collector. He began selling some of his Buffets. Humphrey Bogart, Lauren Bacall, Charles Boyer, Alfred Hitchcock, Kirk Douglas and John Huston all bought a Buffet from Jean, who made a lot of money out of his art collection.

Zanuck bought the rights to *Three Came Home,* Agnes Newton Keith's bestselling memoir of her experiences in a Japanese prison camp from 1942 to 1945. Keith was captured with her British husband and her small son at Sandakan in British Borneo and survived to write her story. Zanuck assigned Nunnally Johnson to adapt the book and to produce the film. Johnson, one of the hottest writers in Hollywood, wrote the screenplay of John Ford's *The Grapes of Wrath* (1940) for which he received the first of two Oscar nominations (*Holy Matrimony* in 1943 was the other). Jean was asked to direct the picture that marked the beginning of a professional collaboration with Johnson that would continue with three other films.

The search for the right cast became top priority. Ingrid Bergman, Ida Lupino and Joan Fontaine were all seen as possibilities to play Agnes Keith, but the three stars were already engaged in other productions. In October, *Three Came Home* was announced as Olivia de Havilland's next film, but due to a schedule conflict with *The Heiress* (1949) she had to be replaced. Finally, Claudette Colbert was assigned the role.

At the end of 1948, Johnson completed the first draft. Once some minor script adjustments were made, Fox dispatched Robert Snody to scout locations and establish a relationship with political and military officials in the remote, foreign locales. It was also Snody's responsibility to have a thorough knowledge of the laws and customs of the regions around Sandakan, Borneo. Snody was accompanied by a second unit crew headed by d.p. Charles G. Clarke, who for four weeks shot landscapes and locations, establishing shots and background plates. According to Clarke, Agnes Keith provided lodging for two of the four crew members and participated in the filming. She seemed very pleased with Johnson's script. However, according to Johnson's wife Nora, Keith found the adaptation too sentimental. She objected to the end of the script where husband and wife, separated for months in different prison camps and then reunited, wept and fell to the ground in a clumsy embrace. "[Mrs. Keith] is English, I supposed she felt they should go forward and shake hands," Nunnally said.[13]

Snody failed to persuade Keith's husband Harry and their ten-year-old George to appear before the cameras in a scene filmed in Sandakan. Mrs. Keith accepted the idea and briefly appeared on a process plate behind Claudette Colbert and another actress as they walked along a pier on their way to the Berhala camp. The 30,000 feet of film shot on location had to be dried out, due to the excessive humidity, before it was shipped to the studio on a chartered plane.

From the footage, stills, props and plants the unit brought back to Hollywood, studio staff were able to construct duplicates of the buildings and prison compounds and create the atmosphere to match the material filmed in Borneo. A replica of the village of Sandakam was erected in a few weeks at a cost of $50,000 with an additional $10,000 spent on landscaping. A rubber factory was built and supplied with real rubber shipped directly from Borneo. Fox's casting department hired a group of California-based Japanese as Japanese soldiers. Two technical advisers were assigned to them—one to teach them to speak Japanese, the other to teach them pidgin English. In addition, SoCal-based Malays, Bajaus, Ukits, Bukitan, Punans, Javanese, Sulus, Sikhs, Pathans and Filipinos were hired as extras to make up Sandakam's population.[14]

On the set, Colbert refused to wear makeup and was clad in plain clothing, following exactly all the directions Jean gave her. "Claudette's performance was realistic and utterly convincing," Jean told Colbert's biographer Lawrence Quirk. He continued:

> And I for one am sick of hearing about how she wouldn't allow her face to get dirtied up or even smudged. She helped do her own makeup, if that is what you want to call it, and her clothes were rumpled and highly appropriate to the fictional situation in which she found herself. As for the traces of lipstick, rouge or other makeup on her face, even in the toughest scenes, the silly carpers forget, that even amidst the worst conditions, women have lipstick or comb or rouge stick handy to try to make themselves at least look passable. And that is exactly the image Colbert presented—rumpled, smudged up, her clothes a mess but kept together with reasonable neatness. I have great respect for her, and saw no traces of vanity throughout the film.[15]

British actor Patric Knowles, who co-starred as her husband, confirmed that *Three Came Home* was not easy, especially for Colbert. Some of the sequences were very tough physically. The emotional level had to be kept at a high pitch. During a particularly moving scene, Colbert cried so profoundly and continuously that it made Mark Keuning, her young son in the film, weep inconsolably at each take. Clayton Ward, the sound man, complained to Jean that the child actor, with his sniffling nose, was coming in over the microphone so loud that it was making Colbert's dialogue inaudible. Jean approached little Mark and asked him what the trouble was. "I've got something in my eyes," replied Mark. "Which eye?" inquired Jean. "Both of them," the boy sobbed.[16]

After testing for the role, Florence Desmond was signed for the second lead. On the day of her screen test, Desmond was nervous in front of a young actress who read the Colbert lines. "When [Negulesco] saw me," the British actress remembered, "he said, 'That's fine, baby—just the way you look now with your brown, shiny face, but please take off your lipstick. I am not going to permit any of the women in this picture to use any makeup. Believe me, baby, this picture is going to make *Snake Pit* look like a drawing room comedy.'" She recalled Jean being considerate and encouraging. "Baby, if you don't

Sessue Hayakawa and Claudette Colbert *in Three Came Home* (1950).

play that part I won't direct the picture," Jean told Desmond before she left the studio. Two days later he called her in Las Vegas, where she was living, saying, "I hope you are not losing all your money on the craps tables in Las Vegas, because you are going to have to come out here to make that picture."[17]

Sessue Hayakawa, cast as the prison camp commandant, also gave a brilliant performance, even though he often forgot his lines. *Three Came Home* took eight weeks to make. To maintain the level of emotional intensity, Jean decided to film it more or less in sequence. He also asked some cast members to follow a strict diet to look thinner and thinner as the shooting progressed. There was a funny moment on the set when Jean succeeded in teaching a very intelligent monkey how to do a double take. He accomplished the feat by holding a banana up to the chimp's nose, suddenly snatching it away, hiding it, bringing it forth and pretending to eat it, hiding it again, etc. The varying expressions of bewilderment on the monkey's face made one of the most hilarious scenes in the picture.

For a scene involving the rape of Colbert's character, Jean was out for realism. The actress was determined to comply, but during one take she injured her spine and cracked a vertebra. She was rushed to a hospital, where she was held for several days. The consequences of that accident left her with chronic back pain so severe that a few months later she had to cancel her trip to the film's New York premiere.

In a note to Jean, Colbert expressed her sense of accomplishment in making that picture. "You know I'm not given to exaggeration so I hope you believe me when I say that working with you has been the most stimulating and happy experience of my entire

5. The Zanuck Touch

career. [I] wished the schedule was longer."[18] Jean responded to those flattering words years later: "My favorite film is *Three Came Home*, much more than *Johnny Belinda*. Claudette Colbert was sensational.... [E]very time I watch that film I cry."[19] *The Hollywood Reporter* noted, "In the direction of Jean Negulesco there is a tremendous power and unerring capacity for sustaining the grim, somber mood of the narrative. His work accounts for performances that are as striking as the material."[20]

Jean was next handed the directorial reins on *The Big Fall*, based on Ernest Hemingway's short story "My Old Man." Casey Robinson purchased the film rights for $45,000 on behalf of 20th Century–Fox. Robinson, considered a master of literary adaptations, did not have much material to work with and was forced to add a number of conflicts to stretch the story into a full motion picture. The original short story, one of the earliest published by Hemingway, was based on what he had observed and heard at the racetracks he had frequented while living in Europe during World War I.

The *Big Fall* script told the story of an unscrupulous jockey, barred from American tracks and forced to seek refuge in Europe. He resumes his career in Italy, but has to flee to France, swindling almost everyone he crosses paths with. Robinson and Negulesco agreed to shift the story to post–World War II Paris, knowing that audiences had more familiarity with that war than World War I.

Before studio shooting began on September 12, 1949, a camera crew spent two and a half summer months in Paris filming at three French tracks—Maison-Lafitte, Auteuil, and Chantilly. Another camera crew spent two months in Italy filming the pastoral scenes which open the film, as well as background footage around the Merano race tracks. The picture had a total of 40 sets, including the interiors of jockey clubs, railroad stations and a half-mile track laid out on the studio back lot for matching shots of the race sequences. A few days into shooting, Jean changed the title of the picture to *Under My Skin*: Under the skin of every soldier and person back home supporting them is a heart prepared to break. According to Jean's adaptation of Hemingway's story, the young fighting men of the world wars were all like innocent children. They believed in defending their countries with all their hearts, only to have their physical bodies ravaged due to their patriotism.[21]

Under My Skin was Jean's third collaboration with John Garfield, cast as the jockey. The star was infatuated with Micheline Presle, his French co-star, who had been signed to a two-picture contract by Fox in August 1948 at $40,000 per film, with the agreement that her name would be changed into Micheline Prelle, since Fox's publicity department found Presle difficult to pronounce. Presle had starred in one of the biggest hits in

Micheline Presle and John Garfield in *Under My Skin* (1950).

France, *Le diable au corp* (*The Devil in the Flesh*, 1947) opposite Gèrard Philipe. Garfield met her while filming *Gentleman's Agreement* during a visit she had paid to 20th Century–Fox.

"When I read the script for the first time I have to admit I was a bit disappointed," Presle wrote in her autobiography. "And when I completed the film, my opinion didn't change. The only good memories I have about that film are the card games with Negulesco in his dressing room on the set. He was a charming and well-educated man. But this memory is tarnished by Bill's [William Marshall] jealousy scenes, that those card games caused."[22] Presle was engaged to actor Marshall, whom she married in Santa Barbara a few days after the beginning of the production. His obsessive jealousy created other problems on set. Presle had a difficult time making love to Garfield for a scene. Everything went well in rehearsals but when it came to shooting the scene, Jean noticed that the French actress seemed slightly upset. He asked her what was wrong. "This is a little embarrassing," Micheline replied. "My husband just walked on the set and is watching me." Marshall had to be escorted off the set, since his presence was responsible for delaying the completion of the scene. In spite of the problem, Garfield raved to a *Collier's* writer about his co-star: "What an actress! ... This dame knows how to play a love scene from 20 feet away."[23] Studio accountant Albert Valentino, the brother of Rudolph Valentino, helped Garfield deliver his Italian lines in the film.

Jean had Dusty make an appearance in a brief romantic scene in a Parisian café, sitting with Garfield. "She brings me luck," he explained to the press. Dusty's presence did not bring much luck to Garfield. During the filming of a scene where he skipped rope while talking to his film son Orley Lindgren, the young actor kept blowing his lines; take after take was required. Finally Jean printed a take, and Garfield asked to take the rest of the day off as he was short of breath. Jean consented but instead of getting some rest, the star went off Beverly Hills to play tennis. After a few sets he suffered myocardial muscle strain, an early manifestation of the heart condition which would cause his death, at age 39, three years later. Jean shot around Garfield for two or three days, but production had to be shut down for three weeks so that the star could get the rest ordered by his physician. "[Garfield] led a rough life and burned himself out," Jean commented years later.

Under My Skin opened in New York on St. Patrick Day, 1950, with mixed reviews and a lukewarm audience reaction. The most common criticism was the sugar-coated Hollywood ending, violating the spirit of Hemingway's story, missing completely the point of no redemption for the main character. While Garfield's strong performance was noted, Jean's direction was described as uninspiring and unconvincing. The film eventually broke even at the box office. When it was released in Spain, new credits were shot, eliminating Hemingway's name, due to his well-known and long-standing anti-fascist views.

Jean's new Fox contract afforded him a new, larger home, exactly what a filmmaker of his caliber was expected to live in. After seeing many properties around Bel Air and Beverly Hills, the Negulescos bought a big house at 904 North Bedford Drive, a few steps from the glamorous Beverly Hills Hotel. The house had belonged to Greta Garbo, who bought it from opera singer Gladys Swarthout. Garbo lived there for 14 years, first with actor John Gilbert, then with conductor Leopold Stokowski. She had put the property up for sale when she decided to quit Hollywood and move to New York. For many months, she had only used a part of the villa that she shared with a maid and a gardener. When

Jean bought it, the huge, mostly abandoned living room was covered by such a thick layer of dried leaves that it took the effort of seven people to clean it up. Garbo was especially proud of two orange trees she had planted with her own hands in the garden adjacent to the house. Jean and Dusty promised her at closing that they would take good care of them. As the Negulescos were in the midst of decorating the new home, Jean was asked to leave for England to direct *The Mudlark*.

In September 1949, Fox optioned for $5000 *The Mudlark*, a novel by American journalist Theodore Bonnet. The author was inspired by a December 14, 1838, event in which 14-year-old Edward Jones was discovered in Buckingham Palace. At the time the queen was not in residence, but the subsequent court case made all the newspapers. Jones was found not guilty of theft and acquitted. The boy broke into the palace three more times, but instead of being put on trial again he was forced to join the Royal Army. *The Mudlark* was in fact the story of a small orphan boy, a "mudlark," who sneaks into Windsor Castle hoping to meet Queen Victoria, who had been in isolation for years after Prince Albert's death. Discovering the boy, the queen suspects some sort of plot and withdraws still further, until Prime Minister Disraeli delivers a moving speech in the House of Commons convincing her to reappear in public. Convinced he had a winning story on his hands, Zanuck bought the full film rights a month later for $75,000 plus a further $2500 based on the book's sales during its first year of publication.

Zanuck offered the film to Jean and the writing chores to Nunnally Johnson, the highest paid screenwriter in Hollywood. On one level, it was a simple tale of an orphan curious about the queen, and on another it was a political story of a country's responsibility to its people. But despite its political content, Zanuck from the beginning seemed to worry mostly about Johnson and Jean's intent to use a variety of British dialects in the film. In a January 1950 memo, he wrote, "Nothing has done more to kill English pictures in America than pronounced British accents. A British picture has got to be simply sensational to get by in this country and overcome the absolute hatred of American audiences for British accents.... A Scottish accent is worst of all. If we load this picture with pronounced accents we are going to be in serious trouble."

Although the picture consisted of interiors that could easily be shot at Fox, Zanuck decided to shoot the film in England where the studio had some money frozen dating back to the war. For this reason it was agreed that the entire cast would all be English except for Irene Dunne, who was chosen to play Queen Victoria. For the role of Prime Minister Disraeli, Alec Guinness and Ralph Richardson were considered; according to Johnson, Guinness campaigned for the part so avidly that he got his wish granted.[24] Guinness then kept himself busy at the New York Public Library studying the life of Disraeli. "I adore Dizzy," he said in an interview about the picture.

On March 4, 1950, Jean, Dusty and Johnson boarded the *Queen Mary* for England. During the crossing, the Negulescos spent time playing cards with Gracie Fields and David Niven. Also aboard was the Don Cossack Chorus which Jean had directed in a Warner Bros. short in 1942.

In London they were greeted with great hostility by the English press, who loathed the idea of an American playing Queen Victoria. Michael Foote, a member of the Labour Party, found the casting "an insult to the British Empire," as well as another example of "Americanization" of the English film industry. Jean's response to the controversy was, "Were the Danes annoyed because Sir Laurence Olivier played Hamlet?" Regardless, multiple press conferences were held to respond not only to the press attacks, but also to the resistance Fox had encountered while obtaining labor permits. In the first press conference held by Negulesco and Johnson, Jean explained that *The Mudlark* was a top-budget production (expected to cost $1,500,000) that needed to do well in America to make it a financial success. Had they made the film with British artists unknown in the States, they would have been faced with sales resistance from the cinema owners whose first question is always "Who's in it?" If they were to cite the names of three British stars unknown to them, the inevitable answer would be, "What do you have with Betty Hutton?"[25]

Fox president Spyros Skouras called a second press conference in London announcing that the idea that his company was trying to keep British star names off the American screens was sheer nonsense. "We are literally starved for new names and new faces and would be only too eager to use British [actors] whenever it is possible," he explained. He added that *The Mudlark* would have provided jobs to British actors, extras and technicians. He said that Irene Dunne was a star of international repute whose talent and ability had never been questioned. Her name at the top of the cast list would play an important part insuring the success of the film wherever it was shown.

In the effort to calm the waters, Fox announced in the English newspapers a search for a British boy, aged about seven, to play the title role. Andrew Ray was eventually cast. The ten-year-old son of the popular radio comedian Ted Ray was an ordinary schoolboy who had never acted professionally. He was at home sick when Ben Lyon, Fox's casting representative, came round intending to audition his older brother, who appeared too old for the part. Young Andrew, however, looked just the right age. Jean gave the boy a screen test and, in agreement with Johnson, cast him. Lyon was also responsible for the casting of blue-eyed, square-jawed, clean-cut Anthony Steel. The British actor had just played his breakthrough role in *The Wooden Horse*, the third most popular film at the British box office in 1950.

By the time Dunne reached England in mid–May, the controversy of her casting had somewhat died down. But any remaining doubts about an American playing the queen were put to rest in a press conference held by Dunne, who charmed the British press.

The Mudlark was scheduled to start filming on May 15, 1950, at Shepperton Studios. Because the Lord Chamberlain refused permission to make the film in Windsor Castle on the grounds that it was Her Majesty's private residence (though there was no objection to exteriors shots being filmed there), interior sets were constructed from official plans and documents. The State Rooms, with their tapestry, pictures and ornaments, were copied exactly. In addition, a perfect replica of the House of Commons was erected on the studio's backlot.

Every morning at seven o'clock sharp, a group of makeup artists, headed by Ben Nye, began transforming Irene Dunne into Queen Victoria; the cost was assessed to be about £2000, an incredible sum at the time for the makeup of only one star. The process was described in detail in a *Life* magazine article.

Among many experts brought in to get all Queen Victoria's physical details exactly right was British actress Helen Hayes, who had portrayed Queen Victoria on stage. Haye stayed on the set all day coaching Dunne to perfectly reproduce the voice of the queen, who had a slight German accent. It was a very difficult task for Dunne, who was born in Louisville, Kentucky. She did not speak with a Southern accent but she did have a drawl at times. Dunne later said that she enjoyed playing the role.

A stunning portrayal was also given by Guinness as Prime Minister Benjamin Disraeli. He chose to wear a wig dyed in a special black color very similar to the prime minister's hair color in his later years. Guinness outdid himself in a moving seven-minute House of Commons speech, the picture's high point. "It was a wonderful shot," Nunnally Johnson told a friend in a letter.

> Because Jean put his camera way at the back of the House of Commons and moved up slowly. I think the speech ran about seven or eight minutes. [Guinness] did it perfectly in rehearsal, and the whole stage crew burst into applause, because it was such a magnificent performance, Then I think there was only one take, only one necessary, and it was done exactly the same way, except that at one point Guinness paused, looked right and left, as if he was so emotionally moved by what he was having to say, that for a moment he was silent. I was telling him when we saw the rushes how wonderful he was, and I said, "What suggested to you to use emotional pause there?" He said, "I forgot my lines." Where another actor would have every reason to say, "I'm sorry, start over again," or "flub," or something, he turned it into an additional advantage of the speech."[26]

Zanuck called that sequence "one of the most effective moments of silence in film history."[27] According to Nunnally Johnson's daughter, Nora, who often visited the set and later wrote a memoir on his father, "Guinness complained during the filming of Jean's lack of direction."[28]

Negulesco said in an interview with a Spanish magazine that the danger of working with Guinness was that his superb acting would often frustrate his colleagues, making feel them amateurish. "He does not become an active part of the cast, but he makes a magnificent solo."[29] Another fine performance was given by Scottish actor Finlay Currie, playing John Brown, the faithful manservant and Queen Victoria's companion and close friend. His perennial drunkenness and irreverence were a nice addition to the plot.

At Alfred Hitchcock's request, his daughter Patricia was cast in a small role as a servant. Constance Smith was preferred by the casting director to a still unknown Audrey Hepburn for the secondary role of Kate Noonan.

The final shot of *The Mudlark*, a reconstruction of the queen's return to London after 15 years of seclusion at Windsor, was skillfully filmed by Jean in cooperation with the War Office, which provided 50 Horse Guards and about 150 Coldstream Guards, who were all provided period mustaches (compulsory in Victoria's day). Five hundred extras in period costumes cheered Dunne's Queen Victoria when she drove by a semi-state landau drawn by gray horses on the Thames embankment opposite the House of Parliament. Jean had to shoot it in a very limited time, since traffic was halted and major roads closed. Ten days later, on July 20, 1950, the picture was finished.

On August 17, *The Mudlark* was shown to Zanuck. "Everybody was pleased," Johnson wrote in a letter to Alec Guinness. "Your scenes with Irene were little masterpieces."[30] The screenwriter mentioned Zanuck's request to cut a scene of Queen Victoria with her grandchildren, in which she examined their dentures—a sequence the producer hated because it slowed the picture down." In her *Modern Screen* column, Hedda Hopper wrote that the picture made Daryl weep every time he saw it, something very hard to believe.

The Mudlark was the movie shown to the king, queen and princesses at the Royal Film performance for that year at the Empire Cinema in London. Queen Mary, who never attended any of the postwar Royal Film performances, was to have a copy of the film sent out to Marlborough House just before the Royal Show to watch it in private.

After the film premiered in front of the royal family, stars and celebrities gathered at the Savoy Hotel for a private supper party (the proceeds went to charity). Claudette

Colbert, Gloria Swanson, Glynis Johns, Valerie Hobson, Ray Milland, James Stewart, Tyrone Power, Richard Todd and Montgomery Clift were among the guests. One of the highlights of the night was Marlene Dietrich singing "Lili Marlene." The American premiere at Hollywood Grauman's Chinese Theatre was followed by an equally glamorous gala benefit for one of the city hospitals.

There were two different cuts of *The Mudlark*; the American one was five minutes longer than the version seen in Britain. Dunne was given star billing in America whereas the British gives equal billing to Guinness. *The Mudlark*'s box office take was very disappointing. *The Hollywood Reporter* noted. "Negulesco has handled the theme with appealing sincerity and conviction and drawn some memorable performances from the players."[31]

While in England, Jean shopped for his new, partially furnished Beverly Hills home. By chance, many of the decorations used for the picture were identical to the needs of his house. To furnish the sets, Jean and his set designers visited the finest antique

Irene Dunne as Queen Victoria in *The Mudlark* (1950).

shops in London—and he was told that, should he desire to keep his outstanding finds, the rental fee during the long shooting schedule would be deducted from the eventual purchase price. The sets were superb and Jean made certain that his house was replete with what he later referred to as "Mudlark furniture."[32]

6

Consistency

"You're an actress, Act!"—Jean Negulesco to Anne Francis

The controversy sparked by *The Mudlark* in England did not last long, but the same cannot be said for *Take Care of My Little Girl*, Negulesco's next project. In February 1950, while Jean was in Europe busy with *The Mudlark*'s pre-production, *Take Care of My Little Girl* was announced. From the beginning, it became the center of a strong debate.

According to studio publicity, Peggy Goodin originally wrote *Take Care of My Little Girl* as her master's thesis at McGill University, then turned it into a novel. It exposed the snobbishness of the college fraternity and sorority system. Fox producer Julian Blaustein encouraged Zanuck to purchase the film rights, which he did, assigning Blaustein the task of an immediate production.

Anatole Litvak was originally announced as the director with Frank McCarthy serving as the associate producer. Then the project was shelved for almost a year. Litvak got involved with a different project and Jean, who had just returned after several months in Europe, was asked to replace him. Pressure was exerted on Fox to cancel the project. Threats were made by members of the Greek societies to scrap the story. The studios ignored the pressure. L.G. Balfour, chairman of the Interfraternity Research and Advisory Council, wrote to Spyros Skouras that the story was "Communistic propaganda and would give comfort to the enemies of the country." In Skouras' reply he mentioned the American right of free expression and the wisdom of withholding judgment until the picture's release. He also reminded Balfour that his studio had made *The Iron Curtain* (1948), the first purely anti–Communist film, the patriotic features *The Fighting Lady* (1944), *The House on 92nd Street* (1945) and *Twelve O'Clock High* (1949) and other pictures which dealt with defects in the American system. "*Take Care of My Little Girl* does not condemn the fraternities and sororities," wrote Skouras, "but it does expose the evils and practices such as segregation and intolerance.... It is un–American, we think, to bar a girl from a sorority because she belongs to a certain religious faith, or happens not to dress as well as her sisters or comes from the wrong side of the railroad tracks. Some of the things that do occur are heartbreaking and wrong." Balfour did not accept Skouras' position, threatening to bring the matter to the attention of the five million fraternity members: "I can assure you that you will not be favorably received."[1] As usual in these situations, the controversy got so much media coverage that it generated more publicity for the picture and resulted into a very strong showing at the box office, out-grossing every 20th Century–Fox premiere in 1950.

Jeffrey Hunter and Jeanne Crain discuss a scene with Negulesco on the set of *Take Care of My Little Girl* (1951).

To assure authenticity, Blaustein employed Goodin as technical advisor on the film, which was scripted by Julius J. and Philip G. Epstein. Goodin worked closely with the screenwriters before and during the shooting. She also advised on costumes with fashion designer Travilla and set design with Lyle Wheeler and Joseph Wright.

Take Care of My Little Girl went into production on October 14, 1950. It revolved around Liz Erikson (Jeanne Crain) as a freshman who gets wise to sorority manipulative scheming. Joe Blake (Dale Robertson), a soft-spoken senior and mature war veteran who is considered an outcast by the rest of the students, opens Liz's eyes about her drunken, womanizing boyfriend Chad Carnes (Jeffrey Hunter).

For Negulesco, it was not an easy task to keep his vivaciously chattering cast of girls placed in front of the camera and remain exactly as they were between scenes. "As relaxed, as cute, as nice and sweet and caring and bantering, as catty and cutting and as cruel as only young persons can be. That way," he proclaimed, "we will have a picture great for its naturalness, for the intolerance of youth which is a very cruel thing, even if it is unconscious. And what we have to tell in this picture is exactly that: the unconscious cruelty of youth. But it must be told without offending the nostalgic memory of millions of American women who once were young and thoughtlessly cruel, too. So we do it lightly. We let it tell itself by peeking indiscreetly through the keyhole of a composite sorority house."[2] The production hired a total of 1200 college-age Hollywood extras. When Jean was asked why he, a foreigner, happened to be directing a subject specific to American life, he replied, "A 'foreigner' has as much a sense of dramatic situations as anyone and may be a little more objective about an American subject. Besides, I have so much experience with Americans. My wife is part Cherokee Indian—and what can be more American than that!"[3] Dusty was often on the set, and had a cameo in the film which ended up on the cutting room floor.

Jeanne Crain arrived on the set six weeks after the birth of her third son and requested a trailer equipped with a nursery where she breastfed her baby between takes and played with her two other children. "I have to take care of my little boys!" became her usual farewell every time she would leave the set. A few days into shooting, Negulesco had to rearrange the film schedule after Dale Robertson was involved in an accident at a golf tournament. The director had to wait until an infection of the actor's foot healed so that he could walk without a limp. Jean Peters later said of her role,

> Ah! The villainess—I was that in *Take Care of My Little Girl*, a sophisticated, snobbish college girl. And to help me in my wickedness, I wore some glamorous clothes, something exceptional for me. I played that part as thought I believed the girl believed she was right.... Jean Negulesco was the director. He seemed to think my approach got results, and I count it one of my favorite parts.[4]

Take Care of My Little Girl received mixed reviews. Some writers thought the picture was one-sided, and *Newsweek* pointed out that "no hint of the novel's objection to religious or racial prejudice sneaks into the movie."[5] On February 4, 1952, Crain and Robertson reprised their roles in a *Lux Radio Theatre* broadcast of the story. The picture was extremely profitable domestically, but it had a very limited release in overseas markets because Fox believed the subject would not arouse much interest outside North America.

On October 13, 1950, just one day before *Take Care of My Little Girl* went into production, a group of 25 Directors Guild members including Negulesco, John Huston, George Seaton, Mark Robson, Richard Brooks, John Sturges, Robert Wise, Robert Parrish, Richard Fleischer, Fred Zinnemann, Joseph Losey, William Wyler, Nicholas Ray, Billy Wilder, Charles Vidor and John Farrow signed a petition in which they called for a special meeting of the Screen Directors Guild of America to reconsider the impeachment of Guild president Joseph L. Mankiewicz. Mankiewicz had not signed the non–Communist oath, therefore becoming a "member not in good standing." They were also trying to avoid his possible inclusion on a "blacklist" of directors that, according to *Daily Variety*, was to be placed in the Guild's quarterly report to studios and producers. Jean was never an active participant in the activities to defend the First Amendment freedoms of their accused friends and colleagues—accused, that is, of being Communists dedicated to infiltrating the motion picture industry as a means to sell propaganda. Nonetheless, he was apt to get involved when people in the industry seemed to be threatened by political repression.

At the end of April 1951, Fox gave Jean a new four-year directorial contract, with options for an additional three years. The news came with the announcement of his becoming the director of *Lydia Bailey*, scheduled to go before cameras the following summer.

In 1947, Kenneth Roberts gave the screen rights to his best-selling novel *Lydia Bailey* to the studio through an agreement which rendered earnings contingent on actual filming and appearances of the picture in theaters. The project was originally handed to producer Sol C. Siegel and was to have been made in England and Jamaica. Linda Darnell, Micheline Presle, Jean Simmons and Susan Hayward were all considered for the role of Lydia, and Victor Mature and Cesar Romero for the male lead. Four years later, the film finally entered into pre-production.

Once Jean was confirmed as director, he started thinking about casting. He thought Errol Flynn would have been the perfect hero for the story, so he made an appointment with the star to discuss the part. Just when he was about to drive to Flynn's house, Negulesco saw Jean Peters in a studio parking lot. Seeing her gave him the idea to ask her to play the role of Lydia opposite Flynn. The proposal made Peters ecstatic because working with Errol was her dream since childhood. Flynn, who was already having trouble with heavy drinking, seemed interested in the part. But then Howard Hughes, who was dating Peters on and off, learned of the possibility of his girlfriend working with Flynn, and he made sure that the casting was not going to happen. When Negulesco went back to the studio, he found a short note from Zanuck: "Cast set for *Lydia Bailey*. Do not approach Errol Flynn or Jean Peters."[6]

Zanuck had in fact confirmed Anne Francis and Tyrone Power as the leads. But Power refused to play the role. Fox put him on suspension; Power said he preferred suspension to doing yet another costume picture. Dale Robinsons, who had worked already with Jean in *Take Care of My Little Girl*, took over the part. In July 1951, crew and cast traveled to Haiti.

"I was completely wrong for the part in *Lydia Bailey*," Anne Francis wrote in her autobiography. "It should have been a flashy, dark-haired actress like Linda Darnell. I was much too blonde and much too young for the character. But it was quite an experience for the first time out, and I learned what Hollywood was all about. I didn't like everything I saw and did, but that's what Hollywood and the studios wanted of me."[7] Problems started immediately. Francis fell off a horse while practicing for a scene. She had to use a cane every time she was not in front of the cameras. She also got a terrible allergic reaction to the dark pancake makeup they applied on her for a scene in which she was disguised as a Haitian native. Then she developed strep throat.

"*Lydia Bailey* was a good book but I can't say the same thing for the film." Jean admitted years later. He continued,

> The subject was the Haitian invasion by Napoleon's army. The producer, a young man, convinced Mr. Zanuck that it could be made inexpensively. It was the first time I had extras that would walk before the cameras, change their hats behind them and walk again to give the impression of an invasion. I had a very good black actor, William Marshall, and a pretty young girl, Anne Francis. One day I entered in her trailer and she was completely naked. She didn't blink an eye. She said, "Yes?" Probably all flustered, I said, "I beg your pardon, and left." I will never forget that she did not blink an eye!"[8]

Francis did blink an eye when she asked for assistance from Jean about the intent of her character for a scene. His answer was, "You're an actress, Act!"[9]—leaving her feeling totally lost.

Lydia Bailey was very loosely based on real persons and events from Haiti's struggle to maintain its independence from France. Led by former slave Toussaint-L'Ouverture, the Haitian people broke free of French-enforced slavery in 1793, but internal strife between whites, blacks and mulattoes plagued the country. In 1802, Napoleon Bonaparte, hoping to reinstate slavery, sent his brother-in-law, Gen. Charles Leclerc, to retake the island. Overpowered by Leclerc's forces, Toussaint agreed to lay down his arms and was eventually captured and taken to France, where he died. The character of "Mirabeau" is

6. Consistency

Dale Robertson and Anne Francis in *Lydia Bailey* (1952).

possibly based on André Rigaud, a mulatto leader who violently opposed Toussaint. Tall and handsome African-American William Marhall, a popular stage and radio actor, made his screen debut as Mirabeau. His convincing performance was praised by reviewers and Fox wasted no time in signing him to a seven-year contract.

Although the picture was not shot on location in Haiti (only some landscapes and background shots), 20th Century–Fox sponsored a four-day press junket to the island, during which the film had its world premiere—the first Hollywood world premiere held outside the continental United States. The country's president, Magloire, hosted a formal reception and a ball for the stars and members of the press. Even with a big fanfare, launch and some positive reviews, *Lydia Bailey* did only mediocre business.

Jean's wife Dusty, reading a *McCall's* magazine in a beauty parlor, discovered the novella *Phone Call from a Stranger* by Ida Alexa Ross Wyle. She was so taken by the plot that she rushed back home to tell Jean about it. He read it and told Nunnally Johnson, who also its potential. He decided to adapt it into a script of four characters aboard a plane en route from New York to Los Angeles: David Trask, a lawyer leaving his wife to commit adultery; Bob Fortess, fleeing from a fatal car crash he caused; stripper Binky Gay, running away from her nasty mother-in-law; and nerdy loudmouth salesman Eddie Hoke, who's madly in love with his wife Marie. The plane crashes and Trask is the only survivor of the four. He makes the phone calls to tell the news, making the memories of the dead a little more pleasant than reality. He also pays a visit to Hoke's wife, a bedridden invalid.

Gary Merrill was cast as Trask, opposite Shelley Winters, Michael Rennie and Keenan

Wynn. Lauren Bacall was Nunnally Johnson's first choice for Binky Gay, but she had to turn it down and accompany her husband Humphrey Bogart to Africa for the filming of *The African Queen* (1951). Shelley Winters, borrowed from Universal, was given the part.

Jean had difficulties in casting Marie Hoke, who turns out to be a paralytic, not the sex bomb her husband made her out to be. Bette Davis was then married to Merrill, and as she recalled,

> Merrill gave the script to me to read one day, I asked who was playing Marie Hoke? Gary said Negulesco hasn't cast it yet. I told him to ask if I could play it. Merrill was flabbergasted because it was such a small part. I said it would be a change of pace for me. I believed in the part more than its length. I have never understood why stars should object to playing smaller parts if they were good ones. Marie Hoke was such a part."[10]

Davis remarked on several occasions that she did not play that part just to help her husband's career. One day Jean received a call from Davis, who told him of her interest in the third-act role. His excited answer was:

> "Listen, Bette, if you do it, I swear that I will lift up your skirt in the middle of Sunset Boulevard and kiss your ass!" I wouldn't even dare to offer her that tiny role! Flattered, Bette asked me a question to which I found the perfect answer.
> "Do you think that people might believe that I accepted this part only to help Gary?"
> "Listen, Gary is an actor who doesn't need his wife's help to be good."
> Relieved, Bette told me: "I agree with you. Tell the studio to contact my agent to write the contract." She later spent her time in a hospital to study the gestures of a paralytic woman ... her way of sitting, moving, her hobbies...reading, knitting—the position of the pulleys, the bed height related to the visitors chair or to a nearby telephone.[11]

For appearing in five scenes, Davis was paid $35,000, as opposed to $1,500 as specified in the original budget.

Bette Davis, Jean Negulesco and Gary Merrill on the set of *Phone Call from a Stranger* (1952).

But dealing with Davis was not a bed of roses. Jean argued that Davis had taken that role just to be closer to Merrill:

> That was still the early phase of their marriage, and she was still ga-ga about him. In fact, that was the third film they did together in a year and a half, and they were Bette's idea, not his. I think he wanted to establish his professional independence apart from her, and with other leading ladies. I don't think she realized that. Not then anyway.[12]

After the first day or two of rushes, Johnson found something overdone and overstated in the way Davis spoke her lines. Jean said he hadn't noticed anything and did not want to get in any arguments with the star. He advised Johnson to go and talk to her personally. Johnson's directorial suggestion made Davis burst into a rage. "You certainly don't expect me to use the same voice or manner of Margo Channing?" Nunnally, terrified, wondered who she was talking about, only realizing later that Margo Channing was her character name in her last big hit *All About Eve*. Merrill tried to mediate this outburst but Davis screamed herself into four days of laryngitis, emerging with a low contralto which fortunately fit the part.[13]

For the first time in his career, Johnson was asked *not* to appear on the set of a film he was producing, since Davis refused to work in his presence. Years later, when Jean was interviewed for a book on Bette Davis, he said that, at the time, both Davis and Joan Crawford:

> were overacting all over the place and there was nothing you could do with them. I tried to get Bette to tone it down, said she was embroidering lines that were very simple and direct, but she wouldn't listen. She prided herself, for heaven's sake, on wearing a shapeless nightgown and bathrobe in the scene, and in knitting away, Granny-style, but it was all so actressy, so overdone! But you couldn't tell her what to do—no, sir![14]

Jean's next picture *Lure of the Wilderness* was a Technicolor remake of director Jean Renoir's *Swamp Water* (1941), based on Vernon Bell's story of a young man who stumbles upon a fugitive from justice hiding in the Okefenokee Swamp in Georgia and his attempts to help clear him of the charges. Meanwhile, the young man falls in love with the fugitive's beautiful and wild daughter.

The picture was produced by Robert Jacks, husband of Darryl Zanuck's daughter Darrylin. The 26-year-old man started in the Fox publicity department, later switched to the story department and gradually moved up to the job of administrative assistant. Working with Negulesco was Jacks' first experience in a long fruitful career as producer, mostly of Western and adventure films for Fox in the 1950s and subsequently television.

Lure of the Wilderness filming started in late October 1951, in Okefenokee Swamp Park in harsh weather conditions near Waycross and Fargo, Georgia. From dawn till dusk, throughout the entire location filming, all members of the production were either wet with sweat or swamp water. The hazards of shooting the picture in the 400,000-acre Okefenokee Swamp were extensive and constant. Gloria Cesar, a professional snake handler, was bitten on both hands by one of her "pets" and had to be rushed to a hospital.

The troupe worked in the heart of the swamp where no tourists and few guides have ever been, most of the time with water up to their waists. Their "alligator patrol" was a constant reminder of that danger. The wardrobe crew carried three extra pairs of khaki pants for Jean, since he would fall into the swamp water more consistently than anyone else. Walter Brennan contracted such severe poison oak reaction that the makeup artists had to mix their body paints with a soothing medical lotion to give him some relief while he was in front of the Technicolor cameras.

Jean and the cast made Waycross their headquarters for the film, traveling into the swamp each day. On the set, Jeffrey Hunter had to keep a tape recorder running to catch the local accent so he could copy it for his character. On coming back to Hollywood after four weeks on location, the troupe looked like a lost war battalion.

The Hollywood set frequently had the appearance of a family affair, Jeffrey Hunter was visited by his wife, actress Barbara Rush, and his parents. Jean Peters played host to her mother and sister from Ohio. On the back lot, filming was finished on a 15-acre recreation of the swamp. Jean Peters recalled, "In *Lure of the Wilderness* I had to be taught the art of handling a bow and an arrow and to pole a boat. Both proved to be fun. Jeffrey Hunter and I had to practice poling on the lake on 20th's back lot. The water was so cold, I made up my mind not to fall in, but we had a couple of narrow squeaks."[15] She added on another occasion, "The real star of the picture is the Okefenokee Swamp and any poor human who thinks otherwise is just kidding himself. With its 180 species of birds, 20 of frogs and toads, 30 of fish, 28 of snakes and 45 of mammals, it's a world apart. Some of those captured on film include panthers, black bears, deer, alligators and others. No I *don't* want to go back there."[16] Negulesco developed a great fondness for Peters, and directed her in two later films. "Peters was superb, gorgeous physically with animal-like movements, like someone who had always lived in the jungle. I admired her and loved her a lot. You couldn't *not* be in love with Jean Peters. She neither wanted to play in any film nor to be a star, but the agents and the producers would fall in love with her and keep casting her in their pictures."

Walter Brennan, Jeffrey Hunter and Jean Peters in *Lure of the Wilderness* (1952).

In February, a few weeks after the film was completed, Peters, Hunter and Brennan were recalled in front of the camera to do two more scenes—on the Fox back lot, not on location. *Lure of the Wilderness*' world premiere was held on July 16, 1952, in Waycross, followed the next day by a gala event in Atlanta, where a four-block section of the city was transformed into a simulated swampland to provide atmosphere for a colorful parade led by stars Brennan, Hunter and Anne Francis.

Boxoffice called Negulesco's work "skillful" and *The Hollywood Reporter* "a splendid megging job" while *Monthly Film Bulletin* was unimpressed. "This time the hand of Negulesco lies too heavily on it."[17]

On February 13, 1952, *Variety* announced that Negulesco "has fixed Feb. 20 as the starting date for filming of *The Last Leaf*, fourth sequence in 20th-Fox's *The Full House*, based on a quintet of O. Henry short stories."[18] Fox had decided to produce *Bagdad on the Subway*, a film in five episodes featuring the contribution of five different filmmakers: Jean, Henry Koster, Henry Hathaway, Henry King and Howard Hawks. Jean's was called *The Last Leaf*, based on a short story originally published in O. Henry's collection *The Trimmed Lamp* (1900). A couple of weeks before the film was shot, Fox changed the title to *O. Henry's Full House*. "It was a film produced by one of the brothers Hakim, at the time Zanuck's son-in-law," recalled Jean. "The story I had to adapt told the fight against death of a woman sick with tuberculosis [Anne Baxter]. She knew that she is going to die when the last leaf, which she sees from a window in her bedroom, will fall from the tree. Her sister [Jean Peters] asks an old painter [Gregory Ratoff] to draw on the wall the soaring leaf. The sick woman starts to recover, thanks to that tiny particle. I wanted Gregory Ratoff so much that I refused to make the picture if he wouldn't be cast in the part. The studio wanted Edmund Gwenn, but I did not find him too close to the character I had imagined. We shot each episode in six days."[19] *The Last Leaf*, 23 minutes long, and the other episodes were introduced by John Steinbeck.

One of the *Last Leaf* scenes was set in an art store. Jean used in the background two of his canvases, a view of a bridge over the Thames and the portrait of a woman. He continued this tradition in many of his future films. "I was nearly thrown out of the movie industry over a dispute on *The Last Leaf*," recalled Jean. "Union rules declared that three painters were required to paint a leaf on a wall."[20]

The film's premiere took place on August 7, 1952, at the Carolina Theatre in O. Henry's birthplace, Greensboro, North Carolina. *The Last Leaf* was found by many to be too melodramatic and not the best episode of the film whose reception was in general scarcely enthusiastic.

In March 1952, Negulesco gave an interesting interview to the *Los Angeles Times* disclosing some details of his job as a filmmaker and advising new film directors. "Have a hunger for knowledge. Have a humble approach in learning what makes photography click." That was the key to success, according to Jean. "The motion picture is a story told to the eyes," he pointed out. "Often you see a picture and although you later forget what the actor said, you remember what the scene looked like." Jean talked about his regular practice of making drawings of all major scenes in advance so that he could get the feel of a scene, determine the best camera angle and how the action should move for the maximum dramatic effect. The day before shooting a sequence, he would make sketches of the action or would have the still man shoot photos under his direction. Afterwards, he would carefully study those sketches and photographs to determine what should be

Gregory Ratoff, Jean Peters and Richard Garrick in the segment "The Last Leaf" from *O. Henry's Full House* (1952).

left out and what should be emphasized. He stressed that teamwork was what counted throughout the process of filmmaking.[21]

Remembering Negulesco's expertise in directing some of the finest musical shorts at Warner, Zanuck assigned him the direction of *Tonight We Sing*. A musical written by Sol Hurok and based on his own life's experiences. It was a fictional biography of the impresario, who had an intense desire to share his love for music. Jean shot some screen tests, but did not like the script, and told Zanuck, who replaced him with Mitchell Leisen.

Zanuck had no objection when in the early summer of 1952, Dore Schary of MGM asked to borrow Negulesco. Schary's intention was to reteam, under Jean's direction, Green Garson and Walter Pidgeon in their eighth collaboration. *My Mother and Mr. McChesney* was the temporary title assigned to the project (changed to *Vicki* during production but released as *Scandal at Scourie*), based on the story "Good Boy" written by Mary McSherry and printed in *Good Housekeeping* in May 1951. Schary hoped that the story of the adoption of a little Catholic orphan by a Protestant couple, provoking the ire of the little Canadian town of Scourie, would be a successful vehicle for his stars and spark the same box office magic as *Mrs. Miniver* (1942) or *Madame Curie* (1943) did a decade earlier. Ten-year-old Donna Corcoran was cast as the young orphan Patsy. Agnes Moorehead, one of Jean's favorite actresses, had a cameo as a French nun.

Jean started shooting on July 14, 1952, on Lot 3 at MGM. The picture, budgeted at $1,148,000, was completed in five weeks. Pidgeon had remarkably finished up his scenes in only four days. *Scandal at Scourie* was a very happy and relaxing experience for everybody.

"I couldn't have had any leading man I would have liked better," Greer said in an interview.²² Little Donna Corcoran recalled, "I had a very happy time making *Scandal at Scourie* with Miss Greer Garson and Mr. Walter Pidgeon. My dearest treasure is a gold necklace with a St. Genesius medal inscribed with *To Donna with Love from Greer Garson*. I never take it off."²³

Jean revealed that Garson had a clause in her contract stating that before each scene the set had to remain silent for five minutes so she could concentrate. This prompted the only clash between the star and the director, who could not waste five minutes each time Garson did a scene. The actress was very understanding and quickly found a different exercise to concentrate herself before appearing before cameras. On the last day of the production, Jean wrote her a moving thank you note. "I know now why people at your studio consider you the lady queen of MGM. Thank you, Vicky [Garson's character name in the film]. Words cannot say the humble joy of being part of *Scourie*, and working with you. It was like getting the jackpot in every scene."²⁴

In an interview with a French magazine, Jean recalled,

> Errol Flynn came on a visit on the set. In the plot, the little girl, who Greer Garson and Walter Pidgeon had adopted, fell into water. After being rescued, she was carried in Garson's arms who was in tears and went to fetch her a new dress. We had a camera placed behind a backless closet to shoot her when she opened the door. Errol Flynn was stark naked in it. You should have seen her expression when she went to get the dress; her jaw dropped followed by a mighty scream! She was so much into the role of the worrying mother. Can you imagine? You open a closet and you find Errol Flynn completely naked! Not bad!²⁵

A very similar prank, this time with Flynn in his underwear in a closet only, was pulled a few years earlier on the set of *That Forsyte Woman* (1949).²⁶

Donna Corcoran, Greer Garson and Walter Pidgeon in a publicity shot *for Scandal at Scourie* (1953).

Once completed, the picture went through several edits. The Production Code Administration was concerned that, in dealing with the subject of religious intolerance, the script portrayed the Catholics much more sympathetically than the Protestants. Therefore, a few changes had to be made to the final cut. On April 16, 1953, *Scandal at Scourie* was screened for the press at Grauman's Egyptian Theatre in Hollywood. Even though the preview audience gave the film a round of applause, reviewers found the picture a tedious tearjerker and a dull copy of the past Garson-Pidgeon hits. Jean received a few honorable mentions. According to *Variety*, his direction "smoothly coordinates and gets the best from the script."[27] *The Hollywood Reporter* agreed: "[He] sensitively imbues a rather fragile story with a warmth that holds throughout its fast 90 minutes, offering an entertaining mixture of laughs and gulps."[28]

Jean called it "a so-so film." Schary was so disappointed that he decided against a lavish Radio City Music Hall premiere, as every previous Garson-Pidgeon film had, opting for a low-profile opening. *Scandal at Scourie* earned $783,000 in the U.S. and Canada and $842,000 elsewhere, resulting in a loss of $333,000.

Negulesco's next three films *Titanic*, *How to Marry a Millionaire* and *Three Coins in the Fountain*, were big hits, making Jean a huge moneymaker for 20th Century–Fox.

Titanic's story was based on the sinking of the White Star line's R.M.S. *Titanic* which, on its maiden voyage from Southampton, England, to New York City, struck an iceberg near Newfoundland. The incident took place shortly before midnight on April 14, 1912, and the vessel sank within three hours. Considered "unsinkable," the *Titanic* was one of the largest and the most luxurious ocean liners of its time.

Jean did a lot of research on the subject along with Fox's research department that worked for months before the start of principal photography. The entire film was shot at the studio. A 20-foot model was created to depict the end of the huge liner in the icy sea. Twenty sets were constructed by Lyle Wheeler and Maurice Ransford from the blueprints used to build the ship. One, at nearly 200 feet long, showed the bridge's chart room, telegraphy room and a stretch of the deck with working lifeboats. Another, the main dining salon, was almost as large with its striking gold- and gilt-leaf paneling which once adorned the main ballroom of the Cornelius Vanderbilt mansion. As for nautical details, from proper commands to customs, Sir Gordon Illingworth, a retired skipper of the *Queen Mary*, was hired on the set as final authority.

Charles Brackett, Richard L. Breen and Walter Reisch were the high-profile screenwriters hired by Zanuck. All navigational details used in the screenplay, including conversations, incidents and general data, were taken verbatim from the published reports of inquiries held in 1912 by the U.S. Congress and the British Board of Trade. Typically for Hollywood productions of that time, historical details were often tailored to the film's storyline resulting in several factual errors and anachronisms. Jean explained on several occasions that the picture told the story of some of the people who were on board, and the disaster served to heighten and emphasize their personal triumphs and sorrows. "We are concerned in this picture, as in every picture, with people—living, breathing, feeling people, but as you consider the overall story, you can't help wonder what might have been."[29]

The Sturgess family (the focus of the story) was fictional but many other characters were based on real people, including Mr. and Mrs. John Jacob Astor, Benjamin Guggenheim and Mr. and Mrs. Isidor Straus. The character of Maude Young (played by Thelma Ritter) was based on the wealthy, outspoken American Molly Brown, one of the estimated

705 survivors. Second Officer Charles Lightoller was played by Edmund Purdom. The only officer to survive the tragedy, he died at age 78 on the day the film was completed.

The plot had a similar format to *Grand Hotel* (1932) with several storylines intertwined or separated. *Nearer My God to Thee* was the picture's working title since *Titanic* was owned by Willy Riber, a German producer who had made a film by that name in 1943. After first changing it into *Passenger List,* producer Charles Brackett was able to get permission to use the name of the ship as the title.

Barbara Stanwyck and Clifton Webb were the stars of the picture along with Ritter, Richard Basehart, Brian Aherne and 23-year-old Robert Wagner. Production began on October 23, 1952. That day Jean arrived on the set extremely tired and sleep-deprived. He asked Webb and Stanwyck to be kind and make an effort to try to do their scenes at their best, otherwise he could fall asleep. Crew and cast was very understanding and the stars delivered their lines impeccably. At the end of the day, Jean thanked everybody: "You've all been very kind, but don't be too nice again, you could get confused, in that case I would be obliged to save the *Titanic* and Darryl Zanuck would never forgive me!"

From the first day, Negulesco and Stanwyck got along splendidly. He recalled,

> She had the humility and the modesty only the greatest actors have. Once in the early days of the shooting, she arrived by car to the studios. The security guard asked her what she was doing there. "My name is Barbara Stanwyck and I am playing in *Titanic.*" He replied, "I'm sorry but extras don't have permission to park their cars inside." Barbara did a U-turn and drove to a parking lot around the corner. I heard this story from some technicians a few days later. So I approached Barbara.
>
> "You're crazy! You should have told him who you really were!"
>
> "He told me he didn't know me, that's all."
>
> It's a very touching story.[30]

Stanwyck was paid $75,000 for eight weeks of work. A similar salary was given to Clifton Webb, who would be directed by Negulesco in another three films. Webb celebrated his birthday on the set but he requested only one candle on the top of the cake so as not to disclose his real age. Between takes, Jean allegedly asked Webb a direct question: "Are you a homosexual?" Webb pulled himself up to his full height and said, "Devout, my boy…. Devout." The anecdote appears in the manuscript of Jean's memoir but it was left out of the book itself, perhaps because it was not true or because Jean or his publisher were unwilling to "out" Webb.[31]

Robert Wagner recalled in his memoir, "*Titanic* was a heavy production logistically, but a pleasant shoot because of the director Jean Negulesco. Jean had a light, very pleasant personality—whenever I think of him, I think of champagne—and was very helpful to a young actor. He was also a talented artist and asked me to sit for a portrait, which I still have on my wall."[32]

After *Titanic* had been shooting for a couple of weeks, Jean throw a party at his house. Wagner escorted Stanwyck, the two spent the entire evening together and from that night on they began a four-year secret relationship, revealed by the actor only after Stanwyck's death.

It was Jean's idea in the editing room to characterize the score of the film by silence. The picture had no background music except for a group of guests singing around a piano, a church service and the ship's band. "Often the key to dramatic punch in a scene is the total absence of sound or motion," said Jean while the film was in pre-production.[33] The solemn hymn "Nearer My God to Thee," played by the band while the ship was going down at the end of the film, was in fact a very intense use of music after so many effective soundless minutes. Stanwyck described to columnist Hedda Hopper the difficulty of shooting that final scene:

> The night we were making the scene of the dying ship in the outdoor tank at Twentieth, it was bitter cold. I was 47 feet up in the air in a lifeboat swinging on the davits. The water below was agitated into a heaving rolling mass and it was thick with other lifeboats full of women and children. I looked down and thought: If one of those ropes snaps now, it's good-bye for you. Then I looked up at the faces lined along the rail—those left behind to die with the ship. I thought of the men

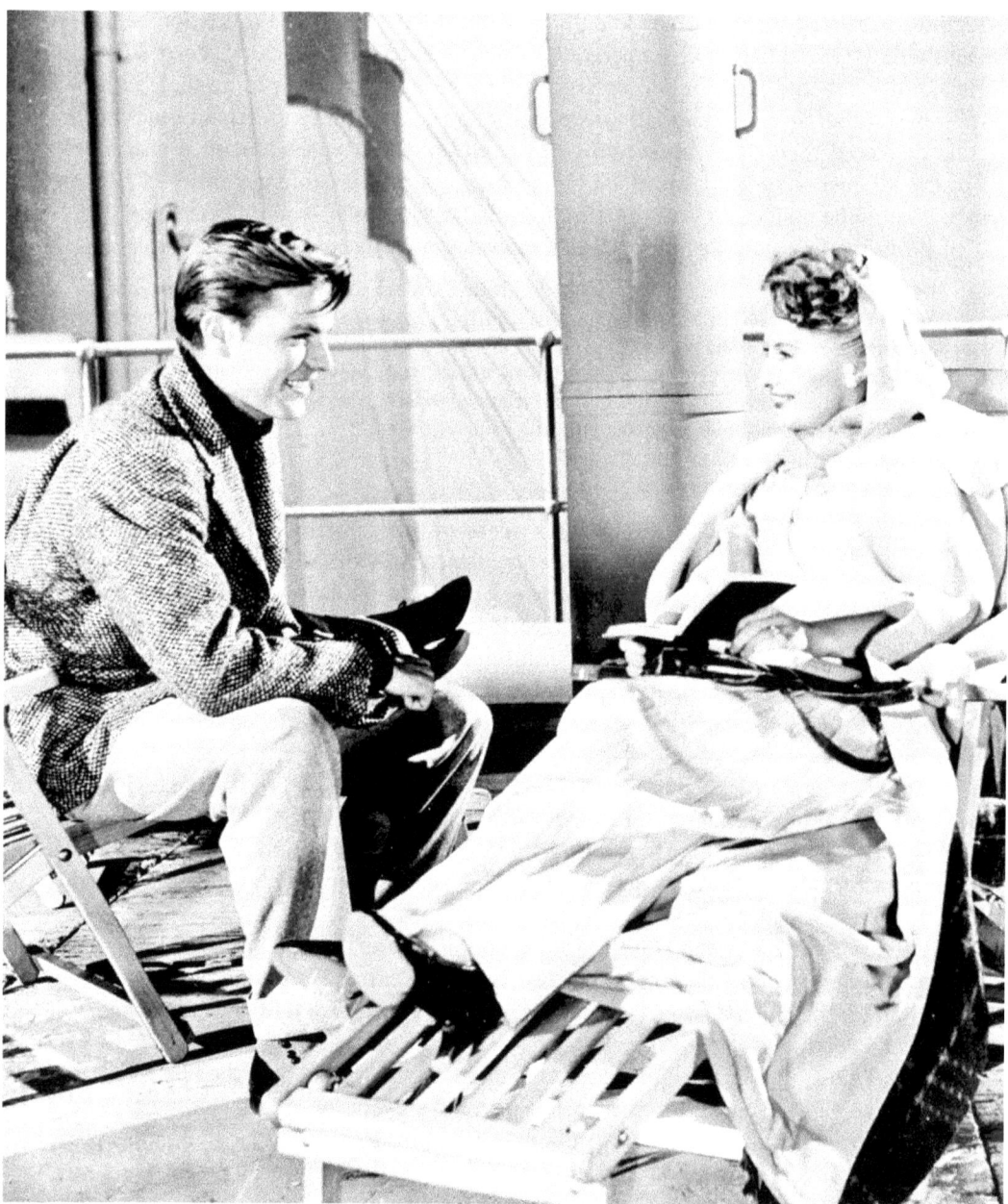

Robert Wagner and Barbara Stanwyck in a scene from *Titanic* (1953).

and women who had been through this thing in our time. We were recreating an actual tragedy and I burst into tears. I shook with great racking sobs and couldn't stop."[34]

The set of *Titanic* became like a big family. At the end of filming, there was a party for cast and crew members, and Jean gave as gifts sketches he had done of everyone.

In the spring of 1953, 20th Century–Fox placed ads in American and British newspapers trying to trace any survivors of the tragedy and invite them to attended a special *Titanic* preview in New York. As reported by *Life* magazine, the reunion was a very tearful occasion. The *Titanic* world premiere was held at the Norfolk Navy Base in Virginia on April 11, 1953, in conjunction with the U.S. Navy Relief Ball.

Titanic's final cost was $1,805,000, which was entirely regained just by a $2,250.000 domestic gross. The film was a hit with audiences worldwide, receiving an Academy Award nomination for Best Art Direction in Black and White and winning an Academy Award for Best Writing, Story and Screenplay.

7

In Glorious CinemaScope!

> [CinemaScope] makes possible the dramatizing of situations which would be confined and imprisoned on the printed page or in a mouthful of dialogue.—Jean Negulesco

In the early 1950s, 20th Century–Fox, like all the Hollywood studios, began experiencing an alarming drop in ticket sales. Studio chiefs were desperate to lure potential moviegoers away from their television sets by offering something the home screen could not. However, it had to be something that did not duplicate the short-term success of 3-D pictures.

CinemaScope was a film process which, through a different system of lenses, allowed widescreen filming. Fox trademarked the name and advertised it as "a new dimensional marvel you see without glasses." The first feature to be completed was *How to Marry a Millionaire*, but Zanuck wanted *The Robe* (1953), his own personal production, to be the first scope picture to be released and get all the publicity. *Millionaire* was released two months later as the second CinemaScope feature.

According to Lauren Bacall, director George Cukor was the first who mentioned to her about a very amusing play by Zoë Akins called *The Greeks Had a Word for It*. The actress, who had a new Fox contract that required her to make at least a film a year, told Zanuck about it. He found the play to be very funny and purchased it. The studio boss paid author Doris Lilly the incredible sum of $50,000 for the title rights to her nonfiction book *How to Marry a Millionaire*. The two stories along with the play *Loco* by Katherine Albert and Dale Eunson were the inspiration for Nunnally Johnson in writing the screenplay of *How to Marry a Millionaire*. The plot was about three fortune huntresses, Pola, Loco and Schatze, pretending to be wealthy in order to find a millionaire husband. They rented a lavishly furnished Manhattan penthouse where they gave parties to lure rich men. While writing the script, Johnson had in mind Bacall, Betty Grable and rising star Marilyn Monroe to play the girls.

"I based the Betty Bacall character in *How to Marry a Millionaire* on Betty Bacall," said Johnson in an interview. "That was Betty. That was the way she acts, and in this particular case I didn't have any great obligation for reality. We were putting on a charade. Betty Grable is not going to be anything other than Betty Grable, there's no need of asking her to do something else, you know. So you are trying to keep it within her baby-blue eyes kind of comedy thing. And as for Marilyn Monroe, God only knows what she would turn out. I didn't think she was a very good comedienne, but I managed to do one thing which I think made her liked more in that picture than any other. I made her nearsighted. I put her in glasses and she was very self-conscious about this."[1]

Zanuck loved Johnson's script and the casting choices, but was not too thrilled by the idea of making it in CinemaScope, thinking that epic stories like *The Robe* were more suitable for that process. When Jean was assigned to the picture, the initial tests were done in 3-D. Then when the possibility of making the picture in CinemaScope arose, he thought it was a great opportunity and fought alongside Johnson to convince Fox to do it in widescreen. Executives called them "fools" and "dreamers." Eventually Zanuck agreed that *How to Marry a Millionaire* would be filmed in CinemaScope on the condition that Bacall do a screen test. This request was something close to an insult for a professional like her. Johnson explained to her that it was only because she hadn't played comedy before and even though they all knew that she was very capable, a test would ease Zanuck's mind. Bacall did the test under Jean's direction and nobody was disappointed. Grable, who had been one of Fox's leading stars, received top billing on the film, but in the trailer and on posters, she was given second billing after Monroe.

The first time Jean met Marilyn was at Sam Spiegel's New Year's Eve party in Beverly Hills in 1948. She was then a young starlet and even though they shared the same agent, Charles Feldman, they rarely saw each other again until *Millionaire*'s pre-production. Zanuck asked Jean to give her the script personally. She read it, but had major doubts about accepting the part. Zanuck encouraged Jean to meet with her a second time. Monroe was not sold on the idea of wearing horn-rimmed glasses and thought the part of Loco was more suitable for her.

She arrived in Jean's office wearing a shirt much smaller than her size, kept together by a safety pin inserted in the middle of her breasts. He was mesmerized by her looks. In a quiet, childlike, out-of-breath voice, Marilyn said, "Mr. Feldman asked me to see you.... Mr. Feldman said you'll explain to me.... My part."

"Have you read the script, Miss Monroe?"

"Yes."

"And?"

"I don't know.... Who are we?"

"Miss Monroe, you are three beautiful girls ... wishing to marry millionaires and the kind of girls you are, the contents of your ice box explains.... Hot dogs, orchids and champagne. Does that answer your question?"

It didn't.

"What is the *motivation* of my character?"

Now it was all clear. Her Russian coach, Natasha Lytess, had put her up to this.

"The motivation, Miss Monroe? You're as blind as a bat without glasses. That is your motivation."

"That's all?"

"Yes. Marilyn that's all."[2]

Jean gently and persuasively made clear that he had much sympathy for her. "No matter what you do in a picture," he said, "if you pick up a glass of water and drink it, right away it's censorable. You cannot help being the essence of *sax* [as Jean would pronounce "sex" with his thick Romanian accent]. To the whole world you stand for *sax*. So you don't have to sell this goddamn *sax* all the time. In this story, I say, you look just as *saxy* with your glasses on, and then think of how utterly charming you become to the audience when you take off the glasses and the world is a blur and you are bumping into walls and doors and hitting yourself on furniture. This is good for you, I say. This is a whole new dimension of *saxiness* for you."

Marilyn was convinced, and Zanuck scheduled shooting to begin on March 11, 1953, four days after Monroe completed *Gentlemen Prefer Blondes*. On Feldman's advice, Jean tried from the very beginning to put Marilyn at ease in order to get a good performance out of her. For two weeks before filming started, he saw her many times for conversations and dinners. He immediately understood her wish to be taken seriously, so he used his passion for art to win her over. He showed her his paintings and drawings and taught her about the greatest European painters. When she claimed that she could not understand modern art, Jean replied that art is like sex; it isn't something one understands but something one feels. Slowly Marilyn came to trust him and he became her friend and confidant. She affectionately called him Johnny and allowed him to paint her portrait. Marilyn told him about a dream she occasionally had when she was a little girl, in which she would meet her mother in a church completely naked, unnoticed by the other worshippers, and would attend the service nude sitting next to her mother.

Remembering how Alec Guinness had complained on the *Mudlark* set about Jean's lack of direction, Johnson asked Negulesco to let him rehearse lines with the actors before each scene. Jean agreed and the cast was pleased.

Marilyn loved rehearsing. "She rehearses forever," Jean said. "But there is a reason for this. She thinks slowly and carefully. She is not one of the quick types like a Bacall. She has a slow tempo. You have to adjust to her tempo. You have to do much rehearsing with her. And when she has learned a scene finally, memorized the lines, and you have to make a change—ah, this is murder. She hates to change it. But if a director is willing to take trouble to feel out her tempo and go at her pace, she will give you a superb performance."[3]

Marilyn Monroe and John Negulesco on the set of *How to Marry a Millionaire* (1953).

Bacall and Grable, who had not met before, became very chummy. "Betty Grable was a funny, outgoing woman, totally professional and easy," Bacall wrote in her memoir. "Marilyn was frightened, insecure—trusted only her coach and was always late.... Grable and I decided we'd try to make it easier for her, make her feel she could trust us. I think she finally did."[4]

On the first day of the shoot, a group of reporters and photographers was allowed on the set, all looking for Monroe, who was on time. Soon, though, she began coming late. Late on the set, late for interviews, late for any appointment she made. Jean patiently tried to explain to her the trouble she created every time she would show up late but besides an apology, her only answer was, "But mentally I was with you at the right time."[5]

On the first day, Jean found a congratulation note from Nunnally Johnson:

> At last the great day has come. You alone know how they have fought to keep us from making this picture.... So now the great day has come at last, and we have overcome all opposition, let us go forward and make this the finest picture that was ever turned out in the entire history of CinemaScope. Let's make them eat their words.... Godspeed on this great crusade."[6]

The filming of *Millionaire* proceeded smoothly and Jean was very enthusiastic. He wrote in an article:

> CinemaScope offers a director some positive advantages. It broadens his horizons and makes possible the dramatizing of situations which would be confined and imprisoned on the printed page or in a mouthful of dialogue. No director has the power to portray with montage or long shots the magnitude and spirit of New York City as we have done in this picture with a single shot of the city's skyline at dusk. The single picture was so moving that audiences at the CinemaScope demonstrations applauded it, as though it were a symphony orchestra.[7]

Bacall recalled, "[I]t was a new experiment for everyone, it was difficult. One had to keep the actors moving and not too close together, as the screen was long and narrow. You shot longer scenes in CinemaScope, five or six pages without a stop, and I like that— it felt closer to the stage and better for me."[8]

But probably not for Monroe. She couldn't do what she was called upon to do. She would look past Jean's chair toward her coach Natasha Lytess waiting for her approval. Jean knew that when Marilyn demanded another take, he didn't have to turn around to know that Lytess had shaken her head. Sometimes the star demanded 15 takes or more, often irritating the other actors who knew they had to be good in every take because there was no telling which one Jean would select. David Conover, an old friend of Marilyn's, described how sometimes Negulesco mocked Marilyn's literary pretensions. Once Jean asked her what she was reading and she told him Tolstoy. Jean told her that she shouldn't be seen reading such stuff, that it might get her into trouble. Marilyn was confused. Jean told her that people would think she was a radical—Red. Monroe reported the exchange to Conover, stating that Negulesco seemed upset that she didn't know what Communists were, wondering if they maybe weren't a Russian ball club.[9]

Bacall and Grable would arrive on the set bringing new ideas for their parts, little details or changes they had envisioned. Marilyn was methodical, following exactly any direction she had been given about her character. In a scene where she was asleep in bed, a stunned Jean realized that she was completely nude under the sheets. "The script said nude," she said, "so I am nude."

Jean told the *Los Angeles Times*, "Grable is so genuine. She has such a wise realization of her limitations and such a sense of humor. And considering that she's been a star for so long, her unpretentiousness is refreshing. Lauren Bacall brings poise and experience beyond her years to everything she plays. She has a quiet way of accepting adversity which is appealing in any woman." On Monroe, he added, "I was surprised to find out how hard she worked and how much she wanted to give a good performance."[10] He also revealed that off the set, Marilyn was spending all her income on singing and dancing classes, striving to be a more complete artist. In *Millionaire*, the three co-stars were teamed up with four male actors: David Wayne, the millionaire who Marilyn would snare, Rory Calhoun who would fall into Grable's trap, and Cameron Mitchell, a prey for Bacall after refusing William Powell.

In a March 2, 1953, letter by censor Joseph Breen, it was revealed that only some of the wardrobe changes for the three stars had approval. Breen points out that two Bacall costumes might result in "unacceptable breast exposure," depending on the lighting and camera angle. So Jean's work became harder because in each scene, he and his cinematographer had to be careful how the lights were positioned, avoidance revealing any transparency through the actresses' costumes. On the girls' penthouse set, Jean placed on displayed some of the drawings he sketched when he visited Mexico in 1939, and some paintings from his own collection.

How to Marry a Millionaire was completed in a month. The world premiere was held on November 4, 1953, at the Fox Wilshire Theatre in Hollywood with scores of leading stars, executives and civic notables attending. It was an unprecedented event. For five blocks on each side of the theater, traffic was being diverted. A howling, overenthusiastic mob of fans was inside and outside with policemen having a tough time holding them back. As celebrities filed into the house, their entrances was accompanied by screams, applause and rushing to get an autograph. The aisle of the auditorium was jammed with photographers and reporters. An impeccably elegant Jean, with Dusty on his arm, was one of the first to arrive, followed by Mitzi Gaynor, Debbie Reynolds, Jeffrey Hunter, Barbara Rush, Rock Hudson and Shelley Winters. At 9:05 p.m. came the big moment: the arrival of Marilyn Monroe. She was accompanied by Nunnally Johnson, Lauren Bacall and Humphrey Bogart. Jean was a nervous wreck that day:

> We were not sure that people would appreciate it. We had doubts they would accept a shot of a hot dog as big as the Empire State Building. The entire film industry was there, all the studio executives and greats like Cecil B. DeMille. Suddenly, we heard a murmur that quickly became very intense like an avalanche: *Marilyn! Marilyn!* The fans. She arrived in front of the theater. She looked like she was sewn in her dress. Every little muscle of her body.... Very, very beautiful. Some cops had to escort her inside because the public wanted to tear her clothes off. In the auditorium, everybody stepped on their chair to look at her. When I saw Cecil B. DeMille and Henry Cohn step on their chairs, I said to myself, "*We won!* No need to see any movie, she is here...." That night I was offered six different films from different studios.... I accepted an offer from Harry Cohn with Columbia. But I did not like the script he gave me and all of the sudden I was not allowed to eat next to him in the executive cafeteria. Not only that, but he also sent me the bill of what I ate during those three days spent at his studios. I was no longer the hero. That's Hollywood."[11]

The picture Jean refused to make was a musical called *The Pleasure Is All Mine* with Betty Grable. After knowing that Jean had turned it down, she refused to play in it. Immediately, Zanuck put her on suspension. She later changed her mind and the picture was made in 1955 as *Three for the Show*. Another offer that night came from Italian producer Dino De Laurentiis, who wanted Jean to direct *Judith and the Holophernes,* a Biblical-style story starring Italian actress Silvana Mangano. After reading the script, Jean turned it down.

Following the *How to Marry a Millionaire* premiere, a reception was given by the Negulescos for over a hundred guests, including Mon-

Jean Negulesco in a portrait from the early '50s.

roe and Bacall. Within a few months, *How to Marry a Millionaire* grossed $12,000,000 against a cost of $2,500,000. (Other sources indicate a cost of $1,870,000 and a profit of $8,000,000.) The picture was a commercial success *and* a technical success, becoming a milestone in the history of cinema. It popularized widescreen filming which other studios followed with similar systems of their own (Panavision, TechniScope, VistaVision, Cinerama and others).

Jean received from Bacall, Grable and Monroe a notebook binder with a brown cover of Moroccan leather on which his name was engraved in gold. Inside there was only one page with an inscription that read: "Wouldn't that be wonderful if you had the three of us up for dinner?—These pioneers, Loco, Schatze, and Pola."

When Negulesco was not behind a camera, he was a man of many hobbies and interests. Besides painting and sketching, he was an extraordinary chef, cooking gourmet dinners for his friends. He was a skilled card player, but mostly an avid devotee of croquet, a game he learned during a weekend at Zanuck's Palm Springs beach house. Romanian agent Fefe Ferry taught Jean how to play. Negulesco found out that the game could be bitterly competitive, very emotional and loud. Zanuck had learned it through Clifton Webb, who together with Howard Hawks, Tyrone Power, George Sanders, Samuel Goldwyn, restaurateur Mike Romanoff and many others, became addicted to it. They all played on the weekends but they would often transfer the game during the week to the Fox lot. Richard Zanuck, Darryl's youngest son, watched many matches but never played. He remembered Louis Jourdan as the best player, with Howard Hughes and Jean not far behind.[12]

Many friendships were broken on the croquet lawn. Players would get so mad that they would pack up in the middle of a weekend and leave. Apparently Jean got so much into the game that his personality would completely change. Playwright Moss Hart recalled. "I remember Jean Negulesco. Jesus, he was cunning. He could also get so violent! He was always complaining that someone had committed a foul over on his ball. He howled and raged."[13] One of Jean's fits of rage had consequences. On a Sunday in May 1953, a couple of weeks after the shooting of *How to Marry a Millionaire* was completed, Jean lost his temper over some error on the court. He flung his mallet to the turf, and it bounced up and hit Zanuck between his eyes. The bleeding studio chief was rushed to a hospital and given three stitches. Jean was mortified. In a letter to producer Robert Goldstein, Nunnally Johnson commented, "I scarcely need tell you what this did to Mr. Negulesco's emotions. Nevertheless, there seemed to be no need for him to take strychnine, cut his throat, hang himself, and shoot himself, too. For the truth of the matter was that Mr. Zanuck took it very well, contenting himself with putting Mr. Negulesco on layoff. That's why Dusty is now using old cigar butts and things like that to paint with instead of brushes."[14]

It is possible that the reason behind Jean's angry outburst was the trouble he was having with Dusty. Columnist Dorothy Kilgallen wrote in her column that the Negulescos "are writing the Unhappy Ending after all these years." Dusty, who was enjoying a new career as a painter, had expressed her desire to go to Paris to study art and improve her technique. (She had had 15 of her paintings exhibited at a show at the Drouant-David gallery in Paris three years earlier.) Jean opposed her idea because he knew that it would require at least two years of study and practice. This became a cause of constant bickering between the Negulescos. But Dusty was also fed up with Jean's recurrent escapades. Jean's bungalow on the Fox lot, where he invited stars and starlets for lunch, was known as his

Dusty and Jean Negulesco enjoying themselves on a dance floor, circa 1953.

"bangalow." "Poor Dusty," Jerry Wald's wife Connie, commented. "[She] had to put up with a lot."[15]

In May, Dusty left for Paris with Dee Hartford, wife of Howard Hawks. After he explained his conjugal problems to Zanuck, Jean asked him to give him an assignment in Europe so he could be close to his Dusty. Zanuck told him that he had three productions ready to start, one in Sweden, one in Germany and one in Italy. Jean chose Italy, a country he had visited several times. Sol Siegel, the producer of the film (*We Believe in Love*, later changed to *Three Coins in the Fountain*), accepted Jean as director, the two left for Italy to scout locations.

The two men stopped over in New York before departing for Italy and saw *Roman Holiday* (1953) starring Gregory Peck and Audrey Hepburn. Jean liked the picture and wrote a memo to Zanuck telling him that *Roman Holiday* was made on location but in black and white while *Three Coins in the Fountain* was going to be shot in color and CinemaScope. Zanuck resented Jean's memo, since his plan was, once the locations had been scouted, to send a second unit to Rome to film backgrounds and long shots with doubles.

All the scenes, including close-ups and interiors, had to be shot on the Fox lot. He also pointed out that if Negulesco did not agree with his idea, he would gladly take him off the picture. Siegel and Jean were very upset by Zanuck's reaction and by his refusal to shoot the entire film in Italy. The two men asked Sid Rogell, head of studio production, if filming on location would be cheaper than creating studio replicas of some of the locations. The obvious answer was that shooting in Italy would have cost a third less than in Hollywood. When the cost study report was presented to Zanuck, he could not oppose the idea any longer, but according to Jean, resented him thereafter. *Three Coins in the Fountain* became the first CinemaScope picture made on location.

En route to Rome, Jean stopped off in Paris to talk Dusty into reconciliation. "I don't pretend she went to Paris with my blessing," he told columnist Harrison Carroll before leaving. "I thought it was a stupid expense. But Dusty wanted to study painting, and when one of those Cherokee Indian girls makes up her mind, nothing is going to stop her." The couple made up and a few days later Dusty joined Jean in Rome.

The original cast of *Three Coins in the Fountain* included Marilyn Monroe and Frank Sinatra as leads, but Monroe got engaged to Joe DiMaggio and did not want to leave the States. Sinatra turned down the part but later agreed to sing the theme over the title credits. The romantic song became the hit love ballad of the year.

The press had announced that Barbara Stanwyck, Clifton Webb, Gene Tierney, Vittorio Gassman, Jeanne Crain and Louis Jourdan had all set to star in *Three Coins in the Fountain*. Yet only Webb and Jourdan appeared in the final cast, which included Dorothy McGuire, Jean Peters, Maggie McNamara and Rossano Brazzi.

During his first weeks in Italy, Jean filmed breathtaking panoramas of Rome and Venice along with the most famous monuments and landmarks. The cast arrived the first week of August and principal photography began. In a 1961 letter to his colleague and friend Vincente Minnelli, then planning to shoot part of *Two Weeks in Another Town* in Rome, Jean offered some advice:

> I would say that the most difficult and the most important condition of making a picture in Italy is to adapt yourself to their spirit, to their way of working. A small example. This happened to me on location. As I arrive on the set and everything is ready to be done at 9 o'clock —the people are having coffee. Now, your assistant also is having coffee—and if you are foolish enough to start to shout and saying you want to work, right away you'll have an unhappy crew and not the cooperation needed for the picture. But if you have coffee with them, they will work for you with no time limit or no extra expense.[16]

Vittorio Gassman, who was then married to Shelley Winters, was chosen to play the role of Giorgio, a simple romantic Italian guy who fell in love with the character played by Jean Peters. Gassman, a veteran of several Hollywood productions, turned down the role after reading the script. It was a decision he later regretted, since his replacement Rossano Brazzi got a huge career boost out of the movie. Jean and Brazzi had met in Hollywood while the Italian actor was filming *Little Women* (1949). During a lunch at the Beverly Hills Hotel honoring director Roberto Rossellini, Jean promised Brazzi to cast him if ever there was a right part for him. Negulesco uses Brazzi three times (*Three Coins*, *A Certain Smile* and *Count Your Blessings*).

Three Coins in the Fountain, a romantic comedy based on a novel by John Secondari, bore some similarities to *How to Marry a Millionaire*; this time, though, the three women look for love and not for money. Three American girls working in Rome throw their coins in the Trevi fountain and hope for romance. Secretary Dorothy McGuire gradually wins the love of her writer-employer Clifton Webb. Jean Peters, is romanced by a local Italian guy, Brazzi. Maggie McNamara lands herself a prince, Louis Jourdan.

Jean discovered that the best time to work quietly in Rome was between one and four in the afternoon, when the shops were closed and the streets deserted while the Romans rested through the heat of the day. Shooting a key scene at Rome's famous Fontana di Trevi cost 20th Century–Fox ten barrels of water. At that time, some of the Romans living near the world's most beautiful fountain got all their drinking and wash water there. Before Jean was granted permission to film, he had to provide two barrels of water at each of the five streets that converged on the fountain. Romans needing water during the filming of the scenes obtained it from the barrels without interrupting the shooting. In a sequence shot near the landmark, the three women had to throw coins into the fountain to bring them luck. After a few takes, an onlooker told Jean that people traditionally threw the coins over their shoulders, so the scene had to be reshot.

Talking with the American press, Jean said that CinemaScope added greatly to the realism of pictures and to their acceptance abroad. But CinemaScope on location with its vivid colors presented new types of problems. While the women's dresses looked superb when shot indoors under artificial lights, outside in the Roman streets next to the Italian extras, they appeared as they were made for a masquerade ball. Jean told the stars to buy (at local stores) new clothing that was more in line with the current Italian fashion. Some of the interior shots were shot on a Fox stage. The decision to do so was made necessary by a lack of studio-type incandescent lamp abroad.

While Negulesco was abroad, he met with the nine-year-old Neapolitan girl whom he had supported for the past three years under a Foster Parents Plan for War Children. Negulesco brought little Adelina Peluso from Naples to Rome to stay with Dusty and

Jean Peters, Louis Jourdan, Maggie McNamara and Dorothy McGuire in *Three Coins in the Fountain* (1954).

himself. The kid was showered with gifts and permitted to act in one scene of the picture. Her father was killed in an Allied raid on Naples in 1944, and her ailing mother was unable to support her. Jean and Dusty got so attached to the little girl that they were ready to bring her back to America with them, but they understood that it wasn't fair to deprive the sick mother of her child. Back in Rome in 1956, Jean and Dusty hoped to legally adopt the little girl, but they discovered that the antiquated Italian adoption requirements would cause a considerable delay in getting the child to Hollywood with them. So once again, they returned home without her, planning to bring her over to the U.S. as soon as the red tape was cut. It never happened. A few years later, the Negulescos did adopt two orphan girls from Germany.

The total cost of *Three Coins* was $1,700,000. Fox was eager to repeat the commercial success of *How to Marry a Millionaire* but, according to a Zanuck biographer, when a rough cut was showed to the studio's head, he got up and left the screening room without any comment. Jean was so upset that he went out and threw up in the street. The film had to be re-edited and some new dialogue added. Zanuck decided to personally take care of the re-editing that made it into a commercial success.

In his memoir, Jean told a completely different story. The rough cut was showed for three nights in a row to friends in the industry, the crew and studio people. Their reactions were unanimously positive. After it was shown to Zanuck and Spyros Skouras, both left the projection room without a word. The following day, Jean and Siegel were summoned by Zanuck, who with the help of a cutter went through all the scenes that they had edited, cut or changed. Finally, the new edited version was ready. Jean and Siegel watched it and were shocked by the butchery done to their picture. They both signed a memo to Zanuck expressing their disappointment and if he decided to release that new version, they demanded that their names not appear in the credits. Zanuck asked them to rewatch the new cut with him; after the viewing, he told the cutter to put it back as it was originally and ship it to all the American exhibitors, who subsequently raved about the picture.[17]

Three Coins in the Fountain received generally positive reviews, particularly for its color and CinemaScope widescreen cinematography of the Italian filming locations. *Variety* wrote, "Once before, in 20th-Fox's *How to Marry a Millionaire*, director Jean Negulesco CinemaScoped a trio of feminine beauties into a lucrative attraction. In *Three Coins in the Fountain* he repeats this feat but obviously has gained some experience. The film has warmth, humor, a rich dose of romance and almost incredible pictorial appeal."[18]

Jean Negulesco showing the Boxoffice Blue Ribbon Award for Best Picture of the Month for the Whole Family: *Three Coins in the Fountain* (1954).

The picture grossed $5,000,000 domestically and got three Academy Award nominations, including Best Film. Jean received an award nomination for Outstanding Directorial Achievement in Motion Pictures from the Directors Guild and a nomination for the Golden Lion at the Venice Film Festival, where the picture was presented in 1954.

During the four-month period between the completion of *How to Marry a Millionaire* and its November 1953 premiere, Marilyn Monroe co-starred with Robert Mitchum in director Otto Preminger's *River of No Return*. After watching a rough cut with a test audience, Zanuck gathered some of his directors including Jean to ask their opinions. According to Jean, "There were very good scenes for a Western, but no love, no passion, no erotism, and that's what to expect when you announce Marilyn Monroe and Robert Mitchum. She's the symbol of sex, he is the evil." Negulesco suggested a couple of scenes, one in which Marilyn, after falling in the river, is saved by Mitchum, who takes her into a grotto and builds a fire to warm her. Then he starts to massage her naked body wrapped in an old blanket. Zanuck felt that such a scene would never be approved by the censors. Because Preminger was already working on another production and Jean was one of the few available directors with CinemaScope experience, he was asked to shoot the retakes and two extras scenes. One was the grotto sequence he originally proposed. "After the last take in the grotto," Jean recalled,

> Marilyn, because of the humidity, got a cold. Her nose was dripping. Bob Mitchum had in his contract that he would stop working at five sharp. He'd do everything, he'd arrive on the set at nine in the morning, but at five he was done. "Bye kids, I'll see you tomorrow morning." And would leave. And there was nothing we could do. Bastard of a great actor! My assistant approached me: "We have only one shot left, one of him and Marilyn's shoulders." If she fell ill, it could take weeks at an expensive cost. I said: "Set the lights now, I'll go to talk to Bob." Bob is an amazing human being and an amazing friend. But at five…. He was home, he had just taken a shower. He was in shorts with a glass in his hand, looking as handsome as a god.
>
> "Come in, partner."
>
> "Bob I have a favor to ask you…. Listen, everybody is sick on this humid set. Marilyn is going to be sick tomorrow. I have only one scene to shoot. It would take ten minutes."
>
> "Okay, I'll come back and will do it."
>
> At that very moment a door opened, and a woman completely naked, wearing only a small necklace and high heels, brings me the Scotch. I am a painter. I've seen so many naked women that it never impressed me, but there I was not ready to see that stunning lady.
>
> "Is it enough?"
>
> "Yes it's fine."
>
> …I drank my Scotch and said, "Thank you for the drink and the show."
>
> "It's okay, it's okay, any time you want."
>
> He came back and we finished it.[19]

In the grotto scene, under Jean's direction, there was no hint that either Mitchum or Monroe was enjoying the massage, in order to avoid any trouble with the censors—who eventually gave the scene their blessing.

River of No Return was hugely popular, Mitchum's most successful picture to date. Negulesco received no credit for his contribution.

8

La Loren

> "[Sophia Loren] is without a doubt the most extraordinary talent I have ever met."—Jean Negulesco

In May 1954, just after the successful release of *Three Coins in the Fountain,* Jean renegotiated his employment at 20th Century–Fox, signing a new four-year exclusive directorial pact under which his first assignment was the Charles Brackett production *Woman's World.* Co-writer Claude Binyon was originally set to direct the picture, but Zanuck decided that the project needed a more experienced touch and brought Jean in. The film had Fox's highest budget ever on a modern drama: $3,250,000. It would have CinemaScope, seven stars and a script by a pair of Pulitzer Prize–winning playwrights.

Eleanor Parker, Glenn Ford and Charlton Heston were the first names connected to the film. Later, the press announced that Gloria Grahame, Jean Peters and Paul Douglas would also appear. But the final cast included instead Clifton Webb, June Allyson, Lauren Bacall, Van Heflin, Cornel Wilde, Fred MacMurray and Arlene Dahl, who replaced at the last moment Jean Peters, who was down with the flu. Peters' sudden illness almost kiboshed the entire production, because of prior commitments by the majority of his stars.

Negulesco had arranged the film schedule tight as a jigsaw puzzle. If *Woman's World* was not finished by July 1, the director would have seen his cast pulled apart in all directions for other productions. Arlene Dahl had to interrupt a holiday in Europe with her fiancé Fernando Lamas to reach the set by the May 5 starting date.

Jean revealed that casting so many stars in films was not entirely dictated by the market value of their names. It was, in large part, a matter of helping the audience promptly identify the seven leading characters. In *Woman's World,* Allyson, Bacall and Dahl play wives who accompany their husbands (Wilde, MacMurray, Heflin) to New York. The men battle for a top executive position with a big motor company. The final decision is in the hands of sharp-tongued, corporate boss Ernest Gifford (Webb).

In a Zanuck memo to screenwriter Binyon, the studio head demanded that the script build more suspense as to which man gets the job. Zanuck advised the writer to remove any early dialogue that seemed to disqualify any of the three men from the competition.

Production went smoothly thanks to Jean's professional and amicable personality. He was very flirtatious with the three female leads, inviting them to lunch separately, but never going beyond lunch, respecting his adoring Dusty.[1] Allyson noted in her autobiography that close friend Bacall, who always seemed calm and collected off the set, was different when working:

Clifton Webb, June Allyson, Van Heflin, Lauren Bacall, Fred McMurray, Arlene Dahl and Cornel Wilde in a publicity shot for *Woman's World* **(1954).**

> I had seen the real Betty when we filmed *Woman's World* together and we were doing a scene in which we each had to pick up champagne glasses and turn and survey the room. I looked at Betty's glass and her hand was shaking—I couldn't believe it. She saw my look and whispered, off camera, "I am so nervous." That was when I realized Lauren Bacall did not have the inner security she displayed to the world. Inside she was very vulnerable.[2]

Gene Tierney was scheduled to appear in the picture as a movie star besieged by autograph seekers at the 21 Club, but that scene was deleted from the final cut. Apparently the cameo had been offered to Tierney after it was turned down by Marilyn Monroe, who was committed to another picture. The only sign of Tierney left in the picture can be found on the wall of Gifford's house: a portrait of the actress recycled from *Laura* (1944), Clifton Webb's most successful film to date.

Since the main characters in the story worked for an automobile company, Fox got full cooperation from the Ford Motor Company: Ford lent the studio possibly the most expensive "props" ever used in a picture. A Ford X-100 and a Mercury X-800 were experiments in body design with futuristic features. The two car models were not planned as prototypes of production models, but as experiments to see what could be built and what the public would buy. They were under armed guard at all times while at Fox; whenever they were brought on the set, they were under the observation of a Ford representative.

Before starting principal photography at Fox, Jean travelled to New York to shoot the snowy city landscape from a helicopter. Dusty went along and painted the same scenes on canvas. Negulesco used a new CinemaScope camera lens said to give considerably better depth than the lenses he used in his previous two CinemaScope productions. "We got a lot to learn yet about making CinemaScope films," Jean told *Variety*. "Stereophonic sound was still far from perfection, particularly at the shooting end where it's difficult to control sound when a person isn't moving but standing still and turning his head while conversing."[3] Another major problem was the intensity of the special lamps used for CinemaScope filming. For technical reasons they were required to be three times stronger than ordinary lights, making the set extremely hot (the temperature hit 115 degrees). The actors sweat so much that they had to shower immediately after each scene was completed.

Woman's World was neither the hoped-for success nor an Oscar contender. Ticket sales barely recovered the original budget. The picture also suffered from comparisons with *Executive Suite* (1954), released by MGM four months earlier.

While he was completing *Woman's World*, Jean heard that Zanuck was setting up the production of the musical *Daddy Long Legs* in CinemaScope and Technicolor. A first draft of the script had been submitted, the two main stars cast and Henry Koster was assigned to direct. The idea of making a musical was Jean's dream, since he directed musical shorts at Warners at the beginning of his career. "How to get rid of [Koster] became an obsession," recalled Henry Ephron, who wrote the screenplay with his wife Phoebe.

> [Negulesco] called Virginia Zanuck, Spyros Skouras, Sam, the barber who cut Zanuck's hair—nothing worked. Then, Jean got lucky. He heard that Cyd Charisse was having a dinner party. He knew

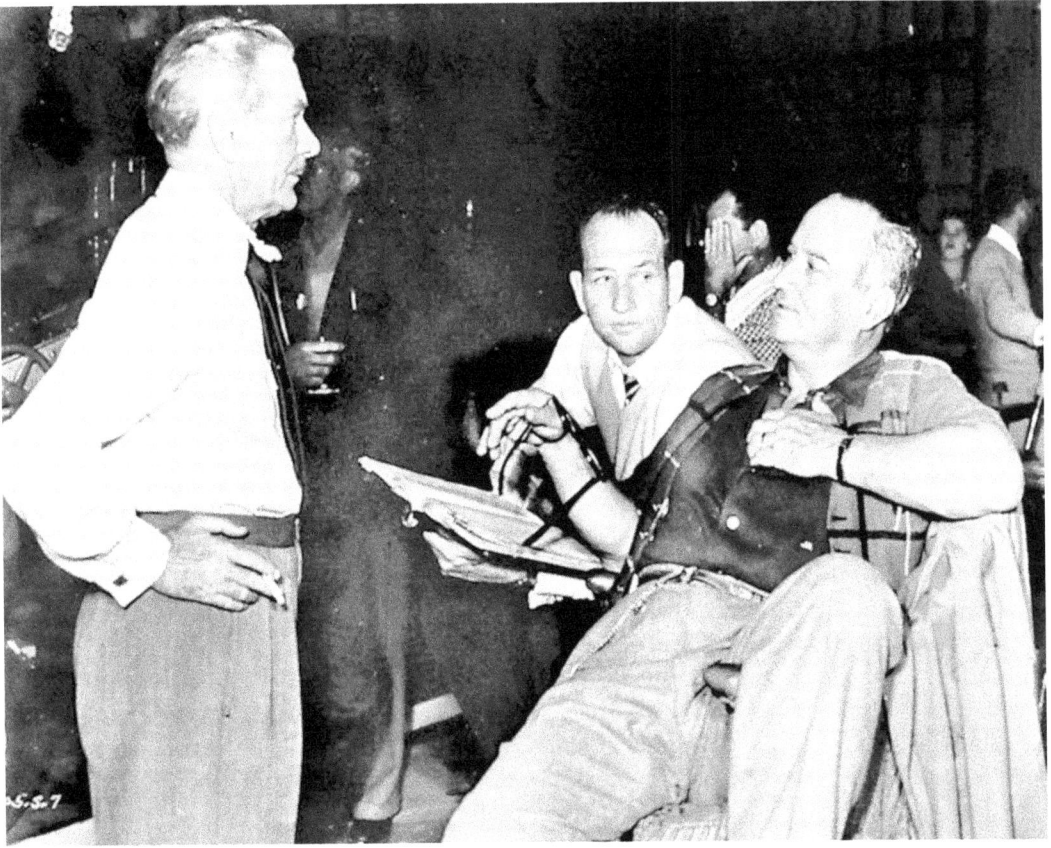

Clifton Webb and Jean Negulesco discuss a scene on the set of *Woman's World* (1954).

she would have Darryl on her right. He briefed her, lectured her over and over again on what to say: Koster, who made his reputation on Deanna Durbin pictures, was all wrong for *Daddy Long Legs*. The only one to direct [Fred] Astaire and [Leslie] Caron was an artist like Negulesco. Negulesco made beautiful pictures—take a look at *Three Coins in the Fountain*. Cyd followed instructions exactly. I don't think she squeezed Zanuck's knees as she talked; she was and is happily married, but she's very beautiful and Zanuck had no more strength against a beautiful woman than any of us do. The next morning Negulesco got the call from Zanuck. It wasn't a mistake. Jean did a fine job and he finally endeared himself to me completely.[4]

Daddy Long Legs was based on a novel by Jean Webster, grand-niece of Mark Twain. The story first appeared as a serial in *Ladies Home Journal* in 1912. Webster later wrote a play based on her novel, which had its Broadway premiere in 1914. A silent film version was made by First National in 1919 starring Mary Pickford and Mahlon Hamilton. 20th Century–Fox acquired the rights for a film released in 1931 with Janet Gaynor, and in 1935 the story was used as the basis of *Curly Top* with Shirley Temple. Sixteen years later, Zanuck planned to remake it as a vehicle for Mitzi Gaynor. Cary Grant, John Lund, Ray Milland, David Niven and Gregory Peck were considered for the main role of Jervis Pendleton. Then, for unknown reasons, the project was shelved until one evening Zanuck saw Fred Astaire and his wife Phyllis dining at Romanoff's and got the idea of making an updated musical version of *Daddy Long Legs*. The next day he called Astaire's agent to explain his plan. While waiting for an answer from the dancer, Zanuck arranged to borrow Leslie Caron from MGM.

In writing the script, the Ephrons went back to the Webb novel, which was written in the form of letters exchanged between a young orphan and her secret benefactor. She calls him "Daddy Long Legs" because the only glimpse she had of him was a long shadow on the orphanage wall. Since Caron was French, the script was updated so that Astaire would discover her during a trip to France and arrange a college education in Massachusetts.

Caron arrived on the set in August. She was shy and very intimidated by Astaire, one of her idols. Every day when she arrived on the set, she would say good morning and shake hands with everyone from Jean to the electricians. According to the Ephrons, the stage hands nicknamed her "The French Corporal." In his autobiography, Astaire described her as a "fine artist, conscientious, apt, serious. She hesitates to attempt anything either in dance or acting unless she is absolutely sure of herself. Leslie will hold up production for many minutes (or hours), on some occasions, until she feels complete control of what's about to do."[5]

Rehearsals started in July 1954, but they got interrupted after a few days because Phyllis Astaire, ill with a terminal disease, entered ah critical stage of her illness and Fred had to be by her side until she died on September 13. Astaire tried to get out of his Fox commitment but friends and relatives urged him to resume work, as the best medicine to ease his grief. In the meantime, Zanuck was ready to find a substitute since too much money and work had already been committed to the project. Canceling it would have been a tremendous loss. Maurice Chevalier was sent a copy of the script and put on standby just in case Astaire would not be ready to come back. Jean and producer Samuel Engel tried to made it as easy as possible for Astaire by rearranging the schedule. For that reason, Caron rehearsed all her solo numbers first.

In early October, Astaire agreed to resume work. Jean, like most of the cast and crew, constantly tried to lift his spirits, assuring him that his performance was perfect without mentioning the loss. Technically, however, it was a bit difficult for Astaire and Caron to perform their musical numbers in CinemaScope. Jean repeatedly ordered, "You've gotta keep those sides filled! You've gotta keep those sides filled!"—especially during the dance scenes, the extremities of the scene had to be filled with movement in order to get the most best CinemaScope results. But Jean was also smart enough to seek out Astaire's advice when shooting the musical numbers, and followed it.

Roland Petit asked Caron if he could be her choreographer in order to work near Astaire, whom he idolized. Producer Engel asked Astaire if the Ballets de Paris directed by Petit could work with him and he agreed. The lavish choreographies cost $800,000 of the $3,500,000 budget. The exterior of Andrew Carnagie's fabulous Fifth Avenue mansion was used as the exterior of Pendleton's residence while the interior, designed by art directors Lyle Wheeler and John DeCuir, was a masterful blend of old and new. The portrait of Astaire as Jervis Pendleton III, in the style of Pablo Picasso, was painted by Jean, who also created the poster for "Julie's" dream appearance at the Paris Opera ballet.

For the millionaire's art collection, Negulesco borrowed genuine pieces from art collector friends, including a Braque, a Picasso and a Matisse. The studio shelled out no rental fees, but had to take out a $200,000 insurance policy for the duration of their use. In addition, Jean borrowed a portrait Claudette Colbert painted of Deborah Kerr's daughter Melanie. Some of Dusty's paintings and Jean's primitive sculptures were also brought in as part of the grand decoration.

Jean's insistence on authenticity extended to the diamond engagement ring Astaire selects for Caron in the picture. The director negotiated the loan of a $250,000 32-carat, pure blue-white, emerald cut diamond ring flown from Paris for the scene. During the shooting, Astaire mentioned to Caron that many of his co-stars (Ginger Rogers, Joan Crawford and Joan Fontaine) worked with him and then went on to win Oscars for acting. Jean ordered a little gold Oscar reproduction for Caron's charm bracelet. When she heard of the gift, the actress refused it, saying, "Thank you, but it would be too pretentious to have one you have not earned." (Caron was twice Oscar-nominated but never won.)

Thelma Ritter and Fred Clark played supporting roles. Jean was particularly fond of Ritter, whom he had previously directed in *Titanic*. "She's a marvelous character actress, so marvelous that when she was not in a scene I had her on the set just to observer her. With only one of her expressions she would make you shout of joy."[6]

Fred Astaire and Leslie Caron in *Daddy Long Legs* (1955).

Many years later, commenting about his experience on the set, cinematographer Leon Shamroy said, "I enjoyed making *Daddy Long Legs*; like its director, Jean Negulesco, it was underrated, and Roland Petit's dance numbers were wonderful. Jean had a rough time; this youth thing they have here has pushed him out. A tragedy: he has a great talent."[7]

The *Daddy Long Legs* world premiere was held on May 4, 1955, at Grumman's Chinese Theatre. The benefit gala opening raised $103,295 for the building fund of St. John's Hospital in Santa Monica. Two other gala premieres followed, one in New York at the Roxy Theatre and a Royal Gala Premiere in London where Caron was presented to Princess Margaret. The critics weren't enthusiastic about the picture and the response from the public was lukewarm. The picture lost almost $1,000,000.

There were talks of Jean directing two new films, 20th Century–Fox's *Dry Martini* and Paramount's *Papa's Delicate Condition*. Both were to star Fred Astaire with a script from the Ephrons; they never materialized.

In January 1955, *Variety* announced that Bryna, Kirk Douglas' production company, had made a deal with United Artists to release his future films. One of the first two productions was *Van Gogh* with Negulesco as director. Jean was very excited to make a biopic about one of his favorite painters, but pre-production was delayed because of differences among the producers. In the meantime, he became involved with a different project, *The Rains of Ranchipur*, and was replaced on *Van Gogh* (later retitled *Lust for Life*) by Vincente Minnelli.

Before working on his next film, the Academy of Motion Picture Arts and Sciences offered Jean the job of producing the live Academy Awards broadcast on March 30, 1955. Jean was flattered to produce such a prestigious show; *Three Coins in the Fountain* was a nominee in three categories including Best Picture. He also voted along with the Board of Directors of the Academy to give an honorary Oscar to Greta Garbo.

"I knew that Garbo would never make an appearance to accept the Oscar, but would she let me come to New York and make a shot of her in her apartment, on her balcony, or any location she would choose?"[8] Jean wrote in his memoir. He even offered to have a writer help prepare her brief thank-you speech, giving Garbo the right to destroy the film and negative if she didn't like what they shot. When Garbo made her decision, it was no. So a scene from *Camille* (1936) was shown at the ceremony, and Nancy Kelly accepted the Oscar in New York on Garbo's behalf.

Right after the Oscars telecast, Jean went back to work on *The Rains of Ranchipur*. Louis Bromfield's novel *The Rains Came* had already been filmed by Fox in 1939; the picture was successfully directed by Clarence Brown and starred Tyrone Power, Myrna Loy and George Brent. Zanuck thought the story was perfect material for a CinemaScope color remake and offered it to Frank Ross, whose production *The Robe* had started the CinemaScope era. Jean agreed with the producer's choice. "When a picture has a really solid story, such as this one, CinemaScope can only make it better than the original. Apart from that, it allows for the necessary new approach."[9] The new adaptation had a $4,000,000 budget. Jean stated in an interview that there were only three women capable of playing Lady Esket: Lana Turner, Ava Gardner and Rita Hayworth. Turner was cast eventually. She had been considered for the secondary role of Fern Simon in the 1939 production, but when the loan-out arrangement between MGM and Fox fell through, Brenda Joyce replaced her.

"Casting is our big problem today," Jean explained in an interview:

> With budgets going up hitting the $1,500,000 and $2,000,000 as an average, who can afford to take a chance on a newcomer? Some do take a chance, of course, but it's a big risk. You have to have an awfully good story to make up for the lack of names. And yet, on the other side, getting the name personalities to work in the picture is becoming tougher than ever. They have formed their own companies and are turning down scripts left and right.[10]

Richard Burton, Fred MacMurray, Michael Rennie and Joan Caulfield completed the cast. Negulesco had hoped to have Ethel Barrymore in the role of the maharani, but Russian stage actress Eugénie Léontovich got the part instead. The story was set in India, but Ross did not receive permission to shoot there. Instead, a company was sent to Pakistan for background shooting prior to the beginning of principal photography, which started on Fox's Stage 16 in August 1955.

A slip in a bathtub nearly prevented Lana Turner from making the picture. The concussion caused her severe headaches and dizzy spells. The actress warned the producers of her condition and a possible delay of her presence on the set. Jean started to shoot everything he could without Turner but after two weeks, he had to close down for a few days, unable to go ahead without her. Zanuck was upset because he wanted the picture completed in time for a Christmas release. Once Turner showed up, she and Jean immediately got along. "She adored her director," recalled her daughter Cheryl. "Jean Negulesco, who was a true artist, painted the most beautiful portrait of her as Lady Esketh."[11] On the other hand, Lana had no chemistry with Burton, whom she described as stuffy and egotistical. Apparently everything started when the leading lady turned down her co-star's advances, a serious affront to the macho Burton. Lana wrote in her autobiography:

> One of the hardest chores for me as an actress is to have to simulate real feeling in love scenes when there is no chemistry between me and the leading man. Burton and I were supposed to be madly in love. He played a dedicated Indian doctor. I was the selfish wife of a titled man who had married me for my money. I would fall in love with the doctor, and he with me…. [Burton] had a bloated self-image. The rest of us joked about his ego and someone even advised wardrobe to make him bigger turbans.[12]

As Dr. Safti, Burton had an official Hindu turban wrapper who was in charge of wrapping the headgear at the right angle. The Welsh star's hair had been darkened for his part. When Hedda Hopper visited the set, she remarked that Burton was the first blue-eyed Hindu she had ever seen. Jean said, "There are some fair-haired Indians around Kashmir. We are taking advantage of that."[13] Nevertheless, according to Turner, Burton strongly resisted Jean's effort to help him deliver a good performance. "You're supposed to be an Indian," he would tell him. "I'm *not* an Indian," Burton would reply loftily."[14] Helen Rose designed Turner's lavish wardrobe. On one occasion there was a small argument between Jean and Lana, who for a scene during a tiger hunt refused to wear a blonde chiffon cocktail dress and a pearl-embroiled sweater, which she found inappropriate for that occasion. Jean maintained that that dress was pertinent because, while the men were hunting, she planned to seduce the doctor. Eventually, Turner got Ross on her side and got to wear what she wanted. Fred MacMurray complained to writer Joe Hyams of being exhausted from carrying Lana Turner around all day on the set. "Actually the carrying isn't so bad, it's the putting down that's tough. I'm tired and my back aches…. When I bent down to get her for the first time I heard a crack and out went my back. From then I was relying upon memories of the day I was younger and stronger."[15]

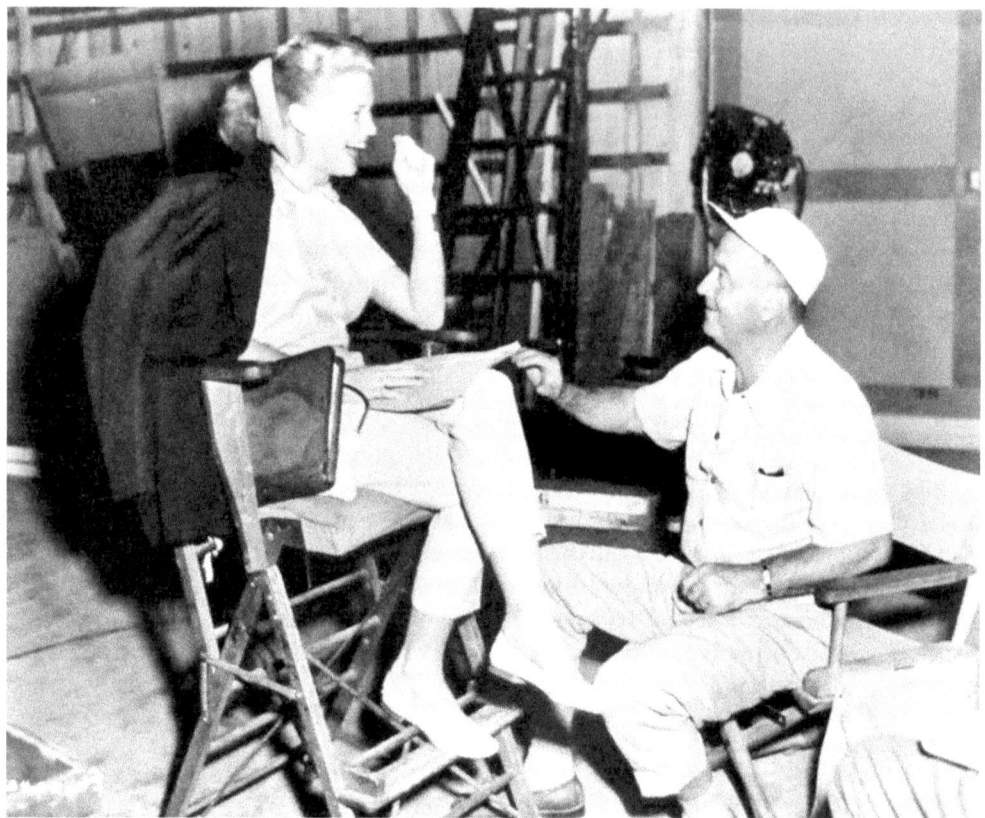

Joan Caulfield and Jean Negulesco on the set of *The Rains of Ranchipur* (1955).

The Rains of Ranchipur was completed in October only five days behind schedule. The budget for the film's special effects was raised from an initial $260,000 to $400,000, due to a costly massive flood and earthquake sequence that got much media attention. The picture performed very poorly after being dismissed by most of the reviewers as a fatuous melodrama. When Burton was asked to comment about the picture's dreadful reviews, he wittily said, "Ah well, they do say it never rains but in Ranchipur."[16]

Jean's only comment about *Ranchipur,* while reminiscing on his career many years later, was, "I'm afraid Louis Bromfield, the author of the novel on which it was based, wasn't very happy with it."[17]

Twentieth Century–Fox bought the screen rights to David Divine's bestselling novel *Boy on a Dolphin* and Alec Coppel was signed to write a screenplay. In November, it was announced that Leon Uris had taken over Coppel's script and that Henry Koster would direct. But in 1956 Jean was handed the direction job and Ivan Moffat assigned to rewrite the script. The following spring, Negulesco made a location scouting trip to Greece. In July, he asked Moffat to inspect the locations he had chosen and to rework some of the scenes to accommodate them.

In the story, an American archaeologist, a rich private collector and a beautiful sponge diver compete for ownership of an ancient Greek statue discovered in the depths of the Aegean Sea. The first to be signed was Clifton Webb as Victor Parmalee (Parmelee was Webb's real middle name and his mother's maiden name), the wealthy art lover obsessed by the statue. It was Webb's fourth and last collaboration with Jean. As the Greek sponge diver, Negulesco had in mind the Italian siren Gina Lollobrigida. Jean flew to Paris, where the actress was starring opposite Anthony Quinn in *The Hunchback of Notre Dame* (1956). During a dinner in a fancy restaurant, the director won over the reluctant Lollobrigida, who was planning to take a sabbatical to have a baby. Robert Mitchum was considered for the role of the archaeologist, but when the production schedule was delayed, the actor got tied up with another film. Once Lollobrigida signed the contract, Cary Grant was offered the male lead. Through his agent, the British star informed Fox that he would have accepted the role only if Sophia Loren would have been his co-star. The two had just completed *The Pride and the Passion* (1957), where they engaged in a tender off-screen romance. Wanting Grant's solid box office name, Zanuck cancelled the contract with Lollobrigida.

Negulesco immediately flew to Rome to discuss terms with Italian producer Carlo Ponti and Loren's agent. Jean's first encounter with Sophia was unforgettable: "The Italian filmmakers when they meet a star, they are smartly dressed with big hats. When I saw her, I was with my entourage and I was wearing jeans. We talked about the story, the costumes, etc. At the end she asked me, 'Where's Mr. Negulesco? You have talked to me for over half an hour. I'm used to directors who look like directors.' 'I do not look like one, but I am one.'"[18]

Loren won Jean over. He came out of that meeting overwhelmed and bewildered, eager to work with her. Later in connection with the film opening, Jean wrote for *The Hollywood Reporter* a witty article entitled, "Impression of Sophia,"

> As for her English, when I was presented to her, her first line was, "Why Negu, you crazy mixed-up kid, how are you?" I couldn't believe my ears. I asked her where she had learned this language and she told me that Frank Sinatra had taught her in Spain. She speaks excellent English with a very colorful accent...
>
> She is without a doubt the most extraordinary talent I have ever met. She can be a clown, a lady. She can listen seriously and talk with great wisdom.
>
> Dancing with Sophia Loren is an experience. She is a born dancer with rhythm in her body. But dancing with her, as I said, is an experience, as she dances completely independently of you and you are just a pivot around which she dances.[19]

Boy on a Dolphin's cast and crew was a mixture of many nationalities. In preparation for a scene in a trendy Athens nightclub, Jean hired as extras all 25 members of the American Ballet Company who were performing in the Greek capital. He also signed the famous Dora Stratou's folk dancers. Finally, Sophia Loren landed in Athens. To celebrate her arrival and the very first American picture ever to be filmed in Greece, Spyros Skouras gave a lavish party.

Four days after the cameras had begun to roll, Cary Grant withdrew from the production. According to Jean, Grant's pregnant wife Betsy Drake, two months earlier was aboard the Italian ocean liner *Andrea Doria* when it collided with another boat. She was safe but lost her baby. Despite the marriage being on the rocks, Grant felt that it was his duty to remain close to his wife who had yet not recovered from the tragedy. Without a leading man, Fox panicked. As Grant's replacement, Jean proposed John Wayne or Van Heflin or any other actor with a strong, masculine body tall enough to be photographed next to the 5'8" Loren. Two days later, Zanuck announced from Hollywood that Alan Ladd had been hired as Grant's replacement with a salary of $290,000. Ladd left immediately but took his time reaching Greece, due to his fear of flying. He crossed the Atlantic by boat and then took a long train ride all over Europe, during which he caught a bug. He arrived at his destination exhausted and gaunt, looking nothing like the glamorous movie star they all remembered. Years later Jean commented on that disastrous casting choice:

> Sophia Loren and Alan Ladd were not probably the most ideal chemical combination ... not because of anything against Alan, but because I don't think Alan was the right man to represent an archaeological man of international repute. Alan is a very fine and capable artist in his right way, but other people were probably more capable for the role—Van Heflin, or Mel Ferrer. Even Cary Grant would have given a charm, a quality. Plus, the fact that the chemistry between two stars is so important.[20]

When Negulesco introduced Ladd to Loren, who was eager to get to know her new co-star, she was so disappointed by the actor's lack of presence that she slowly turned pale. Ladd acted very cold toward the Italian actress, always polite but remaining aloof during the entire shooting. Most likely this was due to a complex about his 5'6" height. In her autobiography, Loren wrote, "Alan Ladd was slightly shorter than me, so to shoot many of the scenes, he had to stand on a stool. It wasn't anyone's fault, but it made him suffer, and he'd created a few too many complexes for himself. I, on my part, acted foolishly and wasn't very kind to him. I enjoyed poking fun at him and I played around all the time, as if life were nothing more than a comedy."[21] Ladd was the only leading man with whom Loren could not make friends.

According to Ladd's biographer, the actor disliked the *Dolphin* script and felt that Jean's camera angle consistently favored Loren. He told the *New York Herald Tribune*, "Negulesco fell in love with her, so she got all the good closeups. All you ever saw of me in most scenes was the back of my neck. I got fed up with it."[22] According to Negulesco, Sophia avoided rehearsing love scenes with him, having Ladd reading his lines with a double sitting with his back to the camera imitating dialogue.

After shooting in Athens, mostly around famous landmarks like the Acropolis, the crew moved to the little rocky island of Hydra. *Boy on a Dolphin* was originally scheduled to be shot in 55mm Cinemascope, but it would have been too difficult to get the enormously heavy 55mm camera into some nearly inaccessible locations. Ultimately the movie was shot in 35mm.

Loren's arrival on the island overlapped with the shipment of Jean's beautiful silver gray 4.9L Ferrari, which he had bought in Rome and planned to use as Clifton Webb's car in the picture. A gorgeous film star and a brand new sports car, both arriving at the same time, created quite a commotion among the local onlookers who had never experienced anything similar on their tiny island.

Hydra did not have the appropriate housing facilities for a cast and crew of nearly 150. So a summer cruise ship was rented at a cost of $2000 a day and anchored at Mandraki Bay, near the harbor, to serve as a floating hotel for the company. A second vessel, the S.S. *Neraida*, owned in prewar years by Mussolini's son-in-law, was used as Parolee's yacht, but also as living quarters for Clifton Webb and his 85-year-old mother Mabel. Alan Ladd had his own private yacht as accommodation.

There were only two houses available for rent on Hydra. One on a hill was occupied by Loren with the costume designer, the hairdresser and the makeup artist. In a second one in the main village, Jean settled with Dusty and Ivan Moffat. Loren wrote of her director:

8. La Loren

Negulesco was cheerful and bursting with life. We got along fine and in the evening he'd take us out fishing on *lampare* [boats used for night fishing]. I loved spending the night out at sea.... Negulesco was enchanted by the landscape, by that sun-drenched, ancient nature that spoke to us about our origins. Whether he wanted to or not, he ended up putting the Mediterranean Sea at the heart of the movie. After all, he was an artist too. Hidden, where I couldn't see him, he sketched some wonderful portraits of me, which he exhibited in a show the following December, once we returned to Rome for the studio shoots.[23]

While shooting in Hydra, Webb was taken ill with a form of pneumonia and had to be rushed back to Athens and confined to bed for a week while Jean shot around him. At the end of the shooting, the production left some money to the municipality plus all the material used like wood, tools and power generators. After the film was released, Hydra received worldwide visibility and became one of the most visited islands of Greece.

The most memorable moment of the shoot was a scene when Sophia lifted her skirt, tucked it between her legs and pinned it to her belt in back before diving into the sea. When she emerged from the freezing water, Jean and all the crew members' jaws dropped, watching her perfect body outlined, including pointed nipples, on her wet, skimpy (but double-lined to avoid censorship) yellow dress. That dress was Jean's creation, inspired by an old photograph he had seen of a Japanese pearl diver. For everybody's pleasure, Negulesco demanded a couple of extra takes. That unforgettable scene made Loren a poster girl and became the symbol of the entire film. *Time* called it the "finest vision since Botticelli painted Aphrodite on her shell."[24]

Sophia Loren and Alan Ladd in *Boy on a Dolphin* (1957).

In December, shooting resumed in Rome at Cinecittà Studios where some of the interiors were completed. In addition, a long and costly sequence was shot in a Roman museum rented for the occasion.

On December 10, 1956, the Galleria Schneider in Rome presented Negulesco's first art exhibition in Italy. On the invitation that showed the silhouette of a little boy riding a big dolphin, a quote of Jean's was printed:

"A Director Enjoys Life Doodling In Pure And Impure Lines...."

The exhibition showed Jean's latest works, mostly sketches and paintings, made in Greece on the set of *Dolphin*. Loren, the guest of honor at the opening, was pleasantly surprised to see many portraits of herself, done by Jean without her knowledge. The event was covered by the international press and was featured in newsreels.

In Rome, Jean was also honored at a dinner given by the High Commission on Tourism, via a plaque lauding the boost he gave Italian tourism with *Three Coins in the Fountain*. The plaque was presented by Commissioner Vittorio Romani at a dinner attended by American press correspondents at a trendy Roman restaurant.

Boy on a Dolphin was completed on schedule by Christmas, at a final cost of $3,500,000. When it was released five months later, it was a solid financial success mostly thanks to the publicity built around Loren and the breathtaking Greek scenery.

While in Greece, Jean and Dusty enjoyed a visit from 12-year-old Chryssoula Yannidaki, a fatherless Greek girl whom they had been supporting for two years through the Foster Parents Plan. The Negulescos' strong desire to have a child was one of the main reasons for Jean to agree to direct without any salary *The Dark Wave*, a documentary about children affected by epilepsy. The Variety Club Foundation to Combat Epilepsy had contacted Spyros Skouras, urging him to sponsor the making of the first picture on epilepsy for theatrical distribution. *The Dark Wave* was scheduled to be a 20-minute color–CinemaScope short. Because of Jean's long experience at Warner Bros. directing shorts along with his ability with CinemaScope, he was the right choice to direct. *The Dark Wave* featured realistic performances from Cornell Borchers, Charles Bickford and Nancy Davis. It was intended to shed light on the seldom discussed disease, aiming to correct some misconceptions about epilepsy and show that there was no reason why sufferers couldn't lead a normal life.

The story unfolded in a typical American town where a 12-year-old girl (Pamela Beaird) becomes an epileptic. At first, her friends, neighbors and even her family shy away from her, but certain salient facts are brought to light by the family doctor and an internationally known specialist, and everyone realizes that the mystery that has so long surrounded the disorder is totally uncalled for. *The Dark Wave* cost $55,000 to produce and was shot at Fox in three days. It was screened for the first time in May 1957 at the Variety Clubs International convention at the Waldorf-Astoria Hotel in New York. When it was theatrically released nationwide by Fox, audiences found it moving and absorbing. It was nominated for two Academy Awards as Best Short Subject (two-reel) and as Best Documentary (short subject).

In May 1957, to give confidence to exhibitors, Spyros Skouros released *The Big Show*, a 110-minute CinemaScope outlining in detail 20th Century–Fox's ambitious program of 55 productions during the next 12 months. The picture illustrated a multi-million-dollar program initiated by the studio to provide audiences with a continuous flow of top-quality entertainment adapted from famous story properties and brought to the screen by a brilliant array of production and star talent. Jean, one of the 19 producers

Dusty and Jean Negulesco at home in Beverly Hills in 1957.

and 14 directors included in the feature, briefly talked about his next project, *A Certain Smile*, based on a best-selling novel by French author Françoise Sagan. *The Big Show* was such an effective gimmick that Skouras, in compliance with thousands of exhibitor requests, made available a special 45-minute version for theater presentation to the public.

Before working on *A Certain Smile*, Jean committed to direct in CinemaScope *Our Love*, a romantic drama with "metaphysical overtones," which he filmed at the end of August 1958. A remake of the 1946 John Payne-Maureen O'Hara tearjerker, *Sentimental Journey*, the new version was from a screenplay by Luther Davis. This version was based upon the original story "The Little Horse" by Neila Gardner White, which appeared first in *Good Housekeeping Magazine* in June 1944.

Later renamed *The Gift of Love*, the production reunited Lauren Bacall and Robert Stack after the highly successful Douglas Sirk melodrama *Written on the Wind* (1956). It was Bacall's first film made following the death of Humphrey Bogart. She reported how hard it was to go back to work without her husband wishing her good luck on her first day, but it was a necessary step for her healing process. She wrote in her memoir, "Not a marvelous picture—a remake, sentimental—but Negulesco would direct and we loved working together."[25]

Bacall played Julie Beck, a devoted wife who, after discovering she has only a short time to live, adopts Hitty, a little orphaned girl, so that her husband Bill Beck, a research scientist, will have someone to love him in the future. Seven-year-old Evelyn Rudie played the child. At such a tender age she was already a precocious young actress, known to millions of television viewers. Jean had previously directed Rudie in *Daddy Long Legs*.

Locations included the Lick Observatory at Mount Hamilton and the Vista del Mar Orphanage located half a mile from the Fox studio in West Los Angeles. Many of the paintings hanging in the Becks' home were part of Jean's art collection including a fine portrait of Bacall which he gave her as a gift when filming was completed. Bacall loved it so much that it hung in the living room of her New York apartment until her death. The portrait was also featured on the cover of *Vogue France* in 1978.

Asked about *The Gift of Love* in a long interview with the Spanish magazine *Film Ideal* in 1965, Jean's reply was, "Honestly, I don't remember of what picture are you talking about?" After he was given more details to refresh his memory, his short comment was, "Oh yes. *Gift* was very successful, it cost very little to make and it was adored by female audiences, who wept and sniveled relating to the story. I worked with Lauren Bacall in four [sic] films. She's great style. She was not a popular beauty as Marilyn but her intellectual appearance was more aimed to a more selected audience."[26]

Robert Stack, Evelyn Rudie and Lauren Bacall in a publicity shot for *The Gift of Love* (1958).

Released to mildly favorable reviews on the weekend of Valentine's Day and marketed as "the perfect date movie," *The Gift of Love* was not as successful as Jean remembered it. It actually flopped, barely recouping its $1,215,000 cost.

That same year, lured by the international success of the French novel *Un certain sourir*, Fox bought the screen rights. The book had created quite a stir in describing the torrid affair between a young student and a much older married man. Before a script was drafted, the Production Code Administration notified the studio that no authorization would be ever granted unless the original Françoise Sagan story first underwent radical changes. The producers hired Frances Goodrich and her husband Albert Hackett, winners of the Pulitzer Prize for their stage adaptation of *The Diary of Anne Frank* (1955), with the intent of transforming Sagan's novel into a suitable story for the screen. The Hacketts toned down most of the sex and the real motivations of the actions of the main characters.

"From my film version of Françoise Sagan's *A Certain Smile,* people seemed to expect a 'dirty' picture, but the writers made it instead into a quite gentle, rather advanced love story,"[27] commented Jean. On another occasion he added:

> If I could have made it with enough independence, probably I'd have shot a completely different film. But let's not forget that I was a studio employee with a weekly salary, and if at the studio there were any problems, those were also my problems. I agree that *A Certain Smile* has not much of Sagan. She herself did not like it and she also wrote an article against it. She was right in saying that that was not her book. Having said that, I still think it was a beautiful picture.[28]

In February 1957, after the names of Rossano Brazzi and Joan Fontaine were confirmed in the cast, Fox announced a worldwide search for a talented new girl for the leading role. According to Hedda Hopper, Jean tried to get Audrey Hepburn but the studio feared higher costs and preferred to give the role to an unknown. Just before the quest was about to begin, Hal Gefsky, an American agent working out of a Paris agency, saw in a French film a young actress named Christine Carrere. Knowing that Fox was about to launch a search for the girl to play the role of Dominique Vallon, Gefsky sent her picture to Hollywood. Carrere was asked to make a test in London. The young woman did not speak a word of English, so she learned the dialogue for the two scenes from the picture phonetically. When she performed before the camera, she almost literally didn't know the meaning of the words she was saying. Producer Henry Ephron and Negulesco looked at it back in Hollywood and said, "That's our girl." The search ended before it began.[29]

For the secondary role of the young boyfriend of Dominique, Jean cast Bradford Dillman after seeing him in Eugene O'Neill's *Long Day's Journey into Night* on stage.

A Certain Smile shot for several weeks on a Fox sound stage in Hollywood. Later the production moved to France where all the exteriors were filmed. "Not for ten billion dollars could we have reproduced here the beauty of France, the scenery and architecture," Jean said to editor Wanda Harris. "We show Paris as we showed Rome in *Three Coins in the Fountain*. The beauty of Yonne Valley, of Villefranche, the small picturesque town of Aix en Provence are all beautiful beyond description."[30] As soon as Negulesco arrived in Paris, he contacted Sagan, to whom he had already sent a copy of the screenplay. The meeting did not turn out to be what he had expected.

> I gave her an appointment in a cafe not too far from where we were shooting. She was sitting on the terrace eating a ham and cheese sandwich in the company of a young man. I approached her a bit confused.

"Miss Sagan?"
"Yes."
"Excuse me, I'm Jean Negulesco. Have you read the script?"
"Yes."
"Did you like it?"
"No."
"Could you tell me why?"
"No."
"Do you want to join me on the set?"
"No."
"Would you allow me to pay for your sandwich?"
"Yes."

She then said to the young man: "It's not him that pays, it's 20th Century–Fox." That was my only interaction I had with Miss Sagan. I am sure she found the picture horrible. But it was really beautiful, because I wanted to show Paris the way I loved it: Rue de Visconti, Place de Furstenberg, Rue de la Seine, Paris at dawn when everybody gets up, when you buy French fries on a paper cone. Actually it was more my youth I wanted to portray. I love this film so much. Unfortunately, something went wrong. Maybe it was the girl. Without any doubts we could have made that picture more erotic, stressing more on the forbidden love of a much older man than on his mistress. I am positive it could have been much better.[31]

Midway through the filming, after looking at rushes, Jean felt that the picture was missing something. His solution was to add a lengthy scene at a trendy Parisian nightclub, where Johnny Mathis sang the title song which was later nominated for an Academy Award.

Rossano Brazzi and Joan Fontaine in *A Certain Smile* **(1958).**

Jean's old friend Joan Fontaine found it very difficult to work; she was ill throughout production. But she persisted and was able to complete the picture. In her autobiography she wrote, "My humor returned briefly when I was told how Mrs. Brazzi has reacted when informed that her husband and Miss Carrere had become romantic on location in the South of France. 'What took him so long?' replied the actor's wife, thoroughly used to the peccadilloes of her handsome Italian husband."[32]

"I seem to work best with Jean Negulesco," Rossano Brazzi said in an interview. "*The Blessing*, which will begin in August—in Paris, I hope—will be my third time with Jean directing. We got to know each other when we made *Three Coins in the Fountain*, and we become fast friends while we were doing *A Certain Smile*. Now I am very happy that he will be with me again in *The Blessing*."[33]

A Certain Smile premiered on July 31, 1958, at New York's Paramount Theatre. Proceeds for the evening's opening went to the Nephrosis Foundation. The same night, the picture debuted in Paris.

Due to its weak script, *A Certain Smile* received mixed reviews. Some found it a sappy soap opera, others a lovely romantic film. Yet all critics agreed on its magnificent scenic beauty, strikingly photographed by Milton Krasner. Commercially the picture was not very successful but it was nominated for three Academy Awards: Best Art Direction, Best Costume Design and Best Song.

9

His Best of Everything

"[Negulesco] was a kick to work with…. He was a big flirt."—Hope Lange

In August 1951, British producer Alexander Korda engaged writer Nancy Mitford to write a treatment based on an idea he supplied. Dissatisfied with her treatment, Korda approved Mitford's request to turn the work into a witty novel, which became *The Blessing*. Four years later, Korda maintained rights to the novel, intending to produce a film adaptation. A script, present in Negulesco's papers, proves that a 132-page draft, dated January 1954, was written by Max Ophuls and Louis Ducreux, but the project was abandoned for unknown reasons. In March 1956, MGM purchased the film rights; two years passed before the studio gave the green light to a production with Sidney Franklin directing from a Karl Tunberg screenplay. In July 1958, Franklin left MGM after many years with the studio and Jean, borrowed from 20th Century–Fox, took over as director. Tunberg revised the script over a dozen times before principal photography began in August 1958.

Count Your Blessings starred Deborah Kerr, Maurice Chevalier, Rossano Brazzi and child star Martin Stephens, who later played in the horror hit *Village of the Damned* (1960). Chevalier was signed at Jean's request; Jean negotiated the actor's salary.

The bulk of the film was filmed in London, Paris and in the French wine country around Bordeaux. The interiors were later completed at MGM in Hollywood. *Count Your Blessings* was a light, sophisticated comedy, handsomely produced with lavish costumes and sets. The script lost much of its originality in the adaptation, partly because of censorship regulations. The atmosphere on the set was very relaxed. The crew and cast happily celebrated the three stars' birthdays (all were born in September). It was Chevalier's 70th, Brazzi's 42nd and Kerr's 37th. Jean presented Deborah with a portrait he had made of her, which had been used as part of the set decoration.[1]

When the picture opened in April 1959, most of the reviewers praised the performances of Chevalier and Kerr, along with Jean's direction, but found the script awfully dull. All seemed to agree with *Variety*: "Jean Negulesco guides his charges competently; but he's handicapped by the slow-paced yarn."[2]

The name Jean Negulesco was often appearing in the list of best dressed men in the Hollywood colony. A lengthy *Chicago Tribune Magazine* article, "Five Dozen Suits!" peeked into "debonair" Jean's wardrobe, which included 60 suits, 69 pairs of sports trousers, 53 waistcoats, 500 ties, three dozen hats, 50 pairs of shoes and heaps of shirts and underclothes. "Negulesco does not have the figure of a Greek Apollo—he is 5 feet 10 inches tall, weighs 170 pounds, and is if anything, a little chunky," the article noted.

9. His Best of Everything

Deborah Kerr, Maurice Chevalier (with hands raised) and Rossano Brazzi in a publicity shot for *Count Your Blessings* (1959).

"But he has a first rate taste for tailoring and color ensembles, and the purse to satisfy his desires."[3] The article went on to describe Jean's favorite color combinations according to the type of event or time of day.

In 1959 Jerry Wald and Jean connected again for their third and last film together, *The Best of Everything,* the story of three girls who share a small New York City apartment and work together at a paperback publishing house. Independent producer Wald had been working for Fox for years; at the studio, he had his own lot, separate from the rest. He often produced three or four pictures simultaneously, more than all the other Fox producers combined. He'd routinely visit all of New York's major publishers, talking to editors about upcoming books with movie potential and scouting for new writers who might have what he needed. In the Simon & Schuster office, Wald was introduced to young author Rona Jaffe, who was about to write a working-girl book. A few months later, while Jaffe was on vacation in California, Wald met her again. They talked about the novel she was planning to write and if the story was as promising as it seemed, Wald expressed his interest in producing a film adaptation. On the train back to New York, Jaffe was impressed by a help-wanted ad in *The New York Times*, "You Deserve the Best of Everything," which, when shortened, became the novel's title. The 437-page book was completed in five months, during which time she constantly updated Wald on her progress. *The Best of Everything* was bought by Fox for $100,000 before the manuscript had been edited. Wald started to announce to the press the stars signed to play in the film. In September 1958, just two weeks after its publication, the novel made *The New York Times*' best-seller list where it remained for five consecutive months.

Since Jaffe decided not to write the screenplay, Wald hired Mann Rubin, whose background was in television writing. Rubin wrote three unsatisfactory drafts and was replaced by Edith Sommer.

Martin Ritt was initially set to direct, but he was replaced by Jean in January 1959 because, reportedly, Ritt was upset with the casting of Suzy Parker. Ritt dismissed this rumor, saying the script wasn't his "cup of tea." Wald considered Jean, now the "master of CinemaScope," a perfect replacement, having fond memories of the great success they had with *Humoresque* and *Johnny Belinda*. *The Best of Everything* seemed to be the right occasion to team up again.

Lee Remick, Hope Lange, Debbie Reynolds and Diane Varsi were some of the first names attached to the project. When asked why he was first casting the girls, Wald told Hedda Hopper that women were always more important because they had to match the boys.

Then Nina Foch, Suzy Parker, Hope Lange and Margaret Leighton were announced as the cast of the production thus far. Robert Evans, was one of the first men signed. A part-time actor and part-time entrepreneur, Evans got his part thanks to Rona Jaffe, who pitched him to Jean.

"'Forget it, Rona, he's a homosexual. It'll show up on the screen.' Listening in on the extension, I wanted to crack up. Jean Negulesco, the director, was talking about me," Evans wrote in his biography. Jaffe had told Evans that one of the novel's main characters, playboy bastard Dexter Key, had been written based on him. "He's a homosexual, Rona," laughed Negulesco. "Everyone knows it. They'll never believe him as a cocksman."[4]

Evans jokingly confirmed Jean's statement, to see Jaffe's surprised face, and then assured her he was straight. In the end, Jaffe's persistence won and Jean reconsidered Evans on the condition he would test for the part, which he did. But Negulesco took a dislike to Evans, getting furious every time the vain actor went into the bathroom. "He's in there combing his hair," Jean would fume.

Brett Halsey was cast as Eddie Davis by Wald. "Very professional ... the kind of actor that comes to the set fully prepared," Jean said of Halsey. Halsey claims to have later met at a party in Malibu the man on whom his character was based; the man complimented him on how well he had played the part.[5]

Louis Jourdan and Brian Aherne did the film because of their friendship with Jean. Wald's other casting choice, heartthrob Stephen Boyd, was about to become a star via his big role in *Ben Hur* (1959) opposite Charlton Heston.

9. His Best of Everything

The female cast took final shape when Fox's contract players Diane Baker, Suzy Parker, Martha Hyer and Hope Lange (whose presence was confirmed at last minute after being announced to star in another Fox production) were all confirmed for the picture. One supporting character, Amanda Farrow, a sexually frustrated editor-in-chief, was left to be cast. Wald had in mind Joan Crawford but Jean argued that the actress would have never accepted such a minor part. But Crawford, who was in dire financial straits, immediately accepted Wald's $65,000 offer for a few days of work. Being directed once again by Jean, someone she trusted, made Crawford's choice easier. She insisted that her name be billed separately from the rest of the cast and demanded that her dressing room–trailer parked inside the stage differently from the trailers of the younger actresses parked outside the stage.

In early May 1959, Jean began filming *The Best of Everything* on location in New York at the new Seagram Building on Park Avenue, followed by numerous other locations in Manhattan and Long Island. The production then moved to the Fox stages, where 35 sets were constructed, including the 37th floor offices of Fabian Publishing and the fabulous apartment set for Louis Jourdan's character. Jean used many of his paintings, and Dusty's, as set decoration.

In spite of all the courtesies extended to Crawford, the actress often misbehaved. On the set she reportedly had problems with Hope Lange. Crawford called her an upstart and accused her of upstaging the veteran actress. Crawford expected Jean to side with her but he was unsympathetic, no longer intimidated by Crawford's whims. He actually made her cry when, in front of everybody, he criticized her "lousy taste" in art, referencing the kitschy big-eyed Margaret Keane paintings she collected.

Joan constantly argued that her character needed more explanations, deeper motivations, but Jean disagreed. When she demanded some time alone before shooting a scene, he told her that he could not spare it. Another tense moment occurred when Crawford and one of the younger actresses were asked to make a trailer to be included in a Fox newsreel. Joan insisted on playing the scene holding a bottle of Pepsi (the company she had just inherited by her late husband, Pepsi-Cola chairman Alfred Steele). Jean objected. But claiming to have Wald's authorization she demanded, "No Pepsi-Cola bottle, Joan Crawford goes home." He replied, "No, Joan. Pepsi-Cola stays but Negulesco goes home." He got up and left the stage.[6] Wald was called to patch things up. He had to explain that she was the star of the picture, not of her product. The trailer was eventually shot without any Pepsi in it. Jean got his revenge in the editing room after Wald complained that the film was too long: He edited out several of Crawford's scenes, including one that was reportedly a superbly acted episode (Crawford rolling into the office in a drunken rage).

Many years later, Crawford commented on her experience. "This was a rather complex semi-movie which was supposed to showcase a whole bunch of up-and coming 20th Century–Fox actors. The youngsters did all right, but for some reason or other I'm proud to say I walked off with the film. Perhaps it was the part—I had all the balls—but I think it was a matter of experience, knowing how to make the most of every scene I had."[7]

The young girls in the cast (Crawford, 55, called them "all those young bitches") loved working with Negulesco. "He was a kick to work with," recalled Hope Lange. "He was a big flirt. He used to call me Miss Slivovitz. At the same time, he was disciplined. He knew what he wanted."[8]

Jean Negulesco and Hope Lange on location in New York City shooting *The Best of Everything* (1959).

"He exactly knew what he wanted us to do," said Diane Baker. "And we just did it. And for that reason I think it was great fun to be in the picture. And you can tell it."[9]

By the end of the shooting, Jean even softened on Robert Evans. The actor was caught by a security guard leaving his trailer at two in the morning with one of the female leads. When Jean found out, he walked into Evans' dressing room and didn't say word.

> Then in his European style, he shrugged. "Robert, one day you are going to be like me." I didn't know what the fuck he was talking about. "When I was your age, all I wanted was to make love to every leading lady I worked with. As I got older, I used to like to *watch* people who make love. Today, now, I like to watch the people who watch the people who make love. Enjoy it while you can, Bob. Everyone's the same. The older you get, the more watching becomes better and better than the doing."[10]

Photographer Bob Willoughby was invited by Fox to work on the set of the film. He later wrote,

> They told me that they were going to make Suzy Parker and Louis Jourdan the new romantic couple *à la* Greta Garbo and John Gilbert (if you can believe that!). Suzy Parker was a very famous fashion model. She had great bones, but not much sex appeal, and Louis Jourdan even less, so although I could take pictures, Jean Negulesco had to get performances out of them, which meant a lot of pull and tug. Negulesco and I hit right off, since we were both passionate about art, and he invited me back to his home to see his collection and to meet his lovely wife, Dusty. Jean had that great facility for drawing a nude with one continuous line, which was phenomenal. He has started out as a painter, and brought this taste of design to his films."[11]

Filming took two months and upon completion, Wald and Jean did a lot of trimming in the editing room after test audiences did not respond too well to the Martha Hyer–Donald Harron coupling. Their sequences were all cut to the bone along with some Crawford scenes considered irrelevant to the plot.

On October 8, 1959, *The Best of Everything* had a sumptuous premiere at New York's Paramount Theatre. To coincide with the opening, Pocket Books scheduled a one-million print run for the novel in paperback, while many outfits worn by the film's young stars were reproduced and sold in department stores across the nation. In spite of lukewarm reviews that dismissed it as a "silly soap opera," the picture was one of the biggest commercial hits of the year with Adele Palmer's costumes and the Alfred Newman-Sammy Cahn theme song "The Best of Everything" getting Oscar nominations. Sad to say, it was the last successful work of Jean's career.

Many critics now consider *The Best of Everything* the mother of all soap operas, a sort of *Sex in the City* of those times. To comply with censorship rules, sex was left to the audience's imagination and words like "abortion" were changed into "operation"; but the spirit of looking for love and rewarding work in New York seems the same.

Jean had acquired the reputation as one of Hollywood best party-givers. As actor George Sanders humorously mentioned in his memoirs,

> Negulesco has a large and comfortable establishment in the heart of Beverly Hills which houses two important collections. One is of paintings of Bernard Buffet and the other is his own waistcoats. He is as happy to show you the one as to wear the other and takes equal pride in both. Jean makes a great host, partly because he is loaded with charm and partly because he is a terrific cook. At all of his parties he provides his guests with wild, unrecognizable Rumanian dishes so cunningly seasoned as to produce a sort of gastronomical conflagration. As strong drink is manifestly the only sensible remedy, the guests are very soon in an advanced state of high spirits and remain so until the early hours of the morning, by which time they are virtually indistinguishable from the gaunt gray masterpieces of Bernard Buffet that surround them on every side.[12]

The October 1959 release of *The Best of Everything* corresponded to an offer Jean received from producer Ray Stark to direct *The World of Suzie Wong,* the love story of an American painter and a young prostitute. Stark had previously worked as a literary and talent agent; *Suzie Wong* marked his first experience as a motion picture producer. He had produced the play written by Paul Osborn, inspired by Richard Mason's original novel; it did excellent business despite poor reviews. Paramount backed the picture in conjunction with Seven Arts. They initially considered hiring British director Jack Clayton, who had recently helmed *Room at the Top* (1959), to direct the film. But it was Jean at the end that was officially hired simultaneously to the casting of William Holden, who had been Stark's client when Stark was an agent. Screenwriter John Patrick was sent to tour Asia for research purposes and to scout locations. Right after New Year's, Jean left for Hong Kong, where principal photography started on January 7, 1960. But in early February, once the crew moved to London's Elstree Studio to film the interiors, the production was shut down officially due to illness of female lead Francis Nuyen, who had created the title role on Broadway. Some sources reported that the picture had been halted because Nuyen had left the set due to clashes with Stark over how her role should be played. Others claimed that the actress was distressed by her rocky relationship with her unfaithful lover Marlon Brando, and that caused a nervous breakdown.

Whatever the case, Stark was forced to conduct a global search for another Suzie. Natalie Wood, Nobu McCarthy, Lisa Liu, Rita Moreno, Grace Chang, Pascale Petit, Charita Soliz and Luz Valdez were all considered. On February 15, Paramount announced the casting of Nancy Kwan (it was her first film experience). She was about to embark in the stage tour of the play before being cast. Only a few days later, the production was again disrupted when Jean was fired and quickly replaced by Richard Quine. Jean's dismissal was due to differences with Stark over portions of the story still to be filmed and over casting choices. On its release, *The World of Suzie Wong* bombed and was panned by the critics as too unbelievable and sentimental.

After leaving the *Suzie Wong* set, Jean stayed in London for a few extra days. He was scheduled to be the guest of honor at the annual dinner of the British Critic's Circle at the Criterion Restaurant, but at the last moment he bowed out due to indisposition.

In February 1960, Jean was informed that he would be getting a star on the famous Hollywood Walk of Fame. It was placed at 6226 Hollywood Blvd, on the south side, between Argyle Avenue and El Centro Avenue. The news was followed by the announcement of the birth of Jean's independent production organization, whose films would be released through United Artists. This was a choice made by many actors and directors tired of being attached to a studio and to their tyrannical orders. As his first independent venture, Jean announced he would produce and direct *Apple Pie Bed* with Maurice Chevalier in a starring roles.

Apple Pie Bed was a romantic and sexy comedy based on the novel *The Midwife of Point Clery* by Flora Sandstorm. Jean had been intending to direct the film since 1957, after he had read the book and bought the rights. In the summer of 1958, he sent a copy of the novel to Marilyn Monroe, explaining that *The Midwife of Point Clery* was fundamentally about sex and he wanted to adapt it into a film for her. He also suggested Monroe give the book to her husband Arthur Miller to read and get his opinion. Marilyn did not show any interest in the project. Jean asked director George Cukor to send the book to Ava Gardner; Jean knew she was busy, but he knew that anything Cukor recommended would have a good chance with Gardner.[13] Nothing came out of it. The part was then offered to Sophia Loren but the Italian actress could not get out of her commitments for other movies to play the part of the midwife. Jean thought to change the locale to England and offered the role to Vivien Leigh. Leigh said she couldn't make it either. While looking for the right cast, a first draft of the script was written by Hugh Herbert. Jean instructed him to move the setting of the film to Forza d'Agrò, a small picturesque Sicilian village near the Strait of Messina, a place he had found while scouting for locations in Italy.

Finally in December 1960, Angie Dickinson, recent winner of a Golden Globe Award for New Star of the Year, was announced as the lead in the cast that included Maurice Chevalier, Agnes Moorehead, Vittorio De Sica, Marcel Dalio and several Italian and French actors. Jean had hoped to cast rising French star and heartthrob Alain Delon, but after a first meeting, the two could not reach a suitable financial agreement.

"I'd much rather make the film here because I hate traveling," was Negulesco's first comment to the Hollywood press. "But our location demanded Sicily."[14]

9. His Best of Everything

Herbert's script, whose title had been changed from *Apple Pie Bed* to *Angela,* proved unsatisfactory. Jean asked Edith Sommer, who had adapted *The Best of Everything,* to take charge. "She's one of the best writers I ever had," Jean commented. Together they agreed to change the title to *Jessica,* the main character's name. The story was a modern rethinking of Aristophanes' comedy *Lysistrata,* set in a Sicilian town whose ladies go on sex strike to make sure that Jessica, a pretty American midwife of whom they are all jealous, will have no future reason for hanging around their town.

Before the shooting began in Italy in the second half of March, Negulesco submitted a copy of the script to the Production Code Administration. He was told that it was quite unsuitable. After some soul-searching and conferences with his colleagues, Jean decided to go ahead and shoot anyway. When the film was completed, he got the approval of the PCA. Jean was very happy with his decision, emphasizing to the press that *Jessica* was substantially the same script he first gave to the PCA and that under other circumstances, the picture probably would have been abandoned or rewritten as to lose the quality which he wanted to have. At the very last moment Vittorio De Sica bowed out and was replaced by Noël-Noël. The French actor was the only member of the cast who did not speak a word of English. He had to deliver all his lines in French which were later dubbed by Jean himself under the supervision of Agnes Moorehead and Dusty. "Watch out," said Moorehead while he was dubbing. "You're beginning to sound like Gregory Ratoff." Dusty told her husband that he had "too much tenor" in his voice.[15]

Angie Dickinson's arrival at the Rome airport was used by Jean as a publicity stunt. He alerted a group of Italian reporters, including a newsreel cameraman, and they showed up on the runway to photograph the actress being warmly welcomed by the director. On the following day, at Jean's suggestion, Dickinson began to learn, with the help of cast member Antonio Cifariello, how to drive a Vespa motorbike, as the script required. The paparazzi chased the couple all over the Italian capital. "Angie Dickinson was a dream," Jean recalled. "She has the softest lips I've ever kissed in my life. I told her by contract you have to kiss me tenderly and sweetly every morning before we start shooting."[16] As customary, Jean used to flirt with all the women on the set, but this time Dusty was with him on location, as the official wardrobe supervisor and the writer of four songs sung by Chevalier. The French actor was cast as a priest who loved to play the guitar. Since Chevalier did not know how to do it, Jean placed two men behind him playing the real music while Chevalier pretended to touch the instrument's strings. While on location for six weeks, the crew lodged in the small village of Forza D'Agrò, where the film was shot. Many members shared a room with local families, while most of the cast stayed in Taormina, one of the most enchanting destinations in Sicily, and a short 20-minute drive from the set.

At one point during filming, Angie Dickinson offered to drive the scooter herself down a twisting road. All went well until, at a sharp curve, the actress lost control and the scooter crashed into a wall. She suffered a cut on her left knee, bruised hands and right hip, and was in shock. She was ordered by a local doctor to stay in bed for two days. Jean decided to use her double for all the remaining scooter scenes.

After a return to Rome, Jean filmed a few final interiors at Cinecittà. Production wrapped on May 30. That same evening, a big dinner in a traditional Roman *trattoria* was organized for the cast and crew.

Jean loved the excitement and enthusiasm he found in Italy. In an interview, he described Rome as the center of the filmmaking world. "Hollywood played a great part

Angie Dickinson and Carlo Croccolo in *Jessica* (1962).

in the development of motion pictures," he told *Variety*, "but the excitement has now vanished and can now only be experienced in Rome."[17]

By acting as his own boss in making *Jessica*, Negulesco claimed that he spent only $50,000 in pre-production including putting the script in shape, scouting Sicilian locations, transatlantic travel, etc. He estimated that working under a studio set-up, the pre-production would have cost over $250,000. To promote *Jessica*, Jean asked painter Bernard Buffet to make a special poster, which became an instant collectable item. After premiering in Los Angeles in the spring of 1962, the film had a very limited domestic release. Jean's plan was to introduce the picture through its soundtrack: According to him, the tune "It's Better to Love" had good possibilities and might generate a buzz around the picture.

Despite the careful marketing strategy, *Jessica* was widely panned by critics and bombed. "Jean Negulesco's *Jessica* is a trite, frivolous variation on the often-exploited 'Lysistrata' theme," wrote *Variety*. The *New York Herald Tribune* called it "very hard to endure." After a few days in release, *Jessica* disappeared from theaters. It was a harsh defeat for Negulesco, who really believed in his project (and had invested in the $1,000,000 budget). "It was a big mistake," he admitted years later, "because you can be producer and director at the same time, those are two things completely different. It is a common mistake nowadays. Everybody wants to do everything. Actors want to be directors; directors want to make music. You don't have the time to concentrate … but at least I had a lot of fun."[18]

While Jean was in Hong Kong in preparation for *Suzie Wong*, Dusty learned from a lawyer about children born during the American occupation of Germany after the war. Those illegitimate children, abandoned by their mothers, were sheltered in special facilities or in hospitals. Dusty got news that in a hospital in Stuttgart there was a three-month-old abandoned girl in the children's ward ready to be adopted. After consulting with Jean, Dusty flew to Germany to adopt Christina. While there, she also heard that in a nearby little town, in a children's shelter house, there was another girl who could be adopted. The idea of having a sister convinced her to also adopt little Gabrielle. This adoption was a complicated process since the identity of her natural mother was known and, according to local law, she had to consent to give her child up for adoption. A contract was finally signed, and Gaby legally adopted.

In May 1961 when all the paperwork was completed, the Negulescos were reunited in Rome with "Tina" and "Gaby." The arrival of the little girls at Rome's airport was warmly celebrated by the Negulescos. (Because of his busy schedule, Jean had not yet met the children.) It was captured by the local press and shown in the Italian newsreels.

During the promotion of *Jessica*, Jean talked about his future possibilities: *The Treasure House of Martin Hews,* based on a novel by E. Phillips Oppenheim; *Sand Against the Wind,* and an original about a girls' reformatory. But *Jessica*'s disappointing reception deterred him from producing any additional pictures.

Jean was very happy to accept producer Jacques Bar's offer to direct a remake of Noël Coward's comedy *Private Lives*. It had already been adapted to the screen in 1931, starring Norma Shearer and Robert Montgomery. This new version was scheduled to be shot in Paris with Brigitte Bardot and Marcello Mastroianni. But MGM cancelled the production.

On August 1, 1962, Jean got an unexpected call from Nunnally Johnson telling him that he was going to be invited to finish a movie in-progress, *Something's Got to Give,* a remake of the successful Leo McCarey picture *My Favorite Wife* (1940) in which a shipwrecked woman presumed dead for years returns home on the eve of her husband's second wedding. Marilyn Monroe, star of the picture, had asked for him as a replacement for George Cukor. The picture had gotten off to a good start with Marilyn loving the script and her co-star Dean Martin. Everything changed when Cukor brought in a new writer to polish the screenplay and add dialogue. Marilyn grew frustrated at having to memorize new scenes every day. She thought her opinion had been ignored and that she'd been betrayed by the studio. Losing interest, she began showing up late. Fox fired her immediately. Then talks resumed between the studio and the blonde star, who agreed to return under certain conditions, including Negulesco as director.

Excited to work again with Monroe, Jean spoke to Peter Levathes, the film's executive producer, suggesting that it would be a good idea to stick to the original unrevised script to please Monroe and to go ahead with the production. But Levathes said that Marilyn had been sued by Fox, after which she had countersued. Therefore, until the matter was cleared by the studio's legal department, Jean was not to have any contact with Monroe. Jean reluctantly agreed.

Three days later, Marilyn was found dead. Jean was devastated. He was suddenly inundated by requests from the press to talk about Marilyn and her sudden death. "She represents to men something we all want in our unfulfilled dreams. She's the girl you'd like to double cross your wife with,"[19] were his words to commemorate the star.

Five days after the tragic event, Negulesco agreed to be interviewed for the TV program CBS Eyewitness News about Monroe. In his Beverly Hills home, a grim-faced Jean appeared before the camera in his first televised interview ever. He reminisced about his relationship with Monroe and his experience on the set of *How to Marry a Millionaire*, explaining to the viewers that she "had something that nobody in her life could catch except the camera."

In June 1963, Jean was called in to shoot a difficult sequence for *The Greatest Story Ever Told* (1965) as a favor for his friend and colleague George Stevens. The picture had fallen behind schedule and different scenes were being shot simultaneously on different sets. Negulesco and British director David Lean were asked to help. Jean directed Dorothy McGuire and Robert Loggia in the Nativity scene. Filming was complicated because the entire picture was shot with a new single-lens Ultra Panavision 70, a new system to Jean who was accustomed to CinemaScope. The movie went unreleased for another two years. Negulesco worked uncredited.

Once his short commitment to *The Greatest Story Ever Told* was completed, Jean moved to Madrid. It was a decision he had in mind for a long time, in agreement with Dusty. It was his opinion that working in Europe was a far more stimulating experience. He had lived through the Golden Era of Hollywood (which was going through major changes with the decadence of the major studios struggling against new independent productions and the fierce competition coming from television); now was the right time to be in Europe, where making films was a relaxing experience, more artistic and sophisticated and less obsessed by box office numbers. Jean left at the end of the summer to find the right house for his family and to discuss the pre-production of *Et Maintenant* (aka *Follies*), a musical he intended to direct starring Laurence Olivier, Cyd Charisse and Tony Martin. Based on a 1929 book by E. Phillips Oppenheim, *The Treasure House of Martin Hews*, the picture was supposed to be a "musical-mystery" filmed in Madrid.

Dusty told columnist Hedda Hopper that they had rented their Beverly Hills house to chess player Ed Lasker and his wife. "We are traveling light to Madrid," Dusty joked, "with two small children, trunks full of photographs, records and paintings, one small Rolls, and a secretary with our casting files. The airplane couldn't make it, and I am not sure we won't sink the boat."[20] Dusty also mentioned a project of her own: a musical called *Paris, Texas* she had finished writing.

Et Maintenant was another project that never saw the light of day: Jean shelved it when 20th Century–Fox producer David Weisbart, who had been the editor of *Johnny Belinda*, asked him to direct a remake of *Three Coins in the Fountain*. Jean had to fly back to Hollywood just when his family was settling into their new Madrid apartment. The good news was that the remake was set to be shot in and around the Spanish capital just like the original film was filmed in Rome. During negotiations in California, Negulesco spent his 64th birthday away from his family, cutting a cake in the company of John Derek and Ursula Andress at the Wilshire House hotel where he was staying.

In March the contract was signed. The picture's budget was to be between three and four million and the shooting set to start on May 1. Negulesco returned immediately to Madrid to find the right locations; he brought with him screenwriter Edith Sommer, to allow her to get a better understanding of the Spanish way of living. As he later would remark,

Fortunately or unfortunately, *Three Coins in the Fountain* was such a hit, and so closely identified with a European capital city, that everyone is tempted to make it a convenient point of reference. But times have changed, and no two cities have the same character or feel.... Everything that happens to our three amorous young ladies will be intimately knitted, I hope with an authentic feeling for the Spanish people and their country. If I succeed, *Three Coins* won't be around like Banquo's ghost, to invoke comparative memories.[21]

Jean started to line up the cast for his new film, which would be titled *The Pleasure Seekers*. Once again the story's troika approach seemed to be a winning combination along with the use of CinemaScope. But Negulesco seemed annoyed by those who called the picture a remake. Jean told the press.

"If a certain resemblance to *Three Coins in the Fountain* begins to suggest itself, think nothing of it.... Edith Sommer has provided us with a script in which the characters are different, the situations are different and the backgrounds and customs are different. The activity takes place in a different moral climate. To be sure, boy meets girl, etc.—but it would take more sophistication than I possess to employ any other basis for a film romance."[22]

He remarked on another occasion, "Instead of Rome, this picture is set in Madrid. And instead of three girls and three men, I am using four. Naturally the problems with American girls living in Madrid are similar to those in *Three Coins,* but this is 1964, so we'll have more difficulties."[23]

Announced for the male leads: Anthony Franciosa, George Chakiris, James Darren and Efrem Zimabalist, Jr. Only Franciosa made it into the picture; the others were replaced. Gardner McKay, Andre Lawrence and Brian Keith eventually filled the other roles.

Pamela Tiffin, Ann-Margret and Carol Lynley in *The Pleasure Seekers* (1964).

The character of Susie Higgins, the most naïve of the three girls, was the most difficult to cast. First Paula Prentiss was announced, then Jill St. John and still later Donna Michelle. Finally Pamela Tiffin was sent to be meet Jean, who immediately liked her. The actress recalled, "I didn't want to do *The Pleasure Seekers.* It was too frivolous and not honest enough for me. Fox suspended me and no other studio could hire me until I gave in. However, I was a good sport and went along."[24]

Off the set, the three stars did not connect with each other. Tiffin, the youngest and least experienced of the bunch, tried to make friends with Lynley and Ann-Margret (with whom she had co-starred in *State Fair* in 1962), but they seemed too competitive and not interested in any sort of camaraderie, especially with another woman. Ann-Margret's uncooperative behavior, playing diva, made the news when she refused to be photographed off-screen with her female co-stars.

According to Tiffin, Anthony Franciosa was very hostile, not knowing how to control his anger, especially with Jean. During a car scene, he got so mad at Jean that he drove off for two hours with Tiffin in his car, scared to death by the crazy speed. In another occasion Jean asked Franciosa to change his tie. The actor got hold of the director's neck and threatened him.

In Madrid, Jean was able to convince the Prado Museum to allow one night's shooting in front of some of their most important paintings. The museum management was worried that the strong lights could damage their masterpieces but Jean assured them that everything would be done very quickly and the result would be enormous publicity for the museum. Jean chose to shoot mostly in front of paintings by El Greco, one of his favorite artists. "When I was a painter, my gods were El Greco and Braque. And right now Bernard Buffet thrills me…. One off the reasons I like Buffet is because his style reminds me of El Greco…."[25]

The last scene on location was filmed in a couple of days on a beach near Malaga on the Costa del Sol where choreographer Bob Sidney hired some gypsies as extras. While shooting, Jean reported that he had been hampered when three gypsies working on the picture were jailed. The Spanish production manager's attempts to spring them failed, and a very exasperated Jean asked why they were involved in something larcenous when they were making good money in his film. "Well, there was this German tourist, a little drunk and showing much money," the Spaniard replied with a characteristic shrug. "They found him irresistible."[26]

There was another unpleasant episode when a bomb exploded in the parking area of the Madrid hotel where the cast and crew was staying. No one was hurt, but it was a great shock for everyone.

The location work was completed on a delayed schedule, so when the production moved back to Hollywood, the crew had only six weeks to complete soundstage interiors in order to avoid going over-budget. Brian Keith and Dina Merrill, who did not have any exterior scenes, were supposed to join the cast, but because of the delay, Merrill dropped out. Gene Tierney stepped in as replacement. The movie marked Tierney's last appearance on the screen. She wrote in her memoir,

> The picture was a melancholy time for me. I had not made it for the money, or for pride, or even a final taste of glory. I had wanted to make the picture to finish the cycle and close the book, and recapture for one last time the fun of making movies had been for me. But the Hollywood I knew was gone. The star system that created me and the other so-called Fox girls no longer existed…. My part in *The Pleasure Seeking* was so undemanding it caused me no difficulty, but not much pleasure."[27]

Once the film was completed, Jean found himself in the middle of a billing order war among all his stars. At the end, Fox decided that Ann-Margret and Carol Lynley would be billed first and second since they were both coming off big hits. Anthony Franciosa and Gardner McKay would follow, and Tiffin got fifth place.

The Pleasure Seekers was scheduled for release in mid–January 1965, but at the last moment the date had to be moved up to Christmas, because Fox had trouble with another film whose release had to be unexpectedly cancelled because of some legal issues. So the picture opened nationwide without much publicity and without an appropriate premiere, seriously hurting the box office.

The film was a critical and a financial disappointment and was generally seen as an inferior remake of *Three Coins in the Fountain*. As with all Jean's previous CinemaScope projects, the glorious cinematography of the colorful Spanish scenery was unanimously lauded. But many considered the script ludicrous.

In February 1965, Jean attended the picture's gala opening in Madrid, sponsored by the Marquesa de Villaverde (General Franco's daughter) for the Spanish Association Against Cancer. "For me this premiere in Madrid is very important since I shot the picture in this capital and in other places here in Spain: Toledo, Segovia, the Costa del Sol…," Jean said to the local press. "But I want to clarify that it was not my intention to do a simple display of Spanish attractions, but to use them to create an effect together with the characters or better to be a colorful background." *The Pleasure Seekers* grossed an estimated domestic $2 million with an additional $1.2 million worldwide, making just a small profit, but nothing compared to *Three Coins,* one of the highest grossing film of 1954. Ann-Margret thought that the film's poor box office performance was caused by audiences who "simply do not envision me as a sophisticated woman of the world."[28]

While Jean was still editing *Pleasure Seekers*, Hollywood columnist Mike Connolly reported in his column, "A new TV series for Gardner McKay? Not if he can't help it. He's got a deal on to star in a movie based on the exciting life of movie director Jean Negulesco."[29] No other details were ever announced.

10

Twilight

"I'm the last of Hollywood's dinosaurs."—Jean Negulesco

Jean and Dusty were both enthusiastic about living in Madrid. Jean told columnist Hedda Hopper that Dusty was particularly happy, joking, "All American women ... every time they take out a cigarette, seven guys break their necks to light it for them."[1]

During his long stay in Madrid, Jean bought a pied-à-terre in London's Mayfair. He was often traveling to the British capital where all the major Hollywood studios had their European headquarters. His house in Beverly Hills was now rented to Rex Harrison, who subleased it to Barbra Streisand and Elliott Gould. In June 1965, Jean was president of the jury at the prestigious San Sebastian Film Festival. On that occasion, he gave a long interview to *Film Ideal*, an established Spanish film magazine, in which he reminisced about his life and career.

In the following year, Jean was invited by the International Executive Service Corps in New York to travel to Turkey advise the Turkish film industry on raising their productions to intentional standards. The IESC, founded in 1964 by David Rockefeller and other American business leaders, was a non-profit organization, still very active today, that sent American executives overseas to help private enterprises in developing countries. The IESC offered advice in the areas of trade and competitiveness, financial services, tourism development, etc. "When I arrived there," Jean recalled, "they were just making films in which the belly dance was much more relevant than the plot, that was always the same: A young man from a rich family would fall in love with a young girl from a poor family. After a few repetitive scenes, they would go to a party, where somebody would perform a belly dance and then another belly dance...."[2] Jean stayed in Turkey nine months; he later called it "an adventurous time filled with Balkan promises." Upon his return, he discussed with Richard D. Zanuck, executive vice-president of 20th Century–Fox in charge of production, a story with a Turkish background which could have been made with local government support. (When a realistic budget was shown to the Turkish authorities, the project fizzled out.) Negulesco's good work was rewarded in March 1967 when he was presented with a silver tray "For Service to Country in the International Executive Corps."

In December 1967, Jean agreed to volunteer his time for the next three months to help a film production and distribution company in Iran. IESC arranged for him to work with Moulin Rouge Co. in Tehran, assisting the company's officials in the selection of subjects for movie production and advising them on establishing contacts with filmmakers in Europe and the U.S. In Iran, Jean was treated like royalty, housed in a penthouse at the Royal Hilton Hotel in Tehran, and provided with a Rolls-Royce and chauffeur. He was also received by the Shah, whom he had previously met at a dinner in Beverly Hills.

On his return to London, where he was now living with Dusty and their daughters, Jean read the book *The Heroes of Yucca* by Michael Barrett. The story, set in Colombia, impressed him so much that afterward he optioned the rights and asked Chester Erskine to adapt it, shifting the setting to Iran. Jean showed a first draft to the Akhavans brothers, partners of Moulin Rouge Co. They liked the idea and agreed to have Negulesco direct *The Heroes,* Iran's first major picture. Beyond the making of the movie, Jean and Mostafa Akhavan stated at a Hollywood press conference in, there were three main goals: to promote Iran as a tourist destination, to promote the country as a filming site, and to develop a native pool of trained filmmakers.

At the beginning, *The Heroes* had a budget estimate of $1.3 million. Jean explained that the picture did not receive any subsidy from the Iranian government, but the use of the army as extras and access to the color laboratories facility, part of the of the Iranian Ministry of Culture and Fine Arts, were offered at no cost.

Once the production was set to start, the Iranian government agreed to invest in it, determined to make Tehran one of the moviemaking capitals of the world. The budget was raised to $2.5 million and Jean was offered a percentage of the worldwide gross.

On October 15, 1968, after forming a pool of local and Italian technicians (including second unit director Franco Prosperi, who brought along many crew members from Cinecittà), Negulesco began principal photography at the 65-acre Moulin Rouge Studio, built by the Akhavan brothers on the outskirts of Tehran. The facility had two soundstages, a Hollywood-type back lot, a small village, woods and a lake. With the exception of a few scenes shot in the desert and in the proximity of some Iranian landmarks, Negulesco filmed most of *The Heroes* there. Originally the picture was supposed to be in Technicolor and CinemaScope, but to lower costs and for practical reasons, it was switched into Panavision. The Akhavan brothers cast Stuart Whitman, Elke Sommer, Curt Jurgens and Jim Mitchum.

The plot involved a disorganized group of six international jewel thieves who become the unofficial guardians of a small Iranian village. When local outlaws attack, looking for the body of their former leader and his treasure map, the invincible six are there to save the day, romance the local females and oppose the outlaws. Shooting started just after a terrible earthquake shook the country and went pretty smoothly, except for an accident involving Elke Sommer: In a rape scene, she overdid it when pretending to kick a heavy .45 automatic out of Stuart Whitman's hand, and wound up with severe bruises on her instep. Jean had to shoot the rest of the rape scene from the ankles up, with Sommer thrashing around on a bed. *The Heroes* was ultimately released as *The Invincible Six.*

Different sources claim that Rudolph Nureyev served as the film's uncredited choreographer, but there's no dance or ballet in the final cut, and there is no real proof that the famous dancer had any involvement with the production. "It's been very exciting. Luckily I still have a great enthusiasm for moviemaking. I hope I never lose it," was Jean's comment on his film.[3]

The Invincible Six premiered in North America in June 1970 without any fanfare, after the producers had difficulty finding a major distributor. Finally, Continental accepted to release it to a limited number of theaters. One of the very few reviews it got was in *Film Bulletin,* who opined that Negulesco "does a creditable job along with second-

Elke Sommer in a dramatic scene from *The Invincible Six* (1970).

unit director Franco Prosperi in handling the abundantly actionful goings-on."[4] The movie disappeared from circulation very quickly in both the U.S. and, a year later, in Europe.

While Jean was still in Iran, it was reported that he would fly to Bucharest for the pre-production work on *The Girl in the Wall,* based on a Sam Roeca screenplay. It was a World War II story of a Romanian girl who helps rescue an American flier, shot down during a bomber raid over the Ploiesti oil fields. The project would have marked Jean's directorial debut in his native Romania. Jean traveled to Romania where he visited all his relatives. With his sister Sabina, he toured the Buftea Film Production Center, Eastern Europe's largest film studio, to see if they would be right for the upcoming project. A few weeks later, the violent events of the Prague Spring had enormous repercussions in Romania, making it impossible to make the film. Decades earlier, Jean had refused to cooperate with the Communist regime in his birth country, so his name, his films and his art were banned from the country until 1989, when his memoir was translated into Romanian.

On July 20, 1969, Jean was in his home in London watching Neil Armstrong walking on the moon when the telephone rang. It was Darryl F. Zanuck calling him from Cannes after nine years of silence. The producer told him that he was making a picture that was in trouble and he needed Jean's immediate help. A few hours later, the director boarded a private plane sent by Zanuck. In Nice, Zanuck's assistant Bill told him that the producer wanted him to read the script of *Hello-Goodbye*, the film they were shooting in Cannes. He was also told that the picture had been shooting for three and a half months with a budget of $8 million, of which $3 million had been already spent. Jean found the script very dull. He also watched what had been shot by Ronald Neame, which was excellent—but it was only one reel.

Negulesco met with Zanuck and could not refuse the generous $5000-a-week salary the producer offered. Negulesco stepped in to direct *Hello-Goodbye*, considering this "an act of love" for Zanuck.

Jean later received a phone call from Zanuck's son Richard, who thanked him for making his father happy. "In the end," said Jean,

> I think I saved the production a couple of million dollars, which the group resented. There's a certain machinery that's set up when you make a film, and it comes to resent the creative end of the production. They keep the books, the budget—it's a whole world apart. It's really better to come in a little over budget or a little under, but never on, because then it looks like you're not only doing your own job, but you're also doing theirs better than they can. You must never undermine the importance of those people.[5]

The film was intended to make a star of French actress Genevieve Gilles, Zanuck's latest mistress; it was her first film experience after working as a model for several Parisian fashion houses. Zanuck had left Hollywood and was currently living in Paris, though he was still nominally the head of Fox. When they first met at Chez Maxim's in Paris, Gilles (whose original name was Gillaizeau) was 19, Zanuck 63. Within a year they became inseparable, even though they acted always with great discretion.

The story, written by Zanuck (under his pseudonym Mark Canfield) and adapted by Roger Marshall, was a romantic comedy that dealt with an old European baron (Curt Jurgens) and his young wife Gilles, who meets a British car salesman, Michael Crawford, whom the baron hires to teach his son about mechanics. The beautiful wife and the visitor have an affair and the forgiving baron eventually falls for an American heiress.

The original director Ronald Neame began shooting on the French Riviera, but within weeks the filmmaker quit because of too much interference from Zanuck, who was constantly on the set, prying. "Irreconcilable differences of opinions on questions of artistic approach between Neame and the pic's producer Andre Hakim," was the official reason for Neame's exit, *Variety* reported.[6]

For the first time in his career, Jean included nudity in his film, something that was becoming a trend in cinema in the late '60s. Jean was not happy about it: "I'm a man who is sorry that censorship has gone," Jean said years later in a BBC interview, "[T]hey gave the illusion ... what you imagine, what is suggested to you is by far more powerful than usually what we see now in TV ... there are so many nude bodies ... which becomes at one moment almost anatomical and embarrassing.... If you suggest instead of showing, [the censors] pass it."[7]

Michael Crawford recalled that Fox had him sign a document that made him responsible for any injury or loss of life, since the British actor agreed to do his own stunts, including driving a Rolls-Royce into a pool. Production assistant Anne Head told Zanuck's biographer that the making of the movie was one solid party. "It was dirty old men at play. Genevieve had a stand-in, who was making it with everybody. All hanky-panky ... I quit."[8] Jean persuaded Head to remain on the film, assuring her that things would change once the company returned to Paris where, at Billancourt Studios, the shooting finished and post-production began.

Producer Milton Sperling years later recalled receiving a call from Jean, who said: "Come out and see this monstrosity with this awful girl."

Sperling said,

> She couldn't act at all. Jean, who had been out of work for three years, had reluctantly taken $5000 a week to make the film. I came on to the set to watch the following scene: Telephone ringing, and Gilles having to come out of the bedroom to the living room and down three steps to answer the phone. Zanuck was at the back smoking his large cigar. Lights—camera—action. Negulesco: "All right, dear, come on." She came down the steps and stumbled on the first step. He said, mildly: "You must look down at the step when you come down the step."
>
> She finally got to the phone, where she was supposed to say: "Hello." She said, "Yes" instead. It was 11 A.M. They wrapped for lunch.
>
> That was the only scene they made that morning.
>
> So I asked Negulesco: "How long is this going on?"
>
> "Forever, I hope," said Negulesco.[9]

Many years later, Jean stated that Gilles was "wonderful" in the picture and "very cooperative." He was optimistic when he started editing the picture with an English editor. The two would meet daily at the studio and tried to keep as much material possible with Michael Crawford, as well as Ira Furstenberg and Vivien Pickles, who played secondary roles, cutting Gilles from all the superfluous scenes. When they showed Zanuck a rough cut, the producer said he did not want to see too much of the other two actresses, claiming that Gilles was the only star. Jean pointed out to him that even if you have the world's greatest actress, you can't center on her. But Zanuck did not want to be contradicted. Jean told him that his work was now over. Zanuck did the final cutting of the film himself, eliminating the other actresses almost entirely.

"Darryl never saw himself as anything but right," was Jean's comment. "He was like Napoleon. He doesn't want to say he lost Elba. He'd say the French weren't good enough."[10]

Zanuck worried that Negulesco could sue him so he told him that he would pay him everything he owed him. Jean, who was very loyal to the producer, had no intention to file a lawsuit. Zanuck paid him off, and with the money Jean bought an apartment in Paris.

Crawford was shattered by how bad all the reviews were. Jean did get a kind word from *The Hollywood Reporter*: "Jean Negulesco's direction is competent; if occasionally haphazard; considering the material given him; a vacillating script and a lovely but wooden leading lady upon which the entire story hinges."[11]

Curt Jurgens and Geneviève Gilles on the set of *Hello-Goodbye* (1970).

10. Twilight

Hello-Goodbye was Jean's biggest screen disappointment, a total catastrophe for everybody who worked on it, and it put 20th Century–Fox one step closer to ruin. Genevieve Gilles never played in another film. Nine months after the release of *Hello-Goodbye*, Jean worked on a new project called *Balzac 3* in which he envisioned a part for Gilles, as he mentioned it in a short letter to Zanuck dated April 15, 1971:

> Dear Darryl,
> Following our telephone conversation, I enclose the screenplay *Balzac 3* which I plan to direct this summer in France and in Italy. Genevieve is ideal for two parts: Michelle and/or Papette. She can play one or both as Peter Sellers is agreeable to play the Duc and Provost as well as Mr. Star.
> We have an interest from Belmondo for Sarasine, the sculptor, and would include Ursula Andres [sic] or Marlene Jobert as the Duchess.
> Samuel Marx, whom you know, is the producer and his partner John Nestor is corresponding with Harry McIntyre regarding a distribution deal which calls for a minimum financial involvement from 20th Century–Fox. A copy of Mr. Nestor's letter will be sent to you.
> Devoted love,
> Jean[12]

Balzac 3 was never made.

In May 1971, Jean wrote a letter to Parviz C. Radji, assistant to Prime Minister Amir-Abbas Hoveyda, enclosing a copy of a letter he wished to be forwarded to His Majesty the Shah of Iran, to make it possible to avoid "unpleasant legal complications." In his letter, Negulesco wrote that *The Invincible Six* was directed with the "full financial backing" of the Central Bank of Iran and that his agreement of 7.5 percent of the gross from the first day the film showed had not been honored, which was "a breach of friendship between our countries." He then asked the shah to "give the necessary orders so that this illegal situation" changed. Two months later, Jean received the amount due him with a note from Radjii stating that there were unlikely to be more, as the "film has been an almost total failure."[13]

Hello-Goodbye was the last picture of Negulesco's filmmaking career. At 71, he was a wealthy man with an amazing art collection and the proud owner of many houses in different parts of the world.

In the 1970s, his name was reportedly attached to two unrealized projects: *Other Winters, Other Springs* in 1973 and *The Rape of the White Dove* in 1976. By then Jean was living in Marbella, on the southern coast of Spain, where he built a house not far from the sea. The decision to move to that beautiful small town, which was about to become a hot spot for the international jet set, came after he and Dusty visited the Seville fair. Upon their return to Madrid, on Orson Welles' suggestion, the Negulescos stopped in Marbella where Dusty fractured her hip in an accident. Forced to stay longer than planned, the couple were hosted for a while by Audrey Hepburn and Mel Ferrer who had just bought a house there. The Negulescos fell in love with Marbella and its surroundings and decided to retire there.

While living in Spain, painting, cooking and traveling became Jean's major activities. Cooking the *sarmalute* accompanied by polenta, a typical Romanian dish, was his forte. His house was always full of friends visiting from all over the world.

Some sources credit Negulesco with starring in the French films *A Police Officer Without Importance* (1973), *Le Joupon Rouge* (1987) and *L'Autre* (1991). Julian Negulesco (no relation) is the star of those films.

In 1982, Jean befriended Malcolm Abbey, a young British director in his early twenties. Abbey asked him to play a small role in his first short film. In *The Barefoot Banker*, set in Marbella, Jean played a gay partygoer amidst the Marbella jet set. Abbey said,

> Negulesco was a mentor to me. Johnny was a very good friend of our family. He taught me very little about making films but a lot about being an artist. He lived 'til he was 93. So I asked him, "Johnny, how are you living this long?"
> "I don't know. All my doctors are dead. Maybe it's the heart-beeps."
> Heart-beeps?
> "I have my own theory. When you're born, God only gives you a certain amount of heart-beeps. If you go jogging, play tennis, all those sports, you use up your heart-beeps and die young. I smoke cigars, drink Cognac, I'm 93 years old."
> "I see. But what about sex, Johnny, don't you use up heart-beeps during sex?"
> I had him cornered, or so I thought. He tilted his head and looked at me as though I was a young fool.
> "Get on the bottom."[14]

Jean would often joke about his good health which he checked every year on his trip back to California. "When I now ask my doctor about a pain, he doesn't give me a pill, he says 'Get used to it!'"[15]

One of the last work offers Jean received was in the early 1980s: Genevieve Gilles invited him to lunch to discuss a project she had in mind. Jean had not heard from her since *Hello-Goodbye* and, intrigued, accepted her invitation. "You know Johnny," Gilles told him, "our picture has been an enormous success in one place…." It was news to Negulesco. The place? "Saudi Arabia."

"I don't know how," said Negulesco, "but she said she had gathered the millions to put into another film. All I had to do was to come up with the property. So I decided to remake my *Mask of Dimitrios*, with Genevieve in the role originally played by Peter Lorre, the newspaperman, made into a newspaperwoman from London who goes to Istanbul. Orson Welles was very interested in playing the Sydney Greenstreet role. But instead, Genevieve decided to sue Virginia Zanuck and the estate for palimony."[16]

Negulesco's name seemed completely forgotten until his biography *Things I Did… and Things I Think I Did* was published in February 1984. The book received positive reviews even though some critics complained about several inaccuracies that called its trustworthiness into question. John Houseman wrote in *The New York Times Book Reviews*, "[Negulesco's] weariness of the Hollywood scene … degenerates into a strange scrapbook of anecdotes, quotations and one-liners that add little or nothing to his story. On the other hand, his book is elegantly presented with dozens of his own well-reproduced drawings, each 'a composition of what a person meant to me.'"[17] Jean's memoir was also translated into French and five years later into Romanian.

Jean was back in the limelight when magazines and newspapers began requesting interviews. In France at the end of 1985, the Cinémathèque Française in Paris hosted a major retrospective of his films. In September 1986 he was a guest at the Festival of the American Film in Deauville where a tribute was held in his honor. He appeared in great shape with amazing energy. He told reporters that part of the secret of his good health was the fact that he never took himself too seriously, and that he never stopped working. "I've a project for a film that I'd like to make, a sort of modern-day *La Bohème*. In the meantime, I'm preparing a sequel to my book *Things I Did…and Things I Think I Did*. This one will deal in more details with the films. I'm also writing a cookbook."[18] During his stay in Deauville, Jean wore a big black cowboy hat that piqued everyone's curiosity. When asked the reason, he replied wittily, "It diverts attention from my face, that with my wrinkles, looks like a Grand Canyon in Colorado."[19] After the festival, Jean traveled to Paris to be decorated by the French Culture Minister Francois Léotard with the Médaille des Arts et Lettres, given to foreign luminaries who had significantly contributed to the enrichment of the French cultural inheritance. It was one of the proudest moments of Jean's life. At 90, he declared, "I'm always looking for a great story. I have one that is good ... and I am negotiating with Metro which owns the rights. It's about reincarnation, a love story."[20]

In the early 1990s, Spain, Jean's second adoptive country, began to celebrate his work. He was first honored at the Festival de Cine of Barcelona, and afterwards, in March 1991, he was the guest of honor at Madrid's Filmoteca Española, which organized a long retrospective of his filmography. Later he was a jury member at the Torremolinos Film Festival in the South of Spain where there was an extensive homage to his career. In July 1991, Jean was spotted wearing an elegant linen suit and a white Panama hat, walking hand in hand with Dusty in the narrow streets of Taormina in Sicily. He had traveled to the Italian island to be the president of the jury of the Taormina Film Festival. His amazing vitality impressed the Italian reporters with whom he joked. "I am the last of Hollywood's dinosaurs, together with Frank Capra, although he is 94 years old and I am only 91. I am still lucky to be on the right side of the grass." Dusty revealed that her husband had fallen in love with all the female stars of his films—something she had tried to cope with all her life with him. When she suspected that Jean got a crush on Sophia Loren during the making of *Boy on a Dolphin,* she decided to have her revenge, traveling around the world using her husband's credit card spending the maximum allowed. "I am still paying the bills," Jean replied. "My weakness for my stars cost me a fortune."

Even in his 90s, Jean never lost his desire to learn new things, like to decipher and practice the secrets of an ancient Chinese painting technique. He also kept an eye peeled for a good story to direct. In an interview with a Spanish magazine, he expressed his wish to make a film based on *Forever,* a 1938 novella by Mildred Cram. "Because it will allow me to make a picture according to my standards," Jean explained, "something of an intimate nature, with two dead characters [reincarnated] living a love story. But it will be very difficult for me to do it. At my age, I should become also my own producer."[21]

In 1993, when Jean's health suddenly deteriorated, he stopped appearing in public. On Sunday, July 18, three days before celebrating his 47th wedding anniversary, he died of heart failure in his Marbella home with Dusty at his bedside. On the 22nd, there was a very private funeral at the Virgen del Carmen cemetery in Marbella where his body was interred.

When Jean's will was read, his origins and his beloved Romania were not forgotten. He remembered how lucky he was when, at

Negulesco in one of his last public appearances in 1992.

the beginning of his career as a painter, he had received financial and moral support from patron of the arts Duncan Phillips. For this reason, he decided to include in his will the creation of the Jean Negulesco Trust Fund, designated for two young Romanians between 18 and 25, talented in any artistic field including music, literature, painting, sculpture, ballet, theater, directing and cinema. The scholarship would allow them to spend three years abroad in an appropriate educational institution, preferably in Paris, Rome or the U.S. In addition, he wished that a part of the money coming from the sale of his collection of paintings (which included works by masters of the twentieth century—Picasso, Modigliani, Lautrec, Buffet and many others) sculptures and art objects, along with his real estate around the world, would be given to some of his Romanian relatives. However, according to Jean's Romanian friend Prof. Manuela Cernat, not all of Negulesco's generous intentions were respected by the will executors. In agreement with his heirs, they dismissed all his wishes related to his country of birth, and liquidated quickly his estate, They refused to have any contact with the Romanian Filmmakers Union, which in 1990 had given Jean an honorary membership and was in possession of a copy of the will.

Eventually Jean's dream came true thanks to on old friend from Craiovia. The academe and former president of the Romanian Filmmakers Union, Mihnea Gheorghiu, set up the Jean Negulescu Foundation, whose mission was to preserve his legacy and give a young man and a young woman the chance to pursue an artistic specialization abroad.

In 1995, Jean's Beverly Hills home, which had four bedrooms in the main house and a two-bedroom guest cottage, was sold for nearly $2 million. All of his other possessions, including his art collection, were auctioned by A.N. Abell in the summer of the same year.

In 1998, Dusty donated to the Margaret Herrick Library in Beverly Hills Jean's personal papers spanning the years 1915 to 1992. The collection consisted of personal correspondence, photographs, scripts, scrapbooks, production material, subject files, legal files, artwork (drawings, sketches, caricatures) and writings (research, various drafts and manuscripts for his autobiography).

According to Malcolm Abbey, Dusty was "sent away" to a nursing home. "Last I heard, and this was 20 years ago, she was severely alcoholic and unable to remember from moment to moment who she was talking to. Very tragic."[22]

Nowadays, Negulesco's legacy as artist and filmmaker is seldom remembered. In Craiova, his birth town, a street has been named after him; the sign reads: "Jan Negulescu—American filmmaker born in Craiova, 1900–1993." One of the last movie theaters in town bearing his name has closed. Some blocks away, the old Negulescu family home still stands, but the new owners removed from its façade a memorial plaque that reminded passersby it was Jean Negulesco's birthplace.

In July 2013, the twentieth anniversary of Jean's death, the Councilor for Culture of Marbella hosted a tribute at the local cemetery—the only public tribute in his honor in recent years.

"If someone would ask me by what right I might enter into Heaven, I'd reply: because I made *Three Came Home*, a picture I truly love."[23] This is how Jean Negulesco wanted to be remembered. Nevertheless, there is much more of Negulesco's artistic heritage that ought to be commemorated—a filmmaker whose life, as he testified repeatedly, was a miracle.

Filmography

As Director

Three and a Day

U.S. B&W 1931; Unreleased

CREDITS: *Producer, Director, Screenplay:* Jean Negulesco; *Photography:* Paul Ivano; *Editors:* Gunther von Frisch, Jean Negulesco

CAST: Mischa Auer (The Painter), Katya Sergava (The Dancer), John Rox (The Farmer)

PLOT: The story of a day in the life of three people: a painter, a ballet dancer and a young farmer.

REVIEWS AND ARTICLES:

The Film Daily September 22, 1931, p. 4; *Variety* September 29, 1931, p. 6; *The New York Times* July 22, 1945

Singapore Woman

A Warner Bros.–First National Picture; U.S. B&W 65 minutes; Released in New York on May 17, 1941

CREDITS: *Producer:* Bryan Foy; *Associate Producer:* Harlan Thompson; *Director:* Jean Negulesco; *Screenplay:* M. Coates Webster, Allen Rivkin; Based on the story "Hard Luck Dame" by Laird Doyle; *Photography:* Ted McCord; *Dialogue Director:* Hugh MacMullan; *Editor:* Everett Dodd; *Art Director:* Charles Novi; *Sound:* Francis J. Scheid; *Gowns:* Damon Giffard; *Makeup:* Perc Westmore; *Technical Advisor:* Louis P. Vincenot; *Music:* Adolph Deutsch; *Musical Director:* Leo F. Forbstein; *Assistant Director:* William Kissell; *Unit Manager:* Jack Saper

CAST: Brenda Marshall (Vicki Moore), David Bruce (David Ritchie), Virginia Field (Claire Weston), Jerome Cowan (Jim North), Rose Hobart (Alice North), Heather Angel (Frieda), Richard Ainley (John Wetherby), Dorothy Tree (Mrs. Bennett), Bruce Lester (Clyde), Connie Leon (Suwa), Douglas Walton (Roy Bennett), Gilbert Emery (Sir Stanley Moore), Stanley Logan (Commissioner), Abner Biberman (Singa), Eva Puig (Natasha), Ian Wolfe (Sidney P. Melrose), Charles Irwin, Ernie Stanton, Lowden Adams, Jack Richardson, Garrett Craig, George Campeau (Reporters), Marten Lamont, Lyle Moraine (Young Men), Harry Cording (Café Proprietor), Chester Gan (Waiter), Gloria Franklin (Eurasian Woman), Anthony Warde (Tough Seaman In Crow's Nest), Frank Hagney (Foreman), David Thursday (Frank), Leyland Hodgson (Sullivan), Maureen Roden-Ryan (Nurse), Louise Brien (Nurse), Ann Edmonds (Telephone Operator), Leonard Mudie (Doctor), Alexis Smith (Miss Oswald's Secretary), Alec Harford (Ship Steward), Louis Vincenot (Malay Policeman)

PLOT: At a Singapore bar, David Ritchie sees a drab, ill-dressed woman whom he recognizes as Vicki Moore and tells his friend about her. Three years earlier, David had been financed by Sir Stanley Moore, wealthy tin magnate, for his rubber-raising experiments. He was visiting Sir Stanley when a disappointed suitor killed himself for love of Vicki, the magnate's daughter. She is now called a "jinx" woman and avoided by everyone. Her father died after losing his wealth, and all connected with her have met with misfortune. When his friends leave, David tries to talk to the reluctant Vicki. His attempts lead to a fight, which develops into a battle royal. David gets Vicki away and takes her to his plantation, hoping that a few quiet days there will help her regain her self-respect. He thinks there is time for the experiment before his fiancée, Claire Weston, arrives for a visit. Next morning, Vicki is defiant and bitter. She believes nothing can kill her jinx and thinks David has an ulterior motive. He makes her look at her dissipated face in a mirror and tells her that a man could feel only pity for her—and he is merely repaying his debt to her father. In David's absence, Vicki looks again into the mirror, then shatters it and runs out into the jungle. When he returns and hears from his servant that she has disappeared, David hurries out into torrential rains. After a long search he finds her being menaced by a crocodile. When Claire arrives, David meets her in Singapore but keeps putting off her visit to his plantation. Claire becomes suspicious, goes to the plantation and meets Vicki, now her old beautiful self. Vicki admits loving David, but offers to give him up. Furious, Claire leaves. David raises $50,000 for improvements on his plantation, but when he hears that the flooded Moore mines could be reclaimed for that amount, he has the work done. The mines are almost ready for operation when Vicki receives a note in answer to which she hurries to Singapore and meets her husband, John Wetherby, who had been reported drowned. He has heard about the mines being reopened and demands his share. Vicki suggests that he should meet David, Wetherby agrees but he drives so carelessly that the car is wrecked and he and Vicki are seriously injured. Wetherby dies, but Vicki recovers. She is heartbroken because she has not heard from David who, believing that Vicki deceived him and may even have been in collusion with Wetherby to obtain the mines, is bitterly angry. But one day he receives a deed signed by Vicki, transferring the tin mines to him. David hurries in search of Vicki, whom he loves. After some time, he finds her in the Singapore café where they had met before. He persuades her that her jinx is all superstition, they will fight it—together. (Original press release source)

REVIEWS:

"[T]he quality of this 'B' from the Warner studios is much higher than a lot of films of this alphabetical order have been of late. It might have been developed into an 'A' had that been the intent and a higher budget figured." *Variety,* May 14, 1941

"Oriental melodrama suffers from an old-fashioned story idea.... Film has little to offer, being handicapped by the script, and the players give their roles a high-strung pitch that is almost nerve-wracking." *The Film Daily,* May 14, 1941

"There is not much to recommend in this melodrama.... [T]he characters do nothing to awaken sympathy. The action is, for most part, slow moving..." *Harrison's Reports,* May 24, 1941

REVIEWS FOR JEAN NEGULESCO:

"[Negulesco] has extracted creditable performances from his cast." *New York Daily News,* May 11, 1941

"*Singapore Woman* is the first feature directed by Jean Negulesco who made a flock of dandy shorts for Vitagraph recently. He has kept the story flowing smoothly, with plenty of atmospheric shots." *Film Bulletin,* March 22, 1941

"Negulesco's artistic pretensions are labored, and the histrionics he inspires, empty." *The Hollywood Reporter,* June 2, 1941

ADDITIONAL REVIEWS AND ARTICLES:

Hollywood Reporter December 2, 1940, p. 2; *Hollywood Reporter* December 10, 1940, p. 3; *Showmen's Trade Review* February 8, 1941, p. 18; *Hollywood Reporter* February 10, 1941, p. 8; *Modern Screen* May 1941 p. 93; *New York Times* May 12, 1941, p. 13; *Motion Picture Daily* May 14, 1941; *Motion Picture Herald* May 17, 1941; *Boxoffice* May 24, 1941; *Motion Picture Herald Product Digest* May 31, 1941, p. 148; *Philadelphia Evening Ledger* May 31, 1941; *The Cleveland Press* June 24, 1941; *The Baltimore Sun* July 9, 1941; *Today's Cinema* October 3, 1941; *The West Wyalong Advocate* January 15, 1942, p. 1; *Le Film du Jour* (France) 1947

The Mask of Dimitrios

A Warner Bros.–First National Picture; U.S. B&W 101 minutes; New York Premiere: June 23, 1944

CREDITS: *Producer:* Henry Blanke; *Executive Producer:* Jack L. Warner; *Director:* Jean Negulesco; *Screenplay:* Frank Gruber; Based on the novel *The Mask of Dimitrios* (published in the U.S. as *A Coffin for Dimitrios*) by Eric Ambler; *Photography:* Arthur Edeson; *Editor:* Frederick Richards; *Dialogue Director:* Herschel Daugherty; *Sound:* Oliver S. Garretson; *Art Director:* Ted Smith; *Set Decorator:* Walter Tilford; *Technical Advisor:* Michael D. Kadri; *Makeup:* Perc Westmore; *Music:* Adolph Deutsch; *Orchestral Arrangements:* Jerome Morross; *Musical Director:*

Leo F. Forbstein; *Assistant Director:* Jack Sullivan

CAST: Sydney Greenstreet (Mr. Peters, also known as Erik Peterson), Zachary Scott (Dimitrios Makropoulos), Faye Emerson (Irana Preveza), Peter Lorre (Cornelius Leyden), Victor Francen (Wladislaw Grodek), Steven Geray (Karel Bulic), Florence Bates (Mme. Chavez), Eduardo Ciannelli (Marukakis), Kurt Katch (Colonel Haki), Marjorie Hoshelle (Anna Bulic), George Metaxa (Hans Werner), John Abbott (Pappas), Monte Blue (Dhris Abdul), David Hoffman (Konrad), George Tobias (Fedor Muishkin), Philip Rock (Boy on Beach), Rita Holland, Rolla Stewart (Girls on Beach), Georges Renavent (Fisherman), Peter Helmers (Reporter), Lal Chand Mehra (Turkish Servant), Jules Molnar (Servant with Tray), Pedro Regas (Turk Morgue Attendant), Nino Pipitone (Turk Hotel Clerk), Eddie Hyans (Turkish Man), Frank Lackteen (Turkish Soldier), Nick Thompson (Porter on Train), Hella Crossley (Bulgarian Hostess), Carmen D'Antonio (Nightclub Dancer), Fred Essler (Bostoff), John Bleifer (Coach Driver), Albert Van Antwerp (Bulgarian Landlord), Edgar Licho (Bulgarian Café Proprietor), Michael Visaroff, Louis Mercier (Bulgarian Policemen), Felix Basch (Vazoff), Leonid Snegoff (Stambulisky), Walter Palm (Butler), Gregory Golubeff (Yugoslav Doorkeeper), Carl Neubert (Male Secretary), Lotte Palfi (Yugoslav Receptionist), Antonio Filauri (Man Across Table), Vince Barnett (Kibitzer), Alfred Paix (Card Player), John Mylong (Druhar), Mary Landa (Flower Girl), Alphonse Martell (Bulgarian Croupier), Ray de Ravenne (French Cabby), Marek Windheim (French Hotel Clerk), Saul Gorss (Shadow Man), Eddie Fields (Conductor), Charles Andre (French Conductor)

PLOT: Cornelius Leyden, a shy Dutch writer, learns from Colonel Haki, chief of the Turkish police, that a stabbed body, washed up on the shore in Istanbul, is identified as that of Dimitrios, an international criminal. Leyden is intrigued and, after seeing the corpse, decides to find out more about the man's past, intending to use his story as the basis for a book. As he travels across Europe collecting small pieces of information, Leyden meets Peters, a stout Englishman, who also displays interest in Dimitrios. The men agree to pool their resources, meeting in Paris on a specific date. There Peters informs Leyden that his real name is Eric Peters, and that he belonged to a smuggling ring in which Dimitrios was involved—and later double-crossed him. Peters also reveals that Dimitrios is still alive, head of a French banking firm. The dead man was actually Konstantin Gollos, a smuggler murdered by Dimitrios. Peters intends to blackmail Dimitrios, using Leyden as the man who can testify that the dead man is not Dimitrios. The writer agrees and on the following day Dimitrios delivers them one million francs for their silence—and then he tries to kill them. In the struggle, Dimitrios is shot dead by Peters, who is wounded himself. The police take Peters into custody while Leyden is released to write the story.

REVIEWS:

"[This] is mostly a conversational piece that too frequently suggests action in the dialog where actually, the film itself practically has none. Talky script slows the pace to a walk." *Variety*, June 7, 1944

"An intriguing melodrama, but not so pleasant by reason of the fact that none of the characters are sympathetic, nor they do anything worthwhile." *Harrison's Reports*, June 10, 1944

"This sort of wordy melodrama calls for refinement in cinematic style, but the writing and direction of this picture betray a rather clumsy conventional approach." *The New York Times*, June 24, 1944

REVIEWS FOR JEAN NEGULESCO:

"This is Jean Negulesco's most effective directorial effort to date, notable for its creation of mood and suspense." *The Hollywood Reporter*, June 6, 1944

"The screenplay of Frank Gruber ... has been directed forcefully by Jean Negulesco." *The Film Daily*, June 8, 1944

"Jean Negulesco has had more interest in the literary original than the imagery which might have been distilled from it." *New York Herald Tribune*, June 24, 1944

ADDITIONAL REVIEWS AND ARTICLES:

Hollywood Reporter November 9, 1943, p. 4; *Hollywood Reporter* November 30, 1943, p. 6; *Hollywood Reporter* December 10, 1943, p. 4; *Hollywood Reporter* January 21, 1944, p. 11; *Motion Picture Herald Product Digest* February 5, 1944, p. 1746; *The Saturday Evening Post* February 19, 1944, p. 37; *Film Daily* June 8, 1944, p. 11; *Motion Picture Herald Product Digest* June 10, 1944, p. 1934; *Boxoffice* June 10, 1944; *Brooklyn Citizen* June 21, 1944; *New York World-Telegram*

June 23, 1944; *New York Sun* June 24, 1944, p. 4; *New York Journal-America* June 24, 1944; *New York Morning Telegraph* June 24, 1944; *New York Daily News* June 24, 1944; *New York Daily Mirror* June 24, 1944; *Brooklyn Citizen* June 25, 1944; *Hollywood Reporter* June 26, 1944, p. 8; *Time* June 26, 1944, p. 94; *New York Motion Picture Critics Reviews* June 26, 1944, p. 324–325; *Staats-Zeitung* June 26, 1944; *Los Angeles Examiner* July 1, 1944; *New Republic* July 10, 1944, p. 44; *Austin American-Statesman* August 20, 1944; *The Cinema* August 30, 1944, p. 14; *Cine-Mundial* September 1944 p. 424; *Today's Cinema* September 8, 1944; *Kinematograph Weekly* September 14, 1944; *Hollywood Reporter* September 29, 1966; *New York World-Telegram* September 29, 1944, p. 20; *Les Lettres Françaises* (France) January 1, 1953; *Cinématographe* (France) July 1979 p. 65; *Telerama* (France) July 28, 1979; *Classic Images* November 1984 p. C10; *Film Score Monthly* February 2003 p. 45–46

NOTES: Former silent film star Pola Negri was considered for a part and Faye Emerson replaced Nancy Coleman in the part of Irana Preveza. Composer Jerome Moross' name was misspelled as "Morross" in the onscreen credits. In 1966, Seven Arts planned a remake starring Rock Hudson, but that film was never produced.

The Conspirators

A Warner Bros.–First National Picture; U.S. B&W 101 minutes; World premiere in Bridgeport, Connecticut, on October 11, 1944

CREDITS: *Producer:* Jack Chertok; *Executive Producer:* Jack L. Warner; *Director:* Jean Negulesco; *Screenplay:* Vladimir Pozner, Leo Rosten; Based on the novel by Frederic Prokosch; *Additional Dialogue:* Jack Moffitt; *Photography:* Arthur Edeson; *Editor:* Rudi Fehr; *Dialogue Director:* Herschel Daugherty; *Sound:* Robert B. Lee; *Technical Advisor:* Henry Da Silva; *Art Director:* Anton Grot; *Set Decorator:* Walter Tilford; *Makeup:* Perc Westmore; *Hair Stylist:* Jean Burt Reilly; *Special Effects:* William McGann, Willard Van Enger; *Montages:* James Leicester; *Gowns:* Leah Rhodes; *Music:* Max Steiner; *Orchestral Arrangements:* Leonid Raab; *Musical Director:* Leo F. Forbstein; *Assistant Directors:* Reginald Callow, Clerence Eurist

CAST: Hedy Lamarr (Irene Duchatel), Paul Henreid (Vincent Van Der Lyn), Sydney Greenstreet (Riccardo Quintanilla), Peter Lorre (Jan Bernassky), Victor Francen (Hugo Von Mohr), Joseph Calleia (Captain Pereira), Carol Thurston (Rosa O'Flynn), Vladimir Sokoloff (Miguel), Eduardo Ciannelli (General Almeida), Steven Geray (Dr. Schmitt), Kurt Katch (Lutzke), Gregory Gaye (Anton Wynat), Louis Mercier (Paulo Leiris), David Hoffman (Antonio), Edward Van Sloan (Dutchman in Cellar), Jean Jacques du Bois (Bobby Benson), Doris Lloyd (Mrs. Benson), Philip Van Zandt (Gomez), William Edmunds (Souvenir Vendor), Serge Krizman (Czech Man), Trudy Glassford (Belgian Girl), Juan Varro (Airport Official), John Arnold, Michael Gastone, Hal Kelly (Custom Officials), Rod De Medici, Jack Chefe, Eddie Abdo (Immigration Officers), John Bleifer (Polish Man), George Sorel (Police Officer), Frederick Brunn, Adrian Droeshout (German Thugs), Roger Neury (Headwaiter), Jacques Lory (Attendant in Pawnshop), Tony Paton (Detective), Oscar Loraine (Deschamps), Christine Gordon (Young Woman), Marguerita Sylva (Older Woman), Isabelle LaMal (French Woman), Walter Bonn (German), Paul Regas (Spaniard), Veronica Pataky (Hungarian Woman), Alexander Sacha (Russian), Billy Roy (Page Boy), Sonya Yarr (Russian Woman), Carla Boehm (German Woman), Leon Belasco (Waiter), Alphonse Martel (Croupier), Frank Reicher (Casino Attendant), Tony Caruso (Young Fisherman), Pedro Regas, Nick Thompson (Older Fishermen), Ludwig Hardt (Refugee), Paul de Corday (Travel Clerk), Robert Tafur (Policeman), Manuel Lopez (Man on the Street), Crane Whitley, Martin Garralaga (Detectives Outside Pawnshop), Carl Neubert, Dick Botiller, Jay Novello (Detectives), Monte Blue (Jennings), Neyle Marx (Portuguese Boy), Ed Hyans (Hotel Manager), Harro Meller (General's Secretary), Fred Nurney (Young Attaché), Arno Frey (General's Attaché), Beal Wong (Japanese Attaché), Luis Alberni (Prison Guard), Saul Gorss (Jorge), Art Miles, Robert Barron (Cell Guards), John Mylong (Commandant), Otto Reichow ("Slugger"), George Macready (Schmitt Con Man), Carmel Myers (Baroness von Kluge), Rafael Storm (Senhor Gamma), Emil Rameau (Prof. Wingby), Leon Lenoir, Erno Verebes (Portuguese Fishermen)

PLOT: Vincent, member of the Dutch Underground Movement, arrives in Lisbon by plane on his way to England. His fight against the Nazis in Holland has been long, but now he is at the gates of freedom. Sitting at a table at a café, watching for a sign which will make known to him one of his confederates, Vincent is startled by a beautiful young woman who begs to sit at his table. Greatly attracted and very curious, he follows her when she leaves. At Estoril, a gambling house, he finds her with Von Mohr of the German Legation. Vincent eventually meets his confederates headed by Quintanilla and aided by Vernasky. All know and admire him as "The Flying Dutchman." The group is about to send an agent to Holland. Vincent is chosen to meet the agent that night. With the day to himself, he plans to learn more about Irene. Waylaying her as she leaves her home, he forces her to accompany him on a drive into the country. Irene is the wife of Von Mohr; she does not love her husband but owes everything to him. She is French and he took her out of a concentration camp and gave her devotion—and freedom. Her sympathies? He remains in ignorance. When Vincent arrives at the room of the agent, he finds him near death, the victim of assassins. "Tell Quintanilla they took the Eagle," he gasps. Suspected of the murder, Vincent is thrown into jail by the Portuguese police. The German Legation works for his conviction but he foils them by escaping and rejoining Quintanilla. Vincent learns that Von Mohr and Irene are members of their organization, and that the stolen Eagle is an underground passport. Quintanilla adds that the killing indicates the presence of a traitor among the small group. That night all the members meet at the casino. The atmosphere is tense. Quintanilla has set a trap which cannot fail to reveal the identity of the traitor. Vincent, challenged by the head of the Portuguese Secret Service, begs not to be arrested. He tells him the real murderer will be caught within a few hours. Von Mohr proves his guilt at the roulette table, but makes his escape. After a terrific chase by Vincent, closely followed by the Portuguese Secret Service man, Von Mohr is finally shot as he tries to board a small boat. The Eagle is found in his possession. Vincent takes it. He will carry it as *his* passport back behind the enemy lines. Standing on the beach on the eve of his departure, Vincent and Irene promise their love to each other and their loyalty to the great conspiracy. (Original press release)

REVIEWS:

"An intriguing spy meller, splendidly cast, richly produced: definitely pulsating entertainment." *The Film Daily,* October 17, 1944

"Picture is filled with overlength footage, both in unnecessary sideline incidents and extended running of relatively unimportant sequences.... [I]t never reaches the dramatic climaxes intended." *Variety.* October 18, 1944

"The adapters have run in a substituted plot worthy of a cartoon strip. The result is a tag end to a tired movie cycle and the waste of such past masters in melodrama as Peter Lorre, Sydney Greenstreet, and Joseph Calleia." *Newsweek,* October 30, 1944

REVIEWS FOR JEAN NEGULESCO:

"[A] dated inept direction which tries desperately to be arty and succeeds only in being irritating." *The Hollywood Reporter,* October 13, 1944

"Jean Negulesco's direction is not always as deft and left as it should be for a melodramatic film of the spy type, where espionage and counterespionage motivate the action." *New York Daily News,* October 21, 1944

"[I]n his stilted direction, Jean Negulesco has pitched the whole thing in a mood of scowling solemnity." *The New York Times,* October 21, 1944

ADDITIONAL REVIEWS AND ARTICLES:

Los Angeles Times October 14, 1943; *Hollywood Reporter* December 1, 1943, p. 1; *Hollywood Reporter* April 6, 1944; *Motion Picture Herald Product Digest* April 15, 1944, p. 1850; *Life* June 9, 1944, p. 65–66; *Modern Screen* September 1944 p. 25; *Women's Home Companion* October 1944 p. 11; *Hollywood Reporter* October 4, 1944 p. 6; *Daily Variety* October 13, 1944, p. 3; *Motion Picture Herald* October 14, 1944, p. 15; *Motion Picture Herald Product Digest* October 15, 1944, p. 2137; *Boxoffice* October 14, 1944; *New York World Telegram* October 20, 1944; *New York Post* October 21, 1944; *New York Sun* October 21, 1944; *Brooklyn Eagle* October 21, 1944; *New York Journal-American* October 21, 1944; *New York Motion Picture Critics* October 23, 1944, p. 204–205; *Brooklyn Citizen* October 23, 1944; *Morning Telegraph New York* October 23, 1944; *New Yorker Staats-Zeitung* October 23, 1944; *Hollywood Reporter* October 24, 1944 p. 14; *Time* November 13, 1944, p. 96; *New Republic* November 13, 1944, p. 627; *Commonweal* November 17, 1944, p. 145; *Today's Cinema* January 19, 1945; *New Statesman* (U.K.) August 4, 1945; *The Evening Standard* (U.K.) August 4, 1945; *The Times* (U.K.) August 6, 1945; *L'Écran Français* (France) February 3, 1948, p. 13; *Le Film Complet* (France) June 17, 1948

Three Strangers

A Warner Bros.–First National Picture; U.S. B&W 92 minutes; Premiered in New York on February 16, 1946

CREDITS: *Producer:* Wolfgang Reinhardt; *Executive Producer:* Jack L. Warner; *Director:* Jean Negulesco; *Assistant Director:* James McMahon; *Screenplay:* John Huston, Howard Koch; *Photography:* Arthur Edeson; *Editor:* George Amy; *Dialogue Director:* Clifford Brooke; *Sound:* C.A. Riggs; *Art Director:* Ted Smith; *Special Effects:* Edwin DuPar; *Technical Advisor:* Fredrik T. Nyquist; *Set Decorator:* Clarence Steensen; *Wardrobe:* Milo Anderson; *Makeup:* Perc Westmore; *Music:* Adolph Deutsch; *Orchestral Arrangements:* Murray Cutter; *Musical Director:* Leo F. Forbstein

CAST: Sydney Greenstreet (Jerome K. Arbutny), Geraldine Fitzgerald (Crystal Shakleford), Peter Lorre (John West), Joan Lorring (Icy Crane), Robert Shayne (Fallon), Marjorie Riordan (Janet Elliott), Arthur Shields (Prosecutor), Rosalind Ivan (Lady Rhea Belladon), John Alvin (Junior Clerk), Peter Whitney (Gabby), Alan Napier (David Shakleford), Clifford Brooke (Senior Clerk), Doris Lloyd (Mrs. Procter), Colin Kenny (Bartender), Holmes Herbert (Sir Robert), Eric Wilton (Bailiff), Keith Hitchcock (Donald Fry), Ian Wolfe (Gillkie), Stanley Logan (Major Beach), Benny Burt (Drunken Stranger), Connie Leon (Flower Woman), Leland Hodgson (Stranger), Norman Ainsley (Mr. Giesing), Olaf Hytten (Guard), Leslie Denison (Detective), Alec Craig (Old Man), Reginald Sheffield (Hotel Clerk), Woodrow Chambls, Tom Pilkington, Creighton Hale (Men in Pub), Leo White, Stanley Mann (Newshawkers), John Burton (Narrator), Cyril Delevanti (Stockbroker's Voice)

PLOT: The three strangers are Crystal Shakleford, an Englishwoman wrapped up in the influence of Kwan Yin, Chinese goddess of human destinies; Jerome Arbutny, a London barrister; and John West, a man of solid background who has deteriorated through the habitual use of alcohol. They meet on the Chinese New Year—and strangely. Crystal picks the men, one at the time, from off the street. Together for the first time but not knowing the others' identities, the trio makes a joint wish for money after Crystal explains that Kwan Yin has the power to grant one's desires. West produces a sweepstakes ticket. He maintains a one-third interest in it and sells the other two-thirds to his new acquaintances. It is through the Grand National that they expect Kwan Yin to grant the wish. Crystal tries to regain the love of her husband; for three years they have been separated and he has fallen in love with another woman. Arbutny has speculated with funds entrusted to his care, and faces imprisonment if the loss is discovered. West, although innocent, is caught up in a murder and is hustled off to jail. On the day the big race is being run, the three strangers again meet in Crystal's apartment. West has been freed from jail, cleared of participation in the murder. Arbutny is there in a last effort to persuade Crystal and West to permit him to dispose of his share in the ticket, so he can obtain funds with which to make up the discrepancy in his client's account. Crystal, determined to stick to the original bargain, refuses to permit Arbutny to dispose of his share in it. At her refusal, he loses control of himself, grabs the bronze statue of Kwan Yin and kills her with it. Then from the radio, West and Arbutny hear they hold the winning ticket—a useless ticket to them for it now connects them to a murder. Hysterical, Arbutny runs into the arms of a police officer and gives himself up. West returns to the companionship of a little Cockney girl who has smoothed his path from time to time. (Original press release source)

REVIEWS:

"Despite an involved, episodic story, this melodrama has a fair share of excitement and suspense." *Harrison's Reports,* February 2, 1946

"[*Three Strangers*] is an oddity among films—so bizarre, indeed, that is not likely to find a very ready audience." *Los Angeles Times,* February 9, 1946

"[A]n interesting experiment that proved a little too difficult to bring off, despite the excellent performances of the three co-stars and the reliable supporting cast." *Newsweek,* March 4, 1946

REVIEWS FOR JEAN NEGULESCO:

"[T]he arty direction of Jean Negulesco is likewise not new. At times, he demands such striking camera angles from the dependable photography by Arthur Edeson that the mechanics of labor made strenuous intrude." *The Hollywood Reporter,* January 23, 1946

"Jean Negulesco's direction is satisfactory." *Variety,* January 30, 1946

"Jean Negulesco has staged more than one sequence in terms of cinematic excitement. But the motion picture is forever falling apart...." *New York Herald Tribune,* February 23, 1946

ADDITIONAL REVIEWS AND ARTICLES: *Los Angeles Times* June 12, 1939; *Monthly Film Bulletin* January 1945 p. 157; *Hollywood Reporter* January 12, 1945, p. 17; *New York Sun* February 15, 1945; *Hollywood Reporter* February 16, 1945, p. 15; *Motion Picture Herald Product Digest* March 17, 1945, p. 2366; *Life* April 2, 1945, p. 49; *Look* May 29, 1945, p. 47; *Kinematograph Weekly* November 29, 1945; *Daily Variety* January 23, 1946, p. 3; *Today's Cinema* November 28, 1945, p. 157; *The Hollywood Quarterly* January 1946 p. 214–16; *Motion Picture Daily* January 23, 1946, p. 7; *Motion Picture Herald Product Digest* January 26, 1946, p. 2817; *Boxoffice* January 26, 1946; *Film Daily* January 28, 1946 p. 8; *L.A. Examiner* February 9, 1946; *The Daily Mirror* (U.K.) February 22, 1946; *New York Times* February 23, 1946, p. 20; *Hollywood Reporter* February 25, 1946, p. 6; *The Daily Telegraph* (U.K.) February 25, 1946; *The New Yorker* March 2 1946 p. 62; *Brooklyn Daily* March 20, 1946; *Theatre Arts* April 1946 p. 213; *Brooklyn Citizen* April 1, 1946; *The Village Voice* November 19, 1985, p. 60; *Dirigido Por* (Spain) October 2013 p. 90

NOTES: Originally the story was entitled *Three Men and a Girl*, Bette Davis and George Brent were expected to star in the film.

Nobody Lives Forever

A Warner Bros.–First National Picture; U.S. B&W 100 minutes; Premiered in New York on October 12, 1946

CREDITS: *Producer:* Robert Buckner; *Executive Producer:* Jack L. Warner; *Director:* Jean Negulesco; *Screenplay:* W.R. Burnett, based on his novel; *Photography:* Arthur Edeson; *Dialogue Director:* Herschel Daugherty; *Editor:* Rudi Fehr; *Art Director:* Hugh Reticker; *Set Decorator:* Casey Roberts; *Sound:* Dolph Thomas; *Special Effects:* William McGann, Willard Van Enger; *Wardrobe:* Milo Anderson; *Makeup:* Perc Westmore; *Music:* Adolph Deutsch; *Orchestral Arrangements:* Jerome Moross; *Musical Director:* Leo F. Forbstein; *Song:* "You Again," music and lyrics by M. K. Jerome and Jack Scholl.

CAST: John Garfield (Nick Blake), Geraldine Fitzgerald (Gladys Halvorsen), Walter Brennan (Pop Gruber), Faye Emerson (Toni Blackburn), George Coulouris (Doc Ganson), George Tobias (Al Doyle), Robert Shayne (Chet King), Richard Gaines (Charles Manning), Dick Erdman (Bellboy), James Flavin (Shake Thomas), Ralph Peters (Windy Mather), Alex Havier (Telesfero), William Edmunds (Mission Attendant), Ralph Dunn (Ben), Grady Sutton (Counterman), Allen Ray (Art), Roger Neury (Headwaiter), Jack Chefe (Waiter), Harry Seymour (Master of Ceremonies), Rudy Friml, Jr. (Orchestra Leader), Fred Kelsey (Railroad Conductor), Wallace Scott (Drunk), Albert Van Antwerp (Tough Waiter), Charles Sullivan (Bartender-Waiter), Paul Power (Hotel Clerk), George Meader (Evans), Virginia Patton (Switchboard Operator), Robert Arthur (Bellhop), Marion Martin (Blonde), Cyril Ring (Blonde's Escort), William Forrest (Mr. Johnson), Adrian Droeshout (Man at Slot Machine), Marion Martin (Lou—Blonde); Joel Friedkin (Storekeeper); Lee Phelps (Police Officer)

PLOT: Honorably discharged from the U.S. Military Hospital, Nick Blake has one thought: to see nightclub singer Toni, his girlfriend. With Al Doyle, faithful henchman of pre-war racketeering days, he goes to the apartment he has loaned Tony—and finds a man's pipe on her dressing table. What has Toni done with $50,000 he had left in her safekeeping? Nick takes Al to the pretentious Toni's Cafe to find out. There the girl and suave Chet King protest that the money was lost in another nightclub venture. King pays up after some "persuasion." Nick and Al take a seaside house. There Pop Gruber, a former racketeer down on his luck, tries to draw him into a confidence deal involving a young widow worth two million dollars. Nick falls in with the plan because of his liking for Pop. He isn't happy about working with Doc Ganson, a doublecrosser, but has no option since Doc found the widow. As a "business executive," and with Al as his "secretary," Nick moves into the hotel where the widow, Gladys Halvorsen, and her business manager Manning are staying. All goes according to plan ... until Toni arrives to embarrass Nick in front of Gladys. Nick realizes he is in love with the widow, and she with him. Nick decides that he will pull out of this scam and will pay Doc his expected share out of his own money. Manning discovers Nick's true identity and warns Gladys. She refuses to believe that Nick is after her money, and even when he confesses she refuses to give him up. Toni tells Doc that after Nick has paid out the expected share, he intends to get away with the widow and the two million. Doc faces Nick with a gun, but Nick disarms him. Yet Nick is uneasy. He tells Al and Pop to tail Doc while he rushes back to the hotel to make sure Gladys is safe. She has disappeared. Pop and Al follow Doc to a shabby dive where the latter's thugs have taken Gladys with the story that Nick is in trouble. Pop leaves Al at the dive and follows the kidnappers to the desolate hideout where the girl is now imprisoned. Nick joins Al, and on the signal from Pop the two speed to the hideout. The rescuers wait for their chance. Guns blaze. Pop pays with his life for his loyalty, but Nick and Gladys are left free to find happiness together. (Original press release source)

REVIEWS:

"Well-directed and acted action thriller melodrama of 'the confidence game' mounted in superb production." *The Film Daily,* September 27, 1946

"Fairly good melodrama. Combining gangsterism with romantic appeal…. The story is not particularly novel, nor the characters … appealing. Yet it has been given a good production and the acting by the leading players is so competent, that one's attention is held well." *Harrison's Reports,* September 28, 1946

"This is a thriller of the conventional American type and has its exciting moments." *Monthly Film Bulletin,* January 1947

REVIEWS FOR JEAN NEGULESCO:

"The direction by Jean Negulesco has a drive and power that would have sold a less interesting script. There are small niceties in his work that cannot be overlooked. He has a lot of story to tell, and he misses none of its points." *The Hollywood Reporter,* September 24, 1946

"Jean Negulesco's direction manages to carry the story along in good fashion most of the way, although he is inclined to be over-obvious in some individual scenes." *Variety,* September 25, 1946

"Jean Negulesco has mounted a melodramatic crescendo in his direction which carries the show across the finish line with considerable impetus." *New York Herald Tribune,* November 2, 1946

ADDITIONAL REVIEWS AND ARTICLES:

The Hollywood Reporter August 6, 1941, p. 1; *The New York Times* August 6, 1941; *Los Angeles Examiner* November 25, 1941; *The Hollywood Reporter* August 25, 1944, p. 8; *The Hollywood Reporter* September 1, 1944, p. 3; *The Hollywood Reporter* September 11, 1944, p. 3; *The Hollywood Reporter* September 30, 1944; *The Hollywood Reporter* November 3, 1944, p. 17; *Motion Picture Herald Product Digest* January 20, 1945, p. 2278; *Motion Picture Herald* September 15, 1945; *Motion Picture Herald Product Digest* February 2, 1946, p. 2830; *Motion Picture Herald Product Digest* September 28, 1946, p. 3221; *Boxoffice* October 5, 1946; *Screenland* October 1946 p. 82; *The New York Times* November 2, 1946, p. 12; *The New Yorker* November 2 1946 p. 101; *The Hollywood Reporter* November 4, 1946, p. 6; *Time* November 18, 1946, p. 104; *Newsweek* November 18, 1946, p. 106; *Today's Cinema* January 1, 1947; *Kinematograph Weekly* January 2, 1947; *The Observer* (U.K.) February 28, 1947; *The Star* (U.K.) February 28, 1947; *The Times* (U.K.) March 3, 1947

Humoresque

A Warner Bros.–First National Picture; U.S. B&W 126 minutes; Premiered in New York on December 25, 1946

CREDITS: *Producer:* Jerry Wald; *Executive Producer:* Jack L. Warner; *Director:* Jean Negulesco; *Screenplay:* Clifford Odets, Zachary Gold; Based on the story by Fannie Hurst; *Photography:* Ernest Haller; *Editor:* Rudi Fehr; *Art Director:* Hugh Reticker; *Montages:* James Leicester; *Sound:* David Forrest, Robert B Lee; *Special Effects:* Roy Davidson, Willard Van Enger; *Set Decorator:* Clarence Steensen; *Dialogue Director:* Herschel Daugherty; *Wardrobe:* Bernard Newman; *Wardrobe for Miss Crawford:* Adrian; *Makeup:* Perc Westmore; *Musical Advisor:* Isaac Stern, *Musical Director:* Leo F. Forbstein; *Music Conductor:* Franz Waxman; *Assistant Directors:* Phil Quinn, Herbert Greene; *Hair Stylists:* Gertrude Wheeler, Della Barnes; *Unit Manager:* Lou Baum; *Music Excerpts:* "Humoresque in G-flat Major" (Opus 101) by Antonín Dvořák; selections from the opera *Carmen,* music by Georges Bizet; "Liebestod" from the opera *Tristan and Isolde* by Richard Wagner; "Zigeunerweisen" by Pablo Sarasate; selections from Violin Concerto in E Minor by Felix Mendelssohn; Violin Concerto in D Major by Peter Ilyich Tchaikovsky; Violin Concerto in D Major, Op. 22 by Henryk Wieniawski; Sonata for Piano and VIolin in A Major by César Franck, Symphonie Espagnole by Édouard Lalo; Piano Concerto in A Major by Edvard Grieg; Piano Concerto by Sergei Prokofiev; Polka by Dmitri Shostakovich; Waltz in A-flat Major by Johannes Brahms; Sonata in G Minor by Johann Sebastian Bach; *Songs:* "Embraceable You," music by George Gershwin, lyrics by Ira Gershwin; "What Is This Thing Called Love?" and "You Do

Something to Me," music and lyrics by Cole Porter.

CAST: Joan Crawford (Helen Wright), John Garfield (Paul Boray), Oscar Levant (Sid Jeffers), J. Carrol Naish (Rudy Boray), Joan Chandler (Gina), Tom D'Andrea (Phil Boray), Peggy Knudson (Florence Boray), Ruth Nelson (Esther Boray), Craig Stevens (Monte Loeffler), Paul Cavanagh (Victor Wright), Richard Gaines (Frederick Bauer), John Abbott (Rozner), Bobby Blake (Paul Boray as a Child), Tommy Cook (Phil Boray as a Child), Don McGuire (Eddie), Fritz Leiber (Hagerstrom), Peg La Centra (Nightclub Singer), Nestor Paiva (Orchestra Leader), Richard Walsh (Teddy), Sylvia Arslan (Gina as a Girl), Ann Lawrence (Florence as a Girl), Charles Kenworthy, Gary Armstrong (Boys on Street), Creighton Hale, Leah Baird (Professors), Louis Quince (Radio Producer), Leo Wonder (Old Violinist), Monte Blue (Furniture Moving Man), Ramon Ros (Engineer), Janet Barrett (Secretary), Jane Harker (Haughty Blonde), Edward Harvey (Butler), Angela Greene (Blonde), John Walsh (Delivery Boy), Esther Michelson (Customer), Frank Elliott (Tailor)

PLOT: It is the birthday of Paul Boray, youngest child of grocery store owner, Rudy Boray and his wife Esther. Rudy takes Paul to a store with the intention of buying him a present. He does his best to interest the boy in toys, but Paul has set his mind on a violin, which has been placed in his hands by Sid Jeffers, an embryo pianist, helping out in his father's store. Enraged by Paul's stubbornness, and the price of the instrument, Mr. Boray escorts his son home without a present. Aware of Paul's tears of frustration and disappointment, Mrs. Boray purchases the violin and Paul is speechless with joy. Mrs. Boray encourages him and assures him of her understanding of his desire for a musical career. During the Great Depression, Paul is oblivious to his struggling family and engrossed in his music; he is stung into action when verbally denounced by his father and brother. He induces Sid Jeffers, now a radio pianist, to get him a job with the broadcasting orchestra. Paul, a perfectionist, quarrels with the conductor over an arrangement and is dismissed. Sid takes him to a fashionable party given by Helen Wright. The beautiful and intelligent Helen is trying to forget her failure in marriage in two ways: by sponsoring young and unrecognized talent and by drinking to excess. She is impressed by Paul's positive character and his mastery of the violin. Deciding to see more of him and teach him the social graces, Helen finances his debut, which is a success. Subsequently she arranges an audition with Hagerstrom, conductor of the New York Philharmonic. Paul resents Helen's efforts even though they are to further his career. As Paul receives recognition in the musical world, Helen becomes vitally important to his life—second only to his music, even though their personalities and habits clash. His mother's warnings of the dangers in associating with Helen are ignored. Tiring of the incessant bickering with Helen and realizing the dangers of an entanglement, Paul leaves on a concert tour and does not communicated with Helen. Though deeply hurt, Helen resumes the affair on Paul's return to New York. Helen's husband, aware of the feelings between his wife and Paul, offers her a divorce, but when Paul asks her to marry him after the divorce, she is undecided. She realizes that they would never be happy together. On the eve of Paul's appearance with Hagerstrom and the Philharmonic, Helen visits Mrs. Boray and meets with bitter opposition. Paul is sincerely worried about Helen's non-appearance at the concert, and when Helen calls him from the beach-house he immediately accuses her of drinking again. She denies it and closes the conversation with, "I love you, darling." Helen pours herself a drink and listens to the concert over the radio while looking at her reflection in the window and the ocean beyond. She takes one drink from the glass, sees her reflection over its brim and, in disgust, sends the glass crashing through the window. As Paul's music reaches a triumphant crescendo, Helen starts through the doors and walks toward the sweeping breakers…. (Original press release source)

REVIEWS:

"There is certainly nothing humorous about the lachrymose *Humoresque*…. It is a rather mawkish lamentation upon the hopelessness of love…. Warner Brothers has wrapped this piteous affair in a blanket of soul-tearing music which is supposed to make it spiritually purgative." *New York Herald Tribune,* December 26, 1946

"A strong romantic tragedy…. Although the story is powerfully dramatic in spots, it is not as good as should have been for such a capable pair of players as Joan Crawford and John Garfield." *Harrison's Reports,* December 28, 1946

"Another film of interminable length about a

musical genius, ...*Humoresque* will probably annoy those who know music, as a film it is an expensive and worthless fake." *The London Times* (U.K.), April 13, 1947

REVIEWS FOR JEAN NEGULESCO:

"There are moments in the direction by Jean Negulesco that are unfortunately 'arty' and therefore intrusive [...] There are times, too, when his dialogue stumbles over its own epigrams. But the faults of Negulesco's work are far outnumbered by its many virtues." *The Hollywood Reporter*, December 23, 1946

"[S]trong direction by Jean Negulesco" *Variety*, December 25, 1946

"Even with Jean Negulesco's sometimes effective direction, *Humoresque* is definitively palling." *The New York Times*, December 26, 1946

ADDITIONAL REVIEWS AND ARTICLES:

Hollywood Reporter September 10, 1945, p. 2; *Hollywood Reporter* December 14, 1945, p. 19; *Motion Picture Herald Product Digest* January 5, 1946, p. 2786; *Hollywood Reporter* February 22, 1946, p. 3; Hollywood Reporter April 12, 1946, p. 15; *Cosmopolitan* November 1946 p. 72; *Motion Picture Herald Product Digest* December 14, 1946, p. 3363–64; *The New York Times* December 22, 1946, p. 44; *Boxoffice* December 26, 1946; *Film Daily* December 26, 1946, p. 11; *Commonweal* December 27, 1947, p. 281; *Motion Picture Herald Product Digest* December 28, 1946, p. 3385–3386; *The New Yorker* December 28, 1946, p. 44; *Hollywood Reporter* December 30, 1946, p. 6; *Photoplay* January 1947 p. 9; *Time* January 13, 1947, p. 97–98; *New Republic* January 20 1947 p. 37; *Good Housekeeping* February 1947 p. 12–13; *Monthly Film Bulletin* April 1947 p. 50; *The Mirror* (U.K.) April 9, 1947;*Today's Cinema* April 11, 1947; *The Sunday Express* (U.K.) April 11, 1947; *Kinematograph Weekly* April 17, 1947; *L'Écran Français* (France) September 30 1947, p. 13; *Mon Film* (France) March 24, 1948, p. 3; *Positif* (France) [October 1971 p. 39; *Image et Son–La Revue du Cinéma* March 1983 p. 106; *Le Monde* (France) September 18, 1986; *Le Nouvel Observateur* (France) September 12 1986; *Le Nouvel Observateur* (France) September 19, 1986; *Le Matin* (France) September 19, 1986; *Radio Times* May 2 1987, p. 19; *Classic Images* May 2005, p. 38; *Sight and Sound* February 2006, p. 89–90

AWARDS AND HONORS:

Academy Awards: U.S. 1947: *Nominated:* Best Music, Scoring of a Dramatic or Comedy Picture, Franz Waxman

Deep Valley

A Warner Bros.–First National Picture; U.S. B&W 104 minutes; Premiered in New York August 22, 1947

CREDITS: *Producer:* Henry Blanke; *Executive Producer:* Jack L. Warner; *Director:* Jean Negulesco; *Screenplay:* Salka Viertel, Stephen Morehouse Avery; Based on the novel by Dan Totheroh; *Photography:* Ted McCord; *Art Directors:* Max Parker, Frank Durlauf; *Set Decorator:* Howard Winterbottom; *Editor:* Owen Marks; *Costumes:* Bernard Newman; *Music:* Max Steiner; *Music Director:* Leo F. Forbstein; *Orchestral Arrangements:* Murray Cutter; *Sound:* C.A. Riggs; *Special Photographic Effects:* William McGann, H.F. Koenekamp; *Makeup:* Perc Westmore; *Assistant Director:* Art Lueker; *Dialogue Director:* John Maxwell; *Unit Manager:* Frank Mattison

CAST: Ida Lupino (Libby Saul), Dane Clark (Barry Burnett), Wayne Morris (Jed Barker), Fay Bainter (Ellie Saul), Henry Hull (Cliff Saul), Willard Robertson (Sheriff Akers), Rory Mallinson (Foreman), Jack Mower (Supervisor), Bob Lowell, Lennie Bremen, Ross Ford, John Alvin (Convicts), William Haade, Clancy Cooper (Guards), Ian MacDonald (Blast Foreman), Ray Teal (Prison Official), Ralph Dunn (Deputy), Eddie Dunn, Harry Strang (Posse)

PLOT: Wretched as the California shack in which they live is the existence of the Saul family. A years-old quarrel separates Mrs. Saul from her husband. She feigns illness and never moves from her upstairs room. embittered and sour, he has no interest in her or anything else. And their daughter Libby spends slavish days and nights in frustration and fear, a prisoner of circumstances. Convict Barry Burnett is working with a construction gang building a road near the Saul place. Fellow feeling stirs within Libby as she watches Barry one day; her sympathy increases when she sees him strike a mocking warder. Jeff Barker, construction job supervisor, visits the house at old Saul's invitation. Libby is torn between her parents and Barry, now confined to a shack on the mountainside for his rebellion. When her father strikes her, she makes for the woods. In the small hut she had planned to make her home, Barry is hiding, a fugitive. The two find a happiness neither has known. But the posse is on his trail. To escape, the couple must have food. Libby sneaks home for supplies, and finds a greatly changed situation: Her parents, shocked by her departure into a realization of the stupid selfishness which has separated them, are striving to re-establish harmony. Some of the sheriff's men are billeted on the place. She cannot get back to Barry. Barry comes to her, desperate but determined. She finds a hiding place for him in a barn loft which has already been searched. But both Jeff Barker and the sheriff are always about. Libby comes to realize that Barry is a born killer—not vindictive, but so aggressive in his fears and rages that he is a menace to society. Mrs. Saul discovers the hideout, and Libby and Barry flee. Barry thrusts Libby away as he tries to escape, realizing that unhappiness would be hers if she stayed with him. The posse's bullets find their mark, and Barry dies in Libby's arms. She is left to face a future which includes her parents' newfound happiness ... and Jeff Barker. (Original press release source)

REVIEWS:

"[T]he film is very well acted.... With a more credibly defined story to support the performances, *Deep Valley* might easily have become an arresting picture." *The New York Times,* August 23, 1947

"A brilliant cast brings conviction and suspense to a somber tale in *Deep Valley*.... So much is so good in this Warner Brothers picture that it is a pity it ravels into a tedious and unresolved ending." *New York Herald Tribune,* August 23, 1947

"It is a rather pathetic picture because everyone concerned with it is obviously trying very hard to do something good, powerful and out of the ordinary. Occasionally this effort brings the picture to life.... But on the whole, *Deep Valley* is reminiscent of many of the solemn little-theater plays of the early '20s: *i.e.,* it is lost in mawkishness and pseudo poetic feeling masquerading as art." *Time,* September 15, 1947

REVIEWS FOR JEAN NEGULESCO:

"Jean Negulesco has never before matched the power of his direction here. It can almost be called a tour de force for gone are his pretensions to artiness. His script makes rare good sense and he misses none of that sense. He concentrates upon obtaining performances that are nothing short of magnificent." *The Hollywood Reporter,* July 30, 1947

"It's strong, uncompromising drama, and Jean Negulesco's direction punches it over forcefully. He sustains a mood of desperation and pending violence that carries the spectator along, and draws performances from the cast that click big." *Variety,* July 30, 1947

"Another first line job of direction is turned by Jean Negulesco in this production which has indications of possessing sleeper qualities." *The Film Daily,* July 30, 1947

ADDITIONAL REVIEWS AND ARTICLES:

Hollywood Reporter September 27, 1946, p. 19; *Independent Film Journal* January 4, 1947, p. 35; *Hollywood Reporter* January 24, 1947, p. 19; *Motion Picture Herald Product Digest* August 2, 1947, p. 23; *Boxoffic* August 2, 1947, *Harrison's Reports* August 2, 1947, p. 122; *Los Angeles Times* August 30, 1947, p. A5; *Baltimore Sun* September 1, 1947, p. 8; *Newsweek* September 1, 1947, p. 77; *Commonweal* September 26, 1947, p. 574; *Modern Screen* October 1947 p. 18; *New Movies* October 1947 p. 11; *Life* February 23, 1948, p. 24; *Today's Cinema* April 16, 1948; *Kinematograph Weekly* April 22, 1948; *Monthly Film Bulletin* May 1948 p. 62

Johnny Belinda

A Warner Bros.–First National Picture; U.S. B&W 102 minutes; Premiered in Hollywood on October 14, 1948

CREDITS: *Producer* Jerry Wald; *Director:* Jean Negulesco; *Screenplay:* Irma von Cube, Allen Vincent; Based on the play by Elmer Harris; *Photography:* Ted McCord; *Art Director:* Robert Haas, Frank Durlauf; *Set Decorator:* William Wallace; *Editor:* David Weisbart; *Wardrobe:* Milo Anderson, Frank Ricci, Patricia Davidson, Marie Blanchard; *Music:* Max Steiner, *Orchestral Arrangements:* Murray Cutter; *Musical Director:* Leo F. Forbestein; *Sound:* Charles Lang; *Special Effects:* William McGann, Edwin DuPar; *Makeup:* Perc Westmore, Frank McCoy; *Hair Stylist:* Betty Belmont, *Assistant Directors:* Mel Dellar, Lee White; *Technical Advisors:* Bruce Caruthers, Elizabeth Gesner; *Dialogue Director:* Felix Jacoves; *Script Supervisor:* Fred Applegate

CAST: Jane Wyman (Belinda McDonald), Lew Ayres (Dr. Robert Richardson), Charles Bickford (Black McDonald), Agnes Moorehead (Aggie McDonald), Stephen McNally (Locky McCormick), Jan Sterling (Stella Maguire), Rosalind Ivan (Mrs. Poggety), Dan Seymour (Storekeeper), Mabel Paige (Mrs. Lutz), Ida Moore (Mrs. McKee), Alan Napier (Defense Attorney), Monte Blue (Ben), Douglas Kennedy (Mountie), James Craven (Interpreter), Richard Taylor (Floyd McQuiggen), Richard Walsh (Fergus

McQuiggen), Joan Winfield (Mrs. Tim Moore), Ian Wolfe (Rector), Holmes Herbert (Judge), Jonathan Hale (Dr. Gray), Ray Montgomery (Tim Moore), Blayney Lewis (Dan'l), Barbara Bates (Gracie Anderson), Frank Hagney, Larry McGrath, Colin Kenny, Lew Harvey, Al Ferguson (Men Reciting Lord's Prayer), Alice MacKenzie (Farm Woman), Frederic Worlock (Prosecutor), Creighton Hale (Bailiff)

PLOT: Life is not easy in the little community on Cape Breton Island in Nova Scotia. For Black McDonald there is a hard existence wrested from the soil. For his sister Aggie there are ceaseless household chores. For his daughter Belinda there is back-breaking toil. And Belinda, a deaf mute, is treated by family and acquaintances alike as an unfeeling non-entity. Village newcomer Dr. Robert Richardson is intelligent and imbued with a stubborn idealism. His office helper and day housekeeper is Stella Maguire, a flighty young lady sought after by the young local men because her father left her a farm. The suitor most likely to succeed seems to be husky Locky McCormick.

Dr. Richardson is shocked to see the treatment accorded to Belinda. He wins the girl's affection and, by simple sign language, takes her on as a patient. Black's changed attitude and the new world opened up by the doctor's books begin to make life worthwhile for Belinda. Locky is rejected by Stella—whose idea that she loves Dr. Richardson is quashed by the doctor himself. After a village jamboree, Locky turns his drunken attentions to Belinda. She resists him fiercely, but the tragic result is that she is with child. Resolute in refusing to name the man, Belinda faces a murderous Black. Once again, Richardson intervenes—and the village, aghast, reasons that he must be the seducer. Black begins to suspect Locky, now married to Stella. Locky kills him during a scuffle, but a storm gives him the chance to escape the consequences of his act. Aggie leaves Belinda and the McDonald farm. The mortgage-holding Pacquet moves in with the auctioneers. Belinda now faces the world alone, but for her child Johnny. Richardson has left, forced to take a staff job with a Montreal hospital in order to exist. Then Stella and Locky, helped by the "Christian" element of the village, win approval to adopt Johnny. When they come to claim Johnny, Belinda kills Locky. Richardson is at Belinda's side at the trial. The case against her is a damning one. Stella finally reveals that Locky was Johnny's father. Belinda has killed, the court agrees, but in self-defense. The town welcomes back Belinda with full respect and honor; while Dr. Richardson claims her as his bride. (Original press release source)

REVIEWS:

"Finely directed by Jean Negulesco, this is a memorable film in which Jane Wyman's performance as Belinda is outstanding ... truly magnificent." *Monthly Film Bulletin,* September 1948

"It is surprising what a good film [Warners has] made.... [T]hey have made a picture which has a novel and genuine theme. And at best they have made it quite moving." *The New York Times,* October 2, 1948

"*Johnny Belinda* is an odd, rather likable blend of believable back-country dramatics and old-fashioned melodramatics." *Time,* October 25, 1948

REVIEW FOR JEAN NEGULESCO:

"Jean Negulesco's direction combines dramatic emphasis and pace with the required sensitivity. His artistry, and that of Jane Wyman who undertakes the difficult acting taste of portraying a deaf mute, give the picture some rare moments which linger long in the memory." *The Hollywood Reporter,* September 14, 1948

"Negulesco's direction was the stamp of a genius." *The Film Daily,* September 14, 1948

"Jean Negulesco's direction never overplays the heartstrings, yet keeps them constantly twanging and evidences a sympathetic instinct that is reflected in the performances." *Variety,* September 15, 1948

ADDITIONAL REVIEWS AND ARTICLES:

Hollywood Reporter October 30, 1946, *Hollywood Reporter* December 5, 1946; *Hollywood Reporter* September 3, 1947 p. 2; *Hollywood Reporter* September 8, 1948 p. 3; *Today's Cinema* September 10, 1948; *Motion Picture Herald* September 11 1948 p. 4310; *Boxoffice* September 18, 1948; *Motion Picture Herald* September 18, 1948, p. 4317; *Harrison's Reports* September 18, 1948, p. 151; *Photoplay* September 1948 p. 22; *Hollywood Reporter* October 5, 1948 p. 6; *McCall's* October 1948 p. 4; *American Cinematographer* October 1948 p. 338–39; *New York Herald Tribune* October 2, 1948; *New York Sun* October 2, 1948; *Collier's* October 2, 1948, p. 41; *New York Daily News* October 2, 1948; *Newsweek* October 4, 1948, p. 85; *The New Yorker* October 9, 1948, 111; *Cue* October 9, 1948; *Hollywood Reporter* October 14, 1948; *Commonweal* October 22, 1948, p. 41; *Life* October 25, 1948, p. 153; *Theatre Arts* October 1948 p. 53, *Liberty* November 1948; *Good*

Housekeeping November 1948 p. 258; *Woman's Home Companion* November 1948 p. 10–11; *The Evening News* (U.K.) December 16, 1948; *The Times* (U.K.) December 20, 1948; *The Daily Express* (U.K.) December 17, 1948; *The Mirror* (U.K.) December 17, 1948; *Nation* December 18, 1948, p. 705; *The Guardian* December 18, 1948; *Sunday Express* (U.K.) December 19, 1948; *The Sunday Times* (U.K.) December 19, 1948; *The Observer* (U.K.) December 20 1948; *Rotarian* January 1949 p. 52; *L'Écran Français* (France) May 10, 1949, p. 11; *Cine Mirror* (France) May 2, 1949; *France Dimanche* (France) May 15, 1949; *Le Soir Illustre* (Belgium) June 23, 1949; *Photoplay* October 1949 p. 32; *Film Complet* (France) March 2, 1950; *Action* May-June 1976; *Photoplay* April 1982, p. 22; *American Cinematographer* October 1984; *Image et Son–La Revue du Cinéma* (France) October 1984 p. 113; *The New York Times* January 31, 2006, p. E3

AWARDS AND HONORS:

National Board of Review, U.S. 1948: *Won:* NBR Award: Top Ten Films; Golden Globes, U.S. 1949: *Won:* Golden Globe: Best Motion Picture–Drama together with *The Treasure of the Sierra Madre* (1948); Best Motion Picture Actress: Jane Wyman; Academy Awards: U.S. 1949; *Won:* Oscar; Best Actress in a Leading Role: Jane Wyman; Academy Awards: U.S. 1949: *Nominated:* Best Picture, Best Actor in a Leading Role: Lew Ayres; Best Actor in a Supporting Role: Charles Bickford; Best Actress in a Supporting Role: Agnes Moorehead; Best *Director:* Jean Negulesco; Best Writing, *Screenplay:* Irma von Cube, Allen Vincent; Best Cinematography, Black and White: Ted McCord; Best Art Direction-Set Decoration, Black and White: Robert Haas, William Wallace; Best Sound Recording: Col. Nathan O. Levinson; Best Film Editing: David Weisbart; Best Music, Scoring of a Dramatic or Comedy Picture: Max Steiner; Photoplay Awards: U.S. 1949: *Won:* Most popular Female Star: Jane Wyman; Venice Film Festival: Italy 1949: *Nominated:* Golden Lion: Jean Negulesco; Writers Guild of America, U.S. 1949: *Nominated:* WGA Award (Screen): Best Written American Drama: Irma von Cube, Allen Vincent

Road House

20th Century–Fox; U.S. B&W 95 minutes; Premiered in New York on November 6, 1948

CREDITS: *Producer:* Edward Chodorov; *Director:* Jean Negulesco; *Screenplay:* Edward Chodorov; Based on the story " Dark Love" by Margaret Gruen and Oscar Saul; *Photography:* Joseph LaShelle, Norbert Brodine; *Music:* Cyril Mockridge; *Musical Direction:* Lionel Newman; *Musical Arrangements:* Herbert Spencer, Earle Hagen; *Art Directors:* Lyle Wheeler, Maurice Ransford; *Set Decorator:* Thomas Little; *Wardrobe Director:* Charles Le Maire; *Costumes:* Kay Nelson; *Makeup:* Ben Nye, Tom Tuttle; *Hair Stylist:* Myrl Stolz, Catherine Reed; *Special Photographic Effects:* Fred Sersen; *Sound:* Alfred Bruzlin, Harry M. Leonard; *Editor:* James B. Clark; *Script Supervisor:* Rose Sternberg; *Fighting Instructor:* Johnny Indrisano; *Songs:* "One for My Baby (and One More for the Road)," music by Harold Arlen, lyrics by Johnny Mercer; "Again," music by Lionel Newman, lyrics by Dorcas Cochran; "The Right Kind," music by Lionel Newman, lyrics by Don George and Charles Henderson

CAST: Ida Lupino (Lily Stevens), Cornel Wilde (Pete Morgan), Celeste Holm (Susie Smith), Richard Widmark (Jefferson "Jefty" Robbins), O.Z. Whitehead (Arthur), Robert Karnes (Mike), George Beranger (Lefty), Ian MacDonald (Police Captain), Grandon Rhodes (Judge), Jack G. Lee (Sam), Tom Moore (Jury Foreman), John Butler (Drunk), James Metcalf (Mr. Green), Clancy Cooper, Robert Foulk, Ray Teal, Chuck Flynn (Policemen), Douglas Gerrard (Waiter), Robert Cherry (Bowling Alley Boy), Harry Seymour (Desk Clerk), Marion Marshall (Millie), Charles Flynn (Policeman at Bus Depot), Kathleen Hughes

PLOT: "Jefty" Robbins owns a road house managed by his lifelong friend Pete Morgan. Another old friend, Susie Smith, is the cashier. To the road house Jefty brings a singer, Lily Stevens. Peter is antagonistic toward her, knowing how soon Jefty tires of his women. But this time, Jefty is seriously attracted, and returns from a visit to his cabin near the Canadian border with a wedding license. Pete and Lily are horror-struck: While Jefty was away, the two fell in love. When Pete breaks the news to his friend, Jefty goes white with rage and tells Pete to get out. Taking the wages due to him from the safe, Pete prepares to leave with Lily for Chicago. At the railway station, Pete is arrested for larceny—the whole amount deposited in the safe by Susie, $2600, has vanished. Pete is found guilty and sentenced to a minimum of two years, but Jefty persuades the judge to parole Pete in his custody. It's quite obvious that Jefty, sore about the wreckage of his plans to marry, has tricked them. He warns Pete that if he tries to leave or resorts to physical violence, he goes to prison for the maximum of ten years. He then suggests that Pete, Lily, Susie and himself spend a few days at his cabin. The atmosphere is tense and on the first night, Jefty, slightly drunk unmercifully taunts the two lovers. Pete can stand the gibes no longer and thrashes him, smashes his rifle and runs with Lily to the Canadian border. While Jefty is nursing his wounds, Susie finds proof that Jefty took the money. She runs after Pete but is followed by Jefty who, knowing the terrain better than they do, catches up with them. Jefty tries to take the evidence of his guilt from Susie. Pete dashes from the bushes, where he and Lily are hiding, and goes for him. There is another savage fight with Jefty emerging as the victor. Lily finds Jefty's revolver on the ground and, as he advances towards her, she implores him to come no nearer. As he is about to pounce on her, she fires, killing him. (Original press release source)

REVIEWS:

"The outline ... is less than inspired, but a climactic twist and a rousing donnybrook between the principals serves as a much-needed catalyst. And the development of characters through an intelligently written script keeps things lively and plausible." *The New York Times,* November 8, 1948

"Good! It is a strong triangle melodrama.... Moreover the production values are good and the performances convincing." *Harrison's Reports,* September 25, 1948

"The action is smooth, and the story is especially interesting where it gives an insight into the various amusements that the road house provides.... The film provides slick entertainment." *Film Monthly Bulletin,* January 1949

REVIEWS FOR JEAN NEGULESCO:

"Jean Negulesco's direction, leisurely and heavy-handed, contributes little in the way of sustained pace." *The Hollywood Reporter,* September 24, 1948

"Jean Negulesco's staging is terse and to the point, knitting the familiar strands of the script into a comparatively engrossing entertainment." *New York Herald Tribune,* November 8, 1948

"Jean Negulesco has masked a thin yarn in some deceptive trappings of reality. He swings his camera over short, sharp chunks of dialogue, searches with his lens in the drab corners of the road house, and builds to a climax in a fine movie chase. Lacking lifelike characters, he gives things a gloss of credibility by keeping his camera on the move." *Time,* November 15, 1948

ADDITIONAL REVIEWS AND ARTICLES:

Los Angeles Times February 11, 1948, p. 19; *Hollywood Reporter* March 1948 p. 15; *Hollywood Reporter* April 30, 1948, p. 15; *Los Angeles Times* May 8, 1948, p. 9; *Screenland* July 1948 p. 8; *Screenland* August 1948, *Motion Picture Herald Product* Digest September 11, 1948, p. 4311; *Daily Variety* September 22, 1948, p. 3; *Film Daily* September 22, 1948, p. 13; *Hollywood Reporter* September 22, 1948, p. 3–4; *Boxoffice* October 2, 1948; *Motion Picture Herald Product Digest* October 2, 1948, p. 4333; *The Film User* November 1950 pp. 651; *Los Angeles Times* November 10, 1948, p. A7; *Hollywood Reporter* November 15, 1948, p. 8–9; *Newsweek* November 15, 1948, p. 93–94; *The New Yorker* November 20, 1948, p. 108; *Today's Cinema* December 1, 1948, p. 14; *The New Republic* December 20, 1948, p. 30; *Rotarian* January 1949 p. 53; *The Observer* (U.K.) April 3, 1949; *The Times* (U.K.) April 4, 1949; *The Daily Telegraph* (U.K.) April 4, 1949; *L'Écran Français* (France) October 3, 1949, p. 13; *Mon Film* (France) February 8, 1950, p. 3 *Cinématographe* (France) February 1983 p. 79; *Image et Son-La Revue du Cinéma* (France) October 1984 p. 85; *Films in Review* May 1986 p. 260; *Dirigido Por* (Spain) February 2011 p. 56–57

The Forbidden Street

Released in the United Kingdom as *Britannia Mews;* 20th Century–Fox; U.S.–U.K. B&W 90 minutes; Premiered in London on February 24, 1949; Released in New York on May 13, 1949

CREDITS: *Producer:* William Perlberg; *Executive Producer:* Darryl F. Zanuck; *Director:* Jean Negulesco; *Screenplay:* Ring Lardner, Jr., based on the novel *Britannia Mews* by Margery Sharp; *Producer's Personal Assistants:* Freddie Fox, Robert E. Dearing; *Photography:* George Perinal; *Art Director:* Andre Andrewjew; *Production Managers:* Ronnie Kinnoch, T.S. Lyndon Haynes; *Assistant Director:* Guy Hamilton; *Camera Operator:* Denys Coop; *Sound Recordist:* Buster Ambler; *Sound Editor:* Ben Hipkins; *Music:* Malcolm Arnold, played by the Royal Philharmonic Orchestra; *Musical Director:* Muir Mathieson; *Costumes:* Renee Pavy; *Assistant Director:* Guy Hamilton

CAST: Dana Andrews (Henry Lambert/Gilbert Lauderdale), Maureen O'Hara (Adelaide Culver), Dame Sybil Thorndike (The Sow Mrs.

Mounsey), Diane Hart (The Blazer Harriet O'Keefe), Anne Butchart (Alice Hambro), Wilfred Hyde-White (Mr. William Culver), Fay Compton (Mrs. Bertha Culver), A. E. Matthews (Mr. Desmond Bly), Anthony Tancred (Treff Culver), Herbert Walton (The Old 'Un), Mary Martlet (Milly Lauderdale), June Allen (Adelaide as a Child), Suzanne Gibbs (Alice as a Child), Heather Latham (The Blazer as a child), Peter Hobbes (Fred Baker), Neil North (Johnny Hambro), Ernest Hare (Policeman), Gwynne Whitby (Miss Bryant), Scott Harold (Benson), Anthony Lamb (Treff as a Child), John Wright's Marionettes

PLOT: Henry Lambert, an impecunious artist, is engaged by Mr. Culver to give drawing lessons to his daughter Adelaide and her cousin Alice. The apartment where he must live was formerly occupied by the family coachman; it's is in the squalid, sordid Britannia Mews, which adjoins the comfortable home of the Culvers. Adelaide falls in love with the drawing master and, defying her family, marries him. They go to live in the Britannia Mews flat when the Culvers move into the country. Soon it becomes clear that Henry is a sensitive artist ruined by drink. But he has one abiding passion: the fashioning of exquisite puppets. Henry and Adelaide quarrel violently when the artist makes insulting remarks, and Adelaide—on the exterior staircase leading to the apartment—gives him the lightest of the pushes. Henry, unsteady with drink, loses his balance and falls to his death. An obscene old hag, Mrs. Mounsey, has witnessed Henry's death, and she blackmails Adelaide and forces her to stay in the Mews. Two years later, Adelaide meets a charming ne'er-do-well, Gilbert Lauderdale, a lawyer now reduced to addressing envelopes. Gilbert, with his legal knowledge, makes short work of Mrs. Mounsey and he is permitted to live in the stable beneath Adelaide's apartment. He is known to everybody in the Mews as "Mr. Lambert." One day Gilbert discovers Henry's lovely puppets and, helped by a famous old puppet master, learns how to operate them and finally opens a tiny puppet theatre in the Mews. A huge success, it's patronized by society. Gilbert and Adelaide have fallen deeply in love, but marriage, he tells her, is impossible; he is already married. When Gilbert's wife comes on the scene, Adelaide insists that he returns to her. Such self-sacrifice is not necessary for it transpires that Mrs. Lauderdale has already divorced Gilbert in the United States. Adelaide is married on the following day and, with the assistance of her brother, is happily reconciled to her joyful parents. (Original press release source)

REVIEWS:
"Little effort has been made to lift the story out of its sentimental sphere and in consequence the performances by the stars are necessary restricted." *Variety,* March 9, 1949

"Those who have read the novel will find little of its character in the film; those who have not will be quite puzzled that such a jigjog thing should have been made." *The New York Times,* May 14, 1949

"[It's] a tiresome and lumbering dramatic exercise for a frozen-faced Maureen O'Hara and an elaborately wing-whiskered Dana Andrews." *Cue,* May 21, 1949

REVIEWS FOR JEAN NEGULESCO:
"[Negulesco] just puts the camera on Maureen, forgets to prod her into animation and acting." *The Daily Express* (U.K.), February 20, 1949

"[Neither the] production resources nor the direction of Jean Negulesco is able to conceal, for very long, that the script is made from the sheerest bits of story." *The Hollywood Reporter,* April 29, 1949

"Negulesco may not have kept the disperse action in much of a unity, but he has reconstructed a slum district of London at the end of last century with vivid pictorial effect." *New York Herald Tribune,* May 14, 1949

ADDITIONAL REVIEWS AND ARTICLES:
Hollywood Reporter June 19, 1946, p. 3; *Variety* August 4, 1948, p. 21; *Variety* May 19, 1948, p. 2; *Variety* December 1, 1948, p. 2; *Variety* December 26, 1948; *Picturegoer* October 9, 1948, p. 8; *Variety* November 30, 1948; *Film Industry* January 13, 1949, p. 17; *Today's Cinema* February 25, 1949, p. 8; *Monthly Film Bulletin* March 1949, p. 38; *Showmen's Trade Review* March 12, 1949, p. 15; *Daily Variety* April 29, 1949, p. 4; *Film Daily* May 3, 1949, p. 6; *Harrison's Reports* May 7, 1949, p. 75; *Boxoffice* May 7, 1949; *Motion Picture Herald* May 7, 1949, p. 4597; *New York Journal of Commerce* May 24, 1949, p. 15; *Newsweek* May 30, 1949, p. 83; *Time* May 30 1949 p. 82; *Los Angeles Times* June 8 1949 p. B7; *L.A. Daily News* June 8, 1949; *Filmland* August 1949 p. 12–13; *Rotarian* October 1949 p. 38; *Hollywood Album* 1954; *Music from the Movies* Spring 1997 p. 30–34

Three Came Home

20th Century–Fox; A Darryl F. Zanuck Presentation; U.S. B&W 106 minutes; Premiered in New York on February 20, 1950

CREDITS: *Producer:* Nunnally Johnson; *Director:* Jean Negulesco; *Screenplay:* Nunnally Johnson; Based on the book by Agnes Newton Keith; *Photography:* Milton Krasner; *Music:* Hugo Friedhofer; *Art Director:* Lyle Wheeler, Leland Fuller; *Set Decorators:* Thomas Little, Fred J. Rode; *Editor:* Dorothy Spencer; *Wardrobe Director:* Charles Le Maire; *Musical Director:* Lionel Newman; *Orchestrator:* Edward Powell; *Makeup:* Ben Nye; *Hair Stylist:* Esperanza Corona; *Special Photographic Effects:* Fred Sersen; *Sound:* E. Clayton Ward, Roger Heman; *Assistant Director:* Saul Wurzel; *Dialogue Director:* Jason Lindsey; *Production Manager:* Robert Snody; *Technical Advisor:* Sylvia Norris

CAST: Claudette Colbert (Agnes Newton Keith), Patric Knowles (Harry Keith), Florence Desmond (Betty Sommers), Sessue Hayakawa (Colonel Michio Suga), Sylvia Andrew (Henrietta Thomas), Phyllis Morris (Sister Rose), Mark Keuning (George Keith), Howard Chuman (Lieutenant Nekata), Drue Mallory, Carol Savage, Virginia Keiley, Mimi Heyworth, Helen Westcott (Prisoners), Devi Dja (Ah Yin), Alex Fraser (Dr. Bandy), Leonard Willey (Governor-General), John Burton, Patrick Whyte, Stanley Fraser, John Shulick (Englishmen), Li Sun (Wilfred), Taka Iwashaiki (Captain), David Matsushama (Evil Guard), Tom Komuro (Japanese Soldier-Secretary), Al Saijo (Japanese Boat Pilot), Jim Hagimori (Japanese Boat Captain), Robert Shirahama (Japanese Doctor), Harry Martin, Pat O'Moore, Clarke Gordon, Douglas Walton, Robin Hughes, John Mantley, James Logan, George Leigh (Australian Prisoners of War), James Yanari, Robert Kino, Yamato Cain Yamasaki, Masaji "Butch" Yamamota, Rollin Moriyama, Hiroshi Neeno, Frank Kobata, Roy Yamadero, George Utsunomiya, Tom Omori, Robert Kishita (Japanese Officers), Frank Kumagai, Sam "Isami" Ono, George Kunitake, Arthur Shira, Otto Han, Yutaka Shimizu, Frank Saito, Bob Matsuo, Frank Emi, John Furukawa, Jim Saito, Bob Oku (Japanese Soldiers), Gene Gondo, Shig Imori, Kurt Hiroshima, Jerry Fujikawa, George Ito, George Natsume, Akira Yoshihara, Yutaka Shimahara, Jimmy Yamaguchi, Albert Hirota, Tom Muramada, Charles Nakauchi, Ralph Nagai, Mas Yoshida (Japanese Guards), Ken Kurose, Giro Murashami (Orderlies), Patricia O'Callaghan, Jean Prescott (English Women), Duncan Richardson, Peter James, Billy Henry (English Boys), Melinda Plowman (English Girl), Campbell Copelin (British Radio Announcer)

PLOT: An onscreen forward reads: "This film is based on the autobiographical book by Agnes Newton Keith who, with her husband and small son, were held prisoners by the Japanese during the greater part of the war."

"Meet the enemy, resist passively, do not cooperate. We are sorry we cannot help you." That is the message that Mrs. Keith and her husband Harry receive when the Japanese approach Sandakan in British North Borneo. When the enemy soldiers arrive, the civilians know that they will receive rough treatment. Mrs. Keith finds that the officer in command of the Japanese Forces, Colonel Suga, is not entirely unsympathetic to her, as a book she has written shows understanding towards Orientals. Soon an edict comes through that the men and women will be taken to separate concentration camps. As time drags on, the prisoners are moved from camp to camp; conditions are appalling and they have to supplement their meager rations as best they can, in order to keep alive. One night when Mrs., Keith, fearing a storm, goes out of the hut to take in laundry, she is molested by a Japanese sentry. She reports the matter and is brutally treated by a junior officer when she refuses to sign a document saying that nothing happened. She is spared further torture by the advent of Colonel Suga. In the spring of 1945, the Allies are pressing and the prisoners are overjoyed as they watch friendly bombers attacking the Japanese headquarters. The end of the war does not bring immediate freedom, but a plane drops pamphlets informing them that Japan has surrendered and urging them to be patient. Colonel Suga, overcome with grief at the news that his wife and children have been killed at Hiroshima, takes George and other starving children to his home and invites them to eat whatever they can find. One morning the prisoners wake to find that their guards have gone. News comes that Allied soldiers are in their way. There are soon tearful and joyous reunions of husbands, wives and children as vans filled with released prisoners, escorted by Allied soldiers, drive into the camp. Mrs. Keith is distraught that her husband is not among them. Then suddenly her face lights up with a new radiance. Laughing uncontrollably, hobbling along on a homemade crutch, Harry Keith literally falls into the arms of his wife. (Original press release source)

REVIEWS:

"Played against realistic settings, which vividly convey the meanness of the jungle prisons, and directed by Jean Negulesco for physical and emotional credibility, *Three Came Home* is a comprehensive film. It will shock you, disturb you, tear your heart out. But it will fill you with a great respect for a heroic soul." *The New York Times,* February 21, 1950

"[This is] a film that vies with the best in documented authenticity and in its untamed emotional tugging.... This is a superbly acted film and one which cannot be questioned for sheer integrity." *Variety,* February 15, 1950

"The story of Mrs Keith ... is here reduced mostly to the level of a screen tear-jerker, though handled at moments with reasonable control and adroitness. Claudette Colbert is miscast as the heroine..." *Monthly Film Bulletin,* February–March 1950

REVIEWS FOR JEAN NEGULESCO:

"In the direction of Jean Negulesco there is a tremendous power and unerring capacity for sustaining the grim, somber mood of the narrative. His work accounts for performances that are as striking as the material." *The Hollywood Reporter*, February 10, 1950

"Here is a superlative script, ably articulated on the screen by Jean Negulesco's direction." *New York Herald Tribune,* February 21, 1950

"...Negulesco works so hard at building up the tension each time that the picture verges at times on old-fashioned melodramatics. At the same time he passes up chance to document the small, disagreeable details of the prison life.... [His] treatment of emotional scenes, notably at the picture's end, is so contrived to wring the last tear from the audience that it comes perilously close to cheapening them." *Time,* February 27, 1950

ADDITIONAL REVIEWS AND ARTICLES:

Los Angeles Times October 30, 1948, p. 6; *Evening News* October 30, 1948, p. 4; *Los Angeles Times* December 20, 1948, p. B6; *Los Angeles Times* April 5, 1949, p. 15; *Hollywood Reporter* April 22, 1949, p. 15; *Motion Picture Daily* May 5, 1949; *Motion Picture Daily* June 27, 1949; *Movie Makers* January 1950 p. 24; *Today's Cinema* February 3, 1950, p. 17; *Film Daily* February 10, 1950, p. 8; *Daily Variety* February 10, 195 p. 3; *Hollywood Reporter* February 10, 1950, p. 3; *Motion Picture Herald Product Digest* February 11, 1950, p. 185; *Harrison's Reports* February 11, 1950, p. 22; *Boxoffice* February 18 1950; *The Observer* (U.K.), February 22, 1950; *The Spectator* (U.K.), February 24 1950, p. 241; *The Daily Express* (U.K.), February 24, 1950; *The Mirror* (U.K.), February 24, 1950; *The Sunday Times* (U.K.), February 26, 1950; *The Times* (U.K.), February 27, 1950, p. 8; *Commonweal* March 3, 1950, p. 557; *Leader Magazine* (U.K.), March 4, 1950, p. 26–27; *The New Statesman and Nation* (U.K.), March 4, 1950, p. 244; *The New Yorker* March 4, 1950, p. 80; *Saturday's Review* March 11, 1950, p. 30–32; *The Daily Notes* March 13, 1950, p. 4; *Life* March 20, 1950, p. 61–62; *The New York Times* March 26, 1950; *Modern Screen* April 1950 p. 115; *Filmland* (New Zealand) April 1950 p. 17; *Films in Review* April 1950 p. 29–30; *Les Lettres Françaises* (France), October 2 1950; *L'Écran Français* (France), October 2, 1950, p. 8; *Films and Filming* October 1959 p. 86; *Image et Son–La Revue du Cinéma* (France), October 1985 p. 34; *The Psychoanalytic Quarterly* January 1993 p. 109–13; *Positif* (France) April 2011 p. 86

NOTES: Jennifer Jones was in talks for Colbert's part. Most of the Japanese soldiers in the film were played by Nisei veterans of the U.S. Army.

Under My Skin

20th Century–Fox; U.S. B&W 86 minutes; Premiered in New York on March 17, 1950

CREDITS: *Producer:* Casey Robinson; *Director:* Jean Negulesco; *Screenplay:* Casey Robinson; Based on the short story "My Old Man" by Ernest Hemingway; *Photography:* Joseph LaShelle; *Art Directors:* Lyle Wheeler, Maurice Hansford; *Set Decorators:* Thomas Little, Walter M. Scott; *Editor:* Dorothy Spencer; *Wardrobe Direction:* Charles Le Maire; *Music:* Daniele Amfitheatrof; *Orchestrators:* Maurice de Packh, Earle Hagen; *Makeup:* Ben Nye; *Special Photographic Effects:* Fred Sersen; *Sound:* George Leverett, Harry M. Leonard; *Hair Stylist:* Esperanza Corona; *Assistant Director:* Saul Wurzel; *Production Manager:* Robert Snody; *Technical Advisors:* André Hakim, Albert Morin, Annie Vivian Power; *Script Supervisor:* Rose Steinberg; *Translators:* Jacques Suremagne, Alberto Valentino; *Songs:* "Stranger in the Night," music by Alfred Newman, lyrics by Mack Gordon, French lyrics by Tanis Chandler; "Viendras tu ce soir?" music by Alfred Newman, lyrics by Jacques Surmagne; "La Seine," music by Guy LaFarge, lyrics by Flavien Monod and Guy LaFarge

CAST: John Garfield (Dan Butler), Micheline Presle (Paule Manet), Luther Adler (Louis Bork), Orley Lindgren (Joe Butler), Noel Drayton (George Gardner), A.A. Merola (Maurice), Ott George (Rico), Paul Bryar (Max), Harry Martin (Drake), Ann Codee (Henriette), Steven Geray (Bartender), Joseph Warfield (Rigoli Italian Jockey), Eugene Borden (Doctor), Loulette Sablon (Nurse), Ernesto Morelli (Hotel Clerk), Hans Herbert (Attendant), Gordon Clark (Barman), Frank Arnold (Official), Elizabeth Flournoy (Mother at Café), Mario Siletti (Italian Officer), Guy Zanette (Porter), Andre Charise (Gendarme), Esther Zeitlin (Flower Woman), Peter Camlin, Andre Charlot (Waiters), Jean Romaine, Beverly Thompson, Monique Chantel, Simone Corday (French Girls), Dusty Anderson (Girl in the Café)

PLOT: Dan Butler, a veteran jockey, rides to victory in a steeplechase race at Merano, Italy, while his 11-year-old son Joe goes wild with excitement. Another spectator, crooked track operator Louis Bork, feels differently. He's been double-crossed and he does not like it. That night Dan sees one of Louis' boys across the street from his hotel and sends Joe to the station to buy two tickets to Paris. Facing the music alone, Dan is manhandled by Louis and his boys. In Paris, Dan and Joe go to a café called Chez Paule to look up an old friend. The friend, meantime, has died, but his pretty young wife Paule, who now owns the cafe, orders Dan out. Dan goes and sees about his baggage, but leaves Joe at the café. Paule takes Joe to her apartment for dinner, where the boy confides he's anxious to return to America. She feels sorry for him and when he falls asleep goes back to the café. Dan breezes into the Chez Paule, but is again greeted bitterly. Paule tells him her husband was killed because of the trouble Dan brought him. She orders him to stay away. A few days pass before Dan and Joe again visit Paule. Louis Bork turns up, wanting the money he lost on the race Dan failed to throw. Dan promises to pay up as soon as he can. Sick with worry, Dan confides in Paule. He doesn't know what to do with his son who idolizes him even though he's broken every rule in the book, Dan gets a job at the Chantilly track and has a bet on a fixed race. Joe realizes that the race was crooked when he sees his father collect his winnings. He accuses his father of being a cheat and Dan takes the weeping boy to the railway station with the idea of sending him home to relatives in America. The next day, Joe returns; he just couldn't leave Dan. Joe and Paule are happy when they learn that Dan has bought a horse for the Gran Prix. They all plan to leave for America after the race. Bork insists that Dan throw the race, but Dan realizes Joe has his heart set on winning, and gets his jockey friend George Gardner to block out any jockey Louis has on his payroll. The race begins, George tries to block out Louis' stooge, but it is George who goes down. Dan comes down the stretch the winner, but as he streaks across the finish line, he crashes into a riderless mount. In the hospital, Joe and Paule see Dan once more, just before he dies. "He meant it about going home, Joe," says Paule. "Don't you think we owe it to him to take him there?" (Original press release source)

REVIEWS:

"Occasionally [*Under My Skin*] gives promise of getting away into the stretch, but then peters out into a slough of absurd sentiment and romance." *Variety,* March 15, 1950

"An interesting horse-racing melodrama [with] many emotional situations." *Harrison's Reports,* March 18, 1950

"The movie is a sentimental tear-jerker, a kind of literature to which Hemingway is not addicted." *The New Republic,* April 3, 1950

REVIEWS FOR JEAN NEGULESCO:

"Jean Negulesco imparts imaginative directorial touches to the proceedings, and gets real action punch from the splendid done steeplechase races." *The Hollywood Reporter,* March 10, 1950

"Jean Negulesco has staged [the story] acutely..." *N.Y. Herald Tribune*, March 18, 1950

"Negulesco has achieved his usual high polished blend of the sentimental and the tough, but in face of the script's inadequacies neither is convincing." *Film Monthly Bulletin,* April-May 1950

ADDITIONAL REVIEWS AND ARTICLES:

Daily Variety July 29, 1949, p. 8; *Hollywood Reporter* September 9, 1949, p. 13; *Los Angeles Times* September 26, 1949, p. 1; *Los Angeles Times* September 30, 1949, p. 1; *Motion Picture Herald Product Digest* March 11, 1950, p. 221;*The New York Times* March 18, 1950, p. 9; *Film Daily*

March 10, 1950, p. 8; *Boxoffice* March 18, 1950; *Cue* March 18, 1950; *The New Yorker* March 25, 1950, p. 100, *Today's Cinema* April 5, 1950; *Christian Century* May 24, 1950, p. 663, *Newsweek* April 3, 1950, p. 79; *Time* April 3, 1959, p. 90; *Commonweal* May 24, 1950, p. 629; *American Cinematographer* June 1950 p. 197; *The Rotarian* July 1950 p. 38; *Les Lettres Françaises* (France) December 2, 1950; *L'Écran Français* (France) December 20, 1950, p. 16; *Hollywood* (Italy), May 5, 1951; *Image et Son-La Revue du Cinéma* (France) October 1985 p. 28

NOTES: *Under My Skin* was originally titled *The Big Fall* and *The Great Fall*.

The Mudlark

20th Century–Fox; A Darryl F. Zanuck Presentation; U.S.–U.K. B&W 94 minutes; Premiered in London on October 30, 1950; Released in New York on December 24, 1950

CREDITS: *Producer:* Nunnally Johnson; *Director:* Jean Negulesco; *Screenplay:* Nunnally Johnson; Based on the novel by Theodore Bonnet; *Music:* William Alwyn played by the Royal Philharmonic Orchestra; *Conductor:* Muir Mathieson; *Photography:* George Perinal; *Art Director:* C. P. Norman; *Special Effects:* W. Percy Day; *Dialogue Coach:* George More O'Ferrall; *Editor:* Thelma Myers; *Sound Recordist:* Bustler Ambler; *Costumes:* Edward Stevenson, Margaret Furse; *Makeup:* Dave Aylott, Ben Nye; *Production Manager:* Frank Bevis; *History Advisor:* Cyril Hartman

CAST: Irene Dunne (Queen Victoria), Alec Guinness (Benjamin Disraeli), Andrew Ray (Wheeler, the Mudlark), Beatrice Campbell (Lady Emily Prior), Finlay Currie (John Brown), Anthony Steel (Lt. Charles McHatten), Raymond Lovell (Sgt. Footman Naseby), Marjorie Fielding (Lady Margaret Prior), Constance Smith (Kate Noonan), Edward Rigby (Watchman), Ronan O'Casey (Slattery), Robin Stevens (Herbert), William Strange (Sparrow), Kynaston Reeves (General Sir Henry Ponsonby), Wilfrid Hyde-White (Tucker), Ernest Clark (Hammond), Eric Messiter (Police Lt. Ash), Albert Whelan (Devoy), Alan Gordon (Disraeli's Valet), Grace Denbeigh Russell (Ross—Queen's Maid), Howard Douglas (Broom), Richmond Nairne (Didbit), George Dillon (Jailer), Leonard Sharp (Ben Fox), Vi Kaley (Mrs. Feeney), Freddie Watts (Iron George), Y. Yanai (Hook), Paul Garrard (Petey), Leonard Morris (Hooker Morgan), Marjorie Gresley (Meg Bownes), Bob Head (Dandy Fitch), Vi Stevens (Mrs. Dawkins), Pamela Arliss (Princess Helena), Ian Selby (Prince Frederick), Barry Jones (Speaker), Arthur Lucas, Joe Cunningham, William Senior (Members of Parliament), Maureen Janes, Patricia Davidson, Rose Howlett, Gertrude Kaye, Edna Morris, Rowena Gregory, Irene Gill, Patricia Hitchcock, Nicholas Amer, Stanley Osborne, Barry Steele (Servants), Peter Drury, Alan Judd, John Stamp (Sentries), Brian Moorhead, Myles Rudge, Patrick Young, Roy Nightingale, Howard Lang, Peter Dunlop, John Fitchin, Neville Gates, Campbell Gray (Footmen)

PLOT: For 15 years, ever since the death of Prince Consort, Queen Victoria has led a life of seclusion in Windsor Castle. Prime Minister Disraeli uses his considerable powers of persuasion to try and bring her closer to her subjects, but to no avail. One evening an orphaned mudlark, Wheeler, inspired by a medallion of the queen, manages to evade the guards and gain admission into the Castle. Hiding behind the curtains during dinner, he falls asleep but his snoring is heard and he is discovered. Questioned by the Castle staff who fear that this incident may be part of another plot to assassinate the queen, Wheeler is rescued by the queen's gillie and friend John Brown. Touched by the boy's interest in the queen and mellowed with whisky, Brown shows Wheeler around the castle and even permits him to sit on the throne. The officer of the day, Lieutenant McHatten, orders Wheeler arrested and he is sent to the Tower. The cunning Disraeli seizes on this incident to provide political capital to carry a government motion for social reform. In a brilliant speech he cites Wheeler, dirty, bedraggled, ignorant, as an example of how the impoverishment people are neglected. He wins the day. Wheeler is brought before Disraeli, who tells him that he is to go to Devonshire to receive a proper education. But at Paddington Station he loses his tutors and makes his way back to Windsor, still determined to see the queen. Disraeli is having an audience with Her Majesty when Wheeler is discovered. At first the queen tells Disraeli to take him away, but the prime minister suggests that this is one of her devoted subjects who regards her literally as the Mother of England. The queen's heart is softened by the open-mouthed awe with which the urchin regards her. Telling her prime minister to look after him, she gives Disraeli her consent to appear before her people again at the opening of a foundling hospital. (Original press release source)

REVIEWS:

"Let there be no illusions about *The Mudlark*. It is not a great picture. But it is a good one, and one that reflects credit on all who were associated with it." *Variety,* November 8, 1950

"The makers of *The Mudlark* treat [the story] solemnly and portentously, degrading the humor to facetiousness and turning the pathos into unctuous sentimentality: the result is, more than anything else, dull." *Monthly Film Bulletin,* December 1950

"*The Mudlark* is a heart-warming tale…. The picture rates high praise for its production quality, direction and acting, and its mixture of comedy, human interest and some excitement should have wide appeal." *Harrison's Reports,* December 2, 1950

REVIEWS FOR JEAN NEGULESCO:

"Negulesco has handled the theme with appealing sincerity and conviction and drawn some memorable performances from the players." *The Hollywood Reporter,* October 31, 1950

"Under the direction of Jean Negulesco, [the picture] reeks of distinction, a quality which comes near to robbing it of energy." *New York Herald Tribune,* December 29, 1950

"When Jean Negulesco … is following the young boy through the impressive expanses of Windsor Castle, he succeeds admirably in making his camera register the boy's astonishment and awe, and he also does pretty well with Finlay Currie, who turns in a fine performance as Victoria's gruff alcoholic gillie." *The New Yorker,* January 6, 1951

ADDITIONAL REVIEWS AND ARTICLES:

The New York Times February 26, 1950; *Variety* March 1, 1950; *Variety* March 6, 1950; *Daily Express* (U.K.), March 6, 1950; *The New York Times* March 19, 1950; *Variety* March 22, 1950; *The Evening Standard* (U.K.) April 4, 1950; *Hollywood Reporter* May 19, 1950, p. 11; *The Times* (U.K.) May 31, 1950; *The New York Times* June 20, 1950; *Hollywood Reporter* June 26, 1950, p. 2; *The New York Times* July 9, 1950, p. 5; *The Daily Mail* (U.K.) July 10, 1950, p. 3; *The Daily Express* (U.K.) July 10, 1950; *Hollywood Reporter* July 21, 1950, p. 11; *Picturegoer* July 22, 1950; *Life* September 11, 1950; *The New York Times* October 3, 1950; *Daily Graphic* (U.K.) October 3, 1950, p. 6; *The Daily Express* (U.K.) October 5, 1950; *The Daily Express* (U.K.) October 6, 1950; *The New York Times Magazine* October 15, 1950, p. 58–59; *The New York Times* October 31, 1950, p. 30; *The Daily Mirror* (U.K.) October 31, 1950; *The Daily Express* (U.K.) October 31, 1950; *Today's Cinema* November 1, 1950, pp. 13; *Boxoffice* November 4, 1950; *The Observer* (U.K.) November 6, 1950; *Today's Cinema* November 10, 1950, p. 7; *The Spectator* (U.K.), November 10, 1950, p. 462; *The Sunday Times* (U.K.) November 12, 1950; *Newsweek* November 13, 1950, p. 100; *Illustrated London News* November 18, 1950; *Hollywood Reporter* November 27, 1950, p. 3; *Daily Variety* November 27, 1950, p. 3; *Film Daily* November 28, 1950, p. 10; *Boxoffice* December 2, 1950; *Compass* December 2, 1950, p. 16; *Picturegoer* December 2, 1950; *Motion Picture Herald Product Digest* December 2, 1950, p. 597; *New York Post* December 10, 1950; *Commonweal* December 22, 1950, p. 278; *Saturday Review* December 23, 1950, p. 29; *Newsweek* December 25, 1950, p. 80; *The New York Times* December 25, 1950, p. 25; *New York World-Telegram* December 26, 1950, p. 23; *New York Post* December 26, 1950, p. 41; *The New York Times* December 29 1950 p. 30; *Film Forum* January 1951; *Films in Review* January 1951 p. 39–41; *Time* January 1, 1951, p. 60; *The Christian Science Monitor* January 9, 1951, p. 5; *Library Journal* January 1, 1951; *The New Yorker* January 6, 1951; *L.A. Examiner* January 3, 1951, sec. 2 p. 7; *The New York Times* January 7, 1951, p. 85; *Film Music Notes* January-February 1951 p. 10–11; *Modern Screen* March 1951 p. 12; *Modern Screen* May 1951 p. 6; *Cine Suisse* (Switzerland) June 6, 1951; *L' Écran Francais* (France) February 20, 1952, p. 9; *The Educational Screen* October 1955, pp. 346; *Illustrated London News* October 18, 1955; *New York Daily News* May 8, 1978, p. 6; *Film Comment* January-February 1980 p. 26

AWARDS AND HONORS:

Picturegoer Award U.K. 1951: *Won:* Gold Medal, Best Actor: Alec Guinness

Academy Awards: U.S. 1952: *Nominated:* Best Costume Design, Black and White: Edward Stevenson, Margaret Furse

Take Care of My Little Girl

20th Century–Fox; U.S. Technicolor 93 minutes; Premiered in Los Angeles on July 6, 1951

CREDITS: *Producer:* Julian Blaustein; *Director:* Jean Negulesco; *Screenplay:* Julius J. Epstein, Philip G. Epstein; Based on the novel by Peggy Goodin; *Photography:* Harry Jackson; *Art Direc-*

tors: Lyle Wheeler, Joseph C. Wright; *Set Decorators:* Thomas Little, Claude Carpenter; *Editor:* William Reynolds; *Wardrobe Director:* Charles Le Maire; *Costumes:* Travilla; *Music:* Alfred Newman; *Associate Music Director:* Ken Darby; *Orchestrator:* Edward Powell; *Makeup:* Ben Nye; *Special Photographic Effects:* Fred Sersen; *Sound:* George Leverett, Harry M. Leonard; *Assistant Director:* Art Lueker; *Technical Advisor:* Peggy Goodin; *Color Consultant:* Monroe W. Burbank; *Songs:* "The Lambs Are Coming," "The Old Maine Bell," "Here's to Our Lizzie," "Nighty Night, Delta Mu," "Sweet Dreams to You, Tri-U," "The Clasp of Hands," "Crown Us Gently, Gently," "To You, Sweetheart," "Lambs Are in the Clover," "Goodnight, Chi Eta, Goodnight" and "My Prince Will Come A'Riding," lyrics by Ken Darby

CAST: Jeanne Crain (Elizabeth Ericson), Dale Robertso (Joe Blake), Mitzi Gaynor (Adelaide Swanson), Jean Peters (Dallas Pruitt), Jeffrey Hunter (Chad Carnes), Betty Lynn (Marge Colby), Helen Westcott (Merry Coombs), Lenka Peterson (Ruth Gates), Carol Brannon (Casey Krause), Natalie Schafer (Mother Clark), Beverly Dennis (Janet Shaw), Kathleen Hughes (Jenny Barker), Peggy O'Connor (June), Marjorie Crosland (Olive Ericson), John Litel (John Ericson), Charlene Hardey (Ellie Stokes), Janet Stewart (Polly), Gail Davis (Thelma), Judy Walsh (Justine), Irene Martin (Marcia), Penny McGuiggan (Helen), Pattee Chapman (Paula), Mary Thomas (Vivian Brooks), Palma Shard (Georgette), Jean Romaine (Rosalyn), Margia Dean (Claire), William A. Mahan (Pete Grayson), Junc Alden (Girl in Gym), Billy Lechner (Bellboy), George Nader (Jack Gruber), Grandon Rhodes (Prof. Benson), Harry Harvey (Clerk), Virginia Hunt (Lyn Hippenstahl), Eleanor Lawson, Shirley Tegge (Freshmen), Charles Conrad (Ticket Agent), Margaret Field (Girl), King Donovan (Cab Driver), Pat Goldin (Porter)

PLOT: Lovely Liz Ericson and her hometown friend Janet Shaw, plain-looking and from humble stock, are deeply impressed with Midwestern University on their arrival as freshmen. At the hotel they meet Adelaide Swanson, the breezy daughter of a wealthy Western businessman. Liz soon gets an invitation from Marge Colby to visit her at Tri U House. The Tri U president and snobbish Dallas Pruitt greet the freshmen; Liz is accepted but not Janet who, broken-hearted, goes home. Liz is taken out by Joe Blake, a senior undergraduate who fought in the war and belongs to no fraternity. She also meets Chad Carnes, an undergraduate with a reputation. One day he asks for Liz's help: It is important for him to graduate and he finds he is unable to do justice to the French paper. With Liz's help, he manages to switch examination papers. Chad, deeply grateful, gives her his fraternity pin. During initiation week, the pledges have to go through many embarrassing ordeals. One evening Liz, set a task, meets Joe, who persuades her to drop into a non-fraternity gathering where a party is taking place. Chad crashes in and accuses Liz of being unfaithful to her sorority. Chad and Joe come to blows. Liz takes off the fraternity pin Chad has given her and leaves it on the mantelpiece. When she arrives home, Liz discovers that there is some concern about Ruth, a shy, plain girl who had been asked to renounce her pledge to Tri U. Liz and Joe find her in the street trying to fulfill her pledge duties. She is in a state of collapse. A doctor finds that she has pneumonia. Liz threatens to turn in her sorority pin but Dallas and the president promise that if she agrees not to do this, Ruth will be welcome back when she recovers. But Liz has had enough of sororities. She shakes her head, gives up her pin and joins Joe, who is waiting for her outside. (Original press release source)

REVIEWS:

"Although the story is treated in a serious vein, it does have its light touches throughout and is further enhanced by a pleasant romantic interest. [It's] a diverting entertainment." *Harrison's Reports,* June 16, 1951

"Lightweight story has a script, however, that has fresh situations and some good dialog; plus an engaging cast of attractive youngsters and pretty Jeanne Crain enhanced by Technicolor." *Variety,* July 13, 1951

"[T]he one passing criticism of the story structure of this film is that it goes by romantic conventions, for all the novelty of its theme…. This film may hurt the sorority business, but it should do the box office plenty of good." *The New York Times,* July 19, 1951

REVIEWS FOR JEAN NEGULESCO:

"…Negulesco has paced his picture well, and if the tempest that seethes in his teapot is less than epic it at least has the virtue of being well brewed." *Saturday Review,* June 2, 1951

"Director Jean Negulesco brings [most of the details] home thoroughly effective touches and fine performances by a hand-picked cast." *The Hollywood Reporter,* June 12, 1951

"The script spreads its material, and particularly its humor, rather thinly and Jean Negulesco's handling is characterless and lacks of definition." *Monthly Film Bulletin,* February 1952

ADDITIONAL REVIEWS AND ARTICLES:
Hollywood Reporter February 28, 1950, p. 2; *New York Herald Tribune* September 25, 1950; *Hollywood Reporter* October 12, 1950, p. 6; *Hollywood Reporter* October 13, 1950, p. 13; *Hollywood Reporter* November 10, 1950, p. 13; *Hollywood Reporter* November 13, 1950, p. 6; *Daily Variety* December 13, 1950; *Hollywood Reporter* December 26, 1950, p. 7; *Screenland* April 1951 p. 28; *Modern Screen* May 1951 p. 104; *Scholastic* May 2, 1951; *Hollywood Reporter* May 29, 1951, p. 2; *Look* June 5, 1951, p. 40–43; *Film Daily* June 13, 1951, p. 7; *Daily Boston Globe* June 16, 1951; *Boxoffice* June 16, 1951, p. 1269; *Motion Picture Herald Product Digest* June 16, 1951, p. 887; *Screenland* July 1951 p. 16; *Los Angeles Examiner* July 7, 1951; *Los Angeles Times* July 7, 1951; *Hollywood Citizen-News* July 10, 1951; *Newsweek* July 16, 1951, p. 85; *New York Times* July 18, 1951, p. 20; *Hollywood Reporter* July 19 1951 p. 1; *New York Herald Tribune* July 19 1951; *Time* July 23, 1951, p. 84; *Commonweal* July 27, 1951; *The New Yorker* July 28, 1951, p. 74; *The Nation* August 11 1951 p. 118; *Picturegoer* February 9, 1952; *Modern Screen* June 1952 p. 56; *Modern Screen* January 1953 p. 47

Phone Call from a Stranger

20th Century–Fox; U.S. B&W 96 minutes; Premiered in New York on January 31, 1952

CREDITS: *Producer:* Nunnally Johnson; *Director:* Jean Negulesco; *Screenplay:* Nunnally Johnson; Based on the *McCall's* story by I.A.R. Wylie; *Music:* Franz Waxman; *Photography:* Milton Krasner; *Art Directors:* Lyle Wheeler, J. Russell Spencer; *Set Decorators:* Thomas Little, Bruce Macdonald; *Editor:* Hugh Fowler; *Wardrobe Director:* Charles Le Maire; *Costumes:* Elois Jenssen; *Orchestrators:* Bernard Mayers; Leonid Raab; *Makeup:* Ben Nye; *Special Photographic Effects:* Ray Kellogg; *Sound:* Eugene Grossman; Roger Heman; *Assistant Director:* Dick Maybery

CAST: Shelley Winters (Binky Gay aka Bianca Carr), Gary Merrill (David Trask), Michael Rennie (Dr. Bob Fortness), Keenan Wynn (Eddie Hoke), Evelyn Varden (Sally Carr), Warren Stevens (Marty Nelson), Beatrice Straight (Claire Fortness), Ted Donaldson (Jerry Fortness), Craig Stevens (Mike Carr), Helen Westcott (Jane Trask), Bette Davis (Marie Hoke), Sidney Perkins (Stewardess), Hugh Beaumont (Dr. Tim Brooks), Thomas Jackson (Mr. Sawyer), Harry Cheshire (Dr. Fletcher), Tom Powers (Dr. Fernwood), Freeman Lusk (Thompson), George Eldredge (Doctor), Nester Paiva (Headwaiter), Elizabeth Flournoy (Hostess), John Hedloe (Ticket Agent), Jack Narz (Flight Announcer), George Nader (Pilot), William Neff (Co-pilot), Robert A. Davis (Henry), John Doucette (Bartender), Cliff Clark (Watchman), Ken Christy (Guard), Betty Jane Howarth (Hat Check Girl), Lillian Hamilton, Ruth Robinson (Nurses), Billy McLean (Bellboy), Jack Daley (Doorman), Keith Hetherington (Travel Agent)

PLOT: After hearing a confession from his wife Jane that she had had an affair with another man, lawyer David Trask decides that he can no longer live with her. He takes a plane to Los Angeles. On the plane he meets Binky Gay, a flashy singer who can't make the grade on Broadway; a quiet troubled doctor, Robert Fortness; and Eddie Hoke, a loud-mouthed, clowning salesman. Bad weather forces the plane down at Las Vegas and while waiting for the weather to improve, the four exchange cards and agree to have a periodical reunion. Fortness confides in Trask that he is on his way to confess to the district attorney that five years ago he cause the death of a fellow doctor and two men in another car when he crashed under the influence of drink. When he learned in the hospital that hey were dead, he declared that the other doctor had been driving. Mrs. Fortness substantiated this, although she knew it to be false. Eddie Hoke is inordinately proud of his beautiful wife Marie and is fond of showing her photographs to the others, who find it hard to imagine what such a lovely girl sees in this wearisome vulgarian. When the plane takes off again, Binky tells Trask that she can't get along with her mother-in-law Sally Carr, an old-time music hall singer. She had left her husband for that reason but was now returning. The plane again runs into bad weather and crashes. There is only one survivor from the four friends, Trask, and he feels it's his duty to call on the relatives of the other three. Mrs. Fortness he finds in great distress. Her son Jerry has run away on learning of his father's death. Track goes in search of the boy and finds him as he is trying to get to South America. He takes Jerry back to his mother and convinces him that his father has been unhappy because he had avoided a manslaughter charge and that this feeling of holding a guilty secret had created a breach between husband and wife; her loyal support of him is proof of her love. Jerry and his mother are reconciled. Then he calls Mrs. Carr, Binky's mother-in-law, who had not yet heard of Binky's death. She informs Trask that Mike, her son, had started divorce proceedings. After painting a wholly untrue portrait of Binky, she is told an equally untrue story by Trask in which Binky's generosity puts Mrs. Carr to shame. Finally Trask visits Mrs. Hoke, a bedridden cripple. She says that her husband was considered vulgar and lacking in taste. She had tired of him and had run away with another man. En route she had an accident that paralyzed her. Her frightened lover had abandoned her but Edie, ever loyal, had rushed to the hospital, forgiven everything and taken her back. Mrs. Hoke suspects that Trask is facing problems of his own. Shaken by her story, Trask tells her of his wife's affair and asks permission to use the telephone. He tells his overjoyed wife that he is coming home. (Original press release source)

REVIEWS:

"*Phone Call from a Stranger* is one of those polished conversation pieces which Hollywood turns out by the dozen and, by some curious alchemy, makes into wonderfully good films." *The Spectator,* January 18, 1952

"Slick is perhaps the best word to describe the [film]. So slick; indeed; is the whole thing—so smooth and efficiently contrived to fit and run with the precision of a beautifully made machine—that it very soon gives the impression of being wholly mechanical; picked up from a storyteller's blueprints rather than from the scroll of life." *The New York Times,* February 2, 1952

"This theatrically written film contains four novelettes for the price of one. The handling is uninteresting and the dialogue's veneer of smartness cannot disguise the hokum of the situations and the stereotyped characters." *Monthly Film Bulletin,* March 1952

REVIEWS FOR JEAN NEGULESCO:

"Taste is Negulesco's distinguishing mark as he weaves *Phone Call* through its many tragic passages without ever permitting them to descend to the maudlin." *The Hollywood Reporter,* January 8, 1952

"Jean Negulesco's direction is strong in handling both players and story." *Variety,* January 9, 1952

"Jean Negulesco's direction breathes vitality into the interpretation of the screenplay and weaves in and out of the time lapses; flashbacks, etc., with the ease and smoothness of a goldfish circling a bowl." *Independent Film Bulletin,* January 28, 1952

ADDITIONAL REVIEWS AND ARTICLES:

Hollywood Reporter February 2, 1951, p. 1; *Hollywood Reporter* August 10, 1951, p. 2; *Hollywood Reporter* August 20, 1951, p. 6; *Hollywood Reporter* August 21, 1951, p. 5.*Hollywood Reporter* August 27, 1951, p. 10; *Hollywood Reporter* August 30, 1951, p. 10; *Hollywood Reporter* September 4, 1951 p. 8; *Hollywood Reporter* September 5, 1951, p. 10; *Hollywood Reporter* September 14, 1951, p. 11; *Motion Picture Daily* January 8, 1952; *Film Daily* January 10, 1952, p. 8; *Boxoffice* January 12, 1952; *Harrison's Reports* January 12, 1952, p. 7; *Motion Picture Herald Product Digest* January 12, 1952, p. 1185; *The Times* (U.K.) January 21, 1952, p. 2; *New York Times* January 31, 1952, p. 23; *Newsweek* February 4, 1952, p. 78–79; *The New Yorker* February 9, 1952, p. 102; *Commonweal* February 11, 1952, p. 471; *The New Republic* February 11, 1952, p. 22; *Picturegoer* February 16, 1952; *Time* February 18, 1952, p. 86; *Los Angeles Examiner* February 21, 1952; *Theatre Arts* March 1952 p. 73; *Cahiers du Cinéma* (France) November 1952; *Les Lettres Françaises* (France) November 30, 1952; *Film Complet* (France) March 5, 1953

AWARDS AND HONORS:

Venice Film Festival: Italy 1952: *Nominated* Golden Lion: Jean Negulesco.

Won Golden Osella: Best Original *Screenplay:* Nunnally Johnson

Lydia Bailey

20th Century–Fox; U.S. Technicolor 89 minutes; World premiere in Port au Prince, Haiti, on May 4, 1952; Premiered in New York on May 30, 1952

CREDITS: *Producer:* Jules Schermer; *Director:* Jean Negulesco: *Screenplay:* Michael Blankfort, Philip Dunne; Based on the novel by Kenneth Roberts; *Photography:* Harry Jackson; *Art Directors:* Lyle Wheeler, J. Russell Spencer; *Editor:* Dorothy Spencer; *Set Decorators:* Thomas Little, Paul S. Fox; *Wardrobe Director:* Charles Le Maire; *Costumes:* Travilla; *Music:* Hugo Friedhofer; *Musical Director:* Lionel Newman, *Orchestrator:* Edward Powell; *Sound:* E. Clayton Ward, Harry M.

Leonard; *Special Photographic Effects:* Fred Sersen, Ray Kellogg; *Choreography:* Jack Cole; *Makeup:* Ben Nye, Harry Maret; *Assistant Director:* Richard Maybery; *Unit Production Manager:* Bill Eckhardt; *Technical Advisors:* Le Roi Antoine, Zori Jannings; *Fencing Instructor:* Fred Cavens; *Color Consultant:* Leonard Doss

CAST: Dale Robertson (Albion Hamlin), Anne Francis (Lydia Bailey), Charles Korvin (Colonel Gabriel D'Autremont), William Marshall (King Dick), Luis Van Rooten (Gen. Charles LeClerc), Adeline de Walt Reynold (Antoinette D'Autremont), Angos Perez (Paul D'Autremont), Bob Evans (Soldier), Gladys Holland (Pauline Bonaparte), Will Wright (Consul), Roy E. Glenn (Mirabeau), Ken Renard (Toussaint L'Ouverture), Juanita Moore (Marie), Carmen de Lavallade, Alvin Ailey (Specialty Dancer), Jack Cole (Dancer), Martin Wilkins (Voodoo Priest), Albert Morin (Lieutenant), William Washington (Deckhand), Clancy Cooper (Codman), Muriel Bledsoe (Ametiste), Mildred Boyd (Marmeline), Marjorie Elliott (Rosida), Suzette Harbin (Floreal), Roz Hayes (Aspodelle), Dolores Mallory (Claircine), Lena Torrence (Attenaire), Frances Williams (Cloryphene), Ken Terrell (Barbe), Louis Mercier (Millet), William Walker (General La Plume), Fred Cavens (Fencing Instructor), Shelby Bacon (King Dick's Son), Rene Beard (Nero), Marcelle Corday (Frenchwoman), Jay Brooks, Joel Fluellen, Phil Thomas (Toussaint's Aides), Eugene Bullard, Paul Bryar (Guards), Alfred Grant (Mirabeau's Aide), Willa Pearl Curtis (Refugee), Joanne Jordan (Lady-in-waiting), Baynes Barron, Maurice Marsac (Sentries), Morris Buchanan (Servant), Elzie Emanuel (Soldier), Vince M. Townsend (General), The Royal Caribbean Singers (Plantation Singers)

PLOT: In the year 1802 the natives of Haiti, having tasted freedom from French rule, determine to resist any new French landing on their shores. A young Boston lawyer, Albion Hamlin, arrives in search of an American girl, Lydia Bailey, whose signature he needs on documents which would turn her dead father's holdings in the U.S. over the government, as stipulated in his will. A powerful native, King Dick, attacks Hamlin, rendering him unconscious. When he recovers, Hamlin convinces King Dick that he is no spy and enlists his help in seeking out Lydia, who lives at the plantation of her fiancé Gabriel D'Autremont, one of Napoleon's agents. To reach the plantation, they must cross jungle country infested by the murderous followers of Mirabeau, a native renegade. Hamlin stains his body with a brown dye and sets out, with King Dick masquerading as his servant. Ambushed by Mirabeau's men, they separate in order to escape. On reaching D'Autremont property, Hamlin finds Lydia who, because of her father's past conduct, has surrendered all her loyalties to the U.S. and considers herself French. She refuses to sign the documents. King Dick is led in as a prisoner but Hamlin vouches for him and he is set free. Native drums beat out a war chant and the aged Madame D'Autremont begs Hamlin to take Lydia away. Lydia offers to sign the documents only if Hamlin will take her native servant Marie back to America where her sweetheart lives. D'Autremont schemes with a traitor, General LaPlume, who is planning to put the Haitian ports in the hands of the French. When LaPlume's body is discovered, bloodhounds are put on the trail and attack King Dick who, with his strength and the enormous stick he carries, beats them off. He runs away from the estate followed by Hamlin. Reaching the coast as French gunboats are shelling shore batteries and knowing that Mirabeau's natives intend to burn down D'Autremont's chateau, Hamlin goes to rescue Lydia. Madame D'Autremont is lying in bed near death, but Hamlin leads Lydia, D'Autremont's young son by a former marriage and Marie out of the chateau just as the natives are closing in. The three white people stain themselves brown. Mirabeau's men set fire to the chateau and search for Lydia, the child and Hamlin. As the pursuers approach, Hamlin sends the two women and the child over a rope bridge which he cuts down when they are safely across. He himself jumps into the cascading water below. Badly wounded, he is picked up by natives loyal to the freedom-loving native General Toussaint L'Overture. That evening Touissant is due at Cap Francais where the French Commandant General LeClerc and his wife Pauline, Napoleon's sister, are giving a ball. There a treaty is to be signed. As Toussaint is leaving, Marie, who with Lydia and the boy has reached Cap Francais in safety, arrives with the news that Toussaint will be shot on arrival. Hamlin takes his place. When D'Autremont at Cap Francais suggests to LeClerc that the American who has come instead of Toussaint should be shot, Lydia leaps to his defense. Eventually it is arranged that Hamlin, under escort, will be conducted to an American ship now in port. As he led away, his old friend King Dick comes to the rescue. Between them they fight off the guards. Receiving word that Hamlin has been captured, Toussaint has no option but to order his men, who surround the town, to burn Cap Francais down. Hamlin is rescuing Lydia, the boy and Marie from their blazing house when D'Autremont sees him and fires. He kills his own boy. Overcome with grief, he allows the other three to escape to the port where King Dick has obtained a boat for them, ready to sail back to America. (Original press release source)

REVIEWS:

"This film has effective moments ... but the story skirts the borders of melodrama a little to closely to allow its complete acceptance." *The London Times,* May 19, 1952

"[T]his period adventure, which merely nods to history on occasion, succeeds in being a briskly paced, swashbuckling yarn..." *The New York Times,* May 31, 1952

"A fast adventure yarn.... Technically, this is one of the best color productions to come out of Hollywood in a long time." *American Cinematographer,* July 1952

REVIEWS FOR JEAN NEGULESCO:

"Jean Negulesco's smooth job of megging keeps the action high and the tempo fast, yet allows full scope for character development so that the personal problems of the principals concerned are always paramount, yet the sweeping historic background is never lost in the individual heroics." *The Hollywood Reporter,* May 28, 1952

"Story seldom lags under Jean Negulesco's breezy direction, which handles the cast from voodoo scenes to chase sequences with equal dexterity." *Variety,* May 28, 1952

"Under Jean Negulesco's direction it is played in the spirit of romantic fiction, with simple, streamlined characters in the hairbreadth escapes in one affray after another." *New York Herald Tribune,* May 31, 1952

ADDITIONAL REVIEWS AND ARTICLES:

Daily Variety September 23, 1946; *Variety* September 25, 1946; *Hollywood Reporter* November 15, 1946; *New York Herald Tribune* February 17, 1947; *Hollywood Reporter* February 26, 1947; *Hollywood Reporter* June 21, 1949, p. 1; *Los Angeles Times* November 9, 1950; *Hollywood Reporter* November 9, 50 p. 1; *Los Angeles Examiner* November 14, 1950; *Los Angeles Time* April 12, 1951; *Hollywood Reporter* May 2, 1951, p. 10; *Boxoffice* May 5, 1951; *Hollywood Reporter* May 14, 1951, p. 4; *Hollywood Reporter* June 4, 1951, p. 1; *Hollywood Reporter* June 6, 1951, p. 2; *Hollywood Reporter* June 8, 1951, p. 11; *Hollywood Reporter* June 11, 1951, p. 4; *Hollywood Reporter* June 19, 1951, p. 4; Hollywood Reporter June 20, 1951, p. 3; *Hollywood Reporter* June 22, 1951, p. 7; *Hollywood Reporter* June 25, 1951, p. 9; *Hollywood Reporter* June 26, 1951, p. 7; *Hollywood Reporter* June 27, 1951, p. 4; *Hollywood Reporter* July 12, 1951, p. 6; *Hollywood Reporter* July 18, 1951, p. 6; *Hollywood Reporter* July 20, 1951, p. 13; *Hollywood Reporter* August 1, 1951, p. 5; *Hollywood Reporter* October 4, 1951, p. 12; *Hollywood Reporter* October 12, 1951, p. 8; *Ebony* January 1, 1952, p. 39; *Motion Picture Herald* March 1, 1952, p. 1255; *Today's Cinema* April 9, 1952, p. 15; *Kinematograph Weekly* April 10, 1952, p. 12; *Hollywood Reporter* April 22, 1952, p. 2; *Motion Picture Herald* May 10, 1952, p. 35; *Jet* May 22, 1952, p. 11; *The New York Times* May 30, 1952, p. 11; *Motion Picture Herald Production Digest* May 31, 1952, p. 1381; *Harrison's Reports* May 31, 1952, p. 86, *Cue* May 31, 1952; *Monthly Film Bulletin* June 1952 p. 81; *Film Daily* June 2, 1952, p. 6; *Newsweek* June 9, 1952, p. 89; *Time* June 16, 1952, p. 98; *The Spectator* (U.K.) June 16, 1952, p. 640; *Saturday Review* June 21, 1952, p. 33; *Los Angeles Examiner* June 28, 1952; *Boxoffice* June 28, 1952, *Picturegoer* July 19, 1952; *Boxoffice* October 4, 1952; *Cahiers du Cinéma* (France) January 1953 p. 20–25

NOTES: The picture was also known with the title *Storm in Haiti.*

Lure of the Wilderness

20th Century–Fox; U.S. Technicolor 93 minutes; World premiere in Waycross, Georgia, on July 16, 1952

CREDITS: *Producer:* Robert L. Jacks; *Associate Producer:* Robert D. Webb; *Director:* Jean Negulesco; *Screenplay:* Louis Lantz; Based on the novel *Swamp Water* by Vereen Bell; *Photography:* Edward Cronjager; *Art Directors:* Lyle Wheeler, Addison Hehr; *Set Decorators:* Thomas Little, Fred J. Rode; *Editor:* Barbara McLean; *Wardrobe Director:* Charles Le Maire; *Costumes:* Dorothy Jeakins; *Music:* Franz Waxman; *Orchestrator:* Leonid Raab; *Makeup:* Ben Nye; *Special Photographic Effects:* Ray Kellogg; *Sound:* Alfred Bruzlin; Harry M. Leonard; *Assistant Directors:* Joe Rickards, Robert D. Webb; *Color Consultant:* Leonard Doss; *Song:* "Starry Hill": music and lyrics by Ken Darby.

CAST: Jean Peters (Laurie Harper), Jeffrey

Hunter (Ben Tyler), Constance Smith (Noreen McGowan), Walter Brennan (Jim Harper), Tom Tully (Zack Tyler), Harry Shannon (Pat McGowan), Will Wright (Sheriff Clem Brink), Jack Elam (Dave Longden), Harry Carter (Ned Tyler), Pat Hogan (Harry Longden), Al Thompson (Shep Rigby), Robert Adler (Will Stone), Sherman Sanders (Square Dance Caller), Robert Karnes (Jack Doran), George Spaulding (Sloane), Walter Taylor (Sheriff Jepson), Ted Jordan (Young Man), Danny Borage (Musician), Norman Field (Deputy Sheriff), George Spaulding (Sloan), Dale Robertson (Narrator)

PLOT: The year is 1910 and the Okefenokee swamp in Georgia is considered a death trap to those living on the outskirts. Young Ben Tyler and his father are searching for two lost trappers when Ben's dog, Careless, spots a deer and swims away. Ben's father tries to dissuade Ben from returning to the swamp to find the dog, as does his fiancée Noreen and the two shiftless Longden brothers, Dave and Harry. But Ben does return and that night is clubbed into unconsciousness. On waking in the morning, he finds himself prisoner of Jim Harper and his daughter Laurie. Careless is with them. Laurie wants to kill Ben, but Jim prevents her. Jim explains that eight years ago he'd been unjustly accused by Dave and Harry Longden of the murder of their brother Bill and a man named Sam Black. Actually Jim had shot Bill in self-defense and the Longdens had murdered Black. When the sheriff allowed a lynch party to get out of hand, Jim fled to the swamp with his wife and daughter. Mrs. Harper had died but Jim and Laurie have existed there ever since. Jim is willing to return if he is given a fair trial. Ben promises to arrange this although Laurie is distrustful of everyone, including Ben. Jim gives a bundle of skins to pay for the legal cost of the trail and shows him the way out of the swamp. On returning home, Ben is turned out of the house by his father when he learns that his son intends to go back to the swamp. After selling the skins, Ben finds that the proceeds are not sufficient to pay the lawyer's fees. He buys Laurie a frock and Jim a box of cigars and, with these presents, returns to the swamp to get more otter skins for the fees. Laurie, delighted with the frock, is fascinated by Ben's description of a dance to be held on the mainland but, fearful that her identity might be discovered, will not accept his invitation. One day, Ben falls on a tree root and is knocked unconscious in the water. Jim's quick intervention saves the boy from being killed by an alligator. At the dance, Ben is furious when he sees that Noreen is dancing continuously with Jack Doran; but suddenly he sees Laurie who has been brought ashore by her father. Now Noreen is jealous. She recognizes the dress Laurie is wearing as one which has been displayed in the shop just before Ben returned to the swamp, and puts two and two together. Furious, Noreen tells Laurie that Ben told her that she and her father were hiding in the swamp. The sheriff and the Longdens challenge Ben, who refuses to lead them to the Harpers. They then subject him to repeat ducklings in the creek and his life is only saved by the appearance of his father. When Ben returns to the swamp with the legal documents, he finds that the Harpers do not trust him. When the documents are proven genuine, they relent. The three head out for the mainland but the Longdens ambush the party, wounding Jim in the leg. Once again Laurie and Jim believe that Ben has trapped them. Only when he exposes himself and is fired on do they believe him. Laurie's knowledge of the swamp proves invaluable. She lured the Longdens on to the quicksand which swallows up Dave. Harry is taken prisoner. At the entrance to the swamp, the sheriff, Ben's father and the local townspeople welcome the party knowing that justice has been done. (Original press release source)

REVIEWS:
"The fascinating background of the great Okefenokee swamp in Georgia, enhanced by Technicolor photography, adds much to the entertainment values of this exciting adventure melodrama.... The direction and acting are competent, and the color photography is pleasing." *Harrison's Reports,* July 26, 1952

"The basic passions with which the novel was concerned do not run as rampant this version as they did in the earlier screen treatment." *Variety,* July 30, 1952

"[W]ith the chilled menace of the swamplands that Fox has got into this film, it hasn't got into a story or acting that carries any conviction at all." *The New York Times,* October 4, 1952

REVIEW FOR JEAN NEGULESCO:
"Jean Negulesco does a splendid megging job, drawing out fine performances from his players and setting a taut, unhurried pace that allows full appreciation of the beauty of the surroundings yet keeps the dramatic story moving along

at an engrossing rate." *The Hollywood Reporter*, July 24, 1952

"A sound; fast-moving; adventure packed scripted was milked for the last drop of his dramatic possibilities by the sterling cast and the skilful direction contributed by Jean Negulesco." *Boxoffice*, August 2, 1952

"This time the hand of Negulesco lies too heavily on it..." *Monthly Film Bulletin*, October 1952

ADDITIONAL REVIEWS AND ARTICLES:

Los Angeles Times September 5, 1951; *Hollywood Reporter* October 9, 1951, p. 1; *Hollywood Reporter* October 31, 1951, p. 1; *Hollywood Reporter* November 2, 1951, p. 15; *New York Times* November 11, 1951; *Hollywood Reporter* November 16, 1951, p. 8; *Hollywood Reporter* November 30, 1951, p. 9; *Hollywood Reporter* January 4, 1952, p. 8; *Hollywood Reporter* January 7, 1952, p. 2; *Hollywood Reporter* February 1, 1952, p. 8; *Hollywood Reporter* February 7, 1952, p. 5; *Hollywood Reporter* April 17 1952 p. 4; *Motion Picture Herald* April 19 1952; p. 1322; *Newsweek* June 30, 1952, p. 100; *Hollywood Reporter* July 11, 1952, p. 11; *Motion Picture Herald Product Digest* July 26, 1952, p. 1461–1462; *Saturday Review* July 26 1952 p. 26; *Motion Picture Daily* July 29 1952; *Film Daily* August 4 1952 p. 10; *Daily Film Renter* August 20 1952 p. 6; *Today's Cinema* August 20, 1952, p. 7; *Kinematograph Weekly* August 21, 1952, p. 20; *Cosmopolitan* September 1952 p. 15–17; *Time* September 8, 1952, p. 108; *Los Angeles Mirror* September 11, 1952; *Los Angeles Times* September 12, 1952; *Los Angeles Examiner* September 12, 1952; *Cleveland Plain Dealer Pictorial Magazine* September 28, 1952, p. 22; *New York Herald Tribune* October 4, 1952; *Film Complet* (France) July 30, 1953

NOTES: The working titles of this film were *Cry of the Swamp*, *Swamp Girl* and *The Land of the Trembling Earth*. 20th Century-Fox originally announced Debra Paget as the film's star.

O. Henry's Full House

20th Century–Fox; U.S. B&W 117 minutes; World premiere in Greensboro, North Carolina, on August 7, 1952

CREDITS: *Producer:* André Hakim; *Directors:* Henry Koster ("The Cop and the Anthem"), Henry Hathaway ("The Clarion Call" [and prologue and narration]), Jean Negulesco ("The Last Leaf"), Howard Hawks ("The Ransom of Red Chief"), Henry King ("The Gift of the Magi"); *Screenplays:* Lamar Trotti ("The Cop and the Anthem"), Richard Breen ("The Clarion Call"), Ivan Goff and Ben Roberts ("The Last Leaf"), Walter Bullock and Philip Dunne ("The Gift of the Magi"), Nunnally Johnson ("The Ransom of Red Chief"); Based on the short stories "The Cop and the Anthem," "The Clarion Call," "The Last Leaf," "The Ransom of Red Chief" and "The Gift of the Magi" by O. Henry; *Photography:* Lloyd Ahern ("The Cop and the Anthem"), Lucien Ballard ("The Clarion Call"), Joe MacDonald ("The Last Leaf" and "The Gift of the Magi"), Milton Krasner ("The Ransom of Red Chief"); *Art Directors:* Lyle Wheeler, Chester Gore, Addison Hehr, Richard Irvine, Joseph C. Wright; *Editors:* Nick DeMaggio ("The Cop and the Anthem," "The Clarion Call and "The Last Leaf"), William B. Murphy ("The Ransom of Red Chief"), Barbara McLean ("The Gift of the Magi"); *Music:* Alfred Newman; *Vocal Director:* Ken Darby; *Orchestrator:* Edward B. Powell; *Sound:* Harry M. Leonard, W.D. Flick, Eugene Grossman, Winston H. Leverett, Alfred Bruzlin; *Unit Manager:* Abe Steinberg; *Assistant Directors:* Dave Silver ("The Clarion Call"), Henry Weinberger ("The Gift of the Magi"), Jasper Blystone and Erich von Stroheim, Jr. ("The Last Leaf"), Paul Helmick ("The Ransom of Red Chief"), Tom Connors, Jr. ("The Ransom of Red Chief"), *Wardrobe:* Sam Benson, Charles Le Maire; *Dialogue Directors:* Lorry Sherwood, Stanley Scheuer; *Unit Manager:* Abe Steinberg; *Songs:* "Bringing in the Sheaves," words by Knowles Shaw; music by George Minor; "De Camptown Races," words and music by Stephen Collins Foster; "O Little Town of Bethlehem," words by Phillips Brooks, music by Lewis M. Redner; "Hark the Herald Angels Sing," words by Charles Wesley; music by Felix Mendelssohn

CAST: John Steinbeck (Narrator)

Prologue: Tyler McVey (O. Henry), Phil Tully (Guard), Carl Betz (Jimmie Valentine), Donna Lee Hickey (Mother), Phil Arnold (Convict), "The Cop and the Anthem": Charles Laughton (Soapy Throckmorton), Marilyn Monroe (Streetwalker), David Wayne (Horace Truesdale), Thomas Browne Henry (Manager)

"The Clarion Call": Dale Robertson (Barney Woods), Richard Widmark (Johnny Kernan), Joyce MacKenzie (Hazel Woods), Richard Rober (Chief of Detectives), Will Wright (Manager), Abe Dinovitch

"The Ransom of Red Chief": Fred Allen (Sam "Slick" Brown), Oscar Levant (William Smith),

Lee Aaker (J.B. Dorset), Irving Bacon (Ebenezer Dorset), Kathleen Freeman (Mrs. Dorset), Gloria Gordon (Ellie Mae)

"The Gift of the Magi": Jeanne Crain (Della Young), Farley Granger (Jim Young), Fred Kelsey (Mr. Schultz—"Santa Claus"), Sig Ruman (Menkie), Harry Hayden (A.J. Crump), Richard Hylton (Bill), Richard Allan (Pete), Fritz Feld (Maurice)

"The Last Leaf": Anne Baxter (Joanna Goodwin), Jean Peters (Susan Goodwin), Gregory Ratoff (Behrman), Richard Garrick (Doctor), Steven Geray (Boris Radolf), Warren Stevens (Druggist), Martha Wentworth (Mrs. O'Brien), Ruth Warren (Neighbor), Bert Hicks (Sheldon Sidney), Don Kohler (Secretary), Beverly Thompson (Girl), Hal J. Smith (Dandy)

PLOT: John Steinbeck introduces each of the five episodes based on short stories by William Sidney Porter, known as O. Henry: "The Cop and the Anthem," "The Clarion Call," "The Ransom of Red Chief," "The Gift of the Magi" and "The Last Leaf":

Negulesco's "The Last Leaf" is the tale of Joanna Goodwin a jilted girl without the will to live because of an unhappy love affair. She watches the leaves wither in the late fall wind. In her delirious state, she starts to believe that she will die when the last leaf falls from a vine on a wall opposite her window. Winter arrives and the leaves are blown away, one by one, until a single leaf remains, persistently sticking to the wall. It doesn't die and its reassuring presence gives Joanna hope. She recovers only to find out, upon close inspection, that the leaf is a creation of Behrman, an impoverished artist who had befriended her and her sister Susan. Behrman did it so that Joanna would hang on to life. The sisters learn that the poor painter had died as a result of his work in the freezing weather, scaling a ladder and painting the leaf at night when Joanna was sleeping. Susan promises to someday tell Joanna just what a great painter Behrman was.

REVIEWS:

"Twentieth Century–Fox has an unbeatable hand in *O. Henry's Full House,* an entrancing collection of five tales by one of America's great story tellers." *The Hollywood Reporter,* August 18, 1952

"Being a mixture of comedy, drama, pathos and melodrama, the picture offers a variety of moods to suit all tastes, although the entertainment quality of the different stories ranges from just fair to good." *Harrison's Reports,* August 23, 1952

"The house is too full…. Five unrelated episodes seem too much for one production. And not all of these adaptations of O. Henry short stories are as sharp and piquant as they might have been." *Picturegoer,* October 11, 1952

REVIEWS FOR JEAN NEGULESCO:

"['The Last Leaf' is] emotionally sure under Jean Negulesco's direction…." *Variety,* August 20, 1952

"The real irony [of the story] lies in the painter's part in the affair, and it's surprising that writers Ivan Goff and Ben Roberts and director Jean Negulesco did not weight the business in his direction." *New York Herald Tribune,* October 17, 1952

"Negulesco's direction of 'The Last Leaf' is at times too emphatic; but he achieves some telling effects…" *Monthly Film Bulletin,* October 1952

ADDITIONAL REVIEWS AND ARTICLES:

Daily Variety October 11, 1943; *Hollywood Reporter* October 14, 1943; *Hollywood Reporter* February 23, 1945, p. 2; *Hollywood Reporter* September 17, 1945, p. 3; *Hollywood Reporter* November 9, 1951, p. 2; *Hollywood Reporter* November 16, 1951 p. 15; *Hollywood Reporter* November 21, 1951, p. 15; *Hollywood Reporter* November 28, 1951, p. 8; *Hollywood Reporter* November 29, 1951, p. 1; *Motion Picture Herald* December 1, 1951; *Hollywood Reporter* January 3, 1952, p. 8; *Hollywood Reporter* January 4, 1952, p. 8; *Motion Picture Herald* January 12, 1952; *Hollywood Reporter January* 11, 1952, p. 14; *Hollywood Reporter* January 14, 1952, p. 4; *Hollywood Reporter* January 24, 1952, p. 6; *Hollywood Reporter* January 27, 1952, p. 7; *Hollywood Reporter* January 28, 1952, p. 2; *Motion Picture Herald* February 2, 1952; *Hollywood Reporter* February 13, 1952, p. 6; *Hollywood Reporter* February 21, 1952, p. 13; *Hollywood Reporter* February 22, 1942, p. 18; *Hollywood Reporter* February 27, 1952, p. 15; *Hollywood Reporter* March 3, 1952, p. 1; *Hollywood Reporter* May 20, 1952, p. 2; *Hollywood Reporter* May 23, 1952, p. 9; *Hollywood Reporter* May 27, 1952, p. 5; *Motion Picture Herald* June 14, 1952, p. 42; *Hollywood Reporter* August 5, 1952, p. 5; *Motion Picture Herald* August 9, 1952, p. 1478 *Hollywood Reporter* August 14, 1952, p. 4; *Motion Picture Daily* August 18, 1952; *Motion Picture Herald Product Digest* August 23, 1952, p. 1501; *Boxoffice* August 23, 1952; *Film Daily* August 26, 1952, p. 6; *Hollywood Reporter* September 5, 1952,

p. 1; *Hollywood Reporter* September 8, 1952, p. 2; *Today's Cinema* September 10, 1952, p. 10; *Daily Film Renter* September 10, 1952, p. 5; *Kinematograph Weekly* September 11, 1952, pp. 16; *Saturday Review* September 13, 1952, p. 34; *Hollywood Citizen-News* September 19. 1952 *The Times* (U.K.) September 22, 1952, p. 2; *Time* September 22, p. 102; *Hollywood Reporter* September 26, 1952, p. 8; *Audio-Visual Guide* October 1952 p. 31; *Films in Review* October 1952 p. 416–417; *Sight and Sound* October-December 1952; p. 77; *The Spectator* (U.K.) October 3, 1952; *New York Times* October 5, 1952; *Newsweek* October 6, 1952, p. 113; *Hollywood Reporter* October 13, 1952, p. 5; *The Tattler* (U.K.) October 15, 1952, p. 144; *Hollywood Reporter* October 17, 1952, p. 3; *New York Times* October 17, 1952, p. 33; *Cue* October 18, 1952; *New York Times* October 26, 1952; *Audio-Visual Guide* November 1952 p. 29; *The Nation* November 22, 1952, p. 475; *Theatre Arts* December 1952 pp. 86; *Audio-Visual Guide* January 1953; p. 14; *Movie* December 1962 p. 21–22; *Cinéma* (France) February 1963 p. 104; *Positif* (France) January 1975

Titanic

20th Century–Fox; U.S. B&W 98 minutes; World premiere in Norfolk, Virginia, on April 11, 1953

CREDITS: *Producer:* Charles Brackett; *Director:* Jean Negulesco; *Screenplay:* Charles Brackett, Walter Reisch, Richard L. Breen; *Photography:* Joe MacDonald; *Art Directors:* Lyle Wheeler, Maurice Ransford; *Special Photographic Effects:* Ray Kellogg; *Set Decorator:* Stuart A. Reiss; *Editor;* Louis Loeffler; *Wardrobe:* Charles Le Maire; *Costumes:* Dorothy Jeakins; *Music:* Sol Kaplan; *Musical Director:* Lionel Newman; *Orchestrator:* Herbert Spencer, Edward B. Powell; *Sound:* Arthur L. Kirbach; Roger Heman; *Makeup:* Ben Nye; *Assistant Director:* Henry Weinberger; *Unit Manager:* Joseph C. Behm; *Property Master:* Don B. Greenwood; *Dialogue Director:* Michael Audley; *Script Supervisor:* Kathleen Fagan; *Technical Advisor:* Commodore Sir Gordon Illingworth; *Song:* "Nearer My God to Thee," words by Sarah Adams; music based on the hymn "Bethany," arranged by Lowell Mason and composed by Sarah Adams

CAST: Clifton Webb (Richard Ward Sturgess), Barbara Stanwyck (Julia Sturgess), Robert Wagner (Gifford Rogers), Audrey Dalton (Annette Sturgess), Thelma Ritter (Maude Young), Brian Aherne (Capt. E.J. Smith), Richard Basehart (George Healey), Allyn Joslyn (Earl Meeker), James Todd (Sandy Comstock), Frances Bergen (Madeleine Astor), William Johnstone (John Jacob Astor), Charles B. FitzSimons (Chief Officer Wilde), Barry Bernard (First Officer Murdock), Harper Carter (Norman Sturgess), Edmund Purdom (Second Officer Lightoller), Christopher Severn (Messenger), James Lilburn (Devlin), Guy Standing, Jr. (George Widener), Hellen Van Tuyl (Mrs. Straus), Roy Gordon (Isidor Straus), Marta Mitrovich (Mrs. Uzcadum), Ivis Goulding (Emma—Maid), Dennis Fraser (Bride), Ashley Cowan (Phillips), Lehmer Graham (Symons), Merry Anders, Gloria Gordon, Melinda Markey (College Girls), Ronald F. Hagerthy, Conrad Feia, Richard West (College Boys), Donald Chaffin, Michael Ferris, Owen McGiveney, John Fraser, Ralph Grosh (Stewards), William Cottrell (Ship Steward), David Hoffman (Webster—Tailor), Gordon Richards (Manager), Robin Camp (Messenger Boy), Robin Hughes, John Dodsworth, Robin Sanders Clark (Junior Officers), David Thursby, Nick Coster, Pat Aherne (Seamen), Camillo Guercio (Mr. Guggenheim), Antony Eustrel (Pelham Sanderson), Alan Marston (Quartermaster), Michael Hadlow (Messenger), Ivan Hayes (Officer), Herbert Deans (Junior Officer), Elizabeth Flournoy (Woman with Baby), Charles Keane (Stoker), Salvador Báguez (Jean Pablo Uzcadum), Eugene Borden (Dock Official), Alberto Morin (Dock Employee), Pat O'Moore, Harry Cording (Relief Men), Mae Marsh (Woman on Lifeboat), Michael Rennie (Narrator)

PLOT: The world's greatest liner, the *Titanic*, steams into Cherbourg in April 1912, on her maiden transatlantic crossing. Julia Sturges and her children Annette, 18, and Norman, 13, look down on the busy quayside. There are escaping from the head of the family Richard Sturges, who is trying desperately to buy his passage. At last Richard persuades a Basque passenger into selling his ticket. Calmly walking from steerage to the first-class dining saloon, Richard confronts his family. Norman and Annette are happy while Julia remains aloof. Alone with Julia, Richard demands to know why she is spiriting the children away from him. Julia's reply is that Annette is becoming a snobbish prig and that she hopes to save Norman before he becomes one too. The next night, Richard tells Julia that he's determined to keep Norman, even if it means going to court. Julia tells him quietly that Norman is not his son. When he learns of the circumstances of his wife's infidelity, Richard vows he will never speak to the boy again. Julia is pacing the deck when he sees George Healey, who is very drunk and in need of help. She takes him to his cabin, where she learns his story: He is an unfrocked Roman Catholic priest now on his way back to America to face his family. Julia seeks out Richard, who is playing marathon bridge rubbers with wise-cracking Maude Young and two other passengers. She pleads with him not to ignore Norman, whose heart is breaking at Richard's indifference, but Richard refuses. Annette has met a young American college boy Giff Rogers, who brings her down to earth by scoffing at her snobbery. An iceberg is spotted dead ahead and an underwater spar rips a gash in the vessel. Captain Smith orders all passengers to don lifebelts and to report to their allotted stations on deck. Richard learns from the captain that there are not enough boats to save the men; he mixes with the passengers and encourages them by his example. Julia is filled with pride at his cool behavior. At this moment everything is forgotten except the love that they had for each other 20 years ago, and they embrace tenderly. After placing Annette and Norman in the lifeboat with Julia, Richard leaves them to help release another lifeboat which has become fouled un the rigging. Giff cuts the boat free but then he falls into the water, injuring himself. He is soon picked by a lifeboat. A woman approaches the lifeboat containing the Sturgesses but there is no more room; Norman gallantly gives her his seat, goes back about the sinking vessel and seeks out his father. Healey, learning that members of the crew are trapped amidships, goes below to say last rites. Norman finds Richard, who is overcome with pride and together they wait for the end. Passengers and crew sing "Nearer My God to Thee" as the *Titanic* sinks into the water. (Original press release source)

REVIEWS:

"The film excels in every department with an extra helping of praise for the sterling performances which were the universal contributions of stars and supporting players alike." *Boxoffice,* April 8, 1953

"Fact and fiction are blended to good advantage in this compelling domestic drama.... The direction is expert, and the acting restrained and void of theatricalism." *Harrison's Reports,* April 18, 1953

"Although maritime disasters are not unique as film fare, Twentieth Century–Fox, abetted by an obviously excellent research staff, a fine cast and a polished script, has fashioned a sometimes moving and often exciting drama...." *The New York Times,* May 28, 1953

REVIEWS FOR JEAN NEGULESCO:

"As tastefully directed by Jean Negulesco; the full tragedy boo the disaster is brought out every nuance of emotion being wrung out of the dramatic moment..." *The Hollywood Reporter*, April 15, 1953

"Negulesco's direction really shines.... [It] takes the players over the dramatic hurdles with a sure hand. The scenes will tear at the heart." *Variety,* April 15, 1953

"The danger before the crash is underplayed, as is the fear afterward, and there is a fine aura of luxury under Jean Negulesco's direction." *New York Herald Tribune,* May 28, 1953

ADDITIONAL REVIEWS AND ARTICLES:

Hollywood Reporter September 8, 1952, p. 4; *Hollywood Reporter* September 11, 1952, p. 2; *Los Angeles Times* September 26, 1952; *Hollywood Reporter* October 13, 1952, p. 2; *Hollywood Reporter* October 22, 1952, p. 6; *Hollywood Reporter* October 24, 1952, p. 13; *Hollywood Reporter* October 29, 1952, p. 8; *Daily Film Renter* November 1952; *Hollywood Reporter* December 5, 1952, p. 6; *Hollywood Reporter* December 9, 1952, p. 6; *Hollywood Reporter* December 22, 1952, p. 4; *The New York Times* December 28, 1952; *Modern Screen* February 1953 p. 89; *Hollywood Reporter* March 20, 1953, p. 10; *Hollywood Reporter* April 9, 1953, p. 4; *Hollywood Reporter* April 13, 1953, p. 8; *Film Daily* April 16, 1953, p. 6; *Motion Picture Herald Product Digest* April 18, 1953, p. 1798; *Los Angeles Times* April 20, 1953; *Time* April 27, 1953, p. 108; *Modern Screen* May 1953; *Films in Review* May 1953 p. 241–242; *Today's Cinema* May 14, 1953, p. 10; *Life* May 18, 1953; *Newsweek* May 18, 1953, p. 108; *Saturday Review* May 23, 1953, p. 30; *The New York Times* May 27, 1953, p. 26; *New York Daily Mirror* May 28, 1953; *The Times* (U.K.) May 29, 1953; *Mein Film* (Austria) May 29, 1953; *The New York Times* May 31, 1953, sec. II p. 1; *Theatre Arts* June 1953 p. 86; *The New Yorker* June 6, 1953, p. 95–96; *The Times* June 17, 1953; *The Star* (U.K.) June 19, 1953; *The Spectator* (U.K.) June 19, 1953; *America* June 20, 1953, p. 326; *The Observer* (U.K.) June 21, 1953;

The Sunday Times (U.K.) June 21, 1953; *Picturegoer* June 27, 1953; *Monthly Film Bulletin* July 1953 p. 103; *Modern Screen* July 1953 p. 16; *Modern Screen* October 1953 p. 96; *Le Soir* (Belgium) April 16, 1954; *Mon Film* (France) September 14, 1955; *Image et Son-La Revue du Cinéma* (France) July 1960; *Focus on Film* October 28, 1977, p. 43–46; *Historical Film of Film Radio and TV* October 1999 p. 421–38; *Cinema Journal* Spring 2008

AWARDS AND HONORS:

National Screen Council and Boxoffice Magazine: U.S. May 1953: *Winner:* Boxoffice Blue Ribbon Award

Academy Awards: U.S. 1954: *Won:* Best Writing; Story and *Screenplay:* Charles Brackett, Walter Reisch, Richard L. Breen

Nominated: Best Art Direction-Set Decoration: Black and White: Lyle R. Wheeler, Maurice Ransford, Stuart A. Reiss

Director Guild of America: U.S. 1954: *Nominated:* DGA Award: Outstanding Directorial Achievement in Motion Pictures: Jean Negulesco

Scandal at Scourie

Metro-Goldwyn-Mayer; U.S. Technicolor 89 minutes; Premiered in New York on May 17, 1953

CREDITS: *Producer:* Edwin H. Knopf; *Director:* Jean Negulesco; *Screenplay:* Norman Corwin, Leonard Spigelgass, Karl Tunberg; Based on the Short Story "Good Boy" by Mary McSherry in *Good Housekeeping*; *Photography:* Robert Planck; *Technicolor Color Consultant:* Henri Jaffa; *Art Directors:* Cedic Gibbons; Wade B. Rubottom; *Editor:* Ferris Webster; *Assistant Director:* Jack Greenwood; *Recording Supervisor:* Douglas Shearer; *Set Decorators:* Edwin B. Willis; Hugh Hunt; *Color Consultant:* Alvord Wiseman; *Special Effects:* A. Arnold Gillespie; *Costumes:* Walter Plunkett; *Hair Styles:* Sydney Guilaroff; *Makeup:* William Tuttle; *Music:* Daniele Amfitheatrof; *Songs:* the traditional airs "Green Sleeves" and "Frère Jacques"

CAST: Greer Garson (Victoria McChesney), Walter Pidgeon (Patrick J. McChesney), Agnes Moorehead (Sister Josephine), Donna Corcoran (Patsy), Arthur Shields (Father Reilly), Philip Ober (B.G. Belney), Rhys Williams (Bill Swazey), Margalo Gillmore (Alice Hanover), John Lupton (Artemus), Philip Tonge (Fred Gogarty), Wilton Graff (Mr. Leffington), Ian Wolfe (Councilman Hurdwell), Michael Pate (the Reverend Williams), Tony Taylor (Edward), Patricia Tiernan (Second Nun), Victor Wood (James Motley), Perdita Chandler (Sister Dominique), Walter Baldwin (Michael Hayward), Ida Moore (Mrs. Ames), Maudie Prickett (Mrs. Holahan), Ivis Goulding (Mrs. O'Russell), Alex Frazer (Wormsley), Matt Moore (Kenston), Charles Watts (Barber), Eugene Borden (Old Man), Rudy Lee (Donald), Max Willenz (Vidocq), Ivan Triesault (Father Barrett), Wayne Farlow, Linda Greer, Kathleen Hartnagel, Warren Farlow (Children), Joann Arnold (Sister Maria), Peter Roman (Freddie), George Davis (Bartender), Vicki Joy Ereutzer (Edith), Claude Guy (Joseph), Gary Lee Jackson (Boy), Jill Martin (Isabella), Coral Hammond (Cecelia), Nolan Leary (Conductor), Owen McGiveney (Clark), Archer MacDonald (Barber Apprentice), Earl Lee (Tweedy Man), Howard Negley (Duggin), Robert Ross (Dr. Parker), John Sherman (Mr. Pringle), Roger Moore (Man)

PLOT: Because seven-year-old Patsy accidentally set fire to Montreal orphanage, she and 60 other Catholic orphans have to find homes throughout Canada. At the little town of Scourie, Ontario, Patsy attracts the notice of charming and childless Vicki McChesney, who takes her in spite of the objections of her husband Patrick to the adoption of a Catholic child by Protestants. Patsy is happy, though wary of Mr. McChesney and tormented by Edward, an orphan who was always her enemy and who has been adopted in the neighborhood. Mr. McChesney's candidacy for the legislature is endangered when his rival, Mr. Belney, suggests that the McChesneys adopted Patsy as a gesture toward the Catholic vote. Mr. McChesney has just told Vicki that Patsy must go. When fire breaks out in the schoolhouse and evidence is brought forward that it is a case of arson, Belney directs suspicion against Patsy. This so enrages Mr. McChesney that he says Patsy wouldn't burn a piece of toast and states he will keep her and defend her, resigning his offices to do so. He and Vicki go happily home to find that Patsy has run away, having overheard Mr. McChesney's previous decision against her. In the meantime, Edward has run away too, leaving a confession that it was he who set the fire to the schoolhouse. They are found safe the next morning. Mr. McChesney convinces Patsy that he wants her: Edward is forgiven and they all go home. (Original press release source)

REVIEWS:

"*Scandal at Scourie* is a drama of warmth and sentiment, tinged with humor ... with acting that is persuasive and a narrative that is reasonably absorbing." *Motion Picture Daily,* April 30, 1953

"There is eye-pleasing Technicolor photography to further beautify the film's tasteful backgrounds and atmosphere." *Boxoffice,* May 2, 1953

"The Victorian Sunday-school sentimentality of this story is presented with shameless winsomeness by a team of MGM's most practiced hands." *Monthly Film Bulletin,* July 1953

REVIEWS FOR JEAN NEGULESCO:
"Jean Negulesco's direction smoothly coordinates and gets the best from the script." *Variety,* April 29, 1953

"Director Jean Negulesco has planned his film for a maximum of warmth and simple emotions.... This is all that any director could do, because there is no script except common romantic movie practice in *Scandal at Scourie* after the first few tentative passes at reality." *The New York Times,* June 16, 1953

"Jean Negulesco has directed ... for the heartthrobs that are carefully planted like juicy plums in this creamy dramatic pudding." *New York Herald Tribune,* June 16, 1953

ADDITIONAL REVIEWS AND ARTICLES:
Hollywood Reporter April 23, 1952, p. 2; *Hollywood Reporter* May 29, 1952 p. 2; *Hollywood Reporter* July 11, 1952, p. 10; *Hollywood Reporter* July 14, 1952, p. 4; *Hollywood Reporter* July 23, 1952, p. 7; *Hollywood Reporter* August 15, 1952, p. 10; *Hollywood Reporter* December 29, 1952, p. 2; *Motion Picture Herald Product Digest* April 11, 1953, p. 1790; *Boxoffice* April 11, 1953; *Hollywood Reporter* April 29, 1953 p. 3; *Harrison's Reports* May 2, 1953, p. 71; *Motion Picture Herald Product Digest* May 2, 1953, p. 1821; *Film Daily* May 7, 1953, p. 6; *Today's Cinema* May 29, 1953, p. 10; *Los Angels Times* June 13, 1953; *America* June 27, 1953, p. 345; *The Spectator* (U.K.) September 18, 1953; *The Daily Mail* (U.K.) September 18, 1953; *The Star* (U.K.) September 18, 1953; *The Mirror* (U.K.) September 18, 1953; *The Daily Telegraph* (U.K.) September 19, 1953; *National Parent-Teacher* October 1953; p. 38; *Picturegoer* October 24 1953

AWARDS AND HONORS:
Parent's Magazine Medal Award: U.S. 1953: Winner

How to Marry a Millionaire

20th Century–Fox; U.S. Technicolor CinemaScope 96 minutes; Premiered in Los Angeles on November 4, 1953

CREDITS: *Producer:* Nunnally Johnson*; Director:* Jean Negulesco; *Screenplay:* Nunnally Johnson; Based on the plays *The Greeks Had a Word for It* by Zoë Akins and *Loco* by Dale Eunson and Katherine Albert; *Photography:* Joe MacDonald; *Camera Operator:* Roy Ivey; *Camera Assistants:* John Van Wormer, Paul Cable, Frank Cory, Jr.; *Art Director:* Lyle Wheeler, Leland Fuller; *Editor:* Louis Loeffler; *Assistant Director:* F.E. Johnson; *Set Decorators:* Walter M. Scott, Stuart Reiss; *Musical Director:* Albert Newman; *Incidental Music:* Cyril Mockridge; *Wardrobe Director:* Charles Le Maire; *Costumes:* Travilla; *Orchestrator:* Edward B. Powell; *Sound:* Alfred Bruzlin, Roger Heman, Charles Kohl; *Sound Editors:* Kenneth Honnold, Del Harris; *Special Photographic Effects:* Ray Kellogg; *Choreographer:* Billy Daniel; *Makeup:* Ben Nye, George Lane, Alan Snyder, Bill Riddle, Dick Hamilton; *Hair Stylists:* Marie Brasselle, Kay Reed; *Unit Manager:* Gaston Glass; *Script Supervisor:* Rose Steinberg; *Color Consultant:* Leonard Doss; *Song:* "New York," music and lyrics by Alfred Newman and Ken Darby

CAST: Betty Grable (Loco Dempsey), Marilyn Monroe (Pola Debevoise), Lauren Bacall (Schatze Page), David Wayne (Freddie Denmark), Rory Calhoun (Eben Salem), Cameron Mitchell (Tom Brookman), Alex D'Arcy (J. Stewart Merrill), Fred Clark (Waldo Brewster), William Powell (J.D. Hanley), George Dunn (Mike—Elevator Operator), Percy Helton (Mr. Benton), Harry Carter (Elevator Operator), Robert Adler (Cab Driver), Tudor Owen (Mr. Otis), Maurice Marsac (Mr. Antoine), Emmett Vogan (Man at George Washington Bridge), Hermine Sterler (Madame), Abney Mott (Secretary), Rankin Mansfield (Bennett), Ralph Reed (Jewelry Salesman), Jan Arvan (Tony), Ivis Goulding (Maid), Dayton Lummis (Justice of the Peace), Van Des Autels (Best Man), Eric Wilton (Butler), Ivan Triesault (Captain of Waiters), Herbert Deans (Steward), George Saurel (Emir), Hope Landin (Mrs. Salem), Tom Greenway (Motorcycle Cop), Charlotte Austin, Merry Anders, Ruth Hall, Lida Thomas, Jane Liddell, Beryl McCutcheon (Models), James Stone (Doorman), Tom Martin (Pete—Doorman), Eve Finnell (Stewardess), Benny Burt (Reporter), Richard Shackleton (Bellboy)

PLOT: Hoping to snare a wealthy husband, gold-digging models Schatze Page, Pola Debevoise and Loco Dempsey rent a lavish Manhattan penthouse apartment which they cannot afford. Loco has a chance encounter with handsome young multi-millionaire Tom Brookman, who helps her with some bags of groceries, but when he meets Schatze he is immediately smitten by her beauty and in spite of her rudeness he persistently calls her. She constantly dismisses him, believing he is poor. Schatze instead pursues J.D. Hanley, a wealthy oil tycoon. The old gent invites the girls to an oil industry event where Pola and Loco met prospective targets. Loco's date is Waldo Brewster, a grouchy married man whom she agrees to accompany on a weekend trip, convinced that they are going to a convention in Maine where she could meet some other rich men. Instead she is taken to his lodge in the mountains. When she realizes his intentions, she demands to return immediately to New York, but she comes down with measles and is bedridden. A good-looking forest ranger named Eben comes to her rescue. When she recovers, Brewster catches the measles. Eben and Loco fall in love but the young woman realizes that the ranger is not rich so she returns to New York with Brewster. Pola heads for Atlantic City, where she is supposed to meet her beau J. Stewart Merrill. Reluctant to wear her glasses in public, she boards the wrong plane. Her seatmate is Freddie Denmark, her landlord, whose wealth is in trouble due to a crooked accountant. The two find they have much in common. Schatze, left alone and without money in New York, decides to accept Hanley's wedding proposal. Loco arrives at the ceremony with Eben, Pola with Freddy. The two girls announce they are both married. Loco had returned to Maine to declare his love to Eben, while Pola and Freddie tied the knot planning to go undercover to clear up his tax troubles. Tom Brookman's arrival at the wedding and Schatze's reaction to his presence convinces Hanley that it is the younger man she really is in love with. He calls off the wedding and Schatze realizes, as her friends did, that marrying for love is better than money. The three couples go to a diner where Tom pulls out of his pocket a huge stack of $1000 bills to pay the check making all three girls faint.

REVIEWS:

"A smartly sophisticated comedy that will delight audiences ... superbly acted and directed." *The Hollywood Reporter*; November 5, 1953

"[This] is a box office natural from all angles—presentation, story, cast, direction, production values, Technicolor photography and above all entertainment values." *Harrison's Reports,* November 7, 1953

"[T]here can be not an iota of doubt as concerns its appeal to the most exciting and mature tastes in motion picture." *Boxoffice,* November 7, 1953

REVIEWS FOR JEAN NEGULESCO:

"Jean Negulesco's direction builds a smart, entertaining show about three models on the prowl for three millionaires." *Variety,* November 11, 1953

"*How to Marry a Millionaire* is measured, not in square feet, but in the size of the Johnson-Negulesco comic invention and the shape of Marilyn Monroe—and that is about as sizable and as shapely as you can get." *New York Herald Tribune,* November 11, 1953

"The glassy expressionless expression, so much a part of Miss Monroe's stock-in-trade, has been put to excellent use by Jean Negulesco." *Saturday Review,* November 28, 1953

ADDITIONAL REVIEWS AND ARTICLES:

Hollywood Reporter August 15, 1952, p. 2; *Motion Picture Herald Product Digest* January 10, 1953, p. 24; *Hollywood Reporter* January 21, 1953, p. 2; *Hollywood Reporter* February 26, 1953, p. 8; *Hollywood Reporter* March 6, 1953, p. 22; *Hollywood Reporter* March 9, 1953, p. 3; *Hollywood Reporter* March 11, 1953, p. 9; *Hollywood Reporter* March 16, 1953, p. 6; *Hollywood Reporter* April 10, 1953, p. 9; *Hollywood Reporter* April 17, 1953, p. 13; *New York Times* April 25, 1953; *Hollywood Reporter* June 30, 1953, p. 9; *Hollywood Reporter* July 1, 1953, p. 1; *Hollywood Reporter* August 25, 1953, p. 6; *Hollywood Reporter* October 21, 1953, p. 2; *Hollywood Reporter* October 22, 1953, p. 2; *Hollywood Reporter* October 30, 1953, p. 11; *Hollywood Reporter* November 4, 1953, p. 4; *Los Angeles Daily News* November 5, 1953; *Los Angeles Times* November 5, 1953; *Los Angeles Herald Express* November 5, 1953; *Film Daily* November 5, 1953, p. 6; *Hollywood Reporter* November 6, 1953, p. 1; *Motion Picture Herald Product Digest* November 7, 1953, p. 24; *Hollywood Reporter* November 10, 1953, p. 3; *New York World-Telegram and Sun* November 10, 1953; *New York Times* November 11,1953 p. 37; *New York Post* November 11, 1953; *New York Daily News* November 11, 1953: *Hollywood Reporter* November 13, 1953, p. 1; *Motion Picture Herald Product Digest* November 14, 1953, p. 2070; *Cue* November 14, 1953, p. 17; *Boxoffice* November 14, 1953; *New York Times* November 15, 1953; *Newsweek* November 16, 1953; *Hollywood Reporter* November 18, 1953, p. 2;

New Yorker November 21, 1953; *Time* November 23, 1953; *Life* November 23, 1953, p. 137–38; *Films in Review* December 1953 p. 535; *Hollywood Reporter* December 2, 1953, p. 2; *Pix* January 2, 1954; *Today's Cinema* January 13, 1954, p. 18; *Kinematograph Weekly* January 14, 1954; p. 17; *Monthly Film Bulletin* February 1954 p. 20; *Hollywood Reporter* February 12, 1954, p. 2; *Hollywood Reporter* February 1, 1954, p. 1; *Il Corriere della sera* (Italy) February 24, 1954; *La Stampa* (Italy) February 26, 1954; *Hollywood Reporter* March 18, 1954, p. 1; *Le Soir* (Belgium) April 2, 1954; *L'Unità* (Italy) April 4, 1954; *Hollywood Reporter* April 6, 1954, p. 4; *Variety* April 7, 1954; *Carrefour* (France) April 12, 1954; *Arts* (France) May 5, 1954; *France*-Observateur (France) May 6, 1954, p. 23; *Le Monde* (France) April 7, 1954; *Cahiers du Cinéma* (France) May 1954 p. 54 *Hollywood Reporter* May 10, 1954, p. 1; *Mon Film* (France) December 1, 1954, p. 8; *TV Guide* September 23, 1961; *Variety* December 5, 1962; *Image et Son-La Revue du Cinéma* (France) December 1962 p. 78; *After Dark* August-September 1981; *Film Reader* n.5 1982 p. 67–75; *Cinéma* (France) April 23, 1986, p. 5; *France-Soir* (France) May 7, 1986; *Positif* (France) October 1986 p. 50; *The Guardian* (U.K.) June 9, 1997, p. 13

AWARDS AND HONORS:
Academy Awards: U.S. 1954: *Nominated:* Best Costume Design: Color: Charles Le Maire, Travilla

Directors Guild of America: U.S. 1954: *Nominated:* DGA Award: Best Written American Comedy; Nunnally Johnson

Bafta Awards: United Kingdom: 1955: *Nominated:* Best Film from any Source: U.S.

Three Coins in the Fountain

20th Century–Fox; U.S. Technicolor CinemaScope 102 minutes; Premiered in New York on May 20, 1954

CREDITS: *Producer:* Sol C. Siegel; *Director:* Jean Negulesco; *Screenplay:* John Patrick; Based on the novel *Coins in the Fountain* by John H. Secondari; *Photography:* Milton Krasner; *Art Directors:* Lyle Wheeler, John De Cuir; *Editor:* William Reynolds; *Set Decorators:* Walter M. Scott, Paul S. Fox; *Wardrobe Direction:* Charles Le Maire; *Costumes:* Dorothy Jeakins; *Sound:* Eugene Grossman; Roger Heman; *Music:* Victor Young; *Orchestra:* Edward B. Powell, Ken Darby, Sidney Cutner, Leo Shuken; *Vocal Director:* Ken Darby; *Makeup:* Ben Nye; *Assistant Director:* Gaston Glass; *Technical Advisor:* Giuseppe Lenzi; *Color Consultant:* Leonard Doss; *Songs:* "Three Coins in the Fountain," music and lyrics by Jule Styne and Sammy Cahn; sung by Frank Sinatra; "Anema e core," music by Salve D'Esposito, lyrics by Tito Manlio; "Nanni," music and lyrics by Franco Silvestri; "O ciucciariello," music by Nino Oliviero, lyrics by Roberto Murolo

CAST: Clifton Webb (John Frederick Shadwell), Dorothy McGuire (Miss Frances), Jean Peters (Anita Hutchins), Louis Jourdan (Prince Dino di Cessi), Maggie McNamara (Maria Williams), Rossano Brazzi (Giorgio Bianchi), Howard St. John (Burgoyne), Kathryn Givney (Mrs. Burgoyne), Cathleen Nesbitt (Principessa), Vincent Padula (Dr. Martinelli), Mario Siletti (Bartender), Alberto Morin (Waiter), Dino Bolognese (Headwaiter), Tony De Mario (Waiter in Venice), Jack Mattis (Consulate Clerk), Willard Waterman (Mr. Hoyt), Zachary Yaconelli (Theatrical Ticket Agent), Celia Lovsky (Baroness), Larry Arnold (Waiter in Select Restaurant), Renata Vanni (Anna), Maurice Brierre (Pepe—Shadwell's Butler), Grazia Narciso (Louisa—Maid), Gino Corrado (Butler), Charles La Torre (Chauffeur), Merry Anders (Girl), Norma Varden (Woman at Cocktail Party)

PLOT: Maria Williams arrives in Rome to work as a secretary for an American business firm and to replace Anita Hutchins, who had decided to return to the United States. The girls share an apartment with Miss Frances, who had been working in Rome for the past 15 years as secretary to John Shadwell, a middle-aged, debonair American author known for his impeccable taste and caustic wit. Miss Frances has unrequited affection for him. Anita's decision to return to the States was motivated by the fact that she was in love with Giorgio Bianchi, a young Italian translator employed by her firm; company rules did not permit her to go out with local employees. The couple's defiance of this rule costs Giorgio his job. Anita quits her position and decides to marry him, but their plans come to naught because he did not earn enough to properly support himself. Maria becomes involved with handsome Prince Dino Di Cessi, a notorious playboy-prince whose efforts to take advantage of her are frustrated by Miss Frances. Maria sets out on a shrewd campaign to win Prince Dino's heart and before long he asks her to become his bride. She then confesses how she had won his love and as a result she loses him. Miss Frances; anticipating that her friends are about to be married, decides to leave Shadwell lest she remain an old maid. Her decision to leaves awakens Shadwell's love for her and he proposes. Their plans hit a snag when he learns from his doctor that he had but one year to live. He tries to get out of the marriage proposal through a flimsy excuse but Miss Shadwell sees through it and convinces him that they should remain together come what may. At the same time she tells him of the romantic problems of Maria and Anita. Using his influence, he sees to it that Giorgio is reinstated in his job and that Prince Dino makes up with Maria. It all ends with the three couples meeting and embracing at the Trevi Fountain, where each of the girls had made a wish at the start of the story. (Original press release source)

REVIEWS:

"[*Three Coins in the Fountain* is] at the same time light-hearted and tender-hearted in its appeal to youth and femininity. Seldom has sure box office been combined so skilfully with skilled picturemaking." *The Hollywood Reporter,* May 12, 1954

"[A] film in which the locale comes first. However; the nonsense of its fable crumbles nicely within the picture frame." *The New York Times,* May 21, 1954

"A three-tiered love story ... summer ... Rome ... color ... and CinemaScope. What could you ask? The Answer: a lot more. [F]ar too many trite romantic clichés slow up the work." *Picturegoer,* July 17, 1954

REVIEWS FOR JEAN NEGULESCO:

"In *Three Coins in the Fountain* [Negulesco] ... has gained some experience. The film has warmth; humor; a rich dose of romance and almost incredible pictorial appeal." *Variety,* May 12, 1954

"[Negulesco's] expert touches ... endow [the film] with a sprightly and warm quality, and with a number of situations that are genuinely dramatic." *Harrison's Reports,* May 15, 1954

"Jean Negulesco's direction is perfunctory. He either felt he could do nothing to improve John Patrick's script, or that Milton Krasner's photography, Dorothy Jeakins' clothes and the sets of Walter M. Scott and Paul S. Fox would hide the script's infirmities. Which in fact they frequently do." *Films in Review,* June-July 1954.

ADDITIONAL REVIEWS AND ARTICLES:

Hollywood Reporter March 2, 1953, p. 2; *Hollywood Reporter* March 26, 1953, p. 2; *Hollywood Reporter* July 16, 1953, p. 6; *Hollywood Reporter* July 23, 1953, p. 3; *Hollywood Reporter* August 6, 1953, p. 4; *Hollywood Reporter* August 7, 1953, p. 10; *Los Angeles Times* August 20, 1953; *Hollywood Reporter* August 31, 1953, p. 3; *Hollywood Reporter* September 18, 1953 p. 10; *Hollywood Reporter* December 15, 1953, p. 3. *Hollywood Reporter* December 22, 1953, p. 6; *Hollywood Reporter* January 6, 1954, p. 3; *Hollywood Reporter* January 11, 1954, p. 5; *Variety* February 24, 1954; *Variety* March 4, 1954; *Hollywood Reporter* May 12, 1954, p. 3; *Film Daily* May 12, 1954, p. 6; *Motion Picture Herald Product Digest* May 15, 1954, p. 2293; *Boxoffice* May 15, 1954, p. 30; *New York Times* May 16, 1954; *Boxoffice* May 22, 1954; *Cue* May 22, 1954, p. 15; *Christian Science Monitor Boston* May 25, 1954, p. 4; *Los Angeles Times* May 27, 1954; *The New Yorker* May 29, 1954, p. 52; *America* May 29, 1954, p. 259; *Life* June 7, 1954, p. 151; *Newsweek* May 31, 1954; *Time* May 31, 1954; *Commonweal* June 4, 1954, p. 223; *Saturday Review* June 5, 1954, p 27; *Today's Cinema* June 23, 1954; p. 30; *Monthly Film Bulletin* August 1954; p. 118; *The Evening Standard* (U.K.) August 19, 1954; *The Star* (U.K.) August 20, 1954; *The Spectator* (U.K.) August 20, 1954, p. 221; *Daily Mail* (U.K.) August 20, 1954; *Daily Mail* (U.K.) August 20, 1954; *Financial Times* (U.K.) August 22, 1954: *The Observer* August 22, 1954; *The Sunday Express* August 22, 1954; *The Times* (U.K.) August 23, 1954, p. 10; *The Tatler* (U.K.) September 1, 1954, p. 372; *Cahiers du Cinéma* (France) October 1954 p. 46; *Films and Filming* October 1954 p. 29; *Arts* (France) October 27 1954; *Radio Cinema Télévision* (France) December 1954; *Hollywood Reporter* March 8, 1955, p. 1; *Film Score Monthly* July-August 2005; p. 57

AWARDS AND HONORS:

Venice Film Festival: Italy 1954: *Nominated:* Golden Lion: Jean Negulesco

Academy Awards: U.S. 1955: *Nominated:* Best Picture: Sol C. Siegel; *Win:* Best Cinematography: Color: Milton R. Krasner; *Best Music:* Original Song "Three Songs in the Fountain," music and lyrics by Jule Styne and Sammy Cahn

Directors Guild of America: U.S. 1955: *Nominated:* DG Award: Outstanding *Director:* Jean Negulesco.

Woman's World

20th Century–Fox; U.S. Technicolor CinemaScope 94 minutes; Premiered in New York on September 28, 1954

CREDITS: *Producer:* Charles Brackett; *Director:* Jean Negulesco; *Screenplay:* Claude Binyon, Mary Loos, Richard Sale; Based on the novelette *May the Best Wife Win* by Mona Williams; *Additional Dialogue:* Howard Lindsay, Russel Crouse; *Photography:* Joe MacDonald; *Art Directors:* Lyle Wheeler, Mark-Lee Kirk; *Set Decorators:* Walter M. Scott, Paul S. Fox; *Special Photographic Effects:* Ray Kellogg; *Editor:* Louis Loeffler; *Costumes:* Charles Le Maire; *Makeup:* Ben Nye; *Hair Stylist:* Helen Turpin; *Sound:* Arthur L. Kirbach, Roger Heman; *Sound Editors:* Al Ross, Dick Jenson; *Music:* Cyril J. Mockridge; *Assistant Director:* Henry Weinberger; *Music Conductor:* Lionel Newman; *Orchestra:* Edward B. Powell; *Production Manager:* Buddy Ericsson; *Color Consultant:* Leonard Doss; *Song:* "It's a Woman's World," music and lyrics by Sammy Cahn and Cyril J. Mockridge; sung by the Four Aces.

CAST: Clifton Webb (Ernest K. Gifford), June Allyson (Katie Baxter), Van Heflin (Jerry Talbot), Lauren Bacall (Elizabeth Burns), Fred MacMurray (Sidney Burns), Arlene Dahl (Carol Talbot), Cornel Wilde (Bill Baxter), Elliott Reid (Tony Andrews), Margalo Gillmore (Evelyn Andrews), Alan Reed (Tomaso), David Hoffman (Jerecki), George Melford (Auto Assembly Plant Worker), Eric Wilton (Butler), Conrad Feia (Bellhop), Marc Snow (Waiter), George E. Stone, George Eldredge, Paul Power, William Tannen, Jonathan Hole, Rodney Bell (Executives), George Spaulding (Ship's Captain), Maude Prickett (Mother), Melinda Markey (Daughter), Virginia Maples, Eileen Maxwell, Beverly Thompson (Models), Joyce Newhard, Virginia Carroll, Fritzi Dugan, Jarma Lewis, Marcoreta Hellman (Women in Bargain Basement)

PLOT: A New York tycoon, Ernest K. Gifford, president of a motor car combine, seeks a successor to his general manager, who killed himself with overwork. To help him choose, he brings to the city his three brightest district managers with their wives. From Kansas City come Bill Baxter and Katie, charming and utterly inhibited, from Dallas come Jerry Talbot and his beautiful and ambitious wife Carol and from Philadelphia come Sid Burns and his smart, attractive but unhappy wife Liz. The three candidates and their wives go to a cocktail party also attended by the organization's executives. Gifford makes a gracious speech of welcome which Katie, who has tried to fight off her nervousness with martinis, punctuates with hiccups. Carol makes a play for Gifford; Liz is dignified and correct. Dinner that night is an extension of the cocktail party as Katie's gaucherie embarrasses the whole party while Carol turns on her sex appeal to win over Gifford. Back at the hotel, Katie tearfully apologizes for ruining Bill's chances. Liz, whose marriage is a casualty of Sid's ambition and devotion to his work, rebuffs her husband's advances. The next day, Gifford escorts the men around the factory while the wives are shown the sights by Gifford's nephew Tony Andrews. Gifford has not made up his mind about the appointment, but he listens closely to the men's answers to his question as to what are the quality of the ideal businessman. Knowing the important part the chosen man's wife will play, Gifford asks his sister Evelyn Andrews to act as hostess at his country house for the weekend, at the end of which he would ask for her opinions. When Katie learns of the invitation, she confides to Liz that she spent the money Bill had given her for clothes on a domestic appliance. Liz takes her to a bargain store where, after fighting through hordes of bargain hunters, she gets fitted up. Aboard Gifford's yacht on the way to the house, Carol continues to ply Gifford with her charms and Katie manages to get herself locked in the washroom. Before dinner that night, after Katie has changed her frock because she spilled tea on it, Gifford asks the men how each feels about the job. Bill says he wants it but not at the expense of his wife and family. Jerry says he wants it but not because of his wife's beauty. Sid says he wants it, not mentioning his wife. Gifford announces that he will give his decision after dinner. Carol seeks out Gifford and offers herself in exchange for Jerry's appointment. Gifford draws away, saying that Jerry will not be appointed because of a handicap. Furious, she slams out of the room and tells Jerry what has happened. Jerry, angry at her interference, orders Carol out of his life when she tells him that her body has won him every promotion he has ever had. Before going down to dinner, Liz softens toward Sid and promises to stick with him whatever the decision. Jerry comes down alone. After dinner, Gifford praises all three men and says his new business manager is to be Jerry, who has rid himself of his handicap. Katie, homesick for Kansas City, clings happily to her husband. (Original press release source)

REVIEWS:

"Five or six writers are responsible for the sum total of this exercise; and the best to be said for their invention is that they manage an occasional brittle joke.... The prettiest things in the picture are some CinemaScope shots of New York." *The New York Times,* September 29, 1954

"The entire cast, under Jean Negulesco fine direction, contribute a performance as polished as the entire production.... Charles Brackett has pulled out all stops in giving the picture top-notch production values." *Variety,* September 29, 1954

"[The movie] is as shiny and as beautifully engineered as one of the automobiles manufactured by the mythical colossus in the picture.... *Woman's World* [is] an entertaining movie; even though it betrays certain evidences of being deliberately constructed for success." *Saturday Review,* November 23, 1954

REVIEWS FOR JEAN NEGULESCO:

"Jean Negulesco's direction, taking full advantage of CinemaScope, creates a holiday picture of New York as seen by happily excited visitors." *The Hollywood Reporter,* September 29, 1954

"Jean Negulesco made quite a movie out of a city and three couples in *Three Coins in the Fountain.* He is aiming at something of the same thing again in *Woman's World....* Negulesco derives a little bit of comedy ... and a little bit of suspense out of the contest ... but there is not much of a single quality in this hit and-miss film." *New York Herald Tribune,* September 29, 1954

"Jean Negulesco, who has played mixed double before (*Three Coins in the Fountain*), uses the same formula in Technicolored Manhattan instead of Rome. Shuttling from one couple to the next, he tries to combine broad farce with narrow moralizing on success at humor's expense." *Time,* October 18, 1954

ADDITIONAL REVIEWS AND ARTICLES:

Hollywood Reporter July 2, 1953, p. 2; *Daily Variety* February 2, 1954; *New York Times* February 14, 1954; *Hollywood Reporter* February 19, 1954, p. 3; *Variety* February 24, 1954; *Hollywood Reporter* March 12, 1954, p. 3; *Hollywood Reporter* April 7, 1954, p. 2; *Hollywood Reporter* April 26, 1954, p. 1; Hollywood Reporter May 5, 1954, p. 10; *Hollywood Report* May 7, 1954; *Hollywood Report* May 10, 1954, p. 2; *Boxoffice* May 15, 1954; *Hollywood Reporter* June 11, 1954, p. 6; *Hollywood Reporter* June 22, 1954, p. 2; *Hollywood Reporter* August 6, 1954, p. 7; *New York Daily News* September 29, 1954; *Film Daily* September 30, 1954, p. 10; *Woman's Home Companion* October 1954 p. 10–11; *Motion Picture Herald* Product Digest October 2, 1954, p. 169; *Boxoffice* October 9, 1954; *Harrison's Reports* October 2, 1954, p. 158; *Hollywood Citizen-News* October 9, 1954; *America* October 9, 1954, p. 54; *Cue* October 9, 1954; *Los Angeles Examiner* October 9, 1954; *Newsweek* October 18, 1954, p. 100; *Commonweal* October 29, 1954, p. 94; *Today's Cinema* November 22, 1954, p. 7; *Kinematograph Weekly* November 25 1954 p. 14; *Films in Review* December 1954 p. 544; *Monthly Film Bulletin* January 1955 p. 6; *The Star* (U.K.) January 14, 1955; *The Daily Mirror* (U.K.) January 14, 1955; *The Daily Mail* January 14, 1955; *The Daily Express* (U.K.) January 14, 1955; *The Sunday Times* (U.K.) January 16, 1955; *The Times* (U.K.) January 17, 1955, p. 5; *Financial Times* (U.K.) January 17 1955; *The Spectator* (U.K.) January 21, 1955, p. 72; *The Tattler* (U.K.) January 26, 1955, p. 155; *Films and Filming* February 1955 p. 28; *Picturegoer* (U.K.) February 12, 1955; *Mon Film* (France) July 20, 1955

NOTES: The working title of this film was *May the Best Wife Win,* then changed into *A Woman's World* made into *Woman's World* eventually.

Daddy Long Legs

20th Century–Fox; U.S. DeLuxe Color CinemaScope 126 minutes; Premiered in Los Angeles on May 4, 1955

CREDITS: *Producer:* Samuel G. Engel; *Director:* Jean Negulesco; *Screenplay:* Phoebe Ephron, Henry Ephron; Based on the novel by Jean Webster; *Photography:* Leon Shamroy; *Art Directors:* Lyle Wheeler, John DeCuir; *Set Decorators:* Lyle Wheeler, Walter M. Fox; *Editor:* William Reynolds; *Special Photography Effects:* Ray Kellogg; *Wardrobe Director:* Charles Le Maire; *Modern Wardrobe Designer:* Kay Nelson; *Ballet Costumes Designer:* Tom Keogh; *Music Supervisor and Conductor:* Alfred Newman; *Vocal Supervision:* Ken Darby; *Hong-Kong; Rio Ballet Music:* Alex North; *Orchestrators:* Edward B. Powell, Skip Martin, Earle Hagen, Bernard Mayers, Billy May; *Sound:* Alfred Bruzlin, Harry M. Leonard; *Sound Editor:* Al Ross; *Ballet Choreography:* Roland Petit, Jacqueline Lemoine; *Dances Choreography:* Fred Astaire, David Robel; *Makeup:* Ben Nye; *Hair Stylist:* Helen Turpin; *Assistant*

Directors: Eli Dunn, Morris "Mushy" Harmell; *Color Consultant:* Leonard Doss; *Dialogue Coach:* Michael Audley; *Unit Manager:* Gaston Glass; *Drum Coach:* Roy Harte; *Songs:* "Something's Gotta Give," "Dream," "History of the Beat," "Sluefoot," "Welcome Egghead," "C-A-T Spells Cat," "Daddy Long Legs," "Dancing Through Life" and "That'll Get It When It's Almost Gone": music and lyrics by Johnny Mercer

CAST: Fred Astaire (Jervis Pendleton III), Leslie Caron (Julie Andre), Terry Moore (Linda Pendleton), Thelma Ritter (Alicia Pritchard), Fred Clark (Griggs), Charlotte Austin (Sally McBride), Larry Keating (Ambassador Alec Williamson), Kathryn Givney (Gertrude Pendleton), Kelly Brown (Jimmy McBride), Ray Anthony and His Orchestra (Themselves), Marcie Miller, Tommy Mercer (Band Vocalists), Sara Shane (Pat Withers), Numa Lapeyre (Jean), Ann Codee (Mme. Sevanne), Joseph Kearns (Guide), Larry Kent (Butler), Charles Anthony Hughes (Hotel Manager), Ralph Dumke (Mr. Bronson), Damian O'Flynn (Larry Hamilton), Kathryn Card (Miss Carrington), Harry Seymour (Cab Driver), Hellen Van Tuyl (College Dean), J. Anthony Hughes, Bob Adler (Deliverymen), George Dunn (Chauffeur), Janice Carroll (Athletic Girl Dancer), Virginia Hunter, Eileen Maxwell, Shirley Dobel, Lisa Montell, Diane Jergens, Marjorie Hellen, Liliane Montevecchi (College Girls), Tom Selden (College Boy), Lillian Culver (Lady at Art Gallery), David Hoffman, Paul Bradley (Jewelers), Guy Des Rochers (French Lieutenant), Carleton Young, Paul Power (Commission Members), William Hines (Army Sergeant), Frank Kreig (French Farmer), Ivis Goulding (Dignified Woman), Pat Ferguson (Elevator Boy), Steven Geray (Emile), Percival Vivian (Professor), Tim Johnson (Bellhop), Olan Soule (Assistant Hotel Manager), Gregor Momdjean (Dancer), Gertrude Astor (Art Gallery Patron)

PLOT: Wealthy Jervis Pendleton, sent by the State Department to France, is stranded when the car in which they are travelling becomes stuck. Jervis calls at an orphanage for help and is intrigued by 18-year-old orphan Julie, who has a wonderful way with the younger children. Determined to help her, he seeks the aid of the U.S. ambassador, who is aghast when he hears that Jervis wants to adopt an 18-years-old girl, knowing the interpretation certain Congressmen would place on it. Julie is flown to the U.S. and enters Walston College but is never to know the identity of her benefactor. All Julie knows of him is the shadow of his legs on the wall as he left the orphanage so she calls him Daddy Long Legs. At college, Julie's roommates are Jervis' niece, Linda, and Sally McBride. Grateful for the opportunities coming her way, Julie constantly writes to her benefactor; her letters are intercepted by Griggs, Jervis' right-hand man. Miss Pritchard, Jervis' secretary, cries over them and files them on instructions. Two years later, the file is massive. Miss Pritchard reads a letter in which Julie pathetically begs for a reply and forces Griggs to take up the matter with Jervis. He hardly remembers the girl but consents to read the letters and is utterly charmed. Determined to see his ward, Jervis takes Linda's mother to the college's annual dance. Introduced to Julie, Jervis takes her into the garden where he learns all about her unknown guardian whom she pictures as an old man. Back in New York, Jervis eagerly reads Julie's next letter which tells him about her meeting with "nice Mr. Pendleton." It also mentions Jimmy McBride, who has fallen in love with her, but has been disappointed because a job he wanted as a mine engineer in South Africa has fallen through. Jervis fixes a job for McBride in his Bolivian tin mines to get him out of the way. Next Jervis invites Linda and Julie to spend a weekend with him in New York, but only Julie turns up. Julie and Jervis have a dinner in Julie's hotel apartment and spend a wonderful evening together. In the next room is the ambassador to France and, the following morning when Jervis calls on Julie for breakfast, the ambassador gets the wrong impression. He summons Jervis to his room, and while accepting his explanation points out that a romance between the two is ridiculous because of their difference in age. Jervis phones Julie telling her that has been called away on a State mission. Back in college, Julie is miserable. She writes to Daddy Long Legs imploring to let her see him as she desperately needs his advice. Miss Pritchard opens it and cables Jervis that Griggs is critically ill. She then goes to Walston and introduces herself to Julie as a friend who is to take her to New York to see her guardian. For the meeting with Julie, Jervis insists that Griggs pretend to be Daddy Long Legs. But the young lady who enters the room is not Julie but Linda, who wants Jervis' assistance in breaking down her mother's opposition to her marriage to McBride. Greatly relieved, Jervis promises to pay for their wedding. As Julie and Miss Pritchard reach the Pendleton Mansion, a guide is showing visitors the famous Pendleton collection of paintings. Julie turns and sees Jervis standing beside her. It is only when she sees the resemblance between Jervis and the paintings of her guardian's ancestors that the truth dawns on her. (Original press release source)

REVIEWS:

"The picture is a bit too long and occasionally it's slow—but that's quibbling. Who can get too much of Fred Astaire and Leslie?" *The New York Times,* May 6, 1955

"Of its type *Daddy Long Legs* is a winner and there is a double reason named Astaire and Caron—besides the exquisitely mounted production backgrounds." *The New York Post,* May 6, 1955

"No complaints; please; on the 'ah; another remake' lines. For this bestseller has been taken down from the shelves, dusted and jazzed up into one of the top ranking film musicals of the year." *Picturegoer,* June 25, 1955

REVIEWS FOR JEAN NEGULESCO:

"Jean Negulesco in directing manages to maintain interest in the story despite the many musicalised interruptions." *Variety,* May 4, 1955

"Direction by Jean Negulesco tends to drag out the dramatic moments, but this is completely overcome by the beauty and the splendour of Engel's overall production; with the modern wardrobes by Kay Nelson; the colourful ballet costumes by Tom Keogh and the special photographic effects by Ray Kellogg contributing enormously to the eye-pleasing features." *The Hollywood Reporter,* May 4, 1955

"Jean Negulesco, in directing, manages to maintain interest in the story despite the many musicalized interruptions." *Variety,* May 4, 1955

"[Negulesco achieves] the film musical at its best—a warm story performed by ingratiating people." *Look,* May 17, 1955

ADDITIONAL REVIEWS AND ARTICLES:

Hollywood Reporter December 11, 1951, p. 7; *Hollywood Reporter* January 6, 1954, p. 2; *Hollywood Reporter* August 18, 1954, p. 4; *Hollywood Reporter* October 6, 1954, p. 2; *Hollywood Reporter* October 11, 1954, p. 4; *Hollywood Reporter* October 21, 1954, p. 4; *Hollywood Reporter* October 25, 1954, p. 3; *Hollywood Reporter* October 26, 1954, p. 3; *Hollywood Reporter* November 1, 1954, p. 3; *Hollywood Reporter* November 3, 1954, p. 9; *Hollywood Reporter* November 11, 1954, p. 2; *Hollywood Reporter* November 12, 1954, p. 2; 6; 10; 12; *Hollywood Reporter* November 15, 1954, p. 9; *Hollywood Reporter* November 17, 1954, p. 10; *Hollywood Reporter* November 18, 1954, p. 8; *Hollywood Reporter* November 24, 1954 p. 3; *Hollywood Reporter* November 26, 1954, p. 3; *Hollywood Reporter* November 30, 1954, p. 1; *Hollywood Reporter* December 8, 1954, p. 12; *Hollywood Reporter* December 17, 1954, p. 4; *Hollywood Reporter* December 23, 1954, p. 17; *Hollywood Reporter* December 29, 1954, p. 7; *Hollywood Reporter* December 31, 1954, p. 2; *Hollywood Reporter* January 11, 1955, p. 3; *Hollywood Reporter* January 31, 1955, p. 5; *Hollywood Reporter* February 1, 1955, p. 5; *Hollywood Reporter* March 29, 1955, p. 9; *Hollywood Reporter* May 3, 1955, p. 2; *Film Daily* May 4, 1955, p. 6; *Hollywood Reporter* May 5, 1955, p. 1; *L.A. Mirror-News* May 5, 1955; *Hollywood Reporter* May 6, 1955, p. 3; *Motion Picture Herald Product Digest* May 7, 1955, p. 425; *Harrison's Reports* May 7, 1955, p. 75; *Time* May 9, 1955; *New York Time* May 15, 1955; *New Yorker* May 14, 1955; *Newsweek* May 16, 1955; *Saturday Review* May 21, 1955; *Life* May 23, 1955; *Commonweal* May 27, 1955 p. 207; *Dance Magazine* June 1955; *New York Herald Tribune* June 6, 1955; *Today's Cinema* June 6, 1955, p. 7; *Kinematograph Weekly* June 9, 1955, p. 18; *Boxoffice* June 11, 1955; *America June* 22, 1955, p. 223; *Films in Review* June-July 1955 p. 289–290; *Hollywood Reporter* July 8, 1955, p. 3; *Monthly Film Bulletin* July 1955 p. 100; *Films and Filming* August 1955 p. 17; *Les Lettres Françaises* (France) October 5, 1955; *Mon Film* (France) January 4 1956; *Fillette* (France) October 25, 1956; *Cinéma 39* (France) August-September 1959 p. 101; *Cinéma Hors-Série* (France) December 1980; *Entertainment Weekly* September 27, 1991; *L'Avant-Scène du Cinema* (France) October 2012; *Positif* (France) June 2013

AWARDS AND HONORS:

Academy Awards: U.S. 1956: *Nominated:*

Best Art Direction Color: Lyle Wheeler, John DeCuir; Set Decoration: Walter M. Scott, Paul S. Fox

Best *Music:* Scoring of a Musical Picture: Alfred Newman

Best Song for "Something's Got to Give": Music and lyrics by Johnny Mercer

The Rains of Ranchipur

20th Century–Fox; U.S. DeLuxe Color CinemaScope 104 minutes; Premiered in New York City on December 14, 1955

CREDITS: *Producer:* Frank Ross; *Director:* Jean Negulesco; *Screenplay:* Merle Miller; Based on the novel *The Rains Came* by Louis Bromfield; *Photography:* Milton Krasner; *Music:* Hugo Friedhofer; *Music Conductor:* Lionel Newman; *Art Directors:* Lyle R. Wheeler, Addison Hehr; *Set Decorators:* Walter M. Scott, Paul S. Fox; *Special Photographic Effects:* Ray Kellogg; *Editor:* Dorothy Spencer; *Wardrobe Direction:* Charles Le Maire; *Costumes Designers:* Travilla, Helen Rose; *Orchestrator:* Maurice DePackh; *Choreography:* Stephen Papich; *Assistant Director:* Eli Dunn; *Makeup:* Ben Nye; *Hair Stylist:* Helen Turpin; *Sound:* Alfred Bruzlin, Harry M. Leonard; *Assistant Art Directors:* Qadeer Ghori, Sami Ahmed; *Color Consultant:* Leonard Doss

CAST: Lana Turner (Lady Edwina Esketh), Richard Burton (Dr. Major Rama Safti), Fred MacMurray (Tom Ransome), Joan Caulfield (Fern Simon), Michael Rennie (Lord Alan Esketh), Eugénie Léontovich (Maharani), Gladys Hurlbut (Maude Simon), Madge Kennedy (Emily Smiley), Carlo Rizzo (Mr. Adoani), Beatrice Kraft (Indian Dancer), King Calder (Homer Smiley), Argentina Brunetti (Mrs. Adoani), John Banner (Raschid), Ivis Goulding (Louise), Ram Singh (Major domo), Lou Krugman (Courier), Rama Bai (Lachmaania), Naji Gabbay (Wagonlit Porter), Jugat Bhatia (Headhunter), Phyllis Johannes (Nurse Gupta), George Brand (Mr. Simon), Elizabeth Prudhomme (Nurse Patel), Aly Wassil (Courier), Trude Wyler (Guest), Ram Chandra (Sattar), Bhupesh Guha, Pasupah Murkerjee, Dr. Yalhiraji Iyengar (Musicians), Kan Thi Iyenger (Singer)

PLOT: Lord Alan Esketh and his beautiful American wife Edwina arrive in Ranchipur, India, to buy an Arabian horse from the maharani. Their marriage is purely a matter of convenience. Edwina wanted his title; he wanted her fortune. She has filled her time with one romantic escapade after another and has acquired a reputation which has preceded her to Ranchipur. At a reception in their honor, the guests include Tom Ransome, Edwina's childhood neighbor. He is now an engineer, disillusioned with life and taken to drink. He has escorted a lovely young Fern Simon at her request. In the afternoon she had introduced herself—and her problem—to him. Her mother wanted to push her into a loveless marriage instead of allowing her to return to Iowa to be a teacher. Also present are Mr. Adoani, the maharani's emissary, and his wife; Mr. and Mrs. Smiley, American missionaries; Raschid-Ul-Rahaim, the chief of Police; and a court favorite, the gifted Dr. Safti, whom Alan and the maharani fear will become the next "victim" of the predatory Edwina. Safti is startled but flattered by the obvious invitation in Edwina's eyes. The antagonism the maharani feels for Edwina mounts when the latter insists on joining in an upcoming tiger hunt. She states her disapproval privately to Edwina, revealing that she raised Safti like s son and that his work is vital to the life of Ranchipur. Edwina states that it is time Safti learned about life and love. Alan is injured on the tiger hunt and during his recovery, a passionate attachment between Edwina and Safti develops. The maharani ordered Edwina to leave the country, taking a chance that the doctor would follow her. A monsoon brings with it earthquake and flood. Edwina can't leave and neither can Tom, who had planned to run out on his growing affection for Fern. Safti is all concern for the homeless and injured, and forgets the message that Edwina is ill with fever. He doesn't see her again until she has recovered and the flood waters have receded due to the selfless bravery of Tom, who dynamited the stagnant waters. Edwina, who has been her own victim of love this time, tells the maharani she is leaving—alone. With only a stop to wish the reunited Fern and Tom happiness and a brief moment with Safti, she goes to her car where Alan; who understands her and what she has given up, always waits for her. (Original press release source)

REVIEWS:

"The lavish settings, the striking authentic Indian locale, and the realistic depiction of the havoc and destruction of a violent earthquake all enhanced by CinemaScope and Technicolor, are outstanding features of this elaborate [film]." *Harrison's Reports,* December 17, 1955

"Louis Bromfield's vital, if somewhat stereotyped characters have been toned down to the dimensions of cardboard puppets and, with the exception of Eugenie Leontovich's superb maharani, are mostly played as such." *Monthly Film Bulletin,* February 1956

"This remake starts with the advantage of fine color photography, the breadth of CinemaScope and ... accomplished players.... [T]he spectacle is magnificent." *Films and Filming,* March 1956

REVIEWS FOR JEAN NEGULESCO:

"[His] earthquake and flood sequences alone make the picture worthwhile as b.o.... Negulesco, with an obvious eye to action, may have felt the story itself was least important or perhaps knew he needed such props for a mediocre script." *Variety,* December 14, 1955

"Negulesco and his crew have fashioned a pip of an earthquake and flood." *The New York Times,* December 16, 1955

"Jean Negulesco's direction is, of course, admirable, and if he has exaggerated a bit in his handling of natural phenomena he has used restraint in the all-too-tempting province of Eastern court life. His settings are lavish, but not ridiculous, and his miscegenation is very polite." *The Spectator* (U.K.), February 24, 1956

ADDITIONAL REVIEWS AND ARTICLES:

Hollywood Reporter January 11, 1955 p. 1; 4; *Hollywood Reporter* May 20, 1955 p. 7; *Hollywood Reporter* June 2, 1955 p. 3; *Hollywood Reporter* June 6, 1955 p. 2; *Hollywood Reporter* July 8, 1955 p. 7; *Variety* June 13, 1955; *Hollywood Reporter* August 12, 1955 p. 10; *Hollywood Reporter* August 16, 1955 p. 5; *Hollywood Reporter* August 18, 1955 p. 3; *Hollywood Reporter* August 22, 1955 p. 3; *Hollywood Reporter* August 29, 1955 p. 6; *Hollywood Reporter* August 30, 1955 p. 15; *Hollywood Reporter* September 7, 1955 p. 6; *Hollywood Reporter* September 14, 1955 p. 3; *Hollywood Reporter* September 15, 1955 p. 8; *Hollywood Reporter* September 16, 1955 p. 3; *Hollywood Reporter* September 23, 1955 p. 12; *Hollywood Reporter* November 21, 1955 p. 7; *American Cinematographer* December 1, 1955 p. 709, *Weekly* January 12, 1956 p. 16; *The Film Daily* December 14, 1955; *Hollywood Reporter* December 14, 1955 p. 3; *Boxoffice* December 17, 1955; *Motion Picture Herald Product Digest* December 17, 1955 p. 705; *Christian Science Monitor* December 27, 1955; *Newsweek* January 2, 1956; *America* January 7, 1956; *Today's Cinema* January 11, 1956; *Commonweal* January 13, 1956, p. 380; *Saturday Review* January 21, 1956 p. 42; *Time* January 9, 1956 p. 86; *Hollywood Reporter* February 17, 1956 p. 5; *Film Complet* (France) October 11, 1956; *Mon Film* (France) October 31, 1956; *Film Complet* (France) March 21, 1957; *L'Avant Scène Cinéma* (France) January 2015

AWARDS AND HONORS:

Academy Awards: U.S. 1956: *Nominated:* Best Effects; Special Effects.

Boy on a Dolphin

20th Century–Fox; U.S.–Italy DeLuxe Color CinemaScope 113 minutes; Premiered in New York City and San Francisco on April 10, 1957

CREDITS: *Producer:* Samuel G. Engel; *Director:* Jean Negulesco; *Screenplay:* Ivan Moffat, Dwight Taylor; Based on the novel by David Divine; *Assistant Directors:* Eli Dunn, Carlo Lastricati; *Photography:* Milton Krasner; *Cameraman* Paul Lockwood; *Assistant Cameraman:* Al Lebowitz; *Art Directors:* Lyle R. Wheeler, Jack Martin Smith; *Editor:* William Mace; *Set Decorators:* Bruno Avesani, Ugo Pericle; *Special Photographic Effects:* Ray Kellogg; *Costumes:* Charles Le Maire; *Wardrobe Director:* Franco Salvi, Anna Gobbi; *Makeup:* Henry Vilardo; *Hair Styles:* Catherine Reed; *Sound:* W.D. Flick, Harry M. Leonard, Emmett O'Brien; *Music:* Hugo Friedhofer; *Conductor;* Lionel Newman; *Orchestrator:* Edward B. Powell; *Dialogue Director:* Mike Audley; "Panegyris"; Greek Folk Dances and Songs Society; *Director:* Dora Stratou; *Choreographer:* Yianni Fleury; Music *Director:* Fivos Anoyanakis; Song "Boy in a Dolphin" based on the music by Takis Moranis; Greek text by J. Fermanglou; American lyrics by Paul Francis Webster; Music adapted by Hugo Friedhofer

CAST: Alan Ladd (Dr. Jim Calder), Clifton Webb (Victor Parmalee), Sophia Loren (Phaedra), Alexis Minotis (Government Man), Jorge Mistral (Rhif), Laurence Naismith (Dr. Hawkins), Piero Giagnoni (Niko), Gertrude Flynn (Miss Dill), Charles Fawcett (William B. Baldwin), Charlotte Terrabust (Mrs. Baldwin), Margaret Stahl (Miss Baldwin), Orestes Rallis (Chief of Police), Antonio Maroudas (Singer-Guitarist in Tavern), George Saris (First Mate)

PLOT: While diving for sponges off the Greek island of Hydra, a peasant girl, Phaedra, finds a sunken wooden wreck on which she glimpses a golden statue of a boy mounted on a dolphin, chained to the hull. Struggling to the surface slightly injured, she is helped aboard the boat by her fiancé Rhif, who takes her to Dr. Hawkins. Hawkins extracts a nail which he believes was made 2000 years ago and was probably part of a ship which sank in a storm off Hydra while carrying art treasures to Delos. Believing Phaedra's story of the statue, he consults a reference book and makes a sketch of the statue. Phaedra takes the sketch to Dr. Jim Calder, an American archaeologist who thinks it is one of the many stories brought him by natives anxious to make easy money. Victor Parmalee, a crooked collector, is equally disinterested. Tired and dejected, Phaedra again encounters Calder, shows him the sketch and intrigues him sufficiently for him to make a date with her at a café that evening. While she is waiting for Calder, she meets Parmalee again who, on learning for whom she is waiting, becomes interested. Soon Calder and Parmalee are aware of the other's intention—Calder to deliver the statue to the Greek people and Parmalee to steal it and satisfy his appetite for antiques. Phaedra tells Rhif and Dr. Hawkins about Parmalee's plan to get the statue, for which he will pay generously. Phaedra is to mislead Calder in his search for the statute with fruitless dives in areas away from its true location. Meanwhile, Calder gets an hint from Phaedra's younger brother Niko that Parmalee's yacht is anchored in the remote Mandrake Bay and goes there to confront him. Calder refuses the huge bribe the collector offers him to leave the field clear. Now aware of Phaedra's duplicity, Calder meets her in a tavern where he tells her that he will find the treasure alone using electronic equipment. Making her excuses, Phaedra hurries to impart the news to Parmalee, who sends Phaedra, men and equipment to free the statue from the sunken ship and hide it in a cave. The next morning, Niko offers to show Calder where Phaedra discovered the statue. Underwater, Calder finds evidence that the figure has been recently cut away. Phaedra and the doctor go to Rhif's shack and catch him with a bundle of notes. When Hawkins asks for his share, Rhif strikes him. Rhif orders Phaedra to dance for Calder that night at the tavern, while he transfers the statue to his own boat. That night Phaedra dances with Calder but Niko arrives and informs Calder that Parmalee's yacht has been moved. Later that night, Calder turns on Phaedra, telling her she is stealing something that belongs to her country. Relenting, Phaedra offers to show Calder the cave where the statue is hidden but on diving there they find it has been taken away. Phaedra confronts Rhif who binds and carries her to his boat. Tied to the rail, she makes frenetic signs to Niko, standing on the shore, to cut the ropes holding the statue beneath the vessel. That night Rhif's boat is moored near Parmalee's yacht, where Rhif receives the final payment. A Government vessel, alerted by Calder, shines its searchlight on the yacht and an official comes aboard with Calder and charges Parmalee with contravening the laws by taking Greek treasure out of the country. Parmalee denies ever having set eyes on it. Calder then hauls up the ropes of Rhif's boat to find that both ends has been severed.

Niko cut the figure loose. Soon a procession of boats, led by Niko and bearing the Boy on a Dolphin, sails in triumph into Hydra harbor. Calder has his eye on another treasure: Phaedra. He overtakes her as she runs from him and they embrace passionately. (Original press release source)

REVIEWS:

"Aside from being a visual treat, the picture ... is a colorful and interesting romantic adventure melodrama." *Harrison's Reports,* April 13, 1957

"*Boy on a Dolphin* brings one of the visual treats of the year.... No need to worry much about the story the picture tells. You will be entranced as you simply sit and look." *New York World-Telegram,* April 20, 1957

"A light sophisticated thriller might have been made from this plot, but it is crippled from the start by a weak script, which never knows whether to take itself seriously or not, and the flaccid direction." *Monthly Film Bulletin,* June 1957

REVIEWS FOR JEAN NEGULESCO:

"Jean Negulesco's direction has been most successful in his utilization of the unrivalled beauty of the Grecian backgrounds. He has caught the grace and timeless form of Greek art and made it an integral part of the story." *The Hollywood Reporter,* April 11, 1957

"Director Jean Negulesco has not overextended any of the values, playing tin the right tempo for the locale and likewise playing down the neo-melodramatics." *Variety,* April 17, 1957

"As for the direction by Jean Negulesco, it is in tune with the classical landscape—a stillness of the ages hangs over everything." *New York Herald Tribune,* April 20, 1957

"Unfortunately director Jean Negulesco appears out of sympathy with the Greek way of life. The delight of his story eludes him. Instead of developing the Greek character he tries to invest the story with Hollywood romantic clichés." *Films and Filming,* June 1957

ADDITIONAL REVIEWS AND ARTICLES:

Hollywood Reporter May 17, 1955, p. 6; *Hollywood Reporter* November 2, 1955, p. 3; *Hollywood Reporter* July 16, 1956, p. 2; *Hollywood Reporter* July 26, 1956, p. 3; *Hollywood Reporter* August 24, 1956, p. 1; *Hollywood Reporter* September 19, 1956, p. 17; *Hollywood Reporter* September 21, 1956, p. 15; *Hollywood Reporter* October 19, 1956, p. 2; *Variety* November 14, 1956; *The Times* (U.K.) November 27, 1956; *Variety* December 12, 1956; *Hollywood Reporter* December 21, 1956, p. 34; *Variety* December 26, 1956; *Variety* April 3, 1957;

Hollywood Reporter April 10, 1957, p. 13; *Daily Variety* April 11, 1957, p. 3; *Film Daily* April 11, 1957, p. 6; *Picture Herald Product Digest* April 13, 1957, p. 337; *The New York Times* April 19, 1957, sec. C p. 6–7; *Boxoffice* April 20, 1957; *The New York Times* April 20, 1957, *New York Daily News* April 20, 1957; *Time* April 22, 1957, p. 108; *The Christian Science Monitor Boston* April 30, 1957, p. 4; *Daily Film Renter* April 26, 1957, p. 3; *Today's Cinema* April 26, 1957; *The New Yorker* April 27, 1957, p. 68; *Kinematograph Weekly* May 2, 1957, p. 18; *American Cinematographer* May 1957 p. 299; *Films in Review* May 1957 p. 222–223; *Commonweal* May 3, 1957, p. 127; *America* May 4, 1957, p. 180; *Life Magazine* May 6, 1957; *The Spectator* (U.K.) May 7, 1957; *Saturday Review* May 11, 1957, p. 27; *The Observer* (U.K.) May 12, 1957; *The Sunday Express* May 12, 1957, *News of the World* (U.K.) May 12, 1957; *The Times* (U.K.) May 13, 1957; *Films And Filming* June 1957 p. 24; *Le Soir* (Belgium) June 28, 1957, p. 22; *Mon Film* (France) July 31, 1957; *New York Daily News* August 4, 1957; *Variety* November 27, 1957

AWARDS AND HONORS:

Academy Awards: U.S. 1958: *Nominated:* Best Music: Scoring; Hugo Friedhofer

NOTES: Julie London sound tracked Sophia Loren's singing voice.

The Gift of Love

20th Century–Fox; U.S. DeLuxe Color CinemaScope 105 minutes; Premiered in New York City on February 11, 1958

CREDITS: *Producer:* Charles Brackett; *Director:* Jean Negulesco; *Screenplay:* Luther Davis; Based on the story "The Little Horse" by Nelia Gardner White; *Photography:* Milton Krasner; *Art Directors:* Lyle R. Wheeler, Mark-Lee Kirk; *Editor:* Hugh S. Fowler; *Set Decorators:* Walter M. Scott, Eli Benneche; *Special Photographic Effects:* L.B. Abbott, Emil Kosa, Jr.; *Executive Wardrobe Designer:* Charles Le Maire; *Makeup:* Ben Nye; *Hair Stylist:* Helen Turpin; *Assistant Directors:* Jack Gertsman, Joe Rickards; *Music:* Cyril J. Mockridge; *Music Conductor:* Lionel Newman; *Orchestration:* Edward B. Powell; *Sound:* Charles Peck, Warren Delaplain, Paul Franz; *Sound Editors:* Kenneth Honnold, Dick Jensen, Bob Weatherford; *Color Consultant:* Leonard Doss; *Song:* "The Gift of Love"; music by Sammy Fain; lyrics by Paul Francis Wenbster; sung by Vic Damone

CAST: Lauren Bacall (Julie Reinhardt Beck), Robert Stack (Bill Beck), Evelyn Rudie (Hitty), Lorne Greene (Grant Allan), Anne Seymour (Miss McMasters), Edward Platt (Dr. Miller), Joseph Kearns (Mr. Rynicker), Benjamin Sherman "Scatman" Crothers (Sam the Gardener), Charity Grace (Sarah the Housekeeper), Alena Murray, Trude Wyler, Linne Ahlstrand (Nurses), Sean Meany, Joe Devlin (Waiters), George Chester (Driver), Kay Cole, Nancy De Carl, Michele De Casse, Susan Fielding (Girls), Robert Brubaker (State Trooper), Theresa Harris (Sam's Wife), Judith Woodbury, Myna Cunard (Wives), John Bradford (Air Force Lieutenant), Paul Kruger (Justice of the Peace), Kurt Katch (Professor), Steven Geray (Toy Store Proprietor), Mary Hennessey (Switchboard Operator), Rosemary Ace (Secretary)

PLOT: Brilliant physicist Bill Beck meets Julie Reinhardt, secretary to Dr. Miller, when he calls seeking medical advice for insomnia. From this meeting the two fall deeply in love and, after a brief courtship, are married. Several years later they are still as much in love as ever but one day Julie has a serious heart attack. Told to rest in bed by Dr. Miller, Julie keeps the news of her condition from Bill and pretends that she has broken a bone in her leg. Realizing that her days are numbered, Julie persuades Bill to consent to their adoption of a child. At an orphanage Julie sees an imaginative eight-year-old called Hitty who has three times been returned to the orphanage by couples who cannot understand her. Hitty is taken to the Becks home and soon the adoption formalities are completed. There's great love between Julie and the child; Julie methodically sets out to teach her how to take her place after she has gone. Bill, with his logical mind, is unable to find much common ground with the child, who has an active imagination. Julie and Bill have their first row when Hitty contracts influenza and Julie insists on staying with her instead of attending a lecture with her husband. Soon after, Julie has a fatal heart attack. The shock causes Bill to forget his responsibilities and he stays away from home for three days. When he returns, Hitty devotes herself to him but her attentions and her insistence that Julie still talks to her only serve to twist the knife in Bill's wounded heart and he loses his temper with her. Believing that she is not wanted, Hitty returns to the orphanage. Alone in the once happy house, Bill is troubled by nameless fear which prompts him to phone the orphanage to learn that Hitty has disappeared. He joins the police and the orphanage authorities in the search. A premonition takes him to the top of a cliff where Julie and Hitty first met. He finds the child has fallen from the cliff and is in danger of drowning. As he carries Hitty in his arms to the car, he agrees with her that the spirit of Julie sent him to her rescue. (Original press release source)

REVIEWS:
"Filmed with great human values for both men and women, this is a film that should stir the emotions of every audience." *The Hollywood Reporter,* February 7, 1958

"Sweetness and cuteness flow from [this film] like the luxuriousness that exudes from the beautiful family kitchen, which glistens in color and CinemaScope. And prettiness is in the performances that all the actors give." *The New York Times,* February 11, 1958

REVIEWS FOR JEAN NEGULESCO:
"Jean Negulesco has directed the film sensitively." *New York Herald Tribune,* February 11, 1958

"[He] works with a poignant touch, making the loves so real, so moving, it's a cinch handkerchiefs will be in use." *Variety,* February 12, 1958

"[He] has timed the proceedings with leisurely warmth." *Independent Exhibitors Film Bulletin,* February 17, 1958

ADDITIONAL REVIEWS AND ARTICLES:
Hollywood Reporter August 18, 1957, p. 3; *Hollywood Reporter* August 23, 1957, p. 8; *American Cinematographer* September 1957 p. 562; *Hollywood Reporter* September 18, 1957, p. 9; *Hollywood Reporter* November 22, 1957, p. 7; *Daily Variety* February 7, 1958, p. 3; *Hollywood Citizen-News* February 8, 1958; *Hollywood Examiner* February 8, 1958; *Los Angeles Times* February 8, 1958; *Seattle Post-Intelligencer* February 14, 1958; *Cue* February 15, 1958; *Harrison's Reports* February 15, 1958, p. 26; *Film Daily* February 17 1958 p. 11; *Boxoffice* February 17, 1958; *Motion Picture Herald Product Digest* February 22, 1958, p. 725; *The New Yorker* February 22, 1958, p. 76; *Motion Picture Herald* February 22, 1958, p. 725; *Modern Screen* March 1958; *Time* February 24, 1958; *Christian Science Monitor* March 4, 1958; *Newsweek* March 10, 1958, p. 108; *The Daily Cinema* March 10, 1958, p. 4; *Kinematograph Weekly* March 13, 1958, p. 14; *The Evening Standard* (U.K.) March 13, 1958; *The Evening News* (U.K.) March 13, 1958; *The Star* (U.K.) March 13, 1958; *The Daily Sketch* (U.K.) March 13, 1958; *America* March 15, 1958; *The Sunday Times* (U.K.) March 16, 1958; *The Observer* (U.K.) Match 16, 1958; *The Times* (U.K.) March 17, 1958; *The Financial Times* (U.K.) March 17, 1958; *FilmFacts* March 19, 1958, p. 29–30; *Monthly Film Bulletin* April 1958; *Films and Filming* April 1970 p. 86

A Certain Smile

20th Century–Fox; U.S. Color DeLuxe CinemaScope 106 minutes; Premiered in New York City on July 31, 1958

CREDITS: *Producer:* Henry Ephron; *Director:* Jean Negulesco; *Screenplay:* Frances Goodrich, Albert Hackett; Based on the novel *Un certain sourire* by Françoise Sagan; *Photography:* Milton Krasner; *Art Directors:* Lyle R. Wheeler, John DeCuir; *Editor:* Louis R. Loeffler; *Set Decorators:* Walter M. Scott, Paul S. Fox; *Costumes:* Marry Wills; *Wardrobe Designer:* Charles Le Maire; *Music:* Alfred Newman; *Sound:* Charles Peck, Harry M. Leonard, Bernard Freericks; *Assistant Director:* Arthur Lueker; *Makeup:* Ben Nye; *Hair Stylist:* Helen Turpin; *Unit Manager:* Gaston Glass; *Dialogue Director:* Carl Shain; *Color Consultant:* Leonard Doss; *Song:* "A Certain Smile": music by Sammy Fain; lyrics by Paul Francis Webster; sung by Johnny Mathis

CAST: Rossano Brazzi (Luc Ferrand), Joan Fontaine (Françoise Ferrand), Bradford Dillman (Bertrand Griot), Christine Carère (Dominique Vallon), Eduard Franz (Monsieur Vallon), Katherine Locke (Madame Vallon), Kathryn Givney (Madame Griot), Steven Geray (Denis), Johnny Mathis (Himself), Trude Wyler (Madame Denis), Sandy Livingston (Catherine), Renate Hoy (Mlle. Minot), Muzaffer Tema (Pierre), Carol Van Dyke, Gabriel Del Valle (South Americans), Feridun Colgecan (Hotel Manager), Edit Angold (Cook), David Hoffman (Concierge), Yvette Mimieux, Pat Mitchell, Hernan Belmonte

PLOT: Bertrand Griot, a student at the Sorbonne, plans to marry fellow student Dominique Vallon if he can persuade his mother to lend him part of his inheritance before it is due. Bertrand introduces Dominique to his uncle Luc Bertrand, a middle-aged philanderer, married to beautiful Françoise. Luc agrees to drive the two young people to Bertrand's mother for a dinner. Madam Griot refuses to advance her son the money. Later that evening, Luc takes Dominique into the garden where he kisses her. She responds. Dominique becomes so infatuated with Luc that she refuses to go out with Bertrand, excusing herself on the ground of studying. When Françoise calls Dominique to see if she can be of any assistance, the woman is at first frigid but later consents to go to a party which includes Françoise and Luc. That night before leaving her at the Sorbonne, Luc tells Dominique that he is going to the Riviera and invites her to spend a week with him. Her conscience troubled, Dominique asks Bertrand to visit them at her parents' house during the vacation. Bertrand's arrival on a motorcycle distresses Dominique's mother, whose only son was killed in a motorcycle crash. As he leaves, Dominique begs him to take her with him. He refuses, so she decides to accept Luc's invitation. They have an idyllic week together, and Luc suggests they extend until he is called back to Paris on urgent business. Dominique changes her mind and takes her mother out of the house and in a café she confesses her love for Luc. The following day, Luc telephones Dominique and suggests they do not see each other again. A few days later, in a restaurant, Dominique is broken-hearted when she sees Luc with another woman. She runs out into the street and is hit by a car. Refusing assistance, she staggers on and collapses. Luc takes her to his home to recuperate. Françoise senses that Dominique is the girl with whom Luc spent his holiday. When Dominique recovers, she is fetched home by her father. On the way she tells the old man everything. Françoise threatens to leave Luc for good, but changes her mind when he pleads pitifully for her to remain as his romantic days are over. At the Sorbonne, Bertrand feels that he has successfully put Dominique out of his mind, but as she walks into class, he follows and falls into step beside her. (Original press release source)

REVIEWS:

"[The film has] a slick, forceless, manufactured quality.... Rarely moving." *The New York Times,* August 1, 1958

"A film of magnificent scenic beauty.... The story is somewhat weak dramatically, but on the whole it has enough emotional appeal and charm...." *Harrison's Reports,* August 2, 1958

REVIEWS FOR JEAN NEGULESCO:

"The film tells of people who sin, who suffer for it, and who are capable of feeling remorse. This gives the actors something to act and director Jean Negulesco takes subtle and intelligent advantage of it." *The Hollywood Reporter,* July 30, 1958

"Having so strenuously toned down the amoral aspects of their story, producer Henry Ephron and director Jean Negulesco apparently decided to go whole hog for visual aspects." *Variety,* July 30, 1958

"Director Jean Negulesco and screenwriters Frances Goodrich and Albert Hackett, all competent practitioners, are hard put to it to keep things going." *New York Herald Tribune,* August 1, 1958

ADDITIONAL REVIEWS AND ARTICLES:

Paris Match December 7, 1957; *Hollywood Reporter* February 14, 1958, p. 12; *Hollywood Reporter* February 17, 1958, p. 5; *Hollywood Reporter* February 19, 1958, p. 4; *Hollywood Reporter* April 1, 1958, p. 3; *Hollywood Reporter* May 2, 1958, p. 8; *Ciné Revue* June 13 1958; *The Sunday News* July 13, 1958, sec 2 p. 3; *Film Daily* July 30, 1958, p. 6; *New York World-Telegram* August 1, 1958; *New York Daily News* August 1, 1958; *The Morning Telegraph* August 1, 1958, p. 2; *Motion Picture Herald Product Digest* August 2, 1958, p. 928; *LA Mirror-News* August 9, 1958; *The New Yorker* August 9, 1958, p. 58; *Cue* August 9, 1958; *Time* August 9, 1958, p. 70; *Boxoffice* August 11, 1958; *Newsweek* August 11, 1958, p. 87; *Commonweal* August 15, 1958, p. 6; *America* August 23, 1958, p. 539; *The Daily Cinema* August 25, 1958, p. 7; *Kinematograph Weekly* August 28, 1958, p. 17; *Film Facts* September 17, 1958, p. 137–138; *The Times* (U.K.) September 18, 1958; *Evening News* (U.K.) September 18 1958; *The Evening Standard* (U.K.) September 18, 1958; *The Star* (U.K.) September 18, 1958; *The Daily Mail* (U.K.) September 19, 1958; *The Daily Mirror* (U.K.) September 19, 1958; *News Chronicles* (U.K.), September 19, 1958; *The Daily Sketch* (U.K.) September 19, 1958; *The Observer* (U.K.) September 21, 1958; *News of the World* (U.K.), September 21, 1958; *The Sunday Times* (U.K.) September 21, 1958; *The Financial Times* (U.K.) September 22, 1958; *Films in Review* October 1958; *Films in Review* October 1958 p. 456–457; *Modern Screen* October 1958 p. 8; *Monthly Film Bulletin* October 1958 p. 123; *Films and Filming* October 1958 p. 23; *Les Lettres Françaises* October 30, 1958; *Mon Film* (France) December 31, 1958; *Screenland* January 1959 p. 15–17; *Image et Son-La Revue du Cinéma* (France) December 1959 p. 50; *Film Ideal* (Spain) May 15, 1965, pp. 133–134

AWARDS AND HONORS:

Academy Awards: U.S. 1959: *Nominated:* Best Costumes: Charles Le Maire, Mary Willis; Best Art *Direction:* Lyle R. Wheeler, John DeCuir; Set Decorations: Walter M. Scott, Paul S. Fox; Best *Music:* Song "A Certain Smile": *Music:* Sammy Fain; lyrics: Paul Francis Webster.

NOTES: Italian Actress Lucia Bosè and German Actor Curt Jurgens were originally chosen by the producers as the leads. Actor James

MacArthur was initially cast as "Bertrand"; but had to withdraw because of a previous commitment.

Count Your Blessings

Metro-Goldwyn-Mayer; U.S.–U.K. Metrocolor CinemaScope 102 minutes; Premiered in New York City on April 23, 1959

CREDITS: *Producer:* Karl Tunberg; *Director:* Jean Negulesco; *Screenplay:* Karl Tunberg; Based on the novel *The Blessing* by Nancy Mitford; *Music Composer and Conductor:* Franz Waxman; *Photography:* Milton Krasner, George J. Folsey; *Art Directors:* William A. Horning, Randall Duell, Don Ashton; *Set Decorators:* Henry Grace, Keogh Gleason; *Color Consultant:* Charles K. Hagedon; *Assistant Director:* William Shanks; *Hair Stylist:* Sydney Guilaroff; *Editor:* Harold F. Kress; *Recording Supervisor:* Franklin Milton; *Gowns:* Helen Rose; *Makeup:* William Tuttle, David Aylott

CAST: Deborah Kerr (Grace Allingham), Rossano Brazzi (Charles-Edouard de Valhubert), Maurice Chevalier (Duc de St. Cloud), Martin Stephen (Sigismond "Sigi"), Tom Helmore (Hugh Palgrave), Ronald Squire (Sir Conrad Allingham), Patricia Medina (Albertine), Mona Washbourne (Nanny), Steven Geray (Guide), Lumsden Hare (John), Kim Parker (Secretary), Frank Kreig (Tourist)

PLOT: Grace Allingham's meeting with Captain Charles-Edouard de Valhubert in wartime London is a welcome respite from her ambulance driving duties, even if he comes as a mere messenger from her fiancé, Hugh Palsgrave. The role of messenger is not in keeping with the vibrant and passionate personality of the French officer. A whirlwind romance ends in marriage for the English girl and her Frenchman, but the ensuing nine years keep them apart. Their small son Sigi barely knows his father. For that matter, neither does Grace. When the war ends, Grace and the captain honeymoon, but it's spent nursing Sigi—and Charles—through the measles! In Paris, where they will make their home, Grace finds she is the mistress of great houses and the bearer of a historic name. She also learns that Charles is an incurable flirt—a Frenchman to the core. His uncle, Duc de St. Cloud, tries to impress upon Grace that Charles is just as incurably in love with her and just as incurably a family man. But an episode in the family museum leads her to believe that Charles is unfaithful again. She takes Sigi to England and starts divorce proceedings. This delights Sigi, who visualizes himself being spoiled first by one parent, then the other. He mischievously thwarts every effort made by Charles to contact Grace. But while he is staying with his father in Paris, Charles decides that it is best for the boy to have one permanent home rather than two "half homes" and to prepares to send him back to his mother. He will now see him less frequently and for shorter periods. Not liking this decision, Sigi slips out of the house and disappears. Charles notifies Grace and she arrives from London with her father and Hugh Palgrave, who once again is her fiancé. Sigi is found perched atop a statue in the Place Joffre, and by this time his manipulations to keep his parents apart have been revealed and misunderstandings between Charles and Grace are cleared up. When a crowd in the Place Joffre bursts into the strains of "La Marseillaise," Grace joins in. She has determined to be first and foremost a French wife and mother. (Original press release source)

REVIEWS:

"A humorous, somewhat sophisticated romantic comedy that should go over pretty well with the general run of movie-goers except perhaps, the dyed-in-the-wool action fans." *Harrison's Reports,* April 4, 1959

"[T]his exceedingly brittle comedy-romance … looks gorgeous in color and CinemaScope … but the wit and the flow of the story do not quite match this sheer exquisiteness for the simple reason that there isn't much story, after it has been boiled down." *The New York Times,* April 24, 1959

"*Count Your Blessings* suffers from the conviction that marble and Mercedes magnificence and a Gallic ambiance can together create a comedy style." *Monthly Film Bulletin,* June 1959

REVIEWS FOR JEAN NEGULESCO:

"Negulesco's direction has a sustained and a knowing good humor…" *The Hollywood Reporter,* April 3, 1959

"Jean Negulesco guides his charges competently, but he's handicapped by the slow-paced yarn." *Variety,* April 8, 1959

"This elegantly furnished tastefully Metrocolor film in which director Jean Negulesco has tried to turn Nancy Mitford's nitty-witty high-society farce into a conventional comedy, develops into a fairly funny mildly sophisticated what-is-it, rather like an interpretation of *The Diary of a Chambermaid* with the last six books of the *Odyssey.*" *Time,* April 27, 1959

"Director Jean Negulesco has wisely buttered up the more insubstantial scenes by playing them against fascinating, beautifully photographed Parisian backgrounds." *Films and Filming,* July 1959

ADDITIONAL REVIEWS AND ARTICLES:
Daily Variety August 1, 1951; *Los Angeles Times* May 15, 1954; *The Hollywood Reporter* March 28, 1956; *The Hollywood Reporter* November 8, 1957 p. 3; *The Hollywood Reporter* January 28, 1958 p. 3; *The Hollywood Reporter* June 17, 1958, p. 1; *The Hollywood Reporter* June 20, 1958, p. 2; *The Hollywood Reporter* August 29, 1958, p. 9; *The Hollywood Reporter* November 7, 1958, p. 10; *Daily Variety* April 3, 1959 p. 3; *Motion Picture Herald Product Digest* April 4, 1959 p. 212; *Box Office* April 6, 1959; *Film Daily* April 6, 1959, p. 6; *New York Herald Tribune* April 24, 1959; *Newsweek* April 27, 1959, p. 114; *Commonweal* May 1, 1959; *The New Yorker* May 2, 1954, p. 154; *America* May 9, 1959, p. 314; *The Daily Cinema* May 15, 1959; *Saturday Review* May 23, 1959; *The Daily Herald* (U.K.) June 12, 1959; *The Daily Express* (U.K.) June 12, 1959; *The Daily Telegraph* (U.K.) June 13, 1959; *The Guardian* (U.K.) June 13, 1959; *The Sunday Times* (U.K.) June 14, 1959; *The Sunday Express* (U.K.) June 14, 1959; *The Observer* (U.K.) June 14, 1959; *News of the World* (U.K.) June 14, 1959; *The Times* (U.K.) June 15, 1959; *The Spectator* (U.K.) June 19, 1959; *Image et Son-La Revue du Cinéma* (France) December 1961 p. 149

The Best of Everything

20th Century–Fox; The Company of Artists; A Jerry Wald Production; U.S. DeLuxe Color CinemaScope 121 minutes; Premiered in New York City on October 8, 1959

CREDITS: *Producer:* Jerry Wald; *Director:* Jean Negulesco; *Screenplay:* Edith Sommer, Mann Rubin; Based on the novel by Rona Jaffe; *Photography:* William C. Mellor; *Art Directors:* Lyle R. Wheeler, Jack Martin Smith, Mark-Lee Kirk; *Editors:* Robert Simpson, Hugh Fowler; *Set Decorators:* Walter M. Scott Stuart A. Reiss; *Costumes:* Adele Palmer; *Music:* Alfred Newman; *Orchestrators:* Earle Hagen, Herbert W. Spencer; *Sound:* Alfred Bruzlin. Harry M. Leonard. W.D. Flick; *Makeup:* Ben Nye; *Hair Stylist;* Helen Turpin; *Assistant Director:* Eli Dunn; *Color Consultant:* Leonard Doss; *Song:* "The Best of Everything": words and music by Sammy Cahn and Alfred Newman; sung by Johnny Mathis

CAST: Hope Lange (Caroline Bender), Stephen Boyd (Mike Rice), Suzy Parker (Gregg Adams), Martha Hyer (Barbara Lamont), Diane Baker (April Morrison), Brian Aherne (Fred Shalimar), Robert Evans (Dexter Key), Brett Halsey (Eddie Harris), Donald Harron (Sidney Carter), Sue Carson (Mary Agnes), Linda Hutchings (Jane), Lionel Kane (Paul Landers), Ted Otis (Dr. Ronnie Wood), Louis Jourdan (David Savage), Joan Crawford (Amanda Farrow), June Blair (Brenda), Myrna Hansen (Judy Masson), Alena Murray, Rachel Stephens, Julie Payne (Girls in Typing Pool), Nora O'Mahoney (Scrubwoman), David Hoffman (Joe), Al Austin (Bill), Stephen Gant (Actor), Theodora Davitt (Margo Stewart), Pat Crest (Nancy Stewart), Mary Patricia Cameron (Miss X), Mary Flynn (Nurse), Molly Glessing, Jesslyn Fax (Aunts), Byron Morrow (Executive), John Rockwell (Busboy), Roxanne Delman (Alice Johnson), Wally Brown (Drunk), Joe Bardot, Mike Mahoney (Policemen)

PLOT: The business day is beginning in New York and the shorthand typists stream into the towering skyscrapers. Among them is Caroline Bender, newly graduated and on her way to her first job with Fabian, a leading publishing house. Mary Agnes, head of the typing pool, gives Caroline a test as Mike Rice, an editor, deals with his hangover. Caroline is assigned to Amanda Farrow, whose secretary is absent. Mary Agnes explains the private lives of the other girls, including Barbara Lamont, pretty, worried about her baby and her affairs with married Sidney Carter; Brenda, the office sexpot; Jane, the severe one, and Gregg Adams, the missing one. Caroline daydreams about her fiancé Eddie Davis, who is in Europe. Amanda proves to be an exacting boss. As Caroline emerges from the first encounter, she runs into April Morrison, another new girl. At lunch, Gregg joins them. She is playing truant so that she can be auditioned by David Savage. April is assigned to Mr. Shalimar, editor-in-chief, a wolf in gray flannel. His pass at April during overtime gets him nowhere. Caroline dares to put in a good report on a manuscript rejected by Miss Farrow. Over a drink that evening, she finds that Mike Rice is a devotee of the bottle. He tells her she is better off married than in the cut-throat business world. She agrees. She is only waiting for Eddie to come back from Europe. Caroline moves into the Greenwich Village apartment shared by April and Gregg. One night, when she is working overtime, Eddie phones from London: He has married someone else. Gregg is persuaded to help Amanda with a party on the excuse that she might meet theatrical folk there. She does meet David Savage, and he whisks her away to his apartment. The annual picnic is a disturbing business. Barbara Lemont and Sydney Carter discover that their affair is common knowledge. April Morrison meets Dexter Kay, a rich playboy. Mike tells Caroline her ambition is making her hard. Gregg just sleeps through it; she has not been home before dawn for nights. Gregg tells Amanda she is leaving Fabian's and Amanda says she's a fool. This is soon proven: At the tryout of the play, David tells Gregg she can't make the grade. At Mary Agnes' wedding, Mike and Caroline learn that April is pregnant. Caroline asks Mike up to her apartment for dinner. The phone rings. It is Eddie back from Europe. He tells Caroline he is coming to New York and wants to see her. Mike leaves while she's still on the phone. Caroline helps April prepare for her elopement with Dexter. When she finds out she has been taken to an abortionist, not a minister, she becomes hysterical and falls out of the sports car. At the hospital, April learns she has been cared for by a young doctor from her own part of the world. When Amanda resigns from Fabian's to get married, Shalimar promotes Caroline in her place. Cast off by David, Gregg deteriorates and takes to spying on him from the fire escape. Caroline is startled to find Miss Farrow has come back to her old job. She tells Caroline it was too late to find happiness in her marriage. Caroline meets Eddie at the hotel. She is shocked when he suggests that she becomes his mistress. Gregg is listening outside David Savage's door when a drunk tries to get it open. In her panic at being discovered, she goes out onto the fire escape, trips and falls into her death. It is the end of another day at Fabian's. As Caroline leaves, the girls call out, "Good night, Miss Bender." She is preoccupied. Outside, as dusk descends on New York, she is joined by Mike, who has been waiting for her across the street. (Original press release source)

REVIEWS:

"*The Best of Everything* is a big, glittery, gaudy Hollywood screen spectacle of New York career girls..." *The Hollywood Reporter,* October 8, 1959

"Thus the drama would seem to have all the potboiling appurtenances of Truth—except that it is slick, superficial, one-tracked and glamorously phoney." *Cue,* October 17, 1959

"As it is the film remains an average example of Jerry Wald Americana..." *Monthly Film Bulletin,* December 1959

REVIEWS FOR JEAN NEGULESCO:

"Direction by Jean Negulesco is first-rate, extracting notable performances..." *Harrison's Report,* October 10, 1959

"[I]t must be acknowledged that director Jean Negulesco keeps the women ambulating through the corridors, various smart bars and a few ornate bedrooms with a certain pictorial agility—at least during the first half.... However the picture tackily lumbers onto the plane of soap opera, under Mr. Negulesco's reverential guide." *The New York Times,* October 9, 1959

"Negulesco's direction is firm-handed at keeping the overwrought story from getting overheated and setting character as well as he can in such a crowd." *Variety,* October 14, 1959

"None knows better than [Negulesco] how to blend novelettish glamour, an air of sophistication and a rather spurious kind of heart-ache—the whole mixture amounting of half-truths and synthetic passions." *The Guardian* (U.K.), November 7, 1959

ADDITIONAL REVIEWS AND ARTICLES:

Hollywood *Reporter* November 13, 1957, p. 2; *Hollywood Reporter* December 11, 1957, p. 4; *Hollywood Reporter* December 22, 1958, p. 3; *Hollywood Reporter* January 5, 1959, p. 3; *Hollywood Reporter* March 20, 1959, p. 1; *Hollywood Reporter* March 31, 1959, p. 1; *Hollywood Reporter* May 4, 1959, p. 1; *Hollywood Reporter* May 8,1959 p. 34; *New York Times* May 17, 1959, p. 24; *Hollywood Reporter* July 31, 1959, p. 10; *Daily Variety* October 8, 1959, p. 3; *Film Daily* October 8, 1959, p. 6; *New York Herald Tribune* October 9, 1959; *Motion Picture Herald Product Digest* October 10, 1959, p. 444; *Boxoffice* October 19, 1959; *Saturday Review* October 19, 1959, p. 24; *Newsweek* October 19, 1959, p. 108; *America* October 24, 1959, p. 111–112; *Time* October 25, 1959, p. 59; *Boxoffice* October 26, 1959; *Sunday Review* October 31 1959 p. 24; *Films in Review* November 1959; *Screen Stories* November 1959; *The New Republic* November 2, 1959, p. 22; *The Daily Cinema* November 4, 1959, p. 9; *The Star* (U.K.) November 5, 1959; *The Evening News* (U.K.) November 5, 1959; *The Daily Mail* (U.K.) November 6, 1959; *The Daily Express* (U.K.) November 6, 1959; *The Daily Telegraph* (U.K.) November 7, 1959; *The Sunday Express* (U.K.), November 8, 1959; *The Observer* (U.K.) November 8, 1959; *The Times* (U.K.) November 9, 1959; *La Cinématographie*

Française November 14, 1959; *Illustrated London News* November 28, 1959; *Hollywood Films and Filming* December 1959 p. 24; *Hollywood Reporter* December 17, 1959, p. 2; *Cinéma 44* (France) March 1960 p. 129; *Mon Film* (France) September 1960 p. 57; *Image et Son-La Revue du Cinéma* (France) December 1960 p. 259; *Vanity Fair* March 2004 p. 202–217; *Film Score Monthly* July-August 2005 p. 61; *The Observer* (U.K.) May 8, 2011, p. 37

AWARDS AND HONORS:
Academy Awards: U.S. 1960: *Nominated:* Best Costume Design Color: Adele Palmer; Best Original Song "The Best of Everything," music by Alfred Newman; lyrics by Sammy Cahn

Jessica

Les Films Ariane (Paris); Dear Film (Rome); United Artists; A Jean Negulesco Production; U.S.-Italy-France Technicolor Panavision 112 minutes; Premiered in Rome on January 17, 1962; Premiered in Los Angeles on March 28, 1962

CREDITS: *Producer-Director:* Jean Negulesco; *Co-Director:* Oreste Palella; *Assistant Director:* Ottavio Oppo; *Screenplay:* Edith Sommer, Ennio De Concini; Based on the novel *The Midwife of Point Clery* by Flora Sandstrom; *Photography:* Piero Portalupi; *Art Director:* Giulio Bongini; *Editors:* Renzo Lucidi, Marie-Sophie Dubus; *Costumes:* Dusty Negulesco, Annalisa Nasalli-Rocca; *Sound:* John Kean, Ennio Sensi; *Makeup:* Amato Garbini, Gabriella Borzelli; *Production Supervisor:* Nate H. Edwards; *Director of Production:* Daniele Micheletti; *Music Composer and Conductor:* Mario Nascimbene; *Songs:* "Jessica," "It Is Better to Love" and "Will You Remember": lyrics and music by Marguerite Monnot and Dusty Negulesco; "The Vespa Song": lyrics and music by Dusty Negulesco and Mario Nascimbene; sung by Maurice Chevalier

CAST: Angie Dickinson (Jessica), Maurice Chevalier (Father Antonio), Noël-Noël (Old Crupi), Gabriele Ferzetti (Edmondo Raumo), Sylva Koscina (Nunzia Tuffi), Agnes Moorehead (Maria Lombardo), Marcel Dalio (Luigi Tuffi), Danielle De Metz (Nicolina Lombardo), Antonio Cifariello (Gianni Crupi), Kerima (Virginia Toriello), Carlo Croccolo (Beppi Toriello), Georgette Any (Mamma Parigi), Rossana Rory (Rosa Masudino), Alberto Rabagliati (Pietro Masudino), Angelo Galassi (Antonio Risino), Marina Berti (Filippella Risino), Manuela Rinaldi (Lucia Casabranca), Gianni Glori Musy (Filippo Casabranca), Joe Pollini (Rosario)

PLOT: Jessica, arriving at Forza D'Agrò to become the village midwife, upsets the life of the little village. Jessica's Italian husband was killed in a car accident as they were setting off on their honeymoon; stricken by the loss, she decided to remain in Italy. Father Antonio is alarmed at the effect she has on the men who watch, including Gianni Crupi. He meets her for the first time as Jessica is on her way to attend her first case in the village: Filippella Risino about to give birth to her ninth child. The village's three most important women, Maria Lombardo, Nunzia Tuffi and Lucia Casabranca, converge on Jessica hoping that the beautiful American girl will turn to be a bad midwife, and they will have an excuse to get rid of her. Maria Lombardo reluctantly admits that professionally Jessica is perfect and also loves her work. Jessica returns to the cottage where she lives on the outskirts of the village, and where Mamma Parigi awaits her. Jessica learned from Mamma Parigi that Crupi the old gardener has injured his hand and is too stubborn to call the doctor. On her scooter, Jessica rides to the castle where he works. At first, he is obstinate, but she eventually tricks him into letting her attend to the injury and they become friends. When Jessica rides past the café, the women are filled with resentment and the men with admiration. The following day, the women hold a meeting and decide to resort to the example set in ancient times by Lysistrata: They will go on strike against their husbands. No more babies will be born in Forza d'Angrò and Jessica will have to leave. This proposal is unanimously accepted. That evening, a series of silent refusals resound throughout the village bedrooms. Jessica goes happily to the Lombardo farm with a wedding gift for Nicolina who is soon to be the bride of Gianni Crupi. Meanwhile, Father Antonio calls on Marchese Raumo, who lives in the castle. The priests ask the Marchese to attend Nicolina's wedding. The taciturn young lord has been living like a hermit since his wife was killed during the war. The evening before Nicolina's wedding, her grandmother, Maria Lombardo, extracts a promise from the young bride that she, like all the other women, will delay her husband rights. Much to everyone surprise, the Marchese Raumo comes to the wedding party. He has come only to please old Crupi in return for the old man's promise to attend also. Raumo's attention is immediately taken when he sees Jessica for the first time arriving on old Crupi's arm. She immediately becomes the center of attraction, and Raumo rescues her by taking her off to the garden. There they spend a few happy hours together, and fall a little in love. Jessica is under the impression that Raumo is a fisherman. The next morning, Mamma Parigi tells Jessica that her fisherman is the Marchese Raumo. Jessica feels she has been made a fool of and is furious. She is even more enraged when she discovers from Father Antonio why the women are ostracizing her and their strike against their husbands. To teach the women a lesson, she starts using her charms on the village men conspicuously and flirts with them openly. Father Antonio grows worried about the situation and persuades Raumo, the owner of Jessica's cottage, to give her notice to leave. The priests thinks this will force the girl to leave the village she has turned upside down. Jessica receives the notice, confronts Raumo with it and slaps his face. She sees him again soon afterwards, at the deathbed of old Crupi. Before he dies, they both promise the old man to replant the garden he tended so faithfully. After the burial, Jessica is packing her bags to leave for Rome when Raumo knocks at her door. Father Antonio and Mamma Parigi tactfully withdraw and leave the two young people to settle their differences. They begin by discussing the restoration of Crupi's garden and reconcile. And so, once again the life of the village resumes its peaceful tempo. Jessica can still count on many children being born in Forza d'Agrò, because there were few wives who had been successful in the strike against their husbands. (Original press release source)

REVIEWS:

"*Jessica* is a romantic farce made abroad that applies the Hollywood treatment to a European theme. The hybrid looks like a European movie as it might turn out if filmed in Hollywood. The mixture does not always work.... In fairness, however, it should be noted the United Artists release has some funny situations...." *The Hollywood Reporter,* March 19, 1962

"[*Jessica*] is a curious mixture of schmaltz and suggestiveness of affected pathos and even more affected humor...." *The New York Herald Tribune,* April 20, 1962

REVIEWS FOR JEAN NEGULESCO:

"Mr. Negulesco is responsible for what the advertisements are pleased to call 'a most immodest comedy.' It would not be difficult to think of a harsher description of that." *The Times,* June 15, 1962

"Jean Negulesco, who produced and directed the color camera of Piero Portalupi in such beautiful and authentic locales as Taormina and Forza D'Agro, has captured blue lagoons from terraced heights, ancient castles, Roman ruins, flowered hillsides and villages nestling on the Sicilian crags.... Mr. Negulesco treats the matters lightly, but all the affairs are transparent long before the happy ending." *The New York Times,* April 20, 1962

"The inherent artificiality of Jean Negulesco's treatment is pinpointed by the casting of Maurice Chevalier—of all people—as the village priest (presumably on the principle that one European is much like another), and the strenuous quaintness of the Sicilian locals." *Monthly Film Bulletin,* July 1962

ADDITIONAL REVIEWS AND ARTICLES:

Chicago Daily Tribune December 17, 1960, p. E4; *Variety* January 24, 1962, p. 5; *Boxoffice* January 29, 1962; *Intermezzo* (Italy), February 28, 1962, p. 6; *Variety* March 14 1962; *Harrison's Report* March 24, 1962; *The Film Daily* March 26, 1962, p. 4; *Show* April 1962; *Motion Picture Herald* April 18, 1962, p. 524; *Time* April 20, 1962, p. 97–98; *Films in Review* May 1962 p. 298; *Commonweal* May 4, 1962, p. 153; *The New Yorker* May 19, 1962, p. 182; *Kine Weekly* May 31, 1962, p. 90; *The Daily Cinema* June 4, 1962, p. 6; *Boxoffice* June 4, 1962, p. 90; *The Daily Express* (U.K.) June 14, 1962; *The Evening Standard* (U.K.) June 14, 1962; *The Daily Mail* (U.K.) June 15, 1962; *The Daily Worker* (U.K.) June 16, 1962; The Guardian (U.K.) June 16, 1962; *The Daily Herald* (U.K.) June 16, 1962; *The Daily Telegraph* (U.K.), June 16, 1962; *The Observer* (U.K.) June 17, 1962; *The Sunday Express* (U.K.) June 17, 1962; *The Sunday Times* (U.K.) June 17, 1962, p. 37; *The Spectator* (U.K.) June 22, 1962; *Films and Filming* July 1962 p. 38; *Screen Stories* August 1962; *Image et Son-La Revue du Cinéma* (France) October 1981 p. 302

NOTES: The running time was 100 minutes in Italy and 90 minutes in France, where the film was released in June 1962 as *La Sage-Femme; Le Cure et Le Bon Dieu.*

The Pleasure Seekers

20th Century–Fox; U.S. DeLuxe Color CinemaScope 107 minutes; Premiered in New York City on December 25, 1964

CREDITS: *Producer:* David Weisbart; *Director:* Jean Negulesco; *Screenplay:* Edith Sommer; Based on the novel *Coins in the Fountain* by John H. Secondari; *Photography:* Daniel L. Fapp; *Art Directors:* Jack Martin Smith, Edward Carrere; *Assistant Director:* Joseph Lenzi; *Editor:* Louis R. Loeffler; *Set Decorators:* Walter M. Scott, Stuart A. Reiss; *Costumes:* Renie; *Music Composer and Conductor:* Lionel Newman; *Music Associate:* Alexander Courage; *Orchestrators:* Herbert Spencer, Warren Barker, Billy May; *Sound:* Robert O'Brien, Elmer Raguse; *Choreography:* Robert Sidney, Antonio Gades; *Makeup:* Ben Nye; *Hair Stylist:* Margaret Donovan; *Technical Advisor:* Antonio Gades; *Dialogue Director:* Carl Shain; *Songs:* "The Pleasure Seekers," "Something to Think About," "Everything Makes Music When You're in Love" and "Next Time": music and lyrics by Sammy Cahn and James Van Heusen; sung by Ann-Margret.

CAST: Ann-Margret (Fran Hobson), Anthony Franciosa (Emilio Lacaye), Carol Lynley (Maggie Williams), Gardner McKay (Pete Stenello), Pamela Tiffin (Susie Higgins), Andre Lawrence (Dr. Andrés Briones), Gene Tierney (Jane Barton), Vito Scotti (Neighborhood Man), Isobel Elsom (Doña Teresa Lacayo), Maurice Marsac (José), Shelby Grant (American Girl), Raoul de Leon (Martínez), Brian Keith (Paul Barton), Antonio Gades (Flamenco Dancer), Emilio Diego (Guitarist), Ida Romero (Receptionist), Peter Brocco (Arturo), Ralph Brooks (Party Guest), Warren Parker (Mr. Morton), Cosmo Sardo (Waiter), Shirley Parker (French Girl)

PLOT: Three young American women come to Madrid in search of romance and adventure. Maggie Williams finds a job as a secretary with an American news agency and falls in love with bureau chief Paul Barton, who is married. When Barton eventually realizes that he loves his wife and family more than Maggie, she turns to Pete Stenello, a handsome young reporter who has admired her since her arrival in Spain. Fran, an ambitious, passionate singer and dancer, has a weekend affair with Andrés Briones, a shy provincial doctor who tries not to become involved with Fran but falls in love in spite of himself. Meanwhile, Susie Higgins has an affair with wealthy playboy Emilio Lacaye, who proposes marriage merely to fulfill his romantic desires but later realizes that he loves Susie and makes good his promise. The affairs culminate at a party given by Paul Barton before he and his family return to the United States.

REVIEWS:
"The script is not long on jokes or bright dialogue. It is superficial. The American girls seem to be as shallow as Europeans frequently complain they are. As to further authenticity, Spain may have changed remarkably in the past few years, but some of the very briefs costumes and the freedom with which the American girls move and comport themselves, seem at odds with this very formal, moralistic country." *The Hollywood Reporter,* December 24, 1965

"*The Pleasure Seekers* is someone's strange idea of a good title for a mushy little opus about three little girls in red, white and blue (yep, Americans all), looking for love in Spain." *The New York Herald Tribune,* December 26, 1965

"The silly plot and dialogue desecrate some good color shots of Madrid, Toledo, Flamenco dancing, the Prado Museum and paintings by El Greco." *Cue,* January 2, 1965

REVIEWS FOR JEAN NEGULESCO:
"Jean Negulesco, the director, who was also responsible for *Three Coins,* and Daniel L. Fapp, his cinematographer, have put their color cameras to artistic use in focusing on the Prado and some of its El Greco's and Velasquez masterpieces...." *The New York Times,* December 26, 1964

"[U]nder the direction of Jean Negulesco... a light picture emerges which should strike a popular note at the box office." *Variety,* December 30, 1964

"A fine glossy example of old-style of Century-Fox know how, this new romantic comedy brings Mr. Jean Negulesco back to the type of film he made his own *Three Coins in the Fountain* and *A Woman's World.*" *The Times,* January 28, 1965

ADDITIONAL REVIEWS AND ARTICLES:
Variety March 11, 1964; *Los Angeles Times* June 2, 1964; *Combat* (France), June 26, 1964; *Film Daily* December 24, 1964, p. 4; *Daily News* December 26, 1964; *New York Morning Telegraph* December 26, 1964; *Motion Picture Herald* January 6, 1965, p. 202; *The Daily Cinema* January 13, 1965, p. 5; *Kine Weekly* January 21, 1965, p. 9; *Daily Telegraph* (U.K.) January 22, 1965; *Daily Mail* (U.K.) January 26, 1965; *Daily Express* (U.K.) January 27, 1967; *Christian Science Monitor* January 28, 1965, p. 2; *The Sun* (U.K), January 30, 1965; *Daily Worker* (U.K.) January 30, 1965; *Films in Review* February 1965 p. 116–117; *Monthly Film Bulletin* March 1965 p. 42; *Films and Filming* March 1965 p. 36–37; *The Guardian* Feb-

ruary 5, 1965; *Variety* March 17, 1965; *Fiches du Cinéma* (France) April 1, 1966

AWARDS AND HONORS:
Academy Awards: U.S. 1966: *Nominated:* Best *Music:* Scoring: Adaptation or Treatment: Lionel Newman and Alexander Courtage

The Invincible Six

A Moulin Rouge Production; Released in the U.S. by the Walter Reade Organization, through Continental; U.S.–Iran Technicolor 1969 99 minutes; Premiered in Trenton, New Jersey, on June 10, 1970

CREDITS: *Producer:* Mostafa Akhavan; *Associated Producer:* Morteza Akhavan; *Director:* Jean Negulesco; *Assistant Directors:* Behi Ansary, Masud Kimiai; *Second Unit Director:* Franco Prosperi; *Second Unit Assistant Directors:* Jalal Mogadam, Ray Poor; *Screenplay:* Guy Elmes; *Screen Adaptation:* Chester Erskine; Based on the novel *The Heroes of Yucca* by Michael Barrett; *Photography:* Piero Portalupi; *Camera Operator:* Cesare Alione; *Second Unit Photographers:* Santa Accile, Petros Palian; *Art Director:* Ivan Girard; *Costume Designer:* Shai Nazemi; *Wardrobe Mistress:* Kristin Anderson; *Hair Stylist:* Mirella Sforza; *Production Manager:* Joe Di Balsio; *Editor:* Derek York; *Dubbing Editors:* Michael Hart, Nestor Lovera; *Dubbing Mixer:* Morris Askew; *Sound Mixer:* Peter Sutton; *Sound Recordist:* Bahram Darai; *Stunt Director:* Benito Stefanelli; *Continuity:* Francesca Roberti; *Makeup:* Giannetto De Rossi, Fabrizio Sforza; *Special Effects:* Pasquino Benassati; *Assistant Cameraman:* Michael Delaney; *Advisors:* Fereydoon Hoveyda, Monir Vakily; *Music Composer and Conductor:* Manos Hadjidakis; *Music Arrangements:* Garry Hughes

CAST: Stuart Whitman (Tex), Elke Sommer (Zari), Curt Jurgens (The Baron), Ian Ogilvy (Ronald), Behrooz Vosugi (Jahan), Lon Sutton (Mike), Isarco Ravaioli (Giorgio), James Mitchum (Nazar), Anoush Artin (Police Chief Baruk), Warrene Ott (Shirine), Shai Nazemi (Crown Jewels Guide), Manoocher Naderi (Mayor), Homayoon Bahadoran (Fake Officer), Amir Jafari (Darab), Poori Banai (Jahan's Wife), Iran Dafteri (Malik's Mother), Susan Ghasemi (Village Girl)

PLOT: Bright sunshine sparkles on the jewel-like domes of modern Tehran as a group of international thieves converge on vaults holding the magnificent Crown Jewels. Their aim—to steal some of the magnificence. The result, failure—and death for some. Tex and Ronald escape. Pursued by police, they go to Shiraz where Mike, a third member of the gang, waits. The Baron, an aristocratic German, offers them a ride. Tex and Mike are joined at a cheap hotel by Jahan, a young fugitive, and Giorgio, who is driving a stolen Jeep. The Baron, obviously one of their kind, reappears and joins them. The Invincible Six are complete. Chased into the desert by police, they enter a recently raided village where the police chief and his daughter Shirine are locked in their own jail. Villagers had hanged bandit leader Malik, and the bandits have retaliated. The Six free the chief and Shirine and defend the village against raids led by the new bandit leader Nazar. He wants Malik's amulet, symbol of leadership. Attempts to get outside aid fail. Malik's mistress Zari also comes to the village for the amulet and its clue to Malik's tremendous wealth. Tex changes guard duty with Ronald so he can spend the night with her. Ronald is kidnapped from his post and his tortured body returned to the village. Enraged, Tex and his friends go to the encampment where Nazar, who has stolen the amulet, holds Zari prisoner. They thwart a final bandit attack by blowing up the ammunition stores and rescue Zari. Giorgio is killed. Nagar escapes to the village, kills the police chief and is himself killed. Zara rushes to his body but finds the paper with the secret a smoldering ash. Military help arrives as Tex, Mike, the Baron and Zari go, leaving Jahan behind with Shirine. Where will they go from there? At the fork of the road, the Baron flips a coin. (Original press release source)

REVIEWS:
"This has plenty of rumbustious action to satisfy the uncritical, despite its saggy story, plus unusual location for those who cares. Reliable escapist entertainment." *Kine Weekly,* April 10, 1971

"Very interesting ... but not quite what the action addicts are looking for." *Today's Cinema,* April 16 1971

REVIEWS FOR JEAN NEGULESCO:
"The direction [is] weak and uninvolving." *Monthly Film Bulletin,* 1970

"The director, Jean Negulesco, also a talented painter, decided to shoot in color on lavish natural setting." *Paris-Jour,* November 28, 1970

ADDITIONAL REVIEWS AND ARTICLES:
Variety May 22 1968; p. 16; *Hollywood Reporter* September 9, 1968, p. 4; *Daily News* September

23, 1968, p. 43; *Hollywood Reporter* November 4, 1968, p. 1; *Variety* November 6, 1968; p. 26; *Variety* November 13, 1968; p. 26; *Boxoffice* November 18, 1968; *Hollywood Reporter* November 22, 1968, p. 19; *Backstage* October 3, 1969, p. 24; *Boxoffice* October 13, 1969; *Variety* June 10, 1970; *Le Figaro* (France) June 18, 1970; *Filmfacts* XIV n. 24 July 1971 p. 757; *Image et Son-La Revue du Cinéma* (France) September 1971 p. 120.

NOTES: Alternative titles were *The Heroes*, *The Killer Heros* and *Qahremanan*.

Hello-Goodbye

20th Century–Fox; in association with George W. George and Frank Granat Productions; U.S. DeLuxe Color 1969 107 minutes; Premiered in New York City on July 12, 1970

CREDITS: *Producer:* André Hakim; *Director:* Jean Negulesco; *Screenplay:* Roger Marshall; *Photography:* Henri Decae; *Production Supervisor:* William Kaplan; *Music:* Francis Lai; *Supervising Editor:* Richard Bryan; *Production Manager:* Paul Joly; *Production Designer:* John Howell; *Art Director:* Auguste Capelier; *Unit Manager:* Nicole Farny; *Assistant Director:* Paul Feyder; *Sound Mixers:* Jock May, Jacques Maumont; *Wardrobe Supervisor:* Rosine Delamar; *Makeup:* George Bouba, Odette Berroyer; *Hair Stylist:* Giorgio of Rome; *Special Effects:* Richard Parker; *Camera Operator:* Charles Henri Montel; *Set Dressers:* Pierre Charron, Pamela Cornell; *Casting Director:* Evelyne Janic; *Property Master:* Rene Albouze; *Picture Car Supervisor:* David Watson; *Continuity:* Sylvette Baudrot; *Sound Editors:* Keith Palmer, Francoise Diot; *Assistant Editors:* Tony Price, Renee Richard

CAST: Michael Crawford (Harry England), Genevieve Gilles (Dany), Curt Jurgens (Baron de Choisis), Ira Fürstenberg (Evelyne Rosson), Lon Satton (Cole), Peter Myers (Bentley), Mike Marshall (Paul), Didier Haudepin (Raymond), Vivian Pickles (Joycie), Agathe Natanson (Monique), Georges Bever (Hotel Porter), Denise Grey (Concierge), Jeffry Wickham (Dickie)

PLOT: Harry England, a mechanic turned super-salesman, has one great passion in life: motor cars. Girls come many laps behind a good car in his life. Harry stands outside a casino on the French Riviera, following the wealthy owners inside as they leave their Rolls-Royces, Aston Martins and Lagondas. As usual, one car owner is refused further credit. Quickly Harry introduces himself and offers to buy his Aston Martin with the money changing hands quickly. Happily Harry drives his purchase along the road leading to Paris. Out the window he holds his harmonica which plays as the air rushes through it. Pulling in at a gas station, his expert eye is caught by a vintage Rolls-Royce which has obviously broken down. Its owner is a beautiful young girl, Dany, who asks for a lift to Paris, to which he agrees but with some reluctance. The two travelers become so attracted to each other that on reaching Paris they quickly become lovers. But Dany still remains a big question mark. She is known at Chanel but wears old jeans. Her purse is full of expensive jewelry yet she drinks Algerian wine like a peasant. She insists he take her to Marseilles. Abruptly she leaves, paying their bill but taking his harmonica. Harry returns to Cannes, where a friend tells him that the aristocrat Baron de Choisis wants to see him. Choisis lives in a magnificent chateau with a collection of vintage cars, two sons and, as Harry is shocked to leer, a beautiful wife: Dany. The Baron wants to employ Harry to work on his cars. And his younger son (16) needs to be taught some facts of life. Harry soon realizes that Choisis knows of his continuing romance with Dany but continues to tend the cars with as much loving care as he gives to Dany. Their meetings take place as often as possible in her tiny apartment in Marseilles. Soon he allows himself the luxury of falling in love, but Dany refuses to leave Choisis. The Baron arranges a cruise for himself and his wife, as he always does after one of Dany's affairs de couer. Hearing of the proposed trip, Harry gets drunk and drives to the chateau, where he threatens to smash all the cars, taking the keys thrown challengingly to him by Choisis from an upstairs window. He chooses a Rolls-Royce and drives into the swimming pool. The car sinks and it is only the Baron's instructions to his men which save Harry's life. Months later Harry returns to Cannes to hear the news that Choisis has gone to Africa with a wealthy American, Mrs. Rosson, whom he had just met gambling at the casino. And Dany has left town. She is at Le Havre, about to sail for America. Harry arrives at the French port, haggard and distraught. He sees Dany at the ship's rail with a handsome escort on her arm. As he turns away, Dany suddenly sees him through the crowd. She dashes down the gangplank, leaving a somewhat bewildered man holding her bouquet of roses. She catches up with Harry and they go off together. (Original press release source)

REVIEWS:

"André Hakim's production of *Hello-Goodbye* is elaborate in that the sets and the people are beautiful—rich and/or beautiful and Cannes and the Riviera make for an exquisite backdrop in the hued cinematography." *Variety*, July 8, 1970

"This embarrassing inept, pretty nothing of a movie ... appears to have been designed exclusively for Miss Gilles.... Crawford is totally miscast." *The New York Daily News*, July 13, 1970

"*Hello-Goodbye* is a dopey picture, a waste of money and a slightly evil-minded exercise in the erotic imaginary of automobiles." *The New Yorker*, July 18, 1970

REVIEWS FOR JEAN NEGULESCO:

"Negulesco may have reasonably decided that a discreet, old-fashioned even faintly nostalgic approach would best define the bittersweet mood of his subject." *Monthly Film Bulletin*, September 1970

"Jean Negulesco directs this pseudo-sophisticated piece as if he knows very well that it doesn't really work. And he's absolutely right." *The Guardian*, October 29, 1979

"Jean Negulesco's direction is competent, if occasionally haphazard, considering the material given him, a vacillating script and a lovely but wooden leading lady upon which the entire story hinges." *The Hollywood Reporter*, July 6, 1970

ADDITIONAL REVIEWS AND ARTICLES:

Kine Weekly May 17, 1969; *Variety* August 13, 1969; *The Hollywood Reporter* October 17, 1969; p. 12; *Variety* October 29, 1969; *Boxoffice* November 10, 1969; *Hollywood Citizen-News* November 14, 1969; *Film Bulletin* April 6, 1970, p. 12; *Independent Film Journal* June 24, 1970; *Les Figaro* July 1, 1970; *Saturday Review* July 11, 1970; *The New York Times* July 13, 1970; *Women's Wear Daily* July 13, 1970; *The New York Post* July 13, 1970; *New York Morning Telegraph* July 14, 1970, p. 3; *New York Magazine* July 27, 1970, p. 47; *Motion Picture Herald* July 29, 1970, p. 487; *Kine Weekly* August 15, 1970, p. 10; *Film Information* August-September 1970; *Show* September 3, 1970, p. 42; *Films and Filming* September 1970 p. 82; *Photoplay* October 1970 p. 31; *The Sun* (U.K.) October 29, 1970; *Daily Mail* (U.K.) October 30, 1970; *The Times* (U.K.) October 30, 1970; *News Statement* October 30, 1970; *Fiches du Cinéma* February 1, 1971; *Image et Son-La Revue du Cinéma* (France) September 1971 p. 120; *Travelling* (France) September 1971 p. 35; *Variety* September 12, 1986

NOTES: *Hello and Goodbye* was the film's working title. Gambling expert Bill Paris was hired as technical advisor on the set.

Short Films

Some sources erroneously indicate Jean Negulesco as the director of the shorts: *Freddie Fisher and His Band* (1943) and *The United States Merchant Marine Cadet Corps Band* (1944) but the correct directors are Lloyd French for the first and Bobby Connolly for the latter.

Alice in Movieland

Warner Bros. and the Vitaphone Corp.; U.S. B&W 22 minutes; Released on March 3, 1940

CREDITS: *Producer:* Gordon Hollingshead; *Director:* Jean Negulesco; *Screenplay:* Owen Crump, Cyrus D. Wood; *Original Story:* Ed Sullivan; *Photography:* Ted McCord; *Editor:* Rudi Fehr; *Music:* Walter G. Samuels

CAST: Joan Leslie (Alice Purdee), Nana Bryant (Agatha Winters), Clara Blandick (Grandmother), Clarence Muse (Train Porter), Ronald Reagan, Jane Wyman, Alexis Smith (Themselves)

PLOT: A small-town girl wins a beauty contest winner and sets out for Hollywood. While on the train she falls asleep and dreams she's on a sound stage where screen tests are being done. She goes through the usual routine of makeup, screen tests, and a daily schedule of calling at Central Casting. Then, after disappointing screen tests and a gag pulled by the people on the set fate rebounds in her favor to the extent of her winning an Academy Award. Then she wakes up.

REVIEWS:

"A well-constructed short drama." *Motion Picture Daily*, November 25, 1940

REVIEWS FOR JEAN NEGULESCO:

"Jean Negulesco's skillful direction and capable and sincere performances ... combine to make the screen treatment by Ed Sullivan's original story grand entertainment for the masses." *Showmen's Trade Review,* November 30, 1940

The Flag of Humanity

Warner Bros. and the Vitaphone Corp.; U.S. Technicolor 20 minutes; Released on October 19, 1940

CREDITS: *Producer:* Gordon Hollingshead; *Director:* Jean Negulesco; *Screenplay:* Charles L. Tedford; *Technicolor Photography:* Charles P. Boyle; *Technicolor Color Director:* Natalie Kalmus; *Editor:* Doug Gould; *Art Director:* Charles Novi; *Music:* Howard Jackson

CAST: Nana Bryant (Clara Barton), Fay Helm (Elsie Howard), John Hamilton (James Garfield), Ted Osborn (Dr. Bellows), John Arledge (Jeremy)

PLOT: Clara Barton, a nurse during the Civil War, vows to improve the terrible conditions prevalent in hospitals. In Switzerland she is given a medal by the founder of the Red Cross, and then is made the first president of the American Red Cross by President Garfield.

REVIEWS:

"The short, in color, is an emotion-stirring dramatization of an inspiring chapter in American history." *Motion Picture Daily,* October 18, 1940

REVIEWS FOR JEAN NEGULESCO:

"Jean Negulesco directed expertly." *The Film Daily,* October 25, 1940

"Jean Negulesco direction's is praiseworthy." *Showmen's Trade Review,* October 26, 1940

Joe Reichman and His Orchestra

aka *Joe Reichman and His Band*; Warner Bros. and the Vitaphone Corp.; U.S. B&W 10 minutes; Released on October 26, 1940

CREDITS: *Producer:* Gordon Hollingshead; *Director:* Jean Negulesco; *Photography:* Carl E. Guthrie; *Editor:* Harlod McLernon

CAST: Joe Reichman and His Orchestra (Themselves)

PLOT: Joe Reichman and his orchestra go into their routine when their agent shows up with someone for them to audition for. They play the songs "Little Thoughts," "Reichmania," "Night and Day," "Moonlight Sonata" and "Cachita."

REVIEWS:

"Audiences that appreciate smooth orchestrations will be well pleased with this subject." *The Film Daily,* October 25, 1940

"Most orchestra reels have become routine but this one is above the average in production, photography, direction and entertainment." *Showmen's Trade Show,* November 2, 1940

Jan Garber and His Orchestra

Warner Bros. and the Vitaphone Corp.; U.S. B&W 10 minutes; Released on August 31, 1940

CREDITS: *Producer:* Gordon Hollingshead; *Director:* Jean Negulesco; *Editor:* Jack Killifer

CAST: Jan Garber and His Orchestra (Themselves)

PLOT: A plot of sorts involves the musical numbers being introduced by people from all walks of life dropping whatever they are doing to listen to Jan Garber and His Orchestra. Instrumental numbers include "My Dear" and "Bugle Call Rag." Numbers with vocals include "Lullaby of Broadway," "Ma, He's Making Eyes at Me" and "Where Was I?"

Henry Busse and His Orchestra

Warner Bros. and the Vitaphone Corp.; U.S. B&W 10 minutes; Released on November 30, 1940

CREDITS: *Producer:* Gordon Hollingshead; *Director:* Jean Negulesco; *Photography:* Arthur Todd; *Editor:* Doug Gould; *Art Director:* Charles Novi; *Sound:* David Forrest

CAST: Henry Busse and His Orchestra (Themselves)

PLOT: Henry Busse plays several solos on the trumpet, and a vocalist sings "Hot Lips" and "Along the Santa Fe Trail." Other songs are "Huckleberry Duck" and "Wang Wang Blues."

REVIEWS:

"Good enough band short." *Motion Picture Herald,* January 18, 1941

Skinnay Ennis and His Orchestra

Warner Bros. and the Vitaphone Corp.; U.S. B&W 9 minutes; Released on January 4, 1941

CREDITS: *Producer:* Gordon Hollingshead; *Director:* Jean Negulesco; *Photography:* Ted McCord; *Editor:* Jack Killifer; *Art Director:* Charles Novi; *Sound:* David Forrest

CAST: Skinnay Ennis and His Orchestra (Themselves)

PLOT: Skinnay Ennis and His Orchestra became popular when Bob Hope made them the orchestra for his radio program in 1938. In this short, they play several well-known pieces as they try to get in shape for an audition. Other performers include a jitterbugging couple and a vocalist. The orchestra plays "A Boy a Girl and the Lamplight," "Three Little Words," "Let's Do It" and "The Birth of the Blues."

REVIEWS:
"A good musical full of excellent tunes played by skilled performers." *Motion Picture Herald*, March 8, 1941

REVIEWS FOR JEAN NEGULESCO:
"Jean Negulesco does a good directing job." *The Film Daily*, December 23 1940

The Dog in the Orchard

Warner Bros. and the Vitaphone Corp.; U.S. B&W 20 minutes; Released on January 18, 1941

CREDITS: *Producer:* Gordon Hollingshead; *Director:* Jean Negulesco; *Screenplay:* Owen Crump; *Original Story:* Mary Roberts Rinehart; *Photography:* Sol Polito; *Music:* Howard Jackson

CAST: Howard da Silva (Foster), Barbara Pepper (Emmie), Addison Richards (Sheriff), David Bruce (Deputy), Virginia Sale (Postmistress), Fay Helm (Beulah), Myra Marsh (Mary); Herbert Heywood (Station Agent), Peter Ashley (Farmhand), Conrad Binyon (Boy), Si Jenks, George Ovey (Old Timers), Norma Jean Nilsson (Girl), Leo White (Bookkeeper)

PLOT: The sheriff drops in on Foster, a Midwestern farmer, for a friendly pre-election chat. The slovenly condition of the farmhouse and the howling in the orchard of Foster's wife's dog give rise to the sheriff's suspicions. The farmer satisfactorily says his wife has gone to visit her mother in Indiana, and the sheriff dismisses his doubts as the product of an over-imaginative mind. It isn't until the farmer takes legal steps to sell his farm that the sheriff and his deputy look into the matter and discover the key to the strange behavior of the farmer and the dog.

REVIEWS:
"This compelling story by Mary Roberts Rinehart has been converted into an interesting screen drama, skillfully performed and directed." *Motion Picture Daily*, January 20, 1941

"The cast is good, the story itself is condensed into a continuously actionful narrative, and the suspense is intense from beginning to end." *The Film Daily*, January 22, 1941

REVIEWS FOR JEAN NEGULESCO:
"Jean Negulesco's direction is praiseworthy, for he has handled his assignment in a manner befitting directors more highly acclaimed." *Showmen's Trade Review*, January 18, 1941

NOTES: Mary Roberts Rinehart's original story "The Dog in the Orchard," published in September 1940 by *Cosmopolitan* magazine, was sold to Warner Bros. for $4000.

Cliff Edwards and His Buckaroos

Warner Bros. and the Vitaphone Corp.; U.S. B&W 10 minutes; Released on March 8, 1941

CREDITS: *Director:* Jean Negulesco; *Screenplay:* Nat Hiken; *Photography:* Arthur L. Todd; *Editor:* Doug Gould; *Sound:* David Forrest; *Music:* M.K. Jerome; *Lyrics:* Jack Scholl

CAST: Cliff Edwards (Cliff the Ranch Hand), Mildred Coles (Ellen), Vera Lewis (Mrs. Marshall)

PLOT: Cliff Edwards and a group of singers interpolate several western numbers including "I Can't Get Along, Little Doggie," "My Little Buckaroo," "Home on the Range" and "Give Me a Song of the Plains."

REVIEWS:
"Fair." *Showmen's Trade Review*, March 8, 1941
"I have seen better musical acts and you can get along without this one." *Motion Picture Herald*, August 23 1941

Freddy Martin and Orchestra

Warner Bros. and the Vitaphone Corp.; U.S. B&W 10 minutes; Released on April 12, 1941

CREDITS: *Producer:* Gordon Hollingshead; *Director:* Jean Negulesco

CAST: Freddy Martin and His Orchestra (Themselves)

PLOT: Freddy Martin and His orchestra play "Bye Lo Bye Lullaby," "I Get a Kick Out of You," "Tales from the Vienna Woods," "Say Si Si" and "Jaywalk."

REVIEWS:
"Although neither Martin nor members of his band have much screen personality, interesting effects have been achieved by the camera work." *Motion Picture Daily*, March 27, 1941

"[A] neatly turned out band reel." *The Film Daily*, April 9, 1941

"Fair." *Showmen's Trade Review*, June 14, 1941

Marie Greene and Her Merrie Men

Warner Bros. and the Vitaphone Corp.; U.S. B&W 10 minutes; Released on April 26, 1941

CREDITS: *Producer:* Gordon Hollingshead; *Director:* Jean Negulesco
CAST: Marie Greene, Mary Parker, Billy Daniels (Themselves)
PLOT: When an old-fashioned hotel deteriorates, Marie Greene, one of the maids, decides it needs a little life. She and the boys get busy on a tuneful, rhythmic show. Needless to say, it makes the hotel a success. Songs included are "Gotta Have My Rhythm," "Long, Long Ago," "Over the Waves," "Dixie," "Old Folks at Home," "Camptown Races" and "Alice in Rhumbaland."
REVIEWS:
"Here is a tuneful little number which should please." *Motion Picture Daily,* April 18, 1941
"Here is a subject that entertains every minute, that's well photographed, directed and produced in a manner that puts it above the usual stereotyped hand and vaudeville reel." *Showmen's Trade Review,* May 3, 1941

Hal Kemp and His Orchestra

Warner Bros. and the Vitaphone Corp.; U.S. B&W 10 minutes; Released on June 14, 1941
CREDITS: *Producer:* Gordon Hollingshead; *Director:* Jean Negulesco; *Photography:* Sid Hickox; *Editor:* Everett Dodd; *Art Director:* Charles Novi; *Sound:* David Forrest
CAST: Hal Kemp, Robert Allen, Janet Blair, Randy Brooks, Maxine Grey (Themselves)
PLOT: Hal Kemp's Orchestra performs "The Joke's on You," "Trade Winds," "Begin the Beguine," "I'll Be Missing You" and "The Workout."
REVIEWS:
"Excellent. These Melody Masters are all good and this one is exceptionally so." *Motion Picture Herald,* February 7, 1942
REVIEWS FOR JEAN NEGULESCO:
"It has been well directed ... with plenty of interesting effects, but despite this, it's still just a band." *Showmen's Trade Review,* May 24, 1941
NOTES: *Hal Kemp and His Orchestra* was completed the day before Al Kemp was killed in a car accident. Another short with the same title was made by Paramount in 1938.

Glen Gray and the Casa Loma Orchestra

Warner Bros. and the Vitaphone Corp.; U.S. B&W 10 minutes; Released on August 12, 1942
CREDITS: *Producer:* Gordon Hollingshead; *Director:* Jean Negulesco; *Photography:* Arthur Edeson; *Editor:* Louis Hesse; *Art Director:* Charles Novi; *Sound:* David Forrest
CAST: Glen Gray, the Casa Loma Orchestra (Themselves), Dean Collins, Jewel McGowan (Jitterbug Dancers), Peewee Hunt (Singer)
PLOT: Glen Gray and His Orchestra play "Hep and Happy," "Purple Moonlight," "Broom Street" and "Darktown Strutters' Ball."
REVIEWS:
"In excellent atmospheric background but entirely lacking in novelty interlude which lessens appreciation of the rapid-fire order in which musical numbers are presented, Glen Gray and his musicians deliver an assembly of just so-so numbers." *Showmen's Trade Review,* September 12, 1942
REVIEWS FOR JEAN NEGULESCO:
"Well staged by Jean Negulesco, ace shorts musical director at this lot, Glen Gray combo cashes in on his present popularity." *Variety,* September 2, 1942

Those Good Old Days

Warner Bros. and the Vitaphone Corp.; U.S. B&W 10 minutes; Released on August 16, 1941
CREDITS: *Producer:* Gordon Hollingshead; *Director:* Jean Negulesco; *Screenplay:* Jack Scholl; *Photography:* L. William O'Connell; *Editor:* Louis Hesse; *Art Director:* Charles Novi; *Sound:* Dolph Thomas; *Dance Director:* Matty King
CAST: William T. Orr (Joe La Rue), Jan Clayton (Mrs. Joe La Rue aka Miss Harris), Janet Chapman (Gloria La Rue), Lucia Carroll (Mary La Rue), John Ridgely (Joe La Rue, Jr.), Juanita Stark (Page Girl), Leo White (Dandy), Tom Wilson (Stagehand)
PLOT: Joe La Rue's greatest pleasure is to tell his little granddaughter about the days when he and his wife were the rage of vaudeville. The old-fashioned routines include "Memories," "I Wish I Was in Dixie's Land," "My Old Shack in Dixie," "Who's Your Honey Lamb," "Seaside Finale n. 1" and "Seaside Finale n. 2"
REVIEWS:
"Nostalgic subject about the good old days in vaudeville. Reel uses cutback technique..." *The Film Daily,* September 2, 1941
"Tuneful and nostalgic." *National Board of Review Magazine,* October 1941

The University of Southern California Band and Glee Club

Warner Bros. and the Vitaphone Corp.; U.S. B&W 10 minutes; Released on September 13, 1941

CREDITS: *Producer:* Gordon Hollingshead; *Director:* Jean Negulesco

CAST: The University of Southern California Band

PLOT: The short features a number of popular college songs and well-known military pieces performed by more than 100 band members. The selections are: Notre Dame's "Victory March," "Caisson's Song," "Marine Hymn," "Semper Fidelis," "On Brave Old Army Team" and "Fight On," Yale's "Boola Boola," Michigan's "The Victors" and "She'll Be Coming Round the Mountain" and Stanford's "New Colonial March," "Anchor's Aweigh" and "Stars and Stripes Forever."

REVIEWS:

"Both musician and vocalist do their job in a thoroughly entertaining manner."
Motion Picture Daily, September 8, 1941

"The film moves along briskly and musically."
The Film Daily, September 17, 1941

Carioca Serenaders

Warner Bros. and the Vitaphone Corp.; U.S. B&W 10 minutes; Released on October 25, 1941

CREDITS: *Producer:* Gordon Hollingshead; *Director:* Jean Negulesco; *Photography:* Carl E. Guthrie; *Editor:* Harold McLernon; *Music:* Howard Jackson

CAST: Humberto Herrera, Mayta Palmera, Theodore Rand, Dinora Rego (Themselves)

PLOT: Humberto Herrera and His South American Band, The Serenaders, perform in a Spanish setting, playing Spanish and South American tunes. Mayta Palmera and Theodore Rand dancers do two solos. Dinora Rego sings "Chick-Qui-Boom." Other songs are "Nena," "Ten Paciencia Agostibho" and "Negra baila la conga."

REVIEWS:

"[A] gay and rollicking musical background.... There is some flippant torso-tossing so characteristic of Latin-American dances contributed by good-looking dancers. All in all, should give program a lift." *The Film Daily,* October 31, 1941

"A lively and refreshing musical interlude...."
Showmen's Trade Review, November 15, 1941

At the Stroke of Twelve

Warner Bros. and the Vitaphone Corp.; U.S. B&W 20 minutes; Released on November 15, 1941

CREDITS: *Associate Producer:* Gordon Hollingshead; *Director:* Jean Negulesco; *Screenplay:* Harold Medford; Based on the story "The Old Doll's House" by Damon Runyon; *Photography:* Ted McCord; *Editor:* Everett Dodd; *Sound:* Stanley Jones; *Art Director:* Charles Novi; *Music:* Howard Jackson

CAST: Craig Stevens (Lane McGowan); Elisabeth Risdon (Abigail Ardsley, aka The Old Doll), Knox Manning (Carson), Howard da Silva (Angie the Ox), Ben Welden (Babe), Frank Ferguson (Prosecuting Attorney), Eddie Dunn (Policeman), Faye Emerson (Miss LaMond), Fred Kelsey (Police Sergeant), John Ridgely (Reporter)

PLOT: Lane McGowan, a handsome young racketeer, is chased by a couple of killers and takes refuge in the house of Abigail Ardsley, a wealthy, eccentric old woman. Later that night, one of the gunmen kills the other and frames Lane. He is saved when the old woman appears in court to supply the alibi.

REVIEWS:

"[A]n absorbing entertainment.... An outstanding short subject in its own right...." *Showmen's Trade Review,* November 8, 1941

"[I]t certainly boasts feature-quality photography ... an exceptional example of fast-paced direction and cutting." *American Cinematographer,* November 1941

REVIEWS FOR JEAN NEGULESCO:

"Jean Negulesco's direction is crisp and sure."
The Film Daily, October 31, 1941

"Ably directed and enacted." *Variety,* November 5, 1941

The Gay Parisian (Gâité Parisienne)

Warner Bros. and the Vitaphone Corp.; U.S. Technicolor 20 minutes; World Premiere in Paterson, New Jersey, on December 4, 1941

CREDITS: *Associate Producer:* Gordon Hollingshead; *Director:* Jean Negulesco; *Choreography:* Leonide Massine; *Technicolor Photography:* Ernie Haller; *Editor:* Everett Dodd; *Sound:* David Forrest; *Art Director:* Charles Novi; *Technicolor Color Director:* Natalie Kalmus; *Music:* Jacques Offenbach; *Musical Director:* Efrem Kurtz

CAST: By arrangement with Sol Hurok: Ballet Russe de Monte Carlo (Ballet Dancers), Leonide Massine (The Peruvian), Milada Mladona (The

Glove Seller), Frederic Franklin (The Baron), Nathalie Krassovska (The Flower Girl); Andre Eglevsky (Tortoni–The Dancing Master), Igor Youskevitch (Officer), Lubov Roudenko, Cyd Charisse (Can-Can Dancers), Casimir Kokitch, James Starbuck, Marc Platt, George Zoritch (Dancers)

PLOT: A Peruvian adventurer fascinated by a charming French shop girl creates amusing mayhem in a Parisian café. His flirting with all the girls causes jealousy and his subsequent eviction from the cafe. Ballets included are "Gaîté Parisienne" and "Overture" from "La vie parisienne," "Allegro brillante" from "Mesdames de la Halle," "Polka" from "Le voyages dans la lune," "Galop" from "La vie parisienne," "Waltz" from "Orphèe aux enfers," "March" from "Tromb-al ca-zar," "Waltz" from "La Périchole," "Introduction" from "Robinson Crusoè," "Can Can" from "La vie parisienne," "Can Can" from "Orphée aux enfers," "Barcarolle" from "Les contes d'Hoffman" and "Galop" from "Les contes d'Hoffman."

REVIEWS:
"Here is a different type of screen entertainment, far in advance of the regulation subject from the standpoint of artistry." *Motion Picture Herald*, January 10, 1942

REVIEWS FOR JEAN NEGULESCO:
"Jean Negulesco's direction is perfect." *The Film Daily*, December 3, 1941

"Directed by Jean Negulesco, his work, the costuming and particularly the Technicolor photography are outstanding technical accomplishment." *Showmen's Trade Review*, December 6, 1941

"The presentation is strikingly beautiful and in no small way is Jean Negulesco's direction responsible." *Motion Picture Daily*, December 17, 1941

NOTES: *The Gay Parisian* was nominated for an Academy Award in the category of Best Live Action Short Film (Two-Reel).

Spanish Fiesta (Capriccio Español)

Warner Bros. and the Vitaphone Corp.; U.S. Technicolor 19 minutes; Released on May 16, 1942

CREDITS: *Associate Producer:* Gordon Hollingshead; *Director:* Jean Negulesco; *Choreography:* Leonide Massine, Argentinita; *Technicolor Photography:* Ernest Haller, Allen M. Davey; *Editor:* Everett Dodd; *Sound:* David Forrest; *Art Director:* Charles Novi; *Technicolor Color Director:* Natalie Kalmus; *Music:* Nikolai Rimsky-Korsakov; *Musical Director:* Efrem Kurtz; *Orchestra Arrangements:* Hugo Friedhofer; *Costumes:* Mariano Andreu

CAST: By arrangement with Sol Hurok: Ballet Russe de Monte Carlo (Ballet Dancers), Leonide Massine (Jealous Suitor), Tamara Toumanova (Gypsy Fortune Teller), Frederic Franklin, Nathalie Krassovska, Andre Eglevsky (Dancers)

PLOT: A gypsy girl runs away from her camp and gate-crashes a party of the Spanish aristocracy where she performs the dancers of her people. The thin story is just a pretext for a combination of music, dance and pantomime on the notes of Rimsky-Korsakov's "Capriccio Español."

REVIEWS:
"Cloaked in magnificent Technicolor, the footage is a super-delight to eye, ear and esthetic senses." *The Film Daily*, December 3, 1941

"The entire troupe performs with great skill. The accompanying music by Rimsky-Korsakov has a really fine quality, while the presentation, vividly colored, is compelling in its beauty." *Motion Picture Daily*, December 17, 1941

REVIEWS FOR JEAN NEGULESCO:
"The direction ... brings into focus the individual talent and artistry of Leonide Massine, Alexandra Danilova [sic] and other stars." *Showmen's Trade Review*, December 6, 1941

The Playgirls

Warner Bros. and the Vitaphone Corp.; U.S. B&W 10 minutes; Released on February 21, 1942

CREDITS: *Associate Producer:* Gordon Hollingshead; *Director:* Jean Negulesco

CAST: The Playgirl Band (Themselves), Catherine Lewis (The Playgirls Band Leader), The Navy Blue Sextette (Themselves), Marguerite Chapman, Leslie Brooks, Peggy Diggins, Georgia Carroll, Kay Aldridge, Claire James (Sextette Members), The Ryan Sisters (Themselves)

PLOT: The Playgirls Band, with atmosphere provided by the Navy Blues Sextette, play "Dream of Love," "You Again," "Oh My Darling, Clementine" and "Yankee Doodle."

REVIEWS: "This is a swell short with skids of beautiful girls who know how to sing and harmonize on all kinds of musical instruments." *Motion Picture Herald*, June 27, 1942

Calling All Girls

Warner Bros. and the Vitaphone Corp.; U.S. B&W, One-Reel 20 minutes; Released on February 21, 1942

CREDITS: *Associate Producer:* Gordon Hollingshead; *Director:* Jean Negulesco (uncredited); *Editor:* Louis Hesse; *Choreographer:* Busby Berkeley; *Music* and *Lyrics:* Harry Warren, Al Dubin, Sammy Fain, Irving Kahal

CAST: Owen Crump (Narrator), James Cagney (Chester Kent in footage from *Footlight Parade*), Ruby Keeler (Bea in footage from *Footlight Parade*), The United States of America Navy Band (Themselves in footage from *Footlight Parade*)

PLOT: All the behind-the-scenes labors involved in casting, rehearsing and designing sets for big musical numbers are showed along with examples of the finished product of memorable pictures culled from the Warner archives: "Don't Say Goodnight" from *Wonder Bar* (1934), "Lullaby of Broadway" and "The Shadow Waltz" from *Gold Diggers of 1933* (1933) and "By a Waterfall" and "Shanghai Lil" from *Footlight Parade* (1933).

REVIEWS:
"[T]his is a good, somewhat unusual subject...." *Motion Picture Daily,* January 20, 1942

"The spectacles pictured are among the screen's shining endeavors in this type of entertainment." *Showmen's Trade Review,* January 24, 1942

NOTES: No director is indicated in the credits. Some sources show Lloyd Bacon as the director.

Leo Reisman and His Orchestra

Warner Bros. and the Vitaphone Corp.; U.S. B&W 10 minutes; Released on February 28, 1942

CREDITS: *Associate Producer:* Gordon Hollingshead; *Director:* Jean Negulesco

CAST: Leo Reisman (Himself); Georgia Carroll (Singer)

PLOT: Leo Reisman and his orchestra play "St. Louis Blues," "Make Love with a Guitar," "What Is This Thing Called Love?" and "Take It."

REVIEWS:
"The subject is somewhat static since there are not specialty performers aside from a singer, but the music is so snappy that no one can keep from at least tapping his feet." *Showmen's Trade Review,* March 28, 1942

Carl Hoff and His Orchestra

Warner Bros. and the Vitaphone Corp.; U.S. B&W 10 minutes; Released on January 3, 1942

CREDITS: *Associate Producer:* Gordon Hollingshead; *Director:* Jean Negulesco

CAST: Carl Hoff and His Orchestra (Themselves)

PLOT: Carl Hoff and His Orchestra offer "I Could Use a Dream, "The Blue Danube," "Dark Eyes," "I Know That You Know" and "When Yuba Plays the Rhumba on the Tuba."

REVIEWS:
"The setting is the usual bandstand, but lightning and camera angles make for variety." *Motion Picture Herald,* February 17, 1942

Richard Himber and Orchestra

Warner Bros. and the Vitaphone Corp.; U.S. B&W 10 minutes; Released on April 11, 1942

CREDITS: *Associate Producer:* Gordon Hollingshead; *Director:* Jean Negulesco

CAST: Richard Himber and Orchestra (Themselves)

PLOT: Richard Himber and his musicians perform modern swings including "Lullaby" by Brahms, "Nobody Knows the Trouble I've Seen" and "The Kerr Dance."

REVIEWS:
"A lot of class, but lacked punch in his band." *Motion Picture Herald,* July 4, 1942

REVIEWS FOR JEAN NEGULESCO:
"A treat for both eye and ear, the subject has been capably directed by Jean Negulesco." *Showmen's Trade Review,* June 6, 1942

California Junior Symphony

Warner Bros. and the Vitaphone Corp.; U.S. B&W 20 minutes; Released on April 18, 1942

CREDITS: *Associate Producer:* Gordon Hollingshead; *Director:* Jean Negulesco; *Editor:* Doug Gould; *Art Director:* Charles Novi

CAST: Peter Meremblum (Himself—Orchestra Conductor); The California Junior Symphony Orchestra (Themselves), Jackie Horner (Herself—Orchestra Soloist), Virginia Ellis, Edwina Pierce (Themselves—Violinists), Mary Louise Zeyen (Herself—Cellist), Owen Crump (Narrator)

PLOT: The California Junior Symphony is a juvenile orchestra conducted by Peter Meremblum. About 100 kids, ranging in age from 8 to

18, perform classical pieces and traditional arias including selections from Tchaikovsky, Wagner and Strauss. Eight-year-old Jackie Horner is soloist in Clementi's "Sonatina." "Voice of Spring," "Pop Goes to Weasel" and "America Marches On" are also performed.

REVIEWS:
"Playing of group is nearly letter-perfect, and ably directed by Meremblum.... However was too long." *Variety,* April 22, 1942

"The picture is bit too long and would have been better as a single reel. As it is, the music lovers will enjoy it thoroughly nevertheless." *Showmen's Trade Review,* May 2, 1942

Don Cossack Chorus

Warner Bros. and the Vitaphone Corp.; U.S. B&W 10 minutes; Released on April 25, 1942

CREDITS: *Associate Producer:* Gordon Hollingshead; *Director:* Jean Negulesco

CAST: By arrangement by Sol Hurok: Serge Jaroff (Himself—Chorus Conductor), The Don Cossack Chorus (Themselves)

PLOT: The Don Cossack Chorus, an ensemble of 50 male voices led by Serge Jaroff, sings in picturesque costumes in the courtyard of a Russian village inn. Their songs include "Cossack Song and Dance," "The Evening Bells," "Parting Song," "The Regiment Was Riding" and "Kuban Cossack Song."

REVIEWS:
"This subject should prove a good novelty." *Motion Picture Daily,* April 28, 1942

"Good production values and an entertaining sweep of accompanying action do much to make the vocal offerings of this talented group one of the most entertaining in this series." *Showmen's Trade Review,* May 2, 1942

The Daughter of Rosie O'Grady

Warner Bros. and the Vitaphone Corp.; U.S. B&W 20 minutes; Released on July 4, 1942

CREDITS: *Associate Producer:* Gordon Hollingshead; *Director:* Jean Negulesco; *Screenplay:* Jack Scholl; *Photography:* Ernest Haller; *Music:* Howard Jackson

CAST: Patti Hale (Rosie O'Grady), Frank Wilcox (Henry Van Ness), Al Shean (Old Dann), Peter Caldwell (Dink), Frank Ferguson (Judge), Roland Drew (Doctor), Jean Inness (Governess), Leah Baird (Superintended), Fran Mayo (District Attorney), Fred Kelsey (Policeman), Leo White (Flower Vendor)

PLOT: In New York, Rosie O'Grady, the daughter of a vaudevillian, is taken from her grandfather and placed in an orphanage. Wealthy Henry Van Ness, who is ill, intervenes and backs a show for her and her grandpa. The songs featured are "Sing an Irish Song," "The Sidewalk Dance," "In Central Park," "When Little Old New York Was Young" and "Daughter of Rosie O'Grady."

REVIEWS:
"[A] musical subject that is distinguished by fairly substantial plot, enjoyable melodies ... and a production number. [It's] a welcome departure from the numerous swing sessions" *Motion Picture Daily,* June 3, 1942

"Excellent photography and first-rate cast." *The Film Daily,* June 10, 1942

Emil Coleman and Orchestra

Warner Bros. and the Vitaphone Corp.; U.S. B&W 10 minutes; Released on May 9, 1942

CREDITS: *Associate Producer:* Gordon Hollingshead; *Director:* Jean Negulesco

CAST: Emil Coleman and Orchestra (Themselves)

PLOT: Emil Coleman and his dance orchestra play several musical numbers. Some of the tunes include the performance of a group of dancers. The songs are "Voice of Spring," "Rustle of Spring," "Just One of Those Things," "Mexican Magic," "Voodoo" and "Shalimar."

REVIEWS:
"Cleverly conceived band short directed by Jean Negulesco with comely, graceful dancers taking some of curse away from stilted shots of orchestra musicians in action." *Variety,* May 13, 1942

"Unusual production values and fine examples of odd-angle photography and shadow effects lend emphasis and enjoyment to the fine musical offering of this talented and versatile dance aggregation." *Showmen's Trade Review,* May 16, 1942

"Lovers of popular songs should go wholehog for this short.... The mood is right and the photography superb with many fancy camera angles. The short is high-class of its type." *The Film Daily,* May 25, 1942

The Spirit of Annapolis

Warner Bros. and the Vitaphone Corp.; U.S. B&W 15 minutes; Released on September 5, 1942

CREDITS: *Associate Producer:* Gordon Hollingshead; *Director:* Jean Negulesco; *Photography:* Ted McCord; *Music Supervisor:* Dudley Chambers; *Production Manager:* Phil Quinn

CAST: The U.S. Naval Academy Band, The Annapolis Glee Club (Themselves)

PLOT: A tour of the U.S. Naval Academy at Annapolis provides a look at the training routine of the men who will sail fighting ships. The Naval Academy Band and the Annapolis Glee Club perform "Anchors Aweigh," "Naval Victory March," "The Ramparts We Watch," "Navy Blue and Gold," "Before the Mast" and "Don't Give Up the Ship."

The United States Army Air Force Band

Warner Bros. and the Vitaphone Corp.; U.S. B&W 10 minutes; Released on September 19, 1942

CREDITS: *Producer:* Gordon Hollingshead; *Director:* Jean Negulesco; *Photography:* Ted McCord; *Editor:* Rex Steele; *Sound:* Everett A. Brown; *Music Supervisor:* Dudley Chambers

CAST: The U.S. Army Air Force Band and Chorus (Themselves), Lieutenant Alf Heiberg (Himself—Bandmaster), Lieutenant General Henry H. Arnold (Himself)

PLOT: The U.S. Army Air Force Band and Chorus play martial airs using as their setting several Washington, D.C., locations including the White House lawn. Tunes include "Shout Wherever You May Be, I Am an American," "His Honor March," "Polly Wolly Doodle," "Man of the Hour" and "The Army Air Corps March."

REVIEWS:

"Very nice photographic work greatly enhances this dandy musical reel, which, of course, is mostly dedicated to marches." *Motion Picture Herald,* December 19, 1942

Six Hits and a Miss

Warner Bros. and the Vitaphone Corp.; U.S. B&W 10 minutes; Released on October 24, 1942

CREDITS: *Associate Producer:* Gordon Hollingshead; *Director:* Jean Negulesco; *Photography:* Ted McCord; *Editor:* Lou Hesse; *Dance Director:* Bobby Connolly; *Song:* "You've Got to Know How to Dance," lyrics by Harry Warren, music by Al Dubin

CAST: Six Hit and a Miss (Themselves—Singers), The Dancing Colleens (Themselves), Rudolph Friml, Jr., and His Band (Themselves), Ruby Keeler, Paul Draper (Themselves—Dancers), Marvin Bailey, Pauline Byrne, Vince Degen, Lee Gotch, Mack McLean, Tony Paris, Bill Seckler (Themselves)

PLOT: On an elegant dance floor, Ruby Keeler and Paul Draper handle the dance solos in this musical short featuring the Dancing Colleens. The Six Hits and a Miss sing the vocals to the accompaniment of Rudolph Friml, Jr., and his band. An extended version of "You've Got to Know How to Dance" is featured throughout the short.

REVIEWS:

"[A] sprightly short." *Motion Picture Daily,* November 17, 1942

"Popular musical entertainment is offered at its best in this reel. The film is lavish and eye-filling to a degree that would do justice to a feature musical." *The Film Daily,* November 18, 1942

REVIEWS FOR JEAN NEGULESCO:

"There is a lot of production value in this single reeler [and Negulesco] gets some really fine photographic angles and effects into a continuity that embraces talent of quality and quantity seldom included in briefs." *Showmen's Trade Review,* November 28, 1942

The Spirit of West Point

Warner Bros. and the Vitaphone Corp.; in collaboration with the Unites States Military Academy of West Point; U.S. B&W 20 minutes; Released on November 7, 1942

CREDITS: *Associate Producer:* Gordon Hollingshead; *Director:* Jean Negulesco; *Photography:* Ted McCord; *Music Supervisor:* Dudley Chambers; *Production Manager:* Phil Quinn

CAST: The West Point Band, The West Point Cadet Chapel Choir (Themselves)

PLOT: The graduation ceremonies are shown as an excuse for flashbacks featuring high points in four years of cadet training at West Point: the calisthenics, boxing matches, football games, marching drills, the combat maneuvers and the dress parades. The background music is supplied by the U.S. Military Academy Band and the singing of the Cadet Chapel Choir. The music score includes "The Official West Point March," "The Corps," "Graduation March," "West Point Alma Mater," "Stars and Stripes Forever" and "Oh, Brave Old Army Team."

REVIEWS:

"New treatment for the usual band short…. High-class subject suited for most exhibit." *Variety,* September 30, 1942

"[A] well done but rather ordinary short." *Motion Picture Daily,* November 5, 1942

REVIEWS FOR JEAN NEGULESCO:

"Fast pace and excellent form … under the expert direction of Jean Negulesco…." *The Film Daily,* October 5, 1942

The United States Marine Band

Warner Bros. and the Vitaphone Corp.; U.S. B&W 10 minutes; Released on November 28, 1942

CREDITS: *Producer:* Gordon Hollingshead; *Director:* Jean Negulesco; *Photography:* Ted McCord; *Editor:* James Gibbon; *Sound:* Everett A. Brown; *Music Supervisor:* Dudley Chambers

CAST: The U.S. Marine Band and Chorus (Themselves), Captain William F. Santelmann (Himself—Bandmaster), Thomas Holcomb (Himself)

PLOT: Against the backdrop of the Capitol in Washington, D.C., for the first time on the screen, the U.S. Marine Band and chorus render their martial music, specifically "Marine's Hymn," "Les Preludes," "Song of the Marines" and "Semper Fidelis." Many scenes of the Marines duties afloat, ashore and landing are presented during the performance.

REVIEWS:

"[T]he band does an excellent job." *Motion Picture Trade,* September 28, 1942

REVIEWS FOR JEAN NEGULESCO:

"A great deal of credit for this exceptional subject, which will thrill American people, goes jointly to Jean Negulesco for his direction, and to Ted McCord for beautiful and ingenious photography." *The Film Daily,* September 23, 1942

"Imaginative direction by Jean Negulesco makes this band subject outstanding." *Variety,* September 30, 1942

"Splendid is the direction by Jean Negulesco." *Showmen's Trade Review,* October 3, 1942

AWARDS AND HONORS:

Academy Awards: U.S. 1943: *Nominated:* Best Short Subject, one-reel

Borrah Minevitch and His Harmonica School

Warner Bros. and the Vitaphone Corp.; U.S. B&W 10 minutes; Released on December 26, 1942

CREDITS: *Associate Producer:* Gordon Hollingshead; *Director:* Jean Negulesco; *Photography:* Ted McCord; *Editor:* Doug Gould; *Art Director:* Charles Novi; *Sound:* David Forrest

CAST: Borrah Minevitch and His Harmonica Rascals (Themselves), Leo Diamond (Himself—Harmonica Rascals Member)

PLOT: Harmonica master Borrah Minevitch and his Rascals offer a concert in a rhythmic vein including these favorites: "Always in My Heart," "Bugle Call Rag," "Begin the Beguine" and "American Patrol."

REVIEWS:

"Lighthearted musical short…. The troupe displays its ability with the harmonica by using many of the instruments in different sizes and shapes." *Motion Picture Daily,* January 6, 1943

"Mouth organs are used exclusively in this entertaining short that presents some popular songs." *Motion Picture Herald,* February 21, 1948

The United States Navy Band

Warner Bros. and the Vitaphone Corp.; U.S. B&W 10 minutes; Released on January 15, 1943

CREDITS: *Producer:* Gordon Hollingshead; *Director:* Jean Negulesco; *Photography:* Ted McCord; *Editor:* Rex Steele; *Sound:* Everett A. Brown; *Music Supervisor:* Dudley Chambers

CAST: Lieutenant Charles Brendler (Himself—Bandmaster). The U.S. Navy Band and Chorus (Themselves)

PLOT: In Washington, D.C., the U.S. Navy Band and Chorus perform against the impressive background of the Lincoln Memorial. While "Anchors Aweigh," "Don't Give Up the Ship" and "V Calls for Victory" are played, different Navy divisions are shown in action.

REVIEWS:

"It is a blood-tingling display of the artistry of the Navy band that will stir audiences to their patriotic depths." *The Film Daily,* January 19, 1943

"The offerings are pleasant and inspiring." *Showmen's Trade Review,* February 13, 1943

Army Show

Warner Bros. and the Vitaphone Corp.; U.S. B&W 20 minutes; Released on February 27, 1943

CREDITS: *Associate Producer:* Gordon Hollingshead; *Director:* Jean Negulesco, *Screenplay:* Edward J. Dunstedter

CAST: The United States Army Air Force Band (Themselves), Captain Edward J. Dunstedter (Himself—Bandmaster), William T. Orr, Peter

Lind Hayes (Themselves), Knox Manning (Narrator)

PLOT: The Army Air Force Band under the direction of Captain Edward J. Dunstedter, together with a fine choral group of soldiers, perform six famous tunes of the air services: "The Army Air Corps," "The Bombardier Song," "Stairway to the Stars," "He Wears a Pair of Silver Wings," "Hello, Mom" and "Glide, Glider, Glide."

REVIEWS:
"Rarely do band shorts come better than this." *The Film Daily,* March 8, 1943

REVIEWS FOR JEAN NEGULESCO:
"When you combine good music with good singing and sentimental backgrounds with exciting action—you've got something. And that's what Jean Negulesco has done in this excellent screen version of the radio program *Soldiers with Wings*." *Showmen's Trade Review,* March 13, 1943

NOTES: *Army Show* was based on the popular CBS radio show *Soldiers with Wings*. Some of the footage was filmed at the West Coast Air Force Training Center at Santa Ana, California.

Ozzie Nelson and His Orchestra

Warner Bros. and the Vitaphone Corp.; U.S. B&W 10 minutes; Released on March 27, 1943

CREDITS: *Associate Producer:* Gordon Hollingshead; *Director:* Jean Negulesco; *Photography:* Bert Glennon; *Editor:* Everett Dodd; *Sound:* David Forrest; *Art Director:* Charles Novi

CAST: Ozzie Nelson and His Orchestra (Themselves), Harriet Hilliard, (Herself—Singer)

PLOT: Ozzie Nelson and his orchestra perform in a pictorial rendition of four numbers ("Central Avenue Shuffle," "Come On, Get Up," "Chinatown, My Chinatown" and "I'm Dancing with the Mammas with the Mooh-Lah"), two of which are acted out.

REVIEWS:
"A pleasing band short." *Motion Picture Daily,* April 20, 1943

REVIEWS FOR JEAN NEGULESCO:
"Jean Negulesco deserves a hand for the direction." *The Film Daily,* April 21, 1943

NOTES: Harriet Hilliard, Ozzie Nelson's wife, has been wrongly credited with the singing of the tune "Come On, Get Up" but she actually lip-syncs to Rose Ann Stevens' voice.

The United States Army Band

Warner Bros. and the Vitaphone Corp.; U.S. B&W 10 minutes; Released on April 17, 1943

CREDITS: *Producer:* Gordon Hollingshead; *Director:* Jean Negulesco; *Photography:* Ted McCord; *Editor:* Everett Dodd; *Sound:* Everett A. Brown; *Music Supervisor:* Dudley Chambers

CAST: Captain Thomas F. Darcy, Jr. (Himself—Bandmaster), The U.S. Army Band and Chorus (Themselves)

PLOT: While pictures of Army activity are shown, the U.S. Army Band plays "You're in the Army Now," "The Caissons Go Rolling Along," "Aura Lee," "Pack Up Your Troubles in Your Old Kit Bag," "It's a Long Way to Tipperary," "Over There," "The Girl I Left Behind Me" and "Garyowen." ("Aura Lee," performed in the short as an instrumental melody, would later become "Love Me Tender," an Elvis Presley hit.) It ends showing news footage of troops marching in New York City before embarking on troop ships for Europe.

REVIEWS: "Good musical reel." *Motion Picture Herald,* May 22, 1943

Three Cheers for the Girls

Warner Bros. and the Vitaphone Corp.; U.S. B&W 16 minutes; Released on May 8, 1943

CREDITS: *Producer:* Gordon Hollingshead; *Director:* Jean Negulesco; *Editor:* Louise Hesse; *Choreography:* Busby Berkeley, Bobby Connelly; *Music:* Harry Warren; *Lyrics:* Al Dubin; *Special Number:* M.K. Jerome (composer), Jack Scholl (lyricist)

CAST: Lynn Baggett, Poppy Wilde (Brunette Chorus Girls), Lois January (Brunette in Dressing Room), Dolores Moran (Blonde Chorus Girl), Flower Parry (Blonde in Dressing Room), Dick Powell (Singer Marine Hymn), Allen Jenkins (Marine Sergeant in Chorus), David Carlyle and Chorus (Themselves)

PLOT: The big Busby Berkeley production numbers from Warner Bros. musical hits of the past are brought together. The link between the various performances are a chorus of girls in a dressing room and singing girls who introduce the nostalgic scenes. "The Florodora Chorus of the Screen," "All's Fair in Love and War," "I'll Sing You a Thousand Love Songs," "The Words Are in My Heart," "Shadow Waltz," "Spin a Little Web of Dreams, "Aloha Oe" and "The Song of the Marines" are the numbers shown.

REVIEWS:

"This is top-flight entertainment." *The Film Daily,* June 13, 1943

"Dances and scenic effects from 'million-dollar' productions, forgotten now, but still attractive and spectacular as when first shown." *Showmen's Trade Review* June 19, 1943

The All American Bands

Warner Bros. and the Vitaphone Corp.; U.S. B&W 10 minutes; Released on May 22, 1943

CREDITS: Associate *Producer:* Gordon Hollingshead; *Director:* Jean Negulesco

CAST: Knox Manning (Narrator), Matty Malneck and His Orchestra, Joe Reichman and His Orchestra, Freddy Martin and His Orchestra, Skinnay Ennis and His Orchestra (Themselves)

PLOT: Four popular bands combine their talents. Matty Malneck plays Rossini's "The William Tell Overture"; Joe Reichman follows with Cole Porter's "Night and Day"; Freddy Martin leads his orchestra in Strauss' "Tales from the Vienna Woods," and Skinnay Ennis closes with "The Birth of the Blues."

REVIEWS:

"[O]ne of the best [shorts] of its type released by Warners." *The Film Daily,* May 28, 1943

"This film will appeal to all swing lovers, who like their music sweet, and hot, and moanin' low." *Showmen's Trade Review,* May 29, 1943

NOTES: *The All American Bands* was made up of archive footage from four Warners shorts: *Matty Malneck and His Orchestra* (1940), *Joe Reichman and His Orchestra* (1940), *Freddy Martin and His Orchestra* (1941) and *Skinnay Ennis and His Orchestra* (1941). George Amy was the director of the first short, and Negulesco directed the other three. The film was originally titled *The Bands of All Nations.*

Childhood Days

Warner Bros. and the Vitaphone Corp.; U.S. B&W 10 minutes; Released on June 5, 1943

CREDITS: *Producer:* Gordon Hollingshead; *Directors:* Jean Negulesco and Jack Scholl

CAST: The Alvarez Sisters, Peter Meremblum and the California Junior Symphony Orchestra, Diana Hale (Themselves)

PLOT: Talented youngster Diana Hale (later known as Patti Hale) dances and sings a group of songs with the assistance of the California Junior Symphony Orchestra under the direction of Peter Meremblum: "Childhood," "It's the Good Old American Way," "Three Cheers for the Red, White and Blue," "Tonight We Love," Richard Strauss' "Perpetuum Mobile" and Tchaikovsky's' "Piano Concerto in B-Flat Minor."

REVIEWS:

"*Childhood Days* is an entertaining musical novelty that should appeal to young and old alike." *Motion Picture Daily,* June 16, 1943

"With its content, studded with youth, good music, as well as novelty—plus rich talents, developed in the juvenile players—it will grace any stand in the land." *The Film Daily,* June 17, 1943

"[I]t will offer your audience a pleasing ten minutes if your audience likes child performers. This is not for the arty theater…" *Showmen's Trade Review,* June 26, 1943

The United States Service Bands

Warner Bros. and the Vitaphone Corp.; U.S. B&W 10 minutes; Released on July 24, 1943

CREDITS: *Executive Producer:* Jack L. Warner; *Associate Producer:* Gordon Hollingshead; *Director:* Jean Negulesco; *Photography:* Ted McCord; *Editor:* Rex Steele; *Sound:* Everett A. Brown; *Music Supervisor:* Dudley Chambers

CAST: The U.S. Army Band, the U.S. Navy Band, the U.S. Marine Band, the U.S. Air Force Band (Themselves)

PLOT: The U.S. Army Band, the U.S. Navy Band, the U.S. Marine Band and the U.S. Air Force Band play a group of songs in front of iconic landmark buildings in Washington, D.C. The Air Force Band tees off with "Shout I Am an American" and "Army Air Corps March." Then comes the Navy Band with "Anchors Aweigh" and "Don't Give Up the Ship." The Marine Band follows with "The Marine's Hymn" and "Semper Fidelis." The Army Band closes by playing "The Caissons Go Rolling Along," "Pack Up Your Troubles in Your Old Kit Bag," "It's a Long Way to Tipperary" and "Over There."

REVIEWS:

"One of the best musical shorts yet seen…. Excellent recording and splendid photography…." *Showmen's Trade Review,* July 31, 1943

"Gordon Hollingshead deserves much credit for turning out a rousing short." *The Film Daily,* August 4, 1943

NOTES: *The United States Service Bands* is made up of footage from earlier Negulesco shorts:

The United States Army Air Force Band (1942), *The United States Marine Band* (1942), *The United States Navy Band* (1943) and *The United States Army Band* (1943).

Hit Parade of the Gay Nineties

Warner Bros. and the Vitaphone Corp.; U.S. B&W 10 minutes; Released on September 18, 1943

CREDITS: *Associate Producer:* Gordon Hollingshead; *Director:* Jean Negulesco; *Screenplay:* James Bloodworth; *Choreographer:* Jack Crosby

PLOT: Famous vaudeville songs and acts of the 1890s are featured in this short, including the old favorites "Take Back Your Gold," "Bedelia," "Hello Ma Baby," "The Bowery," "When You Were Sweet Sixteen," "The Band Played On," "In My Merry Oldsmobile," "My Wild Irish Rose" and "Ta-ra-ra Boom-de-ay"

REVIEWS:

"Here is a musical short that will overwhelm the old-timers with a feeling of nostalgia and supply the young folk with a superb musical treat." *The Film Daily,* November 12, 1943

REVIEWS FOR JEAN NEGULESCO:

"Good direction by Jean Negulesco." *Motion Picture Daily,* October 28, 1943

Women at War

Warner Bros. in cooperation with the U.S. Army; U.S. Technicolor 21 minutes; Released on October 2, 1943

CREDITS: *Producer:* Gordon Hollingshead; *Director:* Jean Negulesco; *Screenplay:* Charles L. Tedford; *Technicolor Photography:* Harry Hallenberger; *Technicolor Director:* Natalie Kalmus; *Sound:* Harold S. Hanks; *Music:* William Lava

CAST: Faye Emerson (Anastasia "Stormy" Hart), Dorothy Day (Lorna Travis), Virginia Christine (Mary Sawyer), Marjorie Hoshelle (Sergeant Ramsey), Robert Warwick (Major General "Blood and Thunder" Travis), Murray Mead (Child), Colonel Oveta Culp Hobby (Herself), Art Gilmore (Narrator)

PLOT: The short follows WAC recruits "Stormy" Hart, Lorna Travis and Mary Sawyer from their examinations, throughout the four-week basic training, to graduation day, when Colonel Oveta Culp Hobby congratulates the new members.

REVIEWS:

"Outstanding." *Showmen's Trade Review,* September 29, 1943

AWARDS AND HONORS:

Academy Awards; USA 1944; *Nominated:* Best Short Subject, Two-reel.

Gordon Hollingshead, producer.

NOTES: The short was filmed at Fort Des Moines, Iowa, with Army cooperation. The world premiere was held on September 29, 1943, in Des Moines to promote the sale of war bonds. Over 7000 people attended the event. The short accompanied the feature *Thank Your Lucky Stars.* Members of the Women Army Corps took over the operation of the theater during the-around-the-clock showings.

Cavalcade of Dance

aka *Cavalcade of the Dance with Veloz and Yolanda;* Warner Bros.; U.S. B&W 10 minutes; Released on October 3, 1943

CREDITS: *Associate Producer:* Gordon Hollingshead; *Director:* Jean Negulesco; *Photography:* Ernest Haller; *Editor:* Rex Steele; *Art Director:* Roland Hill; *Sound:* David Forrest; *Narration Written by* James Bloodworth

CAST: Frank Veloz, Yolanda Veloz (Themselves—Dancers), Art Gilmore (Narrator)

PLOT: This short presents some of the highlights in the history of American dancing for the preceding 30 years. Ballroom dancing couple Veloz and Yolanda take the story from the 1914 Maxixe era right up to the present jitterbug era. The numbers heard "Victory Waltz," "Darktown Strutters' Ball," "Dengoso," "Tango Mi Hijo," "Las Chiapanecas" and "Lamento Enclave."

REVIEWS:

"[A]n exceptionally good short." *Motion Picture Daily,* September 27, 1943

"Good dance reel." *Motion Picture Herald,* December 25, 1943

AWARDS AND HONORS:

Academy Awards: U.S. 1944: *Nominated:* Best Short Subject: one reel: Gordon Hollingshead

Sweetheart Serenade

Warner Bros. and the Vitaphone Corp.; U.S. B&W 10 minutes; Released on October 23, 1943

CREDITS: *Associate Producer:* Gordon Hollingshead; *Director:* Jean Negulesco; *Music:* Edward Ward

CAST: Warren Douglas (The Husband), Joyce Reynolds (The Wife), Rudolf Friml, Jr., and His Band (Themselves)

PLOT: The story of a couple, from babyhood

throughout courtship until marriage, built around the song "When You Were a Smile on Your Mother's Lips and a Twinkle in Your Daddy's Eye," performed by Rudolf Friml, Jr., and his band.

REVIEWS:
"Here is a human little tale of a couple in love ... simply done." *The Film Daily*, November 12, 1943

REVIEWS FOR JEAN NEGULESCO:
"Jean Negulesco directed this all-round good short." *Motion Picture Daily*, October 28, 1943

Over the Wall

Warner Bros. and the Vitaphone Corp.; U.S. B&W 20 minutes; Released on December 11, 1943

CREDITS: Associate *Producer:* Gordon Hollingshead; *Director:* Jean Negulesco; *Screenplay:* Jed Earl Repp; *Original Story:* Matt Taylor; *Photography:* Carl Guthrie; *Editor:* Frederick Richards; *Art Director:* Roland Hill; *Sound:* Frank E. Stahl; *Music:* Howard Jackson

CAST: Dane Clark (Benny Vigo), Tom Tully (Father Darcy), Clarence Muse (Sam), William B. Davidson (Warden Ed), Frank Moran (Prisoner with Gift)

PLOT: Father Darcy, a prison chaplain, is being "retired" to a less strenuous parish due to failing health. Over the years he has won the admiration of the inmates and has converted many criminals into good citizens. One, Benny Vigo, has failed to respond to the Father's persuasion and shortly after the priest leaves, Vigo breaks out. Father Darcy, eager to return to the prison, saves Benny from the search party and sneaks him back into the prison through a ruse. Eventually Vigo is converted and Father Darcy resumes his duties among the convicts.

REVIEWS:
"This is an extraordinary well made and well acted short ... a gripping, suspenseful drama." *Showmen's Trade Review*, January 29, 1944

"Slightly overdone in places." *Motion Picture Daily*, February 10, 1944

REVIEWS FOR JEAN NEGULESCO:
"[The] script has been given worthy direction by Jean Negulesco." *The Film Daily*, February 11, 1944

Roaring Guns

Warner Bros. and the Vitaphone Corp.; U.S. Technicolor 19 minutes; Released on February 19, 1944

CREDITS: *Producer:* Gordon Hollingshead; *Director:* Jean Negulesco; *Screenplay:* Ed Earl Repp, Robert Buckner, Warren Duff; *Original Story:* Clements Ripley; *Photography:* Carl Guthrie; *Editor:* Doug Gould; *Art Director:* Charles Novi; *Sound:* C.A. Riggs; *Music:* Howard Jackson; *Musical Director:* Leo F. Forbstein; *Musical Composer:* Max Steiner; *Dialogue Director:* Harold Winston

CAST: Robert Shayne (Jared Whitney), Virginia Patton (Karen Ferris), Stephen Richards [Mark Stevens] (Lance Ferris), Charles Arnt (Colonel Chris Ferris), Norman Willis (Michen–Mine Foreman), Russell Simpson (Farmer Mackenzie), Art Baker (Narrator), Ralph Bucko, Edmund Cobb, Al Haskell (Farmers), Ken Christy (Harrison McCooey), Victor Cox, Curley Dresden, Jack Evans, Ray Jones (Miners), Wade Crosby (Miner Brawling with Lance), Fred Kelsey (Federal Deputy), Kermit Maynard Kingan Bartender), Jack Mower (Jim).

PLOT: In 1877, engineer Jared Whitney is sent to California to supervise at a gold mine which employs hydraulic water monitors to rip mountains apart and wash out remaining gold. This method of mining destroys the land of the ranchers, causing them to rise up in revolt. Whitney is ousted from his job and joins the settlers in their attack against the ruthless mine workers.

REVIEWS:
"Direction, acting and production values in this western are high in quality, and much action, excitement and fisticuffs have been packed into the film's 20 minutes." *Showmen's Trade Review*, February 19, 1944

REVIEWS FOR JEAN NEGULESCO:
"Directed swiftly by Jean Negulesco." *The Film Daily*, February 18, 1944

"It is an exciting story, well told and capably directed by Jean Negulesco." *Motion Picture Daily*, March 9, 1944

NOTES: Much of the footage in *Roaring Guns* was recycled from Warners' *Gold Is Where You Find It* (1938), directed by Michael Curtiz. Robert Shayne, Virginia Patton and Stephen Richards (later became Mark Stevens) played roles originated by George Brent, Olivia de Havilland and Tim Holt.

Grandfather's Follies

Warner Bros. and the Vitaphone Corp.; U.S. B&W 20 minutes; Released on February 26, 1944

CREDITS: *Associate Producer:* Gordon Hollingshead; *Director:* Jean Negulesco; *Screenplay:* Jack Scholl; *Music:* Leo Arnaud

CAST: Lynn Daguette, Jan Clayton, Charles Foy, Angela Greene, Bud Jamison, Fred Kelsey, Virginia Patton, Charles Foy

PLOT: With Niblo's Garden of New York as the setting, this short features a series of impersonations of one-time greats. Recreated are Millie Cavendish, Maggie Cline, Harrigan & Hart, Lillian Russell, Chauncey Olcott, Eddie Foy and the Florodora Girls. Songs from the era of the 1890s include "When the Robins Nest Again," "You Naughty, Naughty Men," "The Mulligan Guard," "While Strolling Through the Park," "Throw Him Down, McCloskey," "Dear Old Girl," "Come Down, Ma Evening Star," "He Goes to Church on Sunday," "Daisy Bell," "In My Merry Oldsmobile," "Come Josephine in My Flying Machine," "On the Banks of the Wabash" and "After the Ball."

REVIEWS:

"Here is one of the most entertaining shorts seen in a long time." *Motion Picture Daily,* February 24, 1944

REVIEWS FOR JEAN NEGULESCO:

"The subject has been capably directed by Jean Negulesco." *Showmen's Trade Review,* February 19, 1944

"The short was given top-flight production with fine direction by Jean Negulesco." *The Film Daily,* February 28, 1944

South American Sway

Warner Bros. and the Vitaphone Corp.; U.S. B&W 10 minutes; Released on March 18, 1944

CREDITS: *Producer:* Gordon Hollingshead; *Director:* Jean Negulesco

CAST: Joe Reichman and His Orchestra, Carl Hoff and His Orchestra, Emil Coleman and His Orchestra, Humberto Herrera and the Serenaders (Themselves)

PLOT: The orchestras of Joe Reichman, Carl Hoff, Emil Coleman and Humberto Herrera provide South American dance numbers, including "Gotta Have My Rhythm," "Cachita," "Mexican Magic," "When Yuba Plays the Rhumba on the Tuba" and "Negra baila la conga."

REVIEWS:

"This is a mildly entertaining reel which might have been improved by breaks in the musical sequence. Too much of one kind of rhythm makes it monotonous." *Motion Picture Daily,* March 27, 1944

"[L]ack of variety holds the picture out of the top flight class." *Showmen's Trade Review,* April 22, 1944

NOTES: *South American Sway* was assembled out of archive footage from Negulesco's shorts *Joe Reichman and His Orchestra* (1940), *Carl Hoff and His Orchestra* (1940), *Carioca Serenaders* (1941) and *Emil Coleman and Orchestra* (1942).

All Star Melody Masters

Warner Bros. and the Vitaphone Corp.; U.S. B&W 10 minutes; Released on July 29, 1944

CREDITS: *Producer:* Gordon Hollingshead; *Director:* Jean Negulesco; *Editor:* Louis Hesse; *Art Director:* Charles Novi, *Sound:* David Forrest

CAST: Hal Kemp, Emil Coleman, Skinnay Ennis, David Rubinoff (Themselves)

PLOT: Four songs numbers, each played by a different band with vocals and specialties interspersed. Hal Kemp offers "Begin the Beguine," Emil Coleman does "Just One of Those Things," Skinnay Ennis delivers the tune "Let's Do It" and David Rubinoff closes with a typical arrangement of "Dark Eyes."

REVIEWS:

"The short is a dish for those with nervous feet." *The Film Daily,* June 24, 1944

"The film will go nicely with almost any feature attraction." *Showmen's Trade Review,* August 19, 1944

NOTES: *All Star Melody Masters* is made up of clips from existing shorts, three directed by Negulesco: *Hal Kemp and His Orchestra* (1941), *Skinnay Ennis and His Orchestra* (1941) and *Emil Coleman and Orchestra* (1942).

Listen to the Bands

Warner Bros. and the Vitaphone Corp.; U.S. B&W 10 minutes; Released on October 7, 1944

CREDITS: *Producer:* Gordon Hollingshead; *Director:* Jean Negulesco

CAST: Glen Gray and the Casa Loma Orchestra, Joe Reichman and His Orchestra, Skinnay Ennis and His Orchestra, Milt Britton and His Orchestra (Themselves)

PLOT: Glen Gray and His Casa Loma band play "Hep and Happy." Joe Reichman gives his version of Beethoven's "Moonlight Sonata." Skinnay Ennis and His Orchestra offer "Three Little Words." Milt Britton concludes with his version of von Suppé's "Poet and Peasant Overture."

REVIEWS:
"A smartly produced band short." *The Film Daily*, October 31, 1944

"This is a hodgepodge of the doings of four different bands." *Showmen's Trade Review*, December 16, 1944

NOTES: *Listen to the Bands* is made up of four clips from previously seen shorts, three directed by Negulesco: *Joe Reichman and His Orchestra* (1940), *Skinnay Ennis and His Orchestra* (1941) and *Glen Gray and the Casa Loma* (1942).

Documentaries

A Ship Is Born

Warner Bros. and the Vitaphone Corp.; Produced in cooperation with the U.S. Maritime Commission and U.S. Coast Guard; U.S. Technicolor 22 minutes; Released on October 10, 1942

CREDITS: *Producer:* Gordon Hollingshead; *Director:* Jean Negulesco; *Screenplay:* Captain Owen Crump; *Photography:* Wilfred M. Cline; *Technicolor Director:* Natalie Kalmus; *Sound:* Charles Lang; *Editor:* Rex Steele; *Music:* William Lava

CAST: Knox Manning (Narrator)

PLOT: The story of the building of one of the Victory ships and the men preparing to sail her. Scenes showing the training of raw recruits for the Merchant Marine and the making of first class seamen are interspersed with details of the construction of the ship.

REVIEWS:
"A collection of vivid and arresting scenes photographed with all the skill that could be brought to the subject.... [O]ne of Warner's ace shorts." *The Film Daily*, November 18, 1942

"A thrilling, exciting and informative subject." *Showmen's Trade Review*, December 5, 1942

REVIEWS FOR JEAN NEGULESCO:
"Ably directed by Jean Negulesco...." *Motion Picture Daily*, November 17, 1942

OTHER ARTICLES AND REVIEWS:
Variety May 27, 1942, p. 28; *The Film Daily* July 23, 1942, p. 7; *Motion Picture Daily* August 26, 1942, p. 2; *Motion Picture Herald* November 14, 1942, p. 1010

AWARDS AND HONORS:
Academy Awards: U.S. 1943: *Nominated:* Best Documentary

NOTES: This patriotic documentary was partially filmed at the United States Maritime Service Training Station in Port Hueneme, California.

The Voice That Thrilled the World

Warner Bros. and the Vitaphone Corp.; U.S. B&W 17 minutes; Released on October 16, 1943

CREDITS: *Associate Producer:* Gordon Hollingshead; *Director:* Jean Negulesco; *Narration Writer:* James Bloodworth; *Photography:* Sid Hickox; *Editor:* Thomas Pratt; *Art Director:* Roland Hill; *Music:* Howard Jackson

CAST: Art Gilmore (Narrator)

PLOT: A brief history of talking films, from George Eastman's first experiments in sound and Thomas Edison's record through the role that Warners played in its development from the first successful early talkies up to 1942. It includes extracts from *The Jazz Singer* (1927), *The Lights of New York* (1928), *On with the Show* (1929), *Disraeli* (1929), *The Show of Shows* (1929), *Dangerous* (1935), *The Story of Louis Pasteur* (1936), *Sergeant York* (1941) and others. All represent various stages in the growth of talking films. The short concludes with the "Grand Old Flag" number from *Yankee Doodle Dandy* (1942).

REVIEWS:
"If ever there was a short subject that deserved feature billing this is it. It is the inspiring story of the sound motion pictures...." *Showmen's Trade Review*, November 6, 1943

"The featurette is extremely interesting and absorbing." *The Film Daily* November 24 1943

REVIEWS FOR JEAN NEGULESCO:
"Jean Negulesco's direction is excellent as is Art Gilmore's commentary." *Motion Picture Daily* November 18, 1943

NOTES: *The Voice That Thrilled the World* was made by Warner Bros. to commemorate their receiving an Academy Award for sound in 1942.

Food and Magic

Warner Bros.; for the United States Government Office of War Information; U.S. B&W 10 minutes; Released on November 18, 1943

CREDITS: *Producer:* Gordon Hollingshead; *Director:* Jean Negulesco; *Screenplay:* James Bloodworth; *Music:* William Lava

CAST: Jack Carson (Mysto the Magician), Faye

Emerson, Fred Kelsey (Audience Members), Bill Kennedy (Husband), Mark Stevens (Grimy Soldier), Dink Trout (Meek Butcher Customer)

PLOT: On a circus midway, Mysto the Magician demonstrates the importance of food and the war effort. He shows to his audience the concept of waste, rationing and price control as articles appear from nowhere and, just as mysteriously, vanish.

REVIEWS AND ARTICLES: *Motion Picture Herald* November 13, 1943, p. 23; *Motion Picture Daily* November 17, 1943, p. 7; *Motion Picture Herald* December 4, 1943, p. 1659; *The Educational Screen* June 1944 p. 244; *Motion Picture Herald* September 30, 1944, p. 54

NOTES: *Food and Magic* was distributed as a public service by War Activities Committee Motion Picture Industry. The film deals with nutrition, conservation of food and the necessity of sharing it.

The Dark Wave

20th Century–Fox; Produced in cooperation with the Variety Club Foundation to combat epilepsy; U.S. DeLuxe Color CinemaScope 23 minutes; Premiered at the Variety Club Foundation at the Waldorf-Astoria Hotel in New York City in May 1956

CREDITS: *Producer:* John Healy; *Director:* Jean Negulesco; *Story and Screenplay:* Eugene Vale; *Photography:* Charles G. Clarke; *Art Directors:* Lyle R. Wheeler, Jack Martin Smith; *Set Decorators:* Walter M. Scott, Stuart Reiss; *Editor:* David Bretherton; *Assistant Director:* David Silver; *Technical Advisor:* Leon Ottinger, Jr., M.D.; *Sound:* Harry M. Leonard, W.D. Flick; *Narrator:* Charles Bickford

CAST: Cornell Borchers, Charles Bickford, Nancy Davis, Russ Conway, Pamela Beaird, Lili Gentle, James O'Rear, Virginia Carroll

PLOT: In a typical modern American town, a 12-year old girl becomes epileptic. At first her family tends to shy away from her, but certain facts are brought to light by the family doctor and a renowned specialist which convince all concerned that the mystery that surrounds the disorder is totally uncalled for.

REVIEWS AND ARTICLES:
Today's Cinema April 17, 1957, p. 10; *Kinematograph Weekly* April 25, 1957, p. 19; *Motion Picture Daily* May 4, 1956, p. 3; *The Film Daily* May 4, 1957, p. 6; *Motion Picture Daily* June 5, 1956, p. 1; *The Hollywood Reporter* June 13, 1956, p. 3; *Films in Review* October 1957; *Film News* October-November 1966

AWARDS AND HONORS:
Academy Awards: U.S. 1957: *Nominated:* Best Short Subject: two-reel: John Healy; Best Documentary; Short Subjects: John Healy

As Second Unit Director or Associate Director

A Farewell to Arms

Paramount; U.S. B&W 90 minutes; Premiered in New York on December 8, 1932

CREDITS: *Producer-Director:* Frank Borzage; *Associate Producer:* Benjamin F. Glazer; *Second Unit Director:* Jean Negulesco; *Assistant Directors:* Lew Borzage, Arthur Jacobson, Charles Griffin; *Screenplay:* Benjamin Glazer, Oliver H.P. Garrett; Based on the novel by Ernest Hemingway; *Photography:* Charles Lang; *Camera Operator:* Robert Pittack; *Assistant Camera:* Clifford Shirpser; *Sound:* Franklin B. Hansen, Harold Lewis; *Editors:* Otho Lovering, George Nicholls, Jr.; *Art Director:* Roland Anderson, Hans Dreier; *Costumes:* Travis Banton, Ed Gross; *Music:* Ralph Rainger, John Leipold, Bernard Kaun, Paul Marquardt, Herman Hand, W. Franke Harling, Milan Roder; *Technical Advisers on War Sequences:* Charles Griffin; *Technical Adviser on Hospital Sequences:* Dr. A. Jardini

CAST: Helen Hayes (Catherine Barkley), Gary Cooper (Lt. Frederic Henry), Adolphe Menjou (Captain Rinaldi), Mary Phillips (Helen Ferguson), Jack La Rue (The Priest), Blanche Friderici (Head Nurse), Mary Forbes (Miss Van Campen), Gilbert Emery (British Major), Henry Armetta (Bonello), Peggy Cunningham (Molly), Doris Lloyd (Nurse), George Humbert (Piani), Agostino Borgato (Giulio), Paul Porcasi (Harry—Headwaiter), Herman Bing (Post Office Clerk), Alice Adair (Café Girl), Fred Malatesta (Manera), Thomas Ricketts (Count Greffi), Robert Cauterio (Gordoni)

PLOT: During World War I, Lieutenant Frederic Henry, an American serving with the Italian ambulance corps, falls in love with Catherine Barkley, an English nurse in a local hospital. The two become inseparable. When Frederic returns to the front, his major, jealous of the relationship, has Catherine transferred to a hospital in Milan. After recovering from an operation, Frederic goes to Milan to be with her. Later she travels to Switzerland to give birth to Frederic's baby. From there, she sends him several letters, but they are all held up by the jealous major. Frederic locates her, arriving to Switzerland just after their baby has been born dead. Catherine is also near death as news comes that the war is over.

REVIEWS:
"Bravely as it is produced for the most part, there is too much sentiment and not enough strength." *The New York Times*, December 9, 1932

"Outstanding love drama based on bestseller packs a strong romantic punch for adult audience.... Tenderly gripping entertainment...." *The Film Daily*, December 10, 1932

"A woman's picture essentially and a box office winner in every respect ... punchy, action full, colourful, romantic, sexy and engagingly realistic." *Variety*, December 13, 1932

OTHER ARTICLES AND REVIEWS:
Film Daily October 1, 1930 p. 6; *Film Daily* August 13, 1931, p. 8; *Hollywood Reporter* June 4, 1932, p. 3; *Film Daily* July 23, 1932 p. 4; *Film Daily* August 3, 1932, p. 6; *Screenland* October 1932 p. 71; *American Cinematographer* November 1932 p. 46; *Hollywood Reporter* November 16, 1932 p. 6; *Hollywood Reporter* November 30, 1932, p. 1–2; *Motion Picture Herald* December 10, 1932, p. 40; *The New York Times* December 18, 1932, p. 7; *Pour Vous* (France) December 29 1932 p. 11; *Stage* January 1933 p. 42; *Vanity Fair* January 1933 p. 62; *New Look* January 1933 p. 47; *Nation* January 4, 1933, p. 28; *HF* 21 January 21, 1933 p. 1; *Kinematograph Weekly* May 4, 1933; *The Cinema Booking Guide Supplement* July 1933 p. 12; *The Picturegoer* October 21, 1933, p. 26; *Cinémonde* (France) October 26, 1933, p. 889; *Pour Vous* (France) November 2, 1933, p. 6; *Cinémonde* (France) July 7, 1934, p. 544; *The New York Times* May 29, 1938, p. 3; *Monthly Film Bulletin* July 1938 p. 183; *Films and Filming* July 1982 p. 31–32; *Time Out London* October 29, 1982, p. 39; *Film Comment* January-February 1995 p. 70–73; *Sight and Sound* May 1997 p. 59; *London Film Festival Catalogue* v.49 2005 p. 95

AWARDS AND HONORS:
National Board of Review: U.S. 1932: *Winner:* NBR Award, Top Ten Films

Academy Awards: U.S. 1934: *Winner:* Best Cinematography: Charles Lang, Jr.; Best Sound Recording: Paramount Studio Sound Department, Franklin B. Hansen. *Nominated:* Best Film; Best Art *Direction:* Hans Dreier, Roland Anderson

Kiss and Make-Up

Paramount; U.S. B&W 80 minutes; Premiered in New York June 28, 1934

CREDITS: *Producer:* B. P. Schulberg; *Director:* Harlan Thompson; *Associate Director:* Jean Negulesco; *Screenplay:* Harlan Thompson, George Marion, Jr., Jane Hinton; Based on the story "Kozmetika" by Istvan Békeffi; *Photography:* Leon Shamroy; *Art Directors:* Hans Dreier, Ernst Fegté; *Sound:* Jack A. Goodrich; *Wardrobe:* Travis Banton; *Songs:* "Corn Beef and Cabbage I Love You," "The Mirror Song" and "Love Divided by Two," words by Leo Robin, music by Ralph Rainger

CAST: Cary Grant (Dr. Maurice Lamar), Genevieve Tobin (Eve Caron), Helen Mack (Anne), Edward Everett Horton (Marcel Caron), Lucien Littlefield (Max Pascal), Mona Maris (Countess Rita), Rafael Storm (Ronaldo), Toby Wing (Consuelo of Claghorne), Dorothy Christy (Greta), Doris Lloyd (Madame Durant), George André Beranger (Valet), Milton Wallace (Maharajah of Baroona), Sam Ash (Plumber), Henry Armetta (Banquet Chairman), Rita Gould (Madame Dupont), Jean Carmen (Maharajah's Wife), Jean Gale, Judith Arlen, Ann Sheridan, Lee-Anne Meredith (Beauticians), Ann Hovey (Lady Rummon-Dray), Julie Bishop (Salon Client)

PLOT: A handsome young surgeon, Dr. Maurice Lamar, whose specialty is making ugly women beautiful, falls in love with Eve Caron, one of his creations. They marry and go on a Mediterranean honeymoon. There, she cannot eat because it might spoil her figure, cannot bathe because salty water is bad for her skin, cannot dress in less than four hours. Lamar is frustrated with her behavior. He decides to go back to Paris determined to give up his business and to win back his faithful secretary, who is about to marry Caron's first husband. In the end, both couples manage to get back together.

REVIEWS:
"Either a gag comedy with a romantic thread or a light romance with gag comedy, but more gags than romance. A nice picture lacking sufficient strength to wow but should do all right. Plot is thin, though sufficient." *Variety*, June 3, 1934

"Harlan Thompson directed with shrewd appeal to feminine patronage." *Motion Picture Daily,* June 12, 1934

"*Kiss and Make-Up* is a first-class lingerie bazaar and a third-rate entertainment. [It] success to a remarkable degree in being dull." *The New York Times,* June 29, 1934

REVIEWS FOR JEAN NEGULESCO:
"The new directing team of Harlan Thompson and Jean Negulesco did exceptionally well." *The Hollywood Reporter,* May 25, 1934

OTHER ARTICLES AND REVIEWS:
Film Daily February 5, 1934, p. 5; *Variety* February 27, 1934, p. 6; *The Hollywood Reporter* March 20, 1934, p. 8; *Daily Variety* April 3, 1934 p. 2; *The Hollywood Reporter* April 4, 1934, p. 7; *Daily Variety* April 20, 1934, p. 3; *The Film Daily* May 1 1934 p. 6; *Motion Picture Herald* May 12, 1934, p. 42; *Hollywood Reporter* May 25, 1934, p. 3; *Daily Variety* June 8, 1934 p. 3; *Daily Variety* June 9, 1934 p. 4; *Motion Picture Herald* June 16, 1934, p. 79; *New York Times* June 29, 1934 p. 17; *L.A. Times* June 29, 1934; *Film Daily* June 30, 1934, p. 4; *New York World-Telegram* June 30, 1934; *New York Sun* July 2, 1934; *New York Evening Post* July 2 1934; *St. Louis Star Times* July 7, 1934; *Harrison's Reports* July 7, 1934; *Cine-Service* July 25, 1934, p. 249; *New Movie Magazine* August 1934; *Monthly Film Bulletin* August 1934 p. 50; *The Times* (U.K.) August 13, 1934; *Kinematograph Weekly* August 16, 1934; *Monthly Film Bulletin* December 1934 p. 100; *The Newcastle Sun* (U.K.) January 4, 1935, p. 3; *The Picturegoer* January 5, 1935, p. 23

Enter Madame!

Paramount; U.S. B&W 83 minutes; Released on November 2, 1934

CREDITS: *Producer:* Benjamin Glazer; *Director:* Elliott Nugent; *Screenplay:* Gladys Lehman, Charles Brackett; Based on the play *Enter Madame!* by Gilda Varesi Archibald and Dorothea Donn-Byrne; *Photography:* Theodor Sparkuhl, William C. Mellor; *Editor:* Hugh Bennett; *Art Directors:* Hans Dreier, Ernst Fegté; *Costumes:* Travis Banton; *Music:* Heinz Roemheld; *Music Director:* Nathaniel W. Finston; *Sound:* M.M. Paggi; *Technical Advisor:* Jean Negulesco; *Songs:* Selections from the operas *Cavalleria Rusticana,* music by Pietro Mascagni, libretto by Guido Menasci and Giovanni Targioni-Tozzetti, *Tosca,* music by Giacomo Puccini, libretto by Giuseppe Giacosa and Luigi Illica; "The Anvil Chorus" and "Miserere" from *Il Trovatore,* music by Giuseppe Verdi, libretto by Salvatore Cammarano

CAST: Elissa Landi (Lisa Della Robbia), Cary Grant (Gerald Fitzgerald), Lynne Overman (Mr. Farnham), Sharon Lynne (Flora Preston), Michelette Burani (Bice), Paul Porcasi (Archimede), Adrian Rosley (The Doctor), Cecilia Parker (Aline Chalmers), Frank Albertson (John Della Robbia), Richard Bonelli (The Singer, Scarpa in *La Tosca*), Wilfred Hari (Tamamoto), Torben Meyer (Carlson), Harold Berquist (Bjorgenson), Wallis Clark (John H. Massey), Fred Malatesta (Hotel Clerk), Anthony Merlo (Ship's Officer), Richard Kline (Stage Manager), Gino Corrado (Waiter), Diana Lewis (Operator), Frank Dunn (Second Stage Manager), Matt McHugh (Reporter), Mildred Booth (Trixie—Woman Reporter), Jack Byron (Joe—Cameraman), Bud Galea (Spoletta on Stage), Clara Lou Sheridan [Ann Sheridan] (Flora's Shipboard Friend)

PLOT: Gerald Fitzgerald marries Lisa Della Robbia, a passionate, moody opera star, only to find himself merely part of her entourage. Tired of trailing her around the theater, and not getting any help from his wife's manager, Gerald realizes that he belongs some place else, letting Lisa tour Europe alone while he stays in America romancing another girl. When divorce papers are about to be served, Lisa returns, upsetting her rival's wedding plans. Husband and wife eventually reconcile.

REVIEWS:
"Swift pace, general good humor and the presence of a hard-working cast.... *Enter Madame!* is still just a farce with music." *The New York Times,* January 12, 1935

"Fairly good adult fare with good cast and production giving values to old domestic play." *The Film Daily,* January 12, 1935

"Comedy, fast-moving and explosive, appears to be the outstanding showmanship quality to back up the picture's entertainment prestige and the cast strength." *Motion Picture Herald,* September 8, 1934

OTHER ARTICLES AND REVIEWS:
Daily Variety October 5, 1934, p. 3; *Motion Picture Herald* October 6, 1934, p. 53; *Hollywood Reporter* October 18, 1934, p. 3; *Daily Variety* October 18 1934; *Motion Picture Daily* October 25 1934 p. 4; *American Cinematographer* November 1934 p. 306; *Motion Picture Herald* November 3, 1934, p. 36; *Monthly Film Bulletin* January 12,

1935, p. 114; *Variety* January 15, 1935, p. 63; *Kinematograph Weekly* January 17, 1935; *The Picturegoer* May 25, 1935, p. 28

Captain Blood

First National Productions Corp.; A Cosmopolitan Production; Warner Bros. Pictures; U.S. B&W 119 minutes; Premiered in New York on December 28, 1935

CREDITS: *Associate Producers:* Gordon Hollingshead, Harry Joe Brown; *Executive Producers:* Jack L. Warner, Hal B Wallis; *Director:* Michael Curtiz; *Screenplay:* Casey Robinson; Based on the novel *Captain Blood: His Odyssey* by Rafael Sabatini; *Photography:* Hal Mohr; *Additional Photography:* Ernest Haller; *Dialogue Director:* Stanley Logan; *Editor:* George Amy; *Art Director:* Anton Grot; *Sound:* C.A. Riggs; *Set Decorators:* Anton Grot, Robey Cooper; *Gowns:* Milo Anderson; *Special Effects:* Fred Jackman; *Music Director:* Leo F. Forbstein; *Musical Arrangements:* Erich Wolfgang Korngold; *Orchestrators:* Hugo Friedhofer, Ray Heindorf; *Assistant Director:* Sherry Shourds; *Second Unit Director:* Jean Negulesco; *Fencing Master:* Fred Cavens

CAST: Errol Flynn (Peter Blood), Olivia de Havilland (Arabella Bishop), Lionel Atwill (Colonel Bishop), Basil Rathbone (Levasseur), Ross Alexander (Jeremy Pitt), Guy Kibble (Hagthorpe), Henry Stephenson (Lord Willoughby), Robert Barrat (Wolverstone), Hobart Cavanaugh (Dr. Bronson), Donald Meek (Dr. Whacker), Jessie Ralph (Mrs. Barlow), Forrester Harvey (Honesty Nuttall), Frank McGlynn, Sr. (the Rev. Uriah Ogle), Holmes Herbert (Capt. Gardner), David Torrence (Andrew Baynes), J. Carrol Naish (Cahusac), Pedro de Cordoba (Don Diego), George Hassell (Governor Steed), Harry Cording (Kent), Leonard Mudie (Baron Jeffreys), Ivan Simpson (Prosecutor), Stuart Casey (Capt. Hobart), Mary Forbes (Mrs. Steed), E.E. Clive (Clerk of the Court), Colin Kenny (Lord Chester Dyke), Maude Leslie (Mrs. Baynes), Gardner James (Branded Slave), Vernon Steele (King James), Reginald Barlow (Dixon), Murray Kinnell (Governor Steed's Clerk), Gunnis Davis (Auction Clerk), Stymie Beard (Page Boy)

PLOT: Peter Blood, an English doctor, is unjustly accused of treason in the time of King James II and deported to Jamaica. There he is offered for sale as a slave to wealthy landowners in Port Royal. Blood is saved by Arabella Bishop who, intrigued by his personality, hides him in her uncle's mines. Blood leads the local slaves in an uprising, steals a Spanish ship while its crew is looting the town, and becomes the most celebrated corsair in the Caribbean. After a series of adventures at sea fighting the tyranny of James II and the French on the side of William of Orange, Blood is pardoned, made governor and ties the knot with Arabella.

REVIEWS:

"The swagger, the glamour, the road to high adventure and romance penned in the Rafael Sabatini original have been caught effectively and thoroughly by Michael Curtiz." *Motion Picture Daily,* December 19, 1935

"[V]isual beauty and a fine, swaggering arrogance in the new version of *Captain Blood.*" *The New York Times,* December 27, 1935

"*Blood* is a spectacular cinematic entry which, while not flawless, is quite compelling." *Variety,* January 1, 1936

OTHER ARTICLES AND REVIEWS:

Motion Picture Herald January 11, 1935, p. 53; *Daily Variety* March 21, 1935 p. 2; *Daily Variety* August 3, 1935, p. 3; *New York Times* August 18, 1935, p. 3; *Motion Picture Herald;* September 28, 1935, p. 344–45; *Daily Variety* October 28, 1935, p. 11; *Daily Variety* October 29, 1935, p. 10; *Daily Variety* November 29, 1935, p. 2; *Film Daily* December 19, 1935, p. 5; *New York Times* December 27, 1935, p. 14; *Newsweek* December 28, 1935, p. 24–25; *Time* December 30, 1935, p. 16; *The Hollywood Reporter* December 31, 1935, p. 4; *Stage* January 1936 p. 32; *Canadian Magazine* January 1936 p. 33; Commonweal January 3, 1936, p. 272; *Scholastic* January 25, 1936, p. 28; *Monthly Film Bulletin* February 1936 p. 27; *Canadian Magazine* February 1936 p. 36; *Today's Cinema* February 5, 1936; *Fortune Magazine* December 1937 p. 112; *Today's Cinema* April 9, 1943; *Kinematograph Weekly* April 15, 1943; *Sight and Sound Supplement* March 1948 p. 8; *Today's Cinema* July 4, 1952, p. 8; *Daily Film Renter* July 7, 1952, p. 77; *Kinematograph Weekly* July 10, 1952, p. 44; *The Velvet Light Trap* June 1971 p. 26–31; *The Hollywood Reporter* January 6, 1987, p. 4; *Films of the Golden Age* Spring 1996 p. 14–15; *Film-Historia* n.2 1999 p. 133–46; *Music from the Movies* Winter 2001, p. 86; *Empire* December 2005 p. 198

Crash Donovan

Universal; U.S. B&W 57 minutes; Released on July 12, 1936

CREDITS: *Associate Producer:* Julius Bernheim; *Director:* William Nigh; *Associate Director:* Jean Negulesco; *Screenplay:* Eugene Solow, Charles Grayson, Karl Detzer; *Original Story:* Harold Shumate; *Photography:* Milton Krasner; *Art Director:* Ralph DeLancey; *Editors:* Hanson T. Fritch, Byron Robinson; *Gowns:* Brymer; *Sound:* Homer G. Tasker; *Special Visual Effects:* John P. Fulton; *Makeup:* Bill Ely; *Assistant Directors:* William J. Reiter, Fred Frank, Ansel Friedberger; *Dialogue Director:* Edward McGregor; *Musical Director:* Herman Heller; *Songs:* "Devoted to You," words by Ned Washington, music by Allie Wrubel; "Wake Up and Sing," words and music by Carmen Lombardo, Charles Tobias and Cliff Friend; "Polly Wolly Doodle," traditional; "Hail to the Highway Patrol"

CAST: Jack Holt (Michael "Crash" Donovan), John King (Johnny Allen), Nan Grey (Doris Tennyson), Eddie Acuff ("Alabam" Thomas), Hugh Buckler (Captain Tennyson), Ward Bond (The Drill Master), James Donlan ("Smokey"), Douglas Fowley (Harris), William Tanned (Tony), Huey White (Fizz), Al Hill (White); Gardner James (Pete), Paul Porcasi (Café Owner), George Stinson (The Singing Detective), Lane Chandler (Henchman)

PLOT: Michael "Crash" Donovan does motorcycle riding stunts at a carnival. He becomes interested in the motorcycle police and joins up. There he meets and fall for Doris Tennyson, the captain's daughter, who is engaged to Johnny Allen. When Michael realizes that it's a real love affair between those two, he gracefully bows out. After fighting a gang of smugglers and saving Johnny's life, Michael decides to quit the force to return to the fairgrounds.

REVIEWS:

"Good program for the masses. The action is fast and at times thrilling" *Harrison's Reports,* July 18, 1936

"The picture is lively and undemanding; like peanut brittle and a pulp-paper magazine, it has its time and pace." *The New York Times,* August 10, 1936

"The film contains plenty of thrills, plenty of laughter and a touch of pathos. The acting is good all round...." *Monthly Film Bulletin,* September 1936

OTHER ARTICLES AND REVIEWS:

Hollywood Reporter March 1936 p. 5; *Hollywood Reporter* April 10, 1936, p. 2; *The London Reporter* April 20, 1936; *Motion Picture Herald* May 30, 1936, p. 33–34; *Hollywood Reporter* June 8, 1936, p. 5; *Daily Variety* July 9, 1936, p. 3; *Hollywood Reporter* July 9, 1936, p. 4; *Motion Picture Daily* July 11, 1936, p. 16; *Motion Picture Herald* July 18, 1936, p. 54; *Film Daily* August 11, 1936, p. 10; *Variety* August 12, 1936, p. 19; *Photoplay* September 1936 p. 54; *Kinematograph Weekly* September 17, 1936; *Motion Picture Herald* September 26, 1936, p. 72; *Boy's Cinema* October 31, 1936, p. 17

NOTES: The film's working titles were *Crashing Through* and *Crashing Donovan*. William Nigh and Jean Negulesco took over from director Edward Laemmle. Nigh directed the dramatic scenes, Negulesco the car racing sequences and retakes.

Paris Calling

Universal; Charles K. Feldman Group Production; U.S. B&W 95 minutes; Premiered in New York on December 4, 1941

CREDITS: *Producer:* Benjamin Glazer; *Director:* Edwin L. Marin; *Road Scene Director:* Jean Negulesco; *Screenplay:* Benjamin Glazer, Charles Kaufman; *Original Story:* John S. Toldy; *Photography:* Milton Krasner; *Art Directors:* Jack Otterson, Martin Obzina; *Editor:* Edward Curtiss; *Set Decorator:* R.A. Gausman; *Assistant Director:* Fred Frank; *Music Director:* H.J. Salter; *Musical Score:* Richard Hageman; *Sound:* Bernard B. Brown, Robert Pritchard; *Gowns.* Madame Pola

CAST: Elizabeth Bergner (Marianne Jannetier), Randolph Scott (Lt. Nicholas "Nick" Jordan), Basil Rathbone (Andre Benoit), Gale Sondergaard (Colette), Lee J. Cobb (Capt. Schwabe), Charles Arnt (Lt. Lantz), Eduardo Ciannelli (Mouche), Elisabeth Risdon (Madame Jannetier), George Renavent (Butler), William Edmunds (Prof. Marceau), Patrick O'Malley (Bruce McAvoy), George Metaxa, Gino Corrado (Waiters), Paul Leyssac (Chief of Underground), Gene Garrick (Wolfgang Schmitt), Paul Bryar (Paul), Otto Reichow (Gruber), Adolph Milar (Gestapo Agent), Marion Murray (Cherie), Grace Lenard (Marie), Yvette Bentley (Simone), Marcia Ralston (Renee), Jeff Corey (Benoit's Secretary), Roland Varno (German Pilot), Ian Wolfe (Thin Workman), Philip Van Zandt (Thick Workman)

PLOT: On the eve of the Germans entering Paris, wealthy Marianne Jannetier is warned by her lover Andre Benoit, a high government official, that she must flee. On the road, the civilians are bombed by the Nazis and Marianne returns to Paris with her dead mother. An underground meeting is going on at her home. She joins the movement and is assigned to a waterfront café on the French coast where messages are transmitted in code via piano music over short wave. There she aids Lt. Nick Jordan, an American aviator serving in the R.A.F., who was left behind when the British evacuated. Before having Jordan rescued by a commando, Marianne shoots Benoit, who had become an important member of the Nazi-controlled government.

REVIEWS:
"*Paris Calling* is an interesting, entertaining spy story with some really competent acting by an actress named Elizabeth Bergner." *Motion Picture Herald Digest,* December 6, 1941

"Director Edwin Marin has built powerful suspense ... [pacing] the story with admirable balance in switching from the romantic to thrilling episodes." *Variety,* December 10, 1941

OTHER ARTICLES AND REVIEWS:
Hollywood Reporter August 8, 1941, p. 9; *Hollywood Reporter* August 20 1941 p. 6; *Hollywood Reporter* August 28,1941 p. 7; *Hollywood Reporter* October 8, 1941, p. 2; *Hollywood Reporter* November 3, 1941, p. 9; *Modern Screen* December 1941 p. 104; *Hollywood Reporter* December 4. 1941 p. 3; *Film Daily* December 4, 1941, p. 5; *Daily Variety* December 4, 1941, p. 3; *Boxoffice* December 6, 1941; *Harrison's Reports* December 13, 1941, p. 199; *Scholastic* January 12, 1942, p. 28; *New York Times* January 25, 1942, p. 5; *Commonweal* January 30, 1942, p. 370; *Photoplay* February 1942 p. 24; *Hollywood Reporter* June 27, 1941, p. 1; *Hollywood Reporter* January 29, 1942 p. 8; *Monthly Film Bulletin* March 1942 p. 34; *American Cinematographer* April 1942 p. 172

Other Work as Uncredited Director

City for Conquest
Warner Bros., 1940, *Director:* Anatole Litvak; Negulesco took over as director during the final four days of filming when Litvak suffered an eye injury.

River of No Return
20th Century–Fox, 1954, *Director:* Otto Preminger; Negulesco directed retakes and a few additional scenes.

The World of Suzie Wong
World Enterprises–Paramount, 1960, *Director:* Richard Quine

Negulesco was originally hired as director. He worked for 30 days before being fired by producer Ray Stark due to disagreements. He was replaced by Richard Quine. Some of his footage remained in the completed film.

The Greatest Story Ever Told
United Artists, 1965, *Director:* George Stevens
When the shooting fell behind schedule, directors Negulesco and David Lean were hired to pitch in.

Other Work as Screenwriter

Expensive Husbands
Warner Brothers; U.S. B&W 62 minutes; Released in New York on November 27, 1937

CREDITS: *Producer:* Bryan Foy; *Associate Producer:* Frank Mandel; *Director:* Bobby Connolly; *Screenplay:* Lillie Hayward, Jean Negulesco, Jay Brennan; *Original Story:* Kyrill de Shishmareff; *Assistant Directors:* Fred Tyler, Arthur Lueker; *Photography:* James Van Trees; *Editor:* Lou Hesse; *Art Director:* Hugh Reticker; *Gowns:* Howard Shoup; *Sound:* Francis J. Scheid; *Music:* Heinz Roemheld; *Dialogue Director:* Jay Brennan

CAST: Patric Knowles (Prince Rupert), Beverly Roberts (Laurine Lynne), Allyn Joslyn (Joe Craig), Gordon Oliver (Ricky Preston), Vladimir Sokoloff (Andrew Brenner), Eula Guy (Trommy), Robert C. Fischer (Joseph), Fritz Feld (Herr Meyer), John Butler (Savage), Ann Codee (Maria), George Humbert (Giovanni), Otto Fries (Frantz), Granville Owen (Announcer), Don Marion (Bus Boy), Jack Mower (Elevator

Man), Rosella Towne (Stenographer), Ellen Clancy (Telephone Operator), Frank Mayo (Motion Picture Director), Sandra Ramoy, Sam Ash, Lester Dorr (Reporters), Elsa Peterson (Icy Lady), Myrtle Stedman (Nurse), Stuart Holmes (Servant)

PLOT: At the suggestion of her press agent, a fading movie star travels to Europe and buys a title in the form of a husband, an impoverished Austrian prince. The ensuing publicity results in her getting a new contract, but the prince initially refuses to go to Hollywood where she again skyrockets to fame. After a series of funny events, the actress discovers that she is in love with her husband and returns to Vienna to be with him, giving up her career.

REVIEWS:

"*Expensive Husbands* is an attempt at light comedy in the lower budget bracket." *Motion Picture Herald*, September 11, 1937

"There is not much to recommend in this program comedy. Only in one or two instances it is amusing; but for the most part one is bored by the continuous dialogue and ordinary plot developments." *Harrison's Reports,* December 11, 1937

"Reasonably amusing romantic comedy for dual trade. Strictly lightweight as to story, production, marquee value and all-round pretensions but acceptable for runner-up spotting." *Variety,* January 12, 1938

OTHER ARTICLES AND REVIEWS:

Motion Picture Herald July 31, 1937, p. 1944; *Daily Variety* September 3, 1937, p. 3; *Hollywood Reporter* September 3, 1937 p. 2; *Motion Picture Daily* September 8, 1937, p. 2; *Film Daily* September 9, 1937 p. 11; *Monthly Film Bulletin* November 1937 p. 246; *Kinematograph Weekly* November 11, 1937; *New York Times* January 8, 1938, p. 19

Other Work as Author or Co-Author

Fight for Your Lady

RKO; U.S. B&W 66 minutes; Released in New York on November 5, 1937

CREDITS: *Producer:* Albert Lewis; *Executive Producer:* Samuel J. Briskin; *Director:* Ben Stoloff; *Screenplay:* Ernest Pagano, Harry Segall, Harold Kusell; *Original Story:* Jean Negulesco, Isabel Leighton; *Photography:* Jack MacKenzie; *Art Directors:* Van Nest Polglase, Carroll Clark; *Editor:* George Crone; *Set Decorator:* Darrell Silvera; *Gowns:* Edward Stevenson; *Musical Director:* Frank Tours; *Sound:* Hugh McDowell, Jr.; *Songs:* "Blame It on the Danube," music by Harry Akst, lyrics by Frank Loesser

CAST: John Boles (Robert Densmore), Jack Oakie (Ham Hamilton), Ida Lupino (Marietta), Margot Grahame (Marcia Trent), Gordon Jones (Mike Scanlon), Erik Rhodes (Anton Spadissimo), Billy Gilbert (Boris), Paul Guilfoyle (Jimmy Trask), George Renavent (Joris), Charles Judels (Felix Janos), Maude Eburne (Nadya), Charles Coleman (Butler), Leona Roberts (Cleaning Lady), Forrester Harvey (Wrestling Referee), Ward Bond (Mr. Walton), Pat Flaherty (Mr. Russell), Sam Harris (Wrestling Match Spectator), Torben Meyer (Hungarian Police Officer), Gino Corrado (Hungarian Waiter), Sidney Bracey (Densmore's Servant), Gerald Oliver Smith (First Creditor), George Nardelli (Club Patron), Paul Power (Café Patron)

PLOT: Bob Densmore, a rich young concert singer, is left by his gold-digging actress fiancée because she is led to believe he has lost his money. Densmore plans to commit suicide by seducing cabaret artist Marietta; her jealous admirer is a notorious duelist who has killed 44 men. Before the sword fight, the singer changes his mind about dying. He will be helped by the intervention of a wrestling trainer.

REVIEWS:

"*Fight for Your Lady* is a B picture that comes closer to being an A than most of the former aspire to … genuinely entertaining." *Variety,* October 20, 1937

"Short in running time but long in amusement quality…. The intent to amuse was undoubtedly inspired by Jean Negulesco and Isabel Leighton in the creation of the original story." *Motion Picture Daily,* September 25, 1937

"Although not startling, the story offers a pleasant combination of comedy and romance…." *Harrison's Reports,* October 9, 1937

OTHER ARTICLES AND REVIEWS:

Hollywood Reporter June 10, 1937, p. 27; *Hollywood Reporter* July 12, 1937, p. 11; *Hollywood Reporter* August 9, 1937, p. 14–15; *Hollywood Reporter* August 10, 1937 p. 13; *Hollywood Reporter*

September 24, 1937, p. 2; *Daily Variety* September 24, 1937 p. 3; *Film Daily* September 28 1937 p. 9; *Monthly Film Bulletin* October 1937; *Motion Picture Herald* October 2, 1937, p. 41; *Motion Picture Herald* November 13, 1937 p. 81; *New York Post* November 19, 1937; *New York Sun* November 19, 1937; *New York Times* November 20, 1937 p. 21; *New York Daily News* November 20, 1937; *New York Daily Mirror* November 20, 1937; *New York World-Telegram* November 20, 1937; *Brooklyn Daily Eagle* December 11, 1937

The Beloved Brat

A Warner Bros.–First National Picture; U.S. B&W 62 minutes; Released in New York on April 30, 1938

CREDITS: *Producer:* Bryan Foy; *Executive Producers:* Hal B. Wallis, Jack L. Warner; *Director:* Arthur Lubin; *Screenplay:* Lawrence Kimble, Wally Klein; Based on the story "Too Much of Everything" by Jean Negulesco; *Assistant Director:* Arthur Lueker; *Editor:* Frederick Richards; *Photography:* George Barnes; *Art Director:* Stanley Fleischer; *Gowns:* Howard Shoup; *Sound:* Francis J. Scheid; *Music:* Howard Jackson; *Dialogue Director:* Frank Beckwith

CAST: Bonita Granville (Roberta Morgan), Dolores Costello (Helen Cosgrove), Donald Crisp (Mr. Morgan), Natalie Moorhead (Mrs. Morgan), Lucille Gleason (Miss Brewster), Donald Briggs (Williams), Emmett Vogan (Jenkins), Loia Cheaney (Mrs. Jenkins), Leo Gorcey (Spike), Ellen Lowe (Anna), Mary Doyle (Miss Mitchell), Paul Everton (Judge Harris), Bernice Pilot (Mrs. White), Stymie Beard (Pinkie White), Meredith White (Arabella White), Gloria Fischer (Boots), Carmencita Johnson (Estella), Priscilla Lyon (Sylvia), Doris Brenn (Jackie), Patsy Mitchell (Betty Mae), Betty Compson (Eleanor Sparks), Victor Wong (Gardener), Al Duval (Cab Driver), Glen Cavender, Jack Mower, Cliff Saum (Firemen), John Harron (Driver), Monte Vandergrift (Officer), Jessie Arnold (Nurse), Gordon Hart (Judge), Mary Avery, Isabelle La Mal (Teachers), Sarah Edwards (Miss Brundage), Douglas Wood (Mr. Butler), William Worthington (Dr. Reynolds), Ottola Nesmith (Mrs. Higgins), Lottie Williams (Maid), Louise Bates (Mrs. Morgan's Guest)

PLOT: Roberta Morgan is the daughter of neglectful parents who are too busy with their own lives to give her decent care and attention. The girl whips herself into a series of fine frenzies, violently rebelling against all the unfeeling people around her. After she accidentally kills a man, Roberta is sent to a corrective house for girls. She is disliked by all the other pupils, but a compassionate and understanding superintendent begins to have a positive influence on her.

REVIEWS:

"Warner Bros. has done a credible job in finding dramatic material in the field of child guidance." *Variety,* January 12, 1938

"*The Beloved Brat* is not entertainment as the word is to denote amusement. Rather it is a human interest document that should prove interesting and educational to adults, particularly parents, and to children." *Motion Picture Herald,* February 19, 1938

"What is mainly wrong with the production from the standpoint of straight entertainment is the fact that the child is given a very unsympathetic part that arouses no compassion on the part of the audience.... Lubin's direction injects sympathy into a greater degree than the writing allowed for." *The Film Daily,* May 5, 1938

OTHER ARTICLES AND REVIEWS:

Daily Variety February 10, 1938, p. 3; *Hollywood Reporter* February 10, 1938, p. 2; *Motion Picture Daily* February 11, 1938, p. 2; *New York Times* March 30, 1938, p. 38; *Harrison's Reports* April 16, 1938, p. 62; *Monthly Film Bulletin* May 1938 p. 134; *New York Mirror* May 1, 1938; *New York Times* May 2, 1938 p. 13; *New York Sun* May 2, 1938; *New York Telegram* May 2, 1938; *New York Journal-American* May 2, 1938; *New York Post* May 2, 1938; *Brooklyn Daily Eagle* May 7, 1938; *Kinematograph Weekly* May 12, 1938; *Billboard* May 14, 1938, p. 15; *Modern Screen* May 1938 p. 22; *Film Index* 1977, p. 370

Swiss Miss

Metro Goldwyn Mayer; Hal Roach Studios; U.S. B&W 72 minutes; Released on May 20, 1938

CREDITS: *Associate Producer:* S.S. Van Keuren; *Director:* John G. Blystone; *Screenplay:* James Parrott, Felix Adler, Charles J. Morton; *Original Story:* Jean Negulesco, Charles Rogers; *Photography:* Norbert Brodine, Art Lloyd; *Photographic Effects:* Roy Seawright; *Editor:* Bert Jordan; *Art Director:* Charles D. Hall; *Set Decorator:* W.T. Stevens; *Wardrobe:* Ernest Schnapps; *Musical Direction:* Marvin Hatley; *Musical Arrangements:*

Arthur Morton; *Choreographer:* Val Raset; *Songs:* "The Cricket Song," "Yo-Ho-Dee-O-Lay-Hee," "I Can't Get Over the Alps" and "Gypsy Song," music by Phil Charig, lyrics by Arthur Quenzer; "Let Me Call You Sweetheart," music and lyrics by Beth Slater Whitson and Leo Friedman

CAST: Stan Laurel (Stan), Oliver Hardy (Ollie), Della Lind (Anna Hoepfel Albert), Walter Woolf King (Victor Albert), Eric Blore (Edward Morton), Adia Kuznetzoff (Franzelhuber), Charles Judels (Emile), Ludovico Tomarchio (Luigi), Franz Hug (Flag Thrower), Jean De Briac (Enrico the Waiter), George Sorel (Joseph the Chauffeur), Charles Gemora (Gorilla), Virginia Dabney (Chambermaid), Doodles Weaver (Taxicab Driver), Sam Lufkin (Peasant), Bob O'Connor (Astonished Swiss Villager), Jack Hill (Townsman)

PLOT: Two American mousetrap salesmen travel to an Alpine village in Switzerland, thinking that to be the most logical place to sell their devices because it's a country of cheese. They sell their entire stock to a cheesemaker, but after ordering an expensive meal in a local hotel they learn that they have been paid with phony money. They are compelled to stay at the hotel to work as waiters under the supervision of a tyrannical chef. Meanwhile, music composer Victor Albert, who hides away in the same hotel to write his greatest opera, is annoyed by the unexpected arrival of his bossy wife. One of the two salesman falls in love with her and she leads him on so that he will help her to win her husband over. But the man discovers the scheme and things don't go as planned.

REVIEWS:

"Just a filler-in and not a very good one.... [S]tory, production, acting and direction suggest a revival of early sound musicals presented with stage technique." *Variety,* May 11, 1938

"[T]he story was not substantial enough for a feature length picture, and so it had to be padded considerably." *Harrison's Reports,* May 21, 1938

"*Swiss Miss* is a bargain excursion in slapstick: a regular ski train, out of season, to the indefensible heights of fantasy." *The New York Times,* June 4, 1938

OTHER ARTICLES AND REVIEWS:

Film Daily October 20, 1937, p. 10; *Hollywood Reporter* November 29, 1937, p. 2–3; *Hollywood Reporter* December 2, 1937, p. 2; *Hollywood Reporter* December 3, 1937, p. 9; *Hollywood Reporter* December 16, 1937 p. 5; *Film Daily* December 17, 1937, p. 12; *Hollywood Reporter* December 28, 1937, p. 3; *Hollywood Reporter* January 11, 1938, p. 7; *Hollywood Reporter* January 13, 1938, p. 3; *Hollywood Reporter* February 2, 1938, p. 9; *Hollywood Reporter* February 8, 1938 p. 3; *Hollywood Reporter February 9, 1938, p. 3; Motion Picture Herald* February 12, 1938, p. 27; *Hollywood Reporter* February 15, 1938, *p. 3; Boxoffice* February 19, 1938; *Hollywood Reporter February 19, 1938 p. 1; Hollywood Reporter* February 26, 1938, p. 1; *Motion Picture Herald* February 26, 1938, p. 16–17; *Hollywood Reporter* May 4, 1938, p. 2; *Motion Picture Herald* May 7, 1938, p. 39; *Film Daily* May 10, 1938, p. 6; *Motion Picture Daily* May 12, 1938, p. 6; *Boxoffice* May 14, 1938; *Billboard* May 21, 1938, *Monthly Film Bulletin* June 1938 p. 162; *Kinematograph Weekly* June 2, 1938, p. 38; *New York World-Telegram* June 6, 1938; *New York Journal-America June 6, 1938; Daily Mirror New York* June 6, 1938; *New York Daily News* June 6, 1938; *Brooklyn Eagle* June 10, 1938; *Newsweek* June 20, 1938, p. 23; *Time* June 20, 1938, p. 18; *Film Weekly* July 23, 1938, p. 21; *Cinémonde* (France) December 21, 1938, p. 1168; *Pour Vous* (France) December 21, 1938 p. 6; *Hollywood Reporter* August 11, 1939 p.

Rio

Universal; U.S. B&W 77 minutes; Released in New York on September 29, 1939

CREDITS: *Director:* John Brahm, *Assistant Director:* Phil Karlson; *Screenplay:* Abel Kandel, Edwin Justus Mayer, Frank Partos, Stephen Morehouse Avery; *Original Story:* Jean Negulesco; *Photography:* Hal Mohr; *Art Directors:* Jack Otterson, Martin Obzina; *Editor:* Philip Cahn; *Set Decorator:* Russell A. Gausman; *Gowns:* Vera West, *Miss Gurie's Gowns:* Madame Pola; *Music:* Frank Skinner; *Musical Director:* Charles Previn; *Sound:* Bernard B. Brown, William Hedgcock; *Choreographer:* Larry Ceballos; *Songs* "Love Opened My Eyes," words and music by Jimmy McHugh; "Heart of Mine," "After the Rain," words and music by Frank Skinner and Ralph Freed

CAST: Basil Rathbone (Paul Reynard), Victor McLaglen (Dirk), Sigrid Gurie (Irene Reynard), Robert Cummings (Bill Gregory), Leo Carrillo (Roberto), Billy Gilbert (Manuelo), Maurice Moscovitch (Old Convict), Irving Bacon ("Mushy"), Samuel S. Hinds (Lamartine), Irving Pichel (Rocco), Ferike Boros (Maria), Lane Chandler (Guard), Gino Corrado (French Waiter), Virginia

Dabney (American Telephone Operator), Valeska Gert (Specialty Number), Eddie Hall (Prison Guard), Frank Reicher (Paris Banker), Harry Worth (Prefect of Police), Franco Corsaro (Bartender)

PLOT: Paul Reynard, a crooked French financier, is given to forging bonds and casually demanding loans of hundreds of millions francs. Arrested during a fancy dinner, he's sentenced to Devil's Island in South America. His wife Irene, formerly a café singer, moves from France to Rio with Dirk, their old servant, to be near him and aid in his escape. But when the financier finally does escape by murdering another convict, he learns that his wife has in the meantime fallen in love with Bill Gregory, a young American engineer. Reynard tries to shoot Gregory, but Dirk interferes and kills Paul.

REVIEWS:
"[A] blend of romance and adventure ... direction and story are sluggish at times, but for the most part it moves at a good clip." *Variety,* October 4, 1939

"Despite the lavish production Universal has given it, and despite the efforts of the cast, *Rio* is not a good entertainment." *Harrison's Reports,* October 14, 1939

"One of those heavy melodramas without an ounce of subtlety or relieving humor." *New York Post,* October 27, 1939

REVIEWS FOR JEAN NEGULESCO:
"Stirring, action-filled drama, skilfully fashioned and geared to score at B.O. [It has] a strong screenplay based on an original story by Jean Negulesco."
The Film Daily, September 26, 1939

"The author Jean Negulesco suggests more of a story in Reynard that one he tells on the screen." *New York Daily News,* October 27, 1939

OTHER ARTICLES AND REVIEWS:
Hollywood Reporter June 29, 1939 p. 1; *Hollywood Reporter* July 10, 1939, p. 1; *Hollywood Reporter* July 15, 1939, p. 6–7; *Hollywood Reporter* July 25, 1939, p. 10; *Motion Picture Herald* September 9, 1939, p. 59; *Hollywood Reporter* September 21, 1939 p. 4; *Daily Variety* September 21, 1939, p. 3; *Motion Picture Daily* September 29, 1939 p. 7; *Motion Picture Herald* October 14, 1939, p. 42–44; *New York Post* October 27, 1939; *Daily Mirror New York* October 27 1939; *New York Herald Tribune* October 27, 1939; *New York World-Telegram* October 27, 1939; *New York Times* October 27, 1939, p. 27; *Brooklyn Daily Eagle* November 10, 1939; *Motion Picture Herald* December 2, 1939, p. 67; *Today's Cinema* February 21, 1940

As Production Assistant or Technical Advisor (Uncredited)

This Is the Night a.k.a. Tonight We Sing
Paramount, 1932, *Director:* Frank Tuttle; Tuttle asked Negulesco to sketch the opening scene set in Paris.

The Phantom President
Paramount, 1932, *Director:* Norman Taurog; Negulesco worked as a production assistant.

The Big Broadcast
Paramount, 1932, *Director:* Frank Tuttle; Negulesco worked as a production assistant.

A Bedtime Story
Paramount, 1933, *Director:* Norman Taurog; Negulesco worked as a production assistant.

The Story of Temple Drake
Paramount, 1933, *Director:* Stephen Roberts; Based on William Faulkner's novel *Sanctuary,* Negulesco was the technical advisor for a rape scene featuring Miriam Hopkins. He sketched a storyboard for it and supervised its shooting.

The Song of Songs
Paramount, 1933, *Director:* Rouben Mamoulian; Negulesco worked as a production assistant.

The Way to Love
Paramount, 1933, *Director:* Norman Taurog; Negulesco worked as a production assistant.

Hearts Divided
Warner Bros., 1936, *Director:* Frank Borzage; Negulesco was the technical advisor, contributing to the final script.

As Producer

The 27th Annual Academy Awards (1955)

Negulesco produced the awards ceremony, which was directed by Bill Bennington in Hollywood and Grey Lockwood in New York.

Jessica (1962)

See Filmography

Radio Programs and Personal Appearances

Here is a list of radio adaptations based on Jean Negulesco films:

"The Mask of Dimitrios," *The Screen Guild Theater*, CBS, April 16, 1945

"Nobody Lives Forever," *Lux Radio Theatre*, CBS, November 17, 1947

"Humoresque," *The Screen Director Playhouse* NBC, April 1951 (Negulesco is credited as the director. He also talks briefly at the end of the broadcast.)

"The Mudlark," *Lux Radio Theatre*, CBS, August 27, 1951

"Take Care of My Little Girl," *Lux Radio Theatre*, CBS, February 4, 1952

"Phone Call from a Stranger," *Lux Radio Theatre*, CBS, January 5, 1953

"Lure of the Wilderness" *Lux Radio Theatre*, CBS, May 25, 1953

The Big Show

20th Century–Fox; CinemaScope, Color with some sequences in B&W, 110 minutes

CREDITS: Director (scene with Spyros Skouras): Robert Rossen.

CAST: Spyros Skouras, Buddy Adler, Darryl F. Zanuck, Henry King, David O. Selznick, Jerry Wald, Stanley Donen, Cary Grant, Deborah Kerr, Leo McCarey, Richard Rodgers, Oscar Hammerstein II, Elia Kazan, Henry Ginsberg, Fred Zinnemann, Jack Holmes, Victor Vicas, Nunnally Johnson, Joanne Woodward, Lee J. Cobb, David Weisbart, Robert Webb, Alfred Newman, Charles Brackett, Philip Dunne, Walter Reisch, Richard L. Breen, Robert Buckner, Anthony Muto, Barbara Rush, Charles Le Maire, Henry Ephron, Walter Lang, Al Lichtman, Edward Dmytryk, Herbert Bayard Swope, Jr., Lyle Wheeler, Henry Koster, Frank Tashlin, Dick Powell, Richard Murphy, Wendell Mayes, Jean Negulesco, Samuel G. Engel, Henry Levin, Janet Gaynor, Pat Boone, Dick Sargent, Terry Moore, May Britt, Kendall Scott, Tami Conner, Anne Marie Duringer, David Hedison, Lili Gentle, Linc Foster, Diane Jergens, Tony Franciosa, Elena Murray, Rachel Stephens, Rick Jason, Patricia Powell, Dolores Michaels, Tommy Sands, Patricia Owens, Alex Harrison, S. Charles Einfeld

PLOT: Fox president Spyros P. Skouras gives the audience a seven-minute talk in which he extols the 55 films his company intends to release in the coming year. *The Big Show* was first shown to North American film exhibitors, stockholders, press representatives, radio and TV opinionmakers, etc. Negulesco talks briefly about his forthcoming film *A Certain Smile*. A 56-minute version of *The Big Show*, designed for the public, was released on August 28, 1957.

Portrait of a Star

U.K., British Movietone Films, B&W, 44 seconds: December 24, 1956

A newsreel showing Negulesco's one-man art show at a Rome gallery. Most of the art shown was inspired by *Boy on a Dolphin* star Sophia Loren, the special guest at the opening.

This Is Your Life: Rossano Brazzi

U.S., NBC, B&W, 30 minutes: April 20, 1960

A TV show in which Negulesco appears as a surprise guest. He talks about his professional relationship with Italian actor Rossano Brazzi, who starred in *Three Coins in the Fountain* (1954), *A Certain Smile* (1958) and *Count Your Blessings* (1959).

Angie Dickinson Arrives in Rome

La Settimana Incom; Italy, Archivio Storico Luce, B&W, one minute: March 1961

This Italian newsreel shows Dickinson's arrival at the Rome airport. She is welcomed by Negulesco, who will direct her in *Jessica*.

Celebration for the end of the shooting of the film *Jessica*

La Settimana Incom; Italy, Archivio Storico Luce, B&W, one minute: May 30, 1961

This Italian newsreel shows a dinner party in a Rome restaurant to celebrate the completion of *Jessica*. Jean, Angie Dickinson, Maurice Chevalier and others appear to be enjoying themselves.

Cinema No!

La Settimana Incom; Italy, Archivio Storico Luce, B&W, one minute: May 12, 1961

This Italian newsreel shows the arrival of Cristiane and Gabrielle. Negulesco's adopted German girls, warmly greeted by the Negulescos at the Rome airport.

Eyewitness News—Marilyn Monroe: Why?

U.S., CBS News, B&W, 26 minutes: August 10, 1962

A TV special about Monroe's death. Negulesco reminisces about their relationship on the *How to Marry a Millionaire* set.

The Barefoot Banker

U.K.–Spain, 16mm, color, 42 minutes: October 1982

A short, produced and directed by Malcolm Abbey, featuring Negulesco playing a gay partygoer amidst Marbella's jet set.

Duplex Direct Deauville

France, France 2 channel, color, 6 minutes, September 10, 1986

Negulesco and Gene Wilder are interviewed by TV anchor France Roche at the Deauville Film Festival.

Talking Pictures

U.K., BBC, color, 50 minutes: January 1988

A TV series of ten 50-minute programs written and presented by Barry Norman. The series tells the story of Hollywood from the coming of sound to the present. Negulesco is interviewed in one of the episodes.

The Reality Trip

U.K., BBC, color, 60 minutes: January 1997.

A documentary on the history of the cinema and the technological innovations that shaped its development. Footage of Negulesco talking about CinemaScope is shown.

Love, Marilyn

U.S., HBO, color, 107 minutes: November 30, 2012

A documentary on Marilyn Monroe featuring many contemporary stars reading from the actress' diaries. A short clip from *Eyewitness News—Marilyn Monroe: Why?* shows Negulesco commenting on Monroe.

Literary Works

Things I Did ... and Things I Think I Did, New York, Linden Press–Simon & Schuster, 1984. Jean Negulesco's autobiography. The book was translated into French and Romanian.

Awards and Honors

Academy Award nomination, 1949, Best *Director: Johnny Belinda* (1948)

Venice Film Festival, 1949, nomination, Golden Lion: *Johnny Belinda* (1948)

Venice Film Festival, 1952, nomination, Golden Lion: *Phone Call from a Stranger* (1952)

Directors Guilds of America, 1954, nomination, Outstanding Directorial Achievement in Motion Pictures: *Titanic* (1953)

Venice Film Festival, 1954, nomination, Golden Lion: *Three Coins in the Fountain* (1954)

Boxoffice Blue Ribbon Award, 1954, Best Picture of the Month for the Whole Family: *Three Coins in the Fountain* (1954)

Directors Guilds of America, 1955, nomination, Outstanding Directorial Achievement in Motion Pictures: *Three Coins in the Fountain* (1954)

Plaque from the Italian High Commission on Tourism, Rome, Italy, December 11, 1956. An award to praise the impetus Negulesco gave to Italian tourism with *Three Coins in the Fountain* (1954)

Boxoffice Blue Ribbon Award, May 1957: Best Picture of the Month for the Whole Family: *Boy on a Dolphin* (1957)

Cross of Commander, Royal Order of George I, Athens, Greece, February 1958

Star on the Walk of Fame, Hollywood, California, February 8, 1960

Silver Tray, For Service to Country in the International Executive Corps, March 30, 1967

Honorary Membership, American-Romanian Academy of Arts and Sciences, Davis, California, 1983

Honorary Diploma, American-Romanian Academy of Arts and Sciences, Davis, California, 1984

Médaille des Arts et Lettres, Paris, France, September 12, 1986

Honorary Membership, Uniunii Cineaștilor din România, Bucharest, Romania, 1990

Honorary Membership, Academei Române, Bucharest, Romania, May 1992

Honorary Citizen of Craiova, Romania, 2000

Projects with Negulesco's Name Attached

Cavalleria Rusticana, Paramount (1932)

Negulesco planned to produce the first grand opera in motion pictures, Mascagni's *Cavalleria Rusticana*, designing all sets and costumes. But studio executives nixed the idea. Two years later it was announced that Negulesco would direct the picture (now re-titled *Chivalry*) starring Mexican tenor José Mojica and Mary Elliss. The film was not produced.

Alice in Wonderland, Paramount (1933)

Paramount planned a production combining live action and animation, possibly in color, Negulesco was supposed to do several animated cartoon sequences. But the picture was shot without any animated characters.

The Man Who Broke His Heart, Paramount (1933)

Negulesco was set to direct this story about Christ on a fishing wharf. The picture was never made.

A Son Comes Home, Paramount (1934)

The Hollywood Reporter announced that Negulesco was signed to direct this picture, which was slated to go into production on June 24, 1934. Arthur Nolan was cast to play the part of the son. The making of the movie was postponed until 1936 when E.A. Dupont directed.

Lesson in Love (the mid–1930s)

Part of a series of six shorts Negulesco agreed to direct for an English company. All were unrealized. An 88-page script marked unproduced and titled *Lesson of Love* is in the Paul Kohler Agency records at the Margaret Herrick Library in Beverly Hills. The scenario reads: Jean Negulesco and Stephen M. Avery from an outline by Stephen Avery and Eric Knight.

New Orleans aka To-Night We Live, Universal (the mid–1930s)

This script, defined as "a romance of New Orleans," was written by Negulesco and sold in October 1935 to Universal, which announced that it was going into pre-production in the summer of 1937. It was never made.

Ed Sullivan's Hollywood, Warner Bros. (1940)

Negulesco was supposed to directed this short subject, described as "a toned poem," supervised by Jack Warner. It was not made.

Filmography (Projects with Negulesco's Name Attached)

The Bells and *The Monkey's Paw*, Warner Bros. (1941)

Two-reel shorts announced but never made. The first was supposed to be an adaptation of a play by Leopold Lewis, the latter a version of the W.W. Jacobs short story.

The Maltese Falcon, Warner Bros. (1941)

Negulesco was assigned to write the script and direct. A few days before starting pre-production, he was replaced by John Huston.

La Bohème, Warner Bros. (1941)

Negulesco was attached to a Technicolor version of Puccini's opera. The picture was never made.

The Curious Mr. Clark and *Ice Frolics*, Warner Bros. (1941)

This two shorts, scheduled to be directed by Negulesco, were never made. *Showmen's Trade Review* (October 4, 1941) reported: "Jean Negulesco is scouting for expert ice skaters and specialty teams for *Ice Frolics,* two-reel Warner Bros. short subject."

I Hear America Singing, Warner Bros. (1942)

Walt Whitman's best-known poems were to be the basis of a two-reel short. Special music was written by Moe Jerome and Jack Scholl. Negulesco was announced as director. The short was never produced.

Adventures of Don Juan, Warner Bros. (1948)

In 1945, according to some Warner Bros. interoffice memos, Raoul Walsh and Negulesco were at different times assigned to direct the film, which was postponed for various reasons.

Lie Down in Darkness (March 1948)

Negulesco and Charles Feldman were supposed to independently produce this story by W. R. Hayes. It was not made.

Young Man with a Horn, Warner Bros. (1950)

Negulesco was announced as the director while the script was in development. The project was later assigned to Michael Curtiz.

I'd Climb the Highest Mountain, 20th Century–Fox (1951)

20th Century–Fox records indicate that in early 1949, Negulesco provided "a memo, research notes, prologue and story" for the project but it is unknown if any of his work was included in the finished screenplay.

Tonight We Sing, 20th Century–Fox (1953)

Zanuck assigned Negulesco to direct this picture, written by Sol Hurok and based on his own life's experiences. Negulesco shot some screen tests, but did not like the script. The project was later given to Mitchell Leisen.

Judith and the Holophernes, I.F.E. (1953)

Negulesco was supposed to direct the first Italian CinemaScope Technicolor film, a Biblical-style story starring Italian actress Silvana Mangano. The picture was never produced.

The Pleasure Is All Mine, Columbia (1953)

Negulesco was supposed to be loaned out by Fox to Columbia to direct this CinemaScope musical comedy starring Betty Grable and Marge and Gower Champion, based on a story by Somerset Maugham. He did not like the script. The picture was made two years later under the title *Three for the Show* (1955).

Jean-Christophe (1956)

Jerry Wald acquired the rights to the French novel written by Nobel Prize winner Romain Rolland. French stars Charles Boyer and Alain Delon were to be the principal actors with Negulesco to direct. The screenplay was drafted by Christopher Isherwood. The picture was never produced.

Lust for Life, MGM (1956)

In 1953, author Irving Stone wanted to make *Van Gogh,* a film based on his book *Lust for Life,* about the famous painter's life, directed by Negulesco and produced by Dino De Laurentiis and Carlo Ponti. But MGM, who bought the rights from Stone in 1946, would not sell them. In 1955 it was announced that Negulesco would directed Kirk Douglas in the MGM film. But pre-production was delayed because of differences among the producers. Negulesco, now busy with a different project, was replaced by Vincente Minnelli.

Untitled project about Naples (1957)

The New York Times announced in January 1957 that after Negulesco completed *Jessica,* he would shoot a film about Napoli, showing the color and beauty of the city, rather than the seedy side usually seen in films shot there. Achille Lauro, mayor of Napoli, seemed very interested in the project. The film was never realized.

Private Lives, MGM (1961)

Noël Coward's stage comedy was adapted for the screen in 1931 with Norma Shearer and Robert Montgomery. Producer Jacques Bar intended to remake it in Paris with Brigitte Bardot and Marcello Mastroianni. Negulesco was attached to the project as director. It was never produced.

Sand Against the Wind and an untitled project about a girls' reformatory (1962)

These unrealized projects were mentioned by Negulesco in a 1962 *Variety* interview.

Follies aka Et Maintenant (1963)

In December 1963, Negulesco and Tony Martin announced they would co-produce *Follies* starring Cyd Charisse, Laurence Olivier and Martin. The film, based on the 1929 book by E. Phillips Oppenheim *The Treasure House of Martin Hews,* was supposed to be a "musical-mystery" filmed in Madrid. It was never made.

Woman of My Life, Columbia (1965)

In February 1965 it was reported by Hedda Hopper that Negulesco "had locked himself in with a writer on his new project for Columbia," based on Ludwig Bemelmans' book *Woman of My Life* about the life of actress and interior decorator Elsie de Wolfe, also known as Lady Mendl.

The Girl in the Wall (1968)

Boxoffice magazine announced that Negulesco had been signed to direct his first picture in his native Romania, to start in the spring. The screenplay would be by Sam Roeca. The film was never made.

Death of a Gunfighter, Universal (1969)

In June 1966, *Variety* announced that Selmur Productions had made a deal with Negulesco to direct a Western based on the Lewis B. Patten novel *Death of a Gunfighter.* A film version of the Patten novel was made in 1969 by Universal, directed by "Allen Smithee" (a pseudonym for Robert Totten and Don Siegel).

Balzac 3 (1971)

In a letter to Darryl Zanuck, Negulesco mentioned a script entitled *Balzac 3* which he planned to direct in the summer of 1971, produced by Samuel Marx. He added that Genevieve Gilles (star of *Hello-Goodbye*) would be ideal for a part, and that Peter Sellers, Jean-Paul Belmondo and Ursula Andress had shown interest. The project was unrealized.

Other Winters, Other Springs (1973)

The Hollywood Reporter announced in October 1973 that Negulesco was getting set for his return to the screen with this picture based on Flora Sandstrom's novel. Gregory Peck and Richard Harris were in talks to play the lead roles.

The Rape of the White Dove (1976)

Screen International reported that Negulesco was talking with producer Albert Caraco of Cinexport about directing this film.

Passion Flower Hotel aka Boarding School (1978)

In 1968, producer Artur Brauner offered Negulesco the chance to direct this film, based on Roger Longrigg's novel. But the director passed, unconvinced by the script. The picture was made ten years later by André Farwagi.

The Mask of Dimitrios (early 1980s)

According to a Darryl F. Zanuck's biographer, Jean planned to remake his 1944 picture with Genevieve Gilles producing and playing the role originally played by Peter Lorre. Orson Welles showed an interest in playing the role originated by Sydney Greenstreet.

La Bohème (1986)

In an interview with the French magazine *Positif,* Negulesco affirmed that he was preparing an adaptation of Puccini's opera, set in 1968 during the student unrest. Placido Domingo would star as Rodolphe. The project was never realized.

Martha (undated)

In the Andrew Marton Papers at the Margaret Herrick Library is this Negulesco treatment, based on the Friedrich von Flotow opera. Many of the pages were revised by Marton.

Forever (1990)

Negulesco often expressed his desire to adapt *Forever,* a 1938 novella by Mildred Cram, but he was unable to find a financier for the project.

Passage Between Two Seas (1991)

Two years prior his death, Negulesco mentioned in several interviews his interest in making a love story set during the historical events related to the construction of the Panama Canal.

Chapter Notes

Chapter 1

1. Alain Garel and François Guerif, "Jean Negulesco: Une Histoire d'Amour," *La Revue du Cinéma*, March 1990, 45.
2. Enric Ripoll-Freixes and Jaime Lopez Gonzalez de Peredo, "Jean Negulesco. Noventa años y en activo," *Cine y Mas*, December 1990, 32.
3. Jean Negulesco, *Things I Did…and Things I Think I Did* (New York: Linden Press/Simon & Schuster, 1984), 17.
4. *Ibid.*, 18–19.
5. "Jean Negulesco. Dossier," *Positif*, October 1986, 43.
6. "100% Hollywood," *Cinematograph*, February 1986, 10.
7. Manuela Cernat, "Jean Negulesco, un pictor ignorat în România de ieri şi de astăzi," 2013, http://www.istoria-artei.ro/resources/files/SCIAAP_2013_Art_05_Cernat.pdf, 110.
8. *Cine y Mas*, December 1990, 33.
9. *Positif*, October 1986, 44.
10. *Ibid.*
11. *Ibid.*
12. "M. Pala and M. Villegas, Negulesco: un espectáculo de las relaciones sociales," *Film Ideal*, 1 August 1965, 514–515.
13. *Positif*, October 1986, 44.
14. Jean Negulesco, *Things I Did…and Things I Think I Did*, 26.
15. "Pictură, sculptură, Lucia Demetrius-Bălăcescu, I. Negulescu," *Rampa*, 14 January 1924.
16. *Positif*, October 1986, 45.
17. *Ibid.*, 45–46.

Chapter 2

1. Hazel Canning, "Queen Marie's Own Artist Here to Paint American Child Types," *The Journal News*, 4 June 1927, 7.
2. Walter Shaw, "Jean Negulesco…Adventurer of the Palette," 300.
3. "Negulesco's Work," *New York Times*, 6 November 1927, C11.
4. J. Négulesco, *Catalog* (New York: The Fisher Press, 1928).
5. J.K., "Further Comment on Art Exhibitions," *New York Times*, 22 April 1928.
6. Margaret Breuning and Jean Negulesco, *New York Evening Post*, 21 April 1928, 14.
7. Ada Rainey, "Negulesco Paintings Sold," *The Washington Post*, 12 February 1929.
8. Manuela Cernat, "Jean Negulesco," 125.
9. "Film 'Bachelor' Sue for Divorce by Wealthy Wife," *San Bernardino County Sun*, 16 December 1932, 4.
10. Alain Garel and François Guerif, *La Revue du Cinéma*, 45.
11. "Hollywood," *Variety*, September 1931, 6.
12. "Jean Negulesco Producing," *The Film Daily*, 22 September 1931, 4.
13. Cristina Piccino, "Un dinosauro milionario," *Il Manifesto*, 24 July 1991, 15.
14. "From Art to Films; or the Career of Jean Negulesco," *New York Times*, 22 July 1945.
15. "Cristina Piccino," *Il Manifesto*, 15.
16. *Oral History Research Project: Jean Negulesco* (New York: Columbia University, June 1959), 5–6.
17. *Talking Pictures: Jean Negulesco Interview*, Transcript (London: BBC, 1988), roll 1.
18. Ben Wasson, *Count no' Count. Flashback to Faulkner* (Jackson: University Press of Mississippi, 1983), 130.
19. Hervé Dumont, *Frank Borzage. The Life and Films of a Hollywood Romantic* (Jefferson, NC: McFarland, 2006), 184.
20. *Ibid.*, 34.
21. "Terms for Negulesco," *The Hollywood Reporter*, 21 February 1933, 2.
22. *Stage* 13 (1935): 41.
23. Geoff Gehman, *Down but Not Quite Out in Hollow-weird: A Documentary in Letters of Eric Knight* (Latham, MD: The Scarecrow Press, 1998), 113.
24. *Ibid.*, 114.
25. "'Kiss and Make Up': Amusing Burlesque on Beauty Game," *The Hollywood Reporter*, 25 May 1934, 3.
26. *Oral History Research Project*, 6.

27. "Chatter," *Variety*, October 1935, 61.
28. *Positif*, October 1986, 46–47.
29. *Ibid*.
30. "News from Studios," *Sunday Times*, 8 March 1936, 13.
31. Jean Negulesco, *Things I Did...and Things I Think I Did*, 175.
32. *Variety*, October 1937, 12.
33. *Oral History Research Project*, 5.
34. Randy Skretvedt, *Laurel and Hardy. The Magic Behind the Movies* (Beverly Hills, CA: Moonstone Press, 1987), 335.
35. Negulesco, *Things I Did...and Things I Think I Did*, 111.
36. Joan Fontaine, *No Bed of Roses* (London: W.H. Allen, 1978), 105.

Chapter 3

1. Daniel Bubbeo, *The Women of Warner Brothers* (Jefferson, NC: McFarland, 2001), 144.
2. Leslie Norton and Frederic Franklin, *Frederic Franklin: A Biography of the Ballet Star* (Jefferson, NC: McFarland, 2007), 71.
3. *Oral History Research Project*.
4. "Shorts," *The Film Daily*, 3 December 1941, 8.
5. *Oral History Research Project*, 3.
6. Alain Garel and François Guerif, *La Revue du Cinéma*, 46.
7. "Negulesco Wins Spur," *Variety*, September 1940.
8. Alain Garel and François Guerif, *La Revue du Cinéma*, 46.
9. "Singapore Woman Misses on Almost Every Count," *The Hollywood Reporter*, 2 June 1941, 3.
10. Charles Higham, *The Celluloid Muse: Hollywood Directors Speak* (London: Angus & Robertson, 1969), 187.
11. Alain Garel and François Guerif, *La Revue du Cinéma*, 46.
12. Charles Higham, *The Celluloid Muse*, 187.
13. *Oral History Research Project*.
14. "'The Mask of Dimitrios': Absorbing Crime Film," *The Hollywood Reporter*, 6 June 1957, 20.
15. *Postif*, October 1986, 47.
16. Veronica Lake, "*Veronica: The Autobiography of Veronica Lake* (New York: The Citadel Press, 1971), 140.
17. Sylvia Shorris and Marion Abbott Bundy, *Talking Pictures* (New York: The New Press, 1994), 338.
18. Hedy Lamarr, *Ecstasy and Me* (London: W.H. Allen, 1967), 99.
19. *Miami Daily News*, 14 July 1944, 10.
20. Alain Garel and François Guerif, *La Revue du Cinéma*, 47–48.
21. Erskine Johnson, "In Hollywood," *Syndicated Column*, 8 May 1944.
22. Stephen D. Youngkin, *The Lost One: A Life of Peter Lorre* (Lexington: The University Press of Kentucky, 2005), 220.
23. "Conspirators Tired and Dated Espionage Drama," *The Hollywood Reporter*, 13 October 1944, 3.
24. Ruth Barton, *Hedy Lamarr, the Most Beautiful Woman in Film* (Lexington: The University Press of Kentucky, 2005), 143.
25. "Correspondence," *The New Republic*, 13 November 1944, 627.
26. "Director-Artist," *Life*, June 1944, 65–66.
27. Harrison Carroll, "Behind the Scenes in Hollywood," *The Gaffney Ledger*, 4 January 1945.
28. *Miami Daily News*, 2 November 1944, 4.
29. Erskine Johnson, "Wolf Picks Ten Best Wolves," *N.Y. World-Telegram*, 29 September 1944, 20.
30. Ted Sennett, *Masters of Menace: Greenstreet and Lorre* (New York: Dutton, 1979), 102.
31. Stephen D. Youngkin, *The Lost One: A Life of Peter Lorre*, 228.
32. *Ibid*.

Chapter 4

1. Oscar Levant, *The Memoirs of an Amnesiac* (New York: Putnam, 1965), 182.
2. Arthur Millier, "Joan Crawford Makes Director Feel Humble," *Los Angeles Times*, 15 December 1946, B1.
3. Roy Newquist, *Conversations with Joan Crawford* (New York: Citadel Press, 1980), 95.
4. Bob Thomas, *Joan Crawford: A Biography* (New York: Simon & Schuster, 1979), 157.
5. David Bret, *Joan Crawford: Hollywood Martyr* (New York: DaCapo Press, 2006), 168.
6. Charles Higham, *The Celluloid Muse*, 189.
7. Jean Negulesco, *Things I Did...and Things I Think I Did*, 137.
8. Oscar Levant, *The Memoirs of an Amnesiac*, 183.
9. Robert Blake, *Tales of a Rascal* (Willowdale, ON: Black Rainbow Publications, 2012), 214.
10. Robert Nott, *He Ran All the Way: The Life of John Garfield* (New York: Limelight, 2003), 186
11. "Assignment in Hollywood," *Good Housekeeping*, February 1947, 13.
12. "'Humoresque' Strong Blend of Emotions and Fine Music," *The Hollywood Reporter*, 23 December 1946, 3.
13. *Film Daily*, 26 December 1946, 11.
14. Charles Higham, *The Celluloid Muse*, 190.
15. Sheilah Graham, *The Garden of Allah* (London: W.H. Allen, 1971), 131–132.
16. Jean Negulesco, *Things I Did...and Things I Think I Did*, 268.
17. Janet Grey, "What's New," *Daily Herald* (UK), 18 May 1950.
18. Rudy Behlmer, *Inside Warner Bros.* (New York: Simon & Schuster–Fireside, 1987), 299–300.
19. *Ibid.*, 271.
20. Jane Wyman, "I Took a Chance," *Hollywood Album* (London: Marston & Co., 1948), 137.
21. Leslie L. Coffin, *Lew Ayres* (Jackson: University Press of Mississippi, 2012), 142.

22. Rudy Behlmer, *Inside Warner Bros.*, 273.
23. Roddy McDowall, *Double Exposure, Take Three* (New York: Morrow, 1993), 115.
24. Jane Wyman, "I Took a Chance," 139.
25. Charles Tranberg, *The Life and Career of Agnes Moorehead* (Albany, GA: Bear Manor Media, 2007), 121.
26. "Jean Negulesco," *Action*, May–June 1976.
27. M. Pala and M. Villegas, *Film Ideal*, 513.
28. Herb A. Lightman, "Johnny Belinda," *American Cinematographer*, October 1948, 358.
29. Laurence J. Quirk, *Jane Wyman: The Actress and the Woman* (New York: Dumber Books, 1986), 100.
30. Jean Negulesco, *Things I Did…and Things I Think I Did*, 127.
31. Bob Thomas, *Clown Prince of Hollywood: The Antic Life and Times of Jack L. Warner* (New York: McGraw-Hill Publishing, 1990), 168.
32. "Johnny Belinda," *The Film Daily*, 14 September 1948, 7.
33. *The Hollywood Reporter*, 14 September 1948, 3.
34. Jean Negulesco, *Things I Did…and Things I Think I Did*, 128.
35. Laurence J. Quirk, *Jane Wyman: The Actress and the Woman*, 104.
36. Scott Eyman, *Ernst Lubitsch: Laughter in Paradise* (New York: Simon & Schuster, 1993), 172–173.

Chapter 5

1. Alain Garel and François Guerif, *La Revue du Cinéma*, 48.
2. *Cine y Mas*, December 1990, 33.
3. Bertrand Tavernier, *Amis Américains: Entretiens avec les Grands Auteurs d' Hollywood* (Arles: Actes Sud, 2008), 599.
4. *Screenland*, July 1948, 8.
5. Michel Perez, "Une vie a Hollywood," *Le Matin*, 7 January 1986, 29.
6. "Vital Statistic," *Road House*, 20th Century-Fox Press Release, 2.
7. Charles Higham, *The Celluloid Muse*, 194.
8. Garel and Guerif, *La Revue du Cinéma*, 51–52.
9. Maureen O'Hara, *'Tis Herself: A Memoir* (London: Simon & Schuster, 2004), 109.
10. Roddy McDowall, *Double Exposure*, 85.
11. Jean Negulesco, *Things I Did…and Things I Think I Did*, 147.
12. *Ibid.*, 259.
13. Nora Johnson, *Flashback* (Garden City, NY: Doubleday, 1979), 158.
14. "Hollywood," *The Daily Notes*, 13 March 1950, 4.
15. Lawrence Quirk, *Claudette Colbert: An Illustrated Biography* (New York: Crown, 1985), 159.
16. *Hollywood Citizen-News*, February 18, 1950.
17. Florence Desmond, *Florence Desmond by Herself* (London: Harrap & Co., 1953), 289–290.
18. "Claudette Colbert to Jean Negulesco," *Jean and Dusty Negulesco Papers*, Margaret Harrick Library, Beverly Hills, CA.
19. M Pala and M. Villegas, *Film Ideal*, 515.
20. "Home Strongly Realistic," *The Hollywood Reporter*, 10 February 1950, 3.
21. Candace Ursula Grisson, *Fitzgerald and Hemingway on Film* (Jefferson, NC: McFarland, 2001), 143.
22. Micheline Presle, *Di(s)gressions: Conversations avec Stéphane Lambert* (Paris: Stock, 2007), 115.
23. Larry Swindell, *Body and Soul: The Story of John Garfield* (New York: Morrow, 1975), 227.
24. Nora Johnson, *Flashback*, 161.
25. "Skouras Defends Use of Dunne as Queen Victoria," *Variety*, March 1950.
26. Nunnally Johnson, *The Letters of Nunnally Johnson* (New York: Knopf, 1981), 62.
27. Gary O'Connor, *Alec Guinness Master of Disguise* (London: Hodder & Stoughton, 1994), 127.
28. Nora Johnson, *Flashback*, 161.
29. M. Pala and M. Villegas, *Film Ideal*, 512.
30. Nunnally Johnson, *The Letters of Nunnally Johnson*, 52.
31. "The Mudlark," *The Hollywood Reporter*, 1 October 1950, 3.
32. Armand Deutsch, "Jean Negulesco," *Architectural Digest*, April 1985, 64–66.

Chapter 6

1. "Pressure on 20th to Forego Pic on College Frat Evils," *Variety*, December 1950.
2. "Vital Statistics," *Take Care of My Little Girl*, 20th Century-Fox Press Release, 2.
3. *Ibid.*
4. "When Hollywood Calls: It's About Face for Jean Peters," *The 7th Hollywood Album* (London: Sampson Low Marston & Co., Ltd., 1953), 138.
5. *Newsweek*, July 1951, 85.
6. Jean Negulesco, *Things I Did…and Things I Think I Did*, 181.
7. Laura Wagner, *Anne Francis: The Life and Career.* (Jefferson, NC: McFarland, 2011), 14.
8. Alain Garel and François Guerif, *La Revue du Cinéma*, 48.
9. Anne Francis, *Voices from Home* (Millbrae, CA: Celestial Arts, 1982), 27.
10. Whitney Stine, *No Guts, No Glory: Conversations with Bette Davis* (London: Virgin Books, 1990), 143.
11. *Positif*, October 1986, 51.
12. Laurence Quirk, *The Passionate Life of Bette Davis* (London: Robson Books, 1994), 343–344.
13. Nora Johnson, *Flashback*, 204.
14. Laurence Quirk, *The Passionate Life of Bette Davis*, 343.
15. "When Hollywood Calls: It's About Face for Jean Peters," 140.
16. Inez Wallace, "Lure of the Wilderness," *Cleveland Pain Dealer Pictorial Magazine*, September 1952, 22.
17. *Monthly Film Bulletin*, October 1952.
18. *Variety*, February 1952.
19. *Positif*, October 1986, 53.
20. Charles Higham, *The Celluloid Muse*, 196.

21. Bob Jakobsen, "Hunger for Knowledge, Advises Film Director," *L.A. Times* 9 March 1952, B3.
22. Nancy Hill-Holtzman, *Los Angeles Herald-Examiner*, 26 September 1984.
23. Donna Corcoran, "Three Times Lucky," *The 8th Hollywood Album* (London: Sampson Low Marston & Co., Ltd., 1954) 29.
24. Michael Troyan, *A Rose for Mrs. Miniver: The Life of Greer Garson* (Lexington: University Press of Kentucky, 1999), 248.
25. Alain Garel and François Guerif, *La Revue du Cinéma*, 49.
26. Michelangelo Capua, *Janet Leigh: A Biography* (Jefferson, NC: McFarland, 2013), 28.
27. *Variety*, April 1953.
28. *The Hollywood Reporter*, 29 April 1953, 3.
29. Harold Heffernan, "Titanic Disaster-Hollywood Aftermath," *The World's News* (Sidney), 28 February 1953, 8.
30. "Jean Negulesco. Dossier," *Positif*, 48.
31. *Jean and Dusty Negulesco Papers*, Margaret Harrick Library, Academy of Motion Picture Arts and Sciences, Beverly Hills, CA.
32. Robert Wagner, *Pieces of My Heart: A Life* (London: Hutchinson, 2009), 58–59.
33. Bob Jakobsen, "Hunger for Knowledge, Advises Film Director," B3.
34. Ella Smith, *Starring Miss Barbara Stanwyck* (New York: Crown Publisher, 1985), 57.

Chapter 7

1. William Froug, *The Screenwriter Looks at the Screenwriter* (New York: Macmillan, 1972), 248.
2. Jean Negulesco, *Things I Did…and Things I Think I Did*, 218–219.
3. Maurice Zolotow, *Marilyn Monroe* (New York: Harcourt, Brace & Co., 1960), 180.
4. Lauren Bacall, *By Myself* (New York: Knopf, 1978), 229.
5. Leo Guild, *Zanuck: Hollywood's Last Tycoon* (Los Angeles: Holloway House, 1970), 155.
6. Nunnally Johnson, *The Letters of Nunnally Johnson*, 103.
7. Martin Quigley Jr., *New Screen Techniques* (New York: Quigley Publishing. Company, 1953), 176.
8. Lauren Bacall, *By Myself*, 229.
9. Sandra Shevey, *The Marilyn Scandal* (London: Sandra Shevey Books, 2007), 174–175.
10. Lydia Lane, "Film Director Admires Honesty More Than Any Other Trait," *Los Angeles Times*, 1 November 1953, 12.
11. Alain Garel and François Guerif, *La Revue du Cinéma*, 50.
12. David L. Smith, *Sitting Pretty: The Life and the Times of Clifton Webb* (Jackson: University Press of Mississippi, 2011), 170.
13. Leonard Mosley, *Zanuck: The Rise and Fall of Hollywood's Last Tycoon* (Boston: Little Brown, 1984), 318.
14. Nunnally Johnson, *The Letters of Nunnally Johnson*, 108.
15. Laura Jacobs, "The Lipstick Jungle," *Vanity Fair*, March 2004, 412.
16. *Vincent Minnelli Papers*, "General Files" (N-Miscellaneous 1961–1966), Margaret Harrick Library, Academy of Motion Picture Arts and Sciences, Beverly Hills, CA.
17. Negulesco, *Things I Did…and Things I Think I Did*, 157–158.
18. *Variety*, May 1954, 6.
19. Alain Garel and François Guerif, *La Revue du Cinéma*, 50–51.

Chapter 8

1. Charles Tranberg, *Fred MacMurray: A Biography* (Albany, GA: BearManor Media, 2007), 154.
2. June Allyson, *June Allyson* (New York: Putnam's 1982), 61.
3. *Variety*, February 1954, 4.
4. Henry Ephron, *We Thought We Could Do Anything* (New York: Norton, 1977), 134.
5. Fred Astaire, *Steps in Time* (New York: Harpers and Brothers, 1959), 311.
6. M. Pala and M. Villegas, *Film Ideal*, 512.
7. Charles Higham, *Hollywood Cameramen* (London: Thames and Hudson, 1970), 32.
8. Jean Negulesco, *Things I Did…and Things I Think I Did*, 211.
9. "Negulesco Redoing 'Rains' Seeks Ethel Barrymore," *Variety*, July 1955.
10. *Ibid.*
11. Cheryl Crane, *Lana: The Memories, The Myths, The Movies* (Philadelphia: Running Press, 2008), 328.
12. Lana Turner, *Lana: The Lady, the Legend, the Truth* (New York: Dutton, 1982), 190–191.
13. Hedda Hopper, "Hedda Visits Set of Oriental Palace to Get Cool," *Chicago Tribune*, 12 September 1955, 16.
14. Lana Turner, *Lana: The Lady, the Legend, the Truth*, 191.
15. Charles Tranberg, *Fred MacMurray: A Biography*, 160.
16. Penny Junor, *Burton:The Man Behind the Myth* (London: Sedgwick & Jackson, 1985), 65.
17. Charles Higham, *The Celluloid Muse*, 197.
18. Garel and Guerif, *La Revue du Cinéma*, 50.
19. Tichi Wilkerson and Marcia Bore, *The Hollywood Reporter: The Golden Era* (New York: Coward-McCann, 1984), 294–295.
20. *Oral History Research Project*, 15.
21. Sophia Loren, *Yesterday, Today, Tomorrow: My Life* (London: Simon & Schuster, 2015), 115.
22. Beverly Linet, *Ladd: The Life, the Legend, the Tragedy* (New York: Arbor House, 1979), 206.
23. Sophia Loren, *Yesterday, Today, Tomorrow: My Life*, 116.
24. *Time*, April 1957, 108.
25. Lauren Bacall, *By Myself*, 306.

26. M. Pala and M. Villegas, *Film Ideal*, 510.
27. Charles Higham, *The Celluloid Muse*, 197.
28. M. Pala and M. Villegas, *Film Ideal*, 521.
29. Helen Louise Walker, "I Was Afraid of Men," *Screenland*, January 1959, 16–17.
30. Wanda Hale, "'Certain Smile' Debuts July 31 N.Y. and Paris," *Sunday News*, 13 July 1958, sec. 2, 3.
31. Garel and Guerif, *La Revue du Cinéma*, 52.
32. Joan Fontaine, *No Bed of Roses*, 254.
33. W. Hale, *Sunday News* sec. 2, p. 3.

Chapter 9

1. Michelangelo Capua, *Deborah Kerr: A Biography* (Jefferson, NC: McFarland, 2013), 118.
2. *Variety*, April 1959, 6.
3. Seymour Korman, "Five Dozen Suits!," *Chicago Tribune Magazine*, September 1954, 34.
4. Robert Evans, *The Kid Stays in the Picture* (London: Hyperion, 1994), 75–76.
5. John B. Murray, *Brett Halsey: Art or Instinct in the Movies* (Baltimore: Midnight Marquee Press 2008), 123–124.
6. Jean Negulesco, *Things I Did...and Things I Think I Did*, 137.
7. Roy Newquist, *Conversations with Joan Crawford* (Secaucus, NJ: 1980), 104–105.
8. Laura Jacobs, *Vanity Fair*, 413.
9. Ibid., 414.
10. Robert Evans, *The Fat Lady Sings* (New York: It Books, 2013), 136.
11. Bob Willoughby, *The Star Makers: On Set with Hollywood's Greatest Directors* (London: Merrell Publishers, 2003), 100.
12. George Sanders, *Memoirs of a Professional Cad* (London: Dean Street Press, 2015), 138.
13. Emanuel Levy, *George Cukor, Master of Elegance* (New York: Morrow, 1994) 238.
14. "Rome Afire with Films Deals," *Variety*, January 1962, 5.
15. Alain Garel and François Guerif, *La Revue du Cinéma*, 52.
16. Ibid.
17. "Rome Afire with Films Deals," *Variety*, 5.
18. Alain Garel and François Guerif, *La Revue du Cinéma*, 52.
19. *Eros Magazine* 1 (Autumn 1962).
20. Hedda Hopper, "Looking at Hollywood," *Chicago Tribune*, date unknown.
21. "Appearance of Yank 'Pleasure' Unit a Reassuring Omen for Spaniards," *Variety*, June 1964, 1.
22. Philip Scheuer, "Negulesco's Pleasure Seekers," *Los Angeles Times*, 2 June 1964, C9.
23. Edda Hopper, "Looking at Hollywood: MacArthur Story to Be Made into Movie," *Chicago Tribune*, 21 April 1964, 16.

24. Tom Lisanti, *Fantasy Femmes of Sixties Cinema* (Jefferson, NC: McFarland, 2001), 84–85.
25. M. Pala and M. Villegas, *Film Ideal*, 521.
26. Irving Noe, "Noe News is Show News," *Valley Sun*, 2 August 1964, 46.
27. Gene Tierney, *Self-Portrait* (New York: Wyden Books, 1979), 240.
28. Ann-Margret, *Ann-Margret: My Story* (London: Orion, 1994), 124.
29. Mike Connolly, *Independent Star-News from Pasadena, California*, 76.

Chapter 10

1. Edda Hopper, "Looking at Hollywood," 6.
2. Alain Garel and François Guerif, *La Revue du Cinéma*, 53.
3. Charles Higham, *The Celluloid Muse*, 197.
4. "The Killer Heros," *Film Bulletin*, April 1970.
5. Stephen M. Silverman, *The Fox That Got Away: The Last Days of the Zanuck Dynasty at 20th Century-Fox* (Secaucus, NJ: Lyle Stuart, 1998), 155.
6. "Ronald Neame Exits: Negulesco Steps in," *Variety*, August 1969.
7. *Talking Pictures: Jean Negulesco Interview*, Transcript (London BBC 1988), roll 1.
8. Stephen M. Silverman, *The Fox That Got Away*, 158.
9. Leonard Mosley, *Zanuck: The Rise and Fall of Hollywood's Last Tycoon*, 494–495.
10. Ibid., 158.
11. John Goff, "'Hello-Goodbye' Seen as a Slim Box-Office Contender, *The Hollywood Reporter*, 6 July 1970, 3.
12. Jean Negulesco to Darryl Zanuck, April 15, 1971.
13. "Correspondence 1968–1971," *Jean and Dusty Negulesco Papers*, Margaret Harrick Library, Academy of Motion Picture Arts and Sciences, Beverly Hills, CA.
14. Malcom Abbey, email correspondence with the author, January 2016.
15. "Just for Variety," *Variety*, September 1983.
16. Stephen M. Silverman, *The Fox That Got Away*, 313.
17. John Houseman, "Royal Rumanian Movie Maker," *New York Times*, 24 February 1985.
18. Anne Head, "Negulesco: Master of the Arts," *Screen International*, 6 September 1986.
19. Bruno Villen, "Jean Negulesco," *Cinématograph*, October 1986, 5.
20. Alain Garel and François Guerif, *La Revue du Cinéma*, 54.
21. *Cine y Mas*, December 1990, 33.
22. Malcom Abbey, email correspondence with the author.
23. Guillermo Vilela, "100% Hollywood," *Cinématopraph*, February 1986, 10.

Bibliography

Allyson, June. *June Allyson*. New York: Putnam's, 1982.
Ann-Margret. *Ann-Margret: My Story*. London: Orion, 1994.
Astaire, Fred. *Steps in Time*. New York: Harpers and Brothers, 1959.
Bacall, Lauren. *By Myself*. New York: Knopf, 1978.
Barton, Ruth. *Hedy Lamarr, the Most Beautiful Woman in Film*. Lexington: The University Press of Kentucky, 2005.
Behlmer, Rudy. *Inside Warner Bros*. New York: Fireside/Simon & Schuster, 1987.
_____. *Memo from Darryl F. Zanuck: The Golden Years at Twentieth Century–Fox*. New York: Grove Press, 1993.
Blake, Robert. *Tales of a Rascal*. Willowdale, ON: Black Rainbow Publications, 2012.
Bret, David. *Joan Crawford: Hollywood Martyr*. New York: DaCapo Press, 2006.
Bubbeo, Daniel. *The Women of Warner Brothers*. Jefferson, NC: McFarland, 2001.
Capua, Michelangelo. *Deborah Kerr: A Biography*. Jefferson, NC: McFarland, 2011.
_____. *Janet Leigh: A Biography*. Jefferson, NC: McFarland, 2013.
Caron, Leslie. *Thank Heaven: My Autobiography*. New York: Viking Adult, 2009.
Coffin, Leslie L. *Lew Ayres*. Jackson: University Press of Mississippi, 2012.
Crane, Cheryl. *Lana: The Memories, The Myths, The Movies*. Philadelphia: Running Press, 2008.
Desmond, Florence. *Florence Desmond by Herself*. London: Harrap & Co., 1953.
Donati, William. *Ida Lupino: A Biography*. Lexington: University Press of Kentucky, 1996.
Dumont, Hervé. *Frank Borzage: The Life and Films of a Hollywood Romantic*. Jefferson, NC: McFarland, 2006.
Ephron, Henry. *We Thought We Could Do Anything*. New York: Norton, 1977.
Evans, Robert. *The Fat Lady Sings*. New York: It Books, 2013.
_____. *The Kid Stays in the Picture*. London: Hyperion, 1994.
Eyman, Scott. *Ernst Lubitsch: Laughter in Paradise*. New York: Simon & Schuster, 1993.
Fallaci, Oriana. *I sette peccati di Hollywood*. Milano: Longanesi, 1958.
Fontaine, Joan. *No Bed of Roses*. London: W.H. Allen, 1978.
Froug, William. *The Screenwriter Looks at the Screenwriter*. New York: Macmillan, 1972.
Gehman, Geoff. *Down but Not Quite Out in Hollowweird: A Documentary in Letters of Eric Knight*. Latham, MD: The Scarecrow Press, 1998.
Graham, Sheilah. *The Garden of Allah*. London: W.H. Allen, 1971.
Grisson, Candace Ursula. *Fitzgerald and Hemingway on Film*. Jefferson, NC: McFarland, 2001.
Guild, Leo. *Zanuck: Hollywood's Last Tycoon*. Los Angeles: Holloway House, 1970.
Harris, Warren G. *Sophia Loren: A Biography*. New York: Simon & Schuster, 1998.
Higham, Charles. *The Celluloid Muse: Hollywood Directors Speak*. London: Angus & Robertson, 1969.
_____. *Hollywood Cameramen*. London: Thames and Hudson, 1970.
Johnson, Nunnally. *The Letters of Nunnally Johnson*. New York: Knopf, 1981.
Junor, Penny. *Burton: The Man Behind the Myth*. London: Sedgwick & Jackson, 1985.
Knight, Arthur, and Eliot Elisofon. *The Hollywood Style*. London: Macmillan, 1969.
Lake, Veronica. *Veronica: The Autobiography of Veronica Lake*. New York: The Citadel Press, 1971.
Lamarr, Hedy. *Ecstasy and Me*. London: W.H. Allen, 1967.
Levant, Oscar. *The Memoirs of an Amnesiac*. New York: Putnam, 1965.
Levy, Emanuel. *George Cukor, Master of Elegance*. New York: Morrow, 1994.
Linet, Beverly. *Ladd: The Life, The Legend, The Tragedy*. New York: Arbor House, 1979.
Lisanti, Tom. *Fantasy Femmes of Sixties Cinema*. Jefferson, NC: McFarland, 2001.
Loren, Sophia. *Yesterday, Today, Tomorrow: My Life*. London: Simon & Schuster, 2015.

McDowall, Roddy. *Double Exposure, Take Three*. New York: Morrow, 1993.

Meyer, William R. *Warner Brothers Directors: The Hard-Boiled, the Comic and the Weepers*. New Rochelle, NY: Arlington House, 1978.

Mosley, Leonard. *Zanuck: The Rise and Fall of Hollywood's Last Tycoon*. Boston: Little Brown, 1984.

Murray, John B. *Brett Halsey: Art or Instinct in the Movies*. Baltimore: Midnight Marquee Press, 2008.

Negulesco, Jean. *Things I Did ... and Things I Think I Did*. New York: Linden Press/Simon & Schuster, 1984.

Newquist, Roy. *Conversations with Joan Crawford*. Secaucus, NJ: 1980.

Norton, Leslie, and Frederic Franklin. *Frederic Franklin: A Biography of the Ballet Star*. Jefferson, NC: McFarland, 2007.

Nott, Robert. *He Ran All the Way: The Life of John Garfield*. New York: Limelight Editions, 2003.

O'Connor, Gary. *Alec Guinness: Master of Disguise*. London: Hodder & Stoughton, 1994.

O'Hara, Maureen. *'Tis Herself: A Memoir*. London: Simon & Schuster, 2004.

Parish, Robert. *The RKO Gals*. London: Ian Allan, 1974.

Presle, Micheline. *Di(s)gressions: Conversations avec Stéphane Lambert*. Paris: Stock, 2007.

Quigley, Martin, Jr. *New Screen Techniques*. New York: Quigley Publishing Company, 1953.

Quirk, Lawrence. *Claudette Colbert: An Illustrated Biography*. New York: Crown, 1985.

_____. *Jane Wyman: The Actress and the Woman*. New York: Dumber Books, 1986.

_____. *The Passionate Life of Bette Davis*. London: Robson Books, 1994.

Rollyson, Carl E. *Dana Andrews: Hollywood Enigma*. Jackson Hole, WY: University Press of Mississippi, 2012.

Sennett, Ted. *Masters of Menace: Greenstreet and Lorre*. New York: Dutton, 1979.

Shevey, Sandra. *The Marilyn Scandal*. London: Sandra Shevey Books, 2007.

Shores, Sylvia, and Marion Abbott Bundy. *Talking Pictures*. New York: The New Press, 1994.

Silverman, Stephen M. *The Fox That Got Away: The Last Days of the Zanuck Dynasty at 20th Century-Fox*. Secaucus, NJ: Lyle Stuart, 1998.

Skretvedt, Randy. *Laurel and Hardy: The Magic Behind the Movies*. Beverly Hills, CA: Moonstone Press, 1987.

Smith, David L. *Sitting Pretty: The Life and Times of Clifton Webb*. Jackson: University Press of Mississippi, 2011.

Smith, Ella. *Starring Miss Barbara Stanwyck*. New York: Crown Publisher, 1985.

Stine, Whitney. *No Guts, No Glory: Conversations with Bette Davis*. London: Virgin Books, 1990.

Strait, Raymond. *Mrs. Howard Hughes*. Los Angeles: Holloway House, 1970.

Swindell, Larrey. *Body and Soul: The Story of John Garfield*. New York: Morrow, 1975.

Tavernier, Bertrand. *Amis Américains: Entretiens avec les Grands Auteurs d'Hollywood*. Arles: Actes Sud, 2008.

Thomas, Bob. *Clown Prince of Hollywood: The Antic Life and Times of Jack L. Warner*. New York: McGraw-Hill Publishing, 1990.

_____. *Joan Crawford: A Biography*. New York: Simon & Schuster, 1979.

Tierney, Gene. *Self-Portrait*. New York: Wyden Books, 1979.

Tranberg, Charles. *Fred MacMurray: A Biography*. Albany, GA: BearManor Media, 2007.

_____. *I Love the Illusion: The Life and Career of Agnes Moorehead*. Albany, GA: BearManor Media, 2007.

Trojan, Michael. *A Rose for Mrs. Miniver: The Life of Greer Garson*. Lexington: University of Kentucky Press, 1999.

Turner, Lana. *Lana: The Lady, the Legend, the Truth*. New York: Dutton, 1982.

Von Gunden, Kenneth. *Alec Guinness: The Films*. Jefferson, NC: McFarland, 1987.

Wagner, Laura. *Anne Francis: The Life and Career*. Jefferson, NC: McFarland, 2011.

Wagner, Robert. *Pieces of My Heart: A Life*. London: Hutchinson, 2009.

Warren, Dough. *Betty Grable: The Reluctant Movie Queen*. London: Robson Books, 1982.

Wasson, Ben. *Count no' Count: Flashback to Faulkner*. Jackson: University Press of Mississippi, 1983.

Wilkerson, Tichi, and Marcia Bore. *The Hollywood Reporter: The Golden Era*. New York: Coward-McCann, 1984.

Willoughby, Bob. *The Star Makers: On Set with Hollywood's Greatest Directors*. London: Merrell Publishers, 2003.

Youngkin, Stephen D. *The Lost One: A Life of Peter Lorre*. Lexington: The University Press of Kentucky, 2005.

Zolotow, Maurice. *Marilyn Monroe*. New York: Harcourt, Brace & Co., 1960.

Index

Abbey, Malcom 2, 130–131, 132
The Adventures of Don Juan 46–47, 215
The Affairs of Adelaide see *The Forbidden Street*
The African Queen 72
Ahern, Brian 23, 47, 53, 79, 113
Akhavan, Mostafa 125
Akins, Zoë 82
Albert, Katherine 82
Alice in Movieland 25, 186
Alice in Wonderland 16, 214
All About Eve 73
The All American Bands 197
All Star Melody Master 200
Allyson, June 93–94
Ambler, Eric 30, 31
And Now Tomorrow 47
Anderson, Ruth Edwin see Negulesco, Dusty
Andress, Ursula 120, 129
Andrews, Dana 57
Angela see *Jessica*
Ann-Margret 121, 122, 123
Apple Pie Bed see *Jessica*
Aristophanes 117
Armstrong, Neil 126
Army Show 195–196
Astaire, Fred 96–97, 98
Astaire, Phyllis 96
Astor, John Jacob 78
Astor, Mary 36
At the Stroke of Twelve 26, 190
Atwill, Lionel 37
Auer, Misha 16
Avery, Stephen M. 19
Avery Morehouse, Stephen 44
Ayres, Lew 47, 48, 50

Bacall, Lauren 58, 72, 82, 83, 84, 85, 86, 87, 93–94, 105–106
Bad Girl 17
Bagdad on the Subway see *O'Henry's Full House*
Baker, Diane 113, 114
Balfour, L. G. 67

Balzac 3, 129
Bar, Jacques 119
Bardot, Brigitte 119
The Barefoot Banker 130, 213
Barnes, Binnie 22, 23
Barnes, George 27
Barrett, Michael 125
Barrymore, Ethel 99
Barton, Clara 25
Basehart, Richard 79
Baxter, Anne 75
A Bedtime Story 16, 211
Bell, Vernon 73
The Bells 215
Belmondo, Jean Paul 129
The Beloved Brat 22, 209
Bemelmans, Ludwig 216
Ben Hur 112
Bergman, Ingrid 58
Bertensson, Serge 54
The Best of Everything 112–115, 179–181
The Best Years of Our Lives 57
Bickford, Charles 50, 53, 104
The Big Broadcast 16
The Big Fall see *Under My Skin*
The Big Show 104–105, 212
Binyon Claude 93
Blair, Charlie 57
Blake, Robert 42
Blanke, Henry 30, 31
Blaustein, Julian 67, 68
The Blessing see *Count Your Blessings*
Bogart, Humphrey 32, 35, 36, 44, 58, 72, 86, 105
La Bohème 29, 130, 215, 217
Bonnet, Theodore 63
Borchers, Cornell 104
Borrah MInevitch and His Harmonica School 195
Borzage, Frank 17, 18, 20
Bosè, Lucia 177
Boy on a Dolphin 100–104, 131, 173–175, 214
Boyd, Stephen 113

Boyer, Charles 58
Brackett, Charles 78, 79, 83
Brâncuși, Constantin 7, 9
Brando, Marlon 47, 116
Brazzi, Rossano 89, 90, 107, 108, 109, 110, 212
Breen, Joseph 78
Breen, Richard L. 85
Brennan, Jay 21
Brennar, Walter 73, 74, 75
Brent, George 98
Breuning, Margaret 13
Britannia Mews see *The Forbidden Street*
Britannica Mews see *The Forbidden Street*
Bromfield, Louis 98, 100
Brooks, Leslie 29
Brooks, Richard 69
Brown, Clarence 98
Bruce, David 28
Bryant, Nana 25
Buffet, Bernard 58, 115, 118
Burnett, W.R. 35
Burton, Richard 99, 100
Busse, Henry 25, 27
Butterworth, Charlie 43

Cagney, James 25
Cahn, Sammy 115
Calhoun, Rory 85
California Junior Symphony 192–193
Calling All Girls 192
Camille 98
Campbell, Dorothy 43
Capitan Blood 20
Capra, Frank 131
Capriccio Español see *Spanish Fiesta*
Carioca Serenade 190
Carl Hoff and His Orchestra 192
Carnegie, Andrew 97
Carrere, Christine 107, 109
Carroll, Harrison 89
Carson, Jack 35

227

Index

Casablanca 32, 33
Caulfield, Joan 99, 100
Cavalcade of Dance 26, 198
Cavalleria Rusticana 18, 214
Cernat, Manuela 6, 132
A Certain Smile 9, 89, 105, 107–109, 212
Cesar, Gloria 73
Chakiris, George 121
Chaney, Lon 48
Chang, Grace 116
Chaplin, Charlie 12, 15
Chapman, Marguerite 29
Charisse, Cyd 95–96, 120
Chertok, Jack 33
Chevalier, Maurice 21, 96, 110, 111, 116, 117, 213
Chivalry 18, 214
Chodorov, Edward 53, 54
Cifariello, Antonio 117
City for Conquest 25, 207
City Lights 15
Clark, Dane 44, 45
Clarke, Charles G. 58
Clayton, Jack 59
Cliff Edwards and His Buckaroos 188
Clift, Montgomery 66
Cobb, Lee J. 53
A Coffin for Dimitrios see *The Mask of Dimitrios*
Cohn, Harry 43, 44, 86
Colbert, Claudette 58–61, 66, 97
Colby, Anita 32, 36, 43
Collier, John 36
Colman, Ronald 47
Compton, Fay 57
Connolly, Bobby 21
Connolly, Mike 123
Conover, David 85
Conover, Harry 43
The Conspirators 32–35
The Cop and the Anthem see *O'Henry's Full House*
Coppel, Alec 100
Corcoran, Donna 76, 77
Cortez, Ricardo 27
Cossack, Don 63
Costello, Dolores 22
Coulouris, George 32
Count Your Blessings 89, 109, 110–111, 178–179, 212
Cover Girl 43
Coward, Noël 119
Craig, Helen 47
Crain, Jeanne 69, 69, 89
Cram, Mildred 131
Crash Donovan 20–21, 205–206
Crashing Through see *Crashing Donovan*
Crawford, Joan 39–42, 73, 113
Crawford, Michael 127, 128
Crisp, Donald 37

Croccolo, Carlo 118
Cry of the Swamp see *Lure of the Wilderness*
Cukor, George 82, 116, 119
Cummings, Robert 23
The Curious Mr. Clark 215
Curly Top 96
Currie, Finlay 65
The Curtain Iron 67
Curtiz, Michael 20, 46, 199, 205

Daddy Long Legs 1, 95–98, 106, 169–171
Dahl, Arlene 93, 94
Dalio, Marcel 116
Dall, John 39
Dangerous 28
Daniels, Bebe 27
Danilova, Alexandra 26, 191
Dantine, Helmut 32
The Dark Love see *Road House*
Dark Victory 32
Darnell, Linda 69, 70
Darren, James 121
Darrieux, Danielle 23
The Daughter of Rosie O'Grady 193
Daves, Delmer 44, 47
David, Emanuel 58
Davidson, Roy 42
Davies, Marion 43
Davis, Bette 18, 27–28, 29, 31, 40, 47, 50, 72–73, 139
Davis, Luther 105
Davis, Nancy 104
Death of a Gunfighter 216
Deep Valley 44–46, 53, 142
Degas 26
de Havilland, Olivia 20, 58, 199
De Laurentiis, Dino 216
Delon, Alain 116, 215
De Mille, Cecil Blunt 86
Derek, John 121
De Shishmareff, Kyrill 21
De Sica, Vittorio 116, 117
Desmond, Florence 59–60
The Devil in the Flesh 62
De Wolfe, Elsie 216
Diaghilev 7
The Diary of Anne Frank 107
Dickinson, Angie 116, 117 118, 212–213
Dieterle, William 27
Dietrich, Marlene 66
DiMaggio, Joe 159
Dinov 6
Disraeli 63
The Dog in the Orchard 26, 188
Domingo, Placido 217
Don Cossack Chorus 193
Donat, Robert 47
Douglas, Kirk 58, 98, 216
Douglas, Paul 93

Doyle, Laird 133
Drake, Betsy 101
Draper, Ruth 12
Dry Martini 98
Ducreux, Louis 110
Duhamel, Georges 7
Duncan, Isadora 12
Dunne, Irene 63–64, 65, 66
Dupont, Ewald André 214
Durant, Tim 23

Ed Sullivan's Broadway 215
Emerson, Faye 35, 136
Emil Coleman and Orchestra 193
Enescu, George 4
Engel, Sam 96, 171
Enter Madame! 18, 19, 204
Ephron, Henry 95, 96, 98, 107, 177
Ephron, Phoebe 96, 98
Epstein, Julius J. 68
Epstein, Philip G. 68
Erskine, Chester 125
Erskine, Johnson 3, 6
Et Maintenant 120, 216
Eunson, Dale 82
Evans, Robert 112, 114
Executive Suite 95
Expensive Husbands 21, 207–208
Eyewitness News 120, 213
Eyman, Scott 52

Fairbanks, Douglas, Sr. 29, 37
Fairbanks, Laetitia 29
A Farewell to Arms 17–18
Farmer, Francis 29
Farrow, John 69
Farwagi, André 217
Faulkner, William 16, 17, 44, 211
Faure, Élie 11, 15
Fehr, Rudy 33
Feldman, Charles K. 53, 56, 83, 84, 215
Ferdinand I, King 6
Ferrer, Mel 102, 129
Ferry, Fefe 87
Field, Gracie 63
Fight for Your Lady 21, 208
The Fighting Lady 67
Fitzgerald, Geraldine 35, 37
The Flag of Humanities 3, 187
Florian, Sabina see Negulescu, Sabina
Flynn, Errol 20, 29, 37, 46, 70, 77
Foch, Nina 112
Follies see *Et Maintenant*
Fontaine, Joan 23, 32, 58, 97, 107, 108, 109
Food and Magic 26, 201–202
Foote, Michael 63
The Forbidden Street 56–57, 146

Ford, Glenn 93
Ford, John 58
Forever 131, 217
Foujita 8
The Four Horsemen of the Apocalypse 10
Fox, Freddie 56
Fox, Sidney 18, 21
Foy, Brian 27
Franciosa, Anthony 121, 122
Francis, Anne 67, 70, 71, 75
Francis, Kay 37
Franklin, Frederic 26
Franklin, Sidney 110
Freddie Fisher and His Band 186
Freddy Martin and Orchestra 188
Fredericks, Ellsworth 50
French, Lloyd 186
Furstenberg, Ira 128

Gable, Clark 28, 53
Gaîté Parisienne see *The Gay Parisian*
Garbo, Greta 62–63, 98, 115
Gardner, Ava 98, 116
Gardner, Nelia 105
Garfield, John 36, 39, 40, 41, 42, 44, 61, 62
Garson, Green 76–77, 78
Gassman, Vittorio 89
The Gay Parisian 26
Gaynor, Janet 86, 96
Gaynor, Mitzi 96
Gentleman's Agreement 62
Gentlemen Prefer Blondes 84
Gershwin, George 39
Gessner, Elizabeth 48
Gheorghiu, Mihnea 132
The Gift of Love 105–107, 175–176
Gilbert, John 62, 115
Gillaizeau, Genevieve see Gilles, Genevieve
Gilles, Genevieve 127, 128, 129, 130, 186, 216
The Girl in the Wall 126, 216
Girls on Probation see *The Beloved Brat*
Give Me Liberty 25
Give Me This Woman see *The Conspirators*
Glazer, Benjamin 16, 17–18, 29, 39
Glen Gray and the Casa Loma Orchestra 189
Goddard, Paulette 43
Goirman, Raliu 36
Gold, Zachary 39
Golden Boy 39
Goldstein, Robert 87
Goldwyn, Samuel 87
Gone with the Wind 26

Goodin, Peggy 67, 68
Goodrich, Frances 107
Gottlieb, Alex 44
Gould, Elliott 124
Grable, Betty 82, 83, 84, 85, 86, 87, 215
Graham, Sheilah 43
Grahame, Gloria 93
Grand Hotel 79
Grandfather's Follies 199–200
Grant, Gary 18–19, 96, 101, 102
Granville, Bonita 22
The Grapes of Wrath 58
The Great Fall see *Under My Skin*
The Greatest Story Ever Told 120, 207
The Greeks Had a Word for It 82
Greenstreet, Sydney 30, 31, 32, 33, 34, 36, 37, 130, 137, 217
Grot, Anton 34
Gruber, Frank 31, 135
Gruen, Margaret 83
Guinness, Alec 63, 65, 66, 84
Gurie, Sigrid 23
Guttman, Lorraine see Brooks, Leslie
Gwenn, Edmund 75

Hackett, Albert 107, 177, 186
Hakim, Andre 75, 127
Hal Kemp and His Orchestra 29, 189, 200
Haller, Ernest 26
Halsey, Brett 112
Hamilton, John 25
Hamilton, Mahlon 96
Hammett, Dashiell 27
Hard Luck Dame see *Singapore Woman*
Hardy, Oliver 21
Harris, Helmer 47
Harris, Richard 216
Harris, Wanda 107
Harrison, Rex 124
Hart, Moss 87
Hartford, Dee 88
Haskin, Byron 20
Hathaway, Henry 75
Havlicek, Winifred see Hayers, Winifred
Hawks, Howard 44, 75, 87, 88
Hayakawa, Sessue 60
Hayers, Suzanne 10, 44
Hayers, Winifred 10, 11, 12, 14, 18, 22–23, 44
Hayes, Helen 17, 18, 64
Hayes, W. R. 215
Hayward, Lillie 21
Hayward, Susan 70
Hayworth, Rita 43, 98
Hearst, William R. 20

Hearts Divided 20, 211
Heflin, Vann 93, 94, 101, 102
The Heiress 59
Hellman, George S. 12
Hello-Goodbye 127–129, 130, 185–186
Hemingway, Ernest 17, 18, 61, 62, 150
Henreid, Paul 32, 33, 34, 35
Henry Busse and His Orchestra 25, 27, 187
Hepburn, Audrey 65, 88, 107, 129
Herbert, Hugh 116, 117
Heroes of Yucca see *The Invincible Six*
Hertz, David 54
Heston, Charles 93, 112
High Sierra 27, 35
Hilliard, Harriet 196
Himber, Richard 27, 192
Hirliceanu, Elena 3, 9
Hit Parade of the Gay Nineties 198
Hitchcock, Alfred 2, 36, 58, 65
Hitchcock, Patricia 65
Hobson, Valerie 66
Holden, William 29, 39, 115
Hollingshead, Gordon 25, 26
Holm, Celeste 54
Holt, Tim 199
Holy Matrimony 58
Hopkins, Miriam 16–17, 37, 211
Hopper, Hedda 65, 80–81, 99, 107, 112, 120, 124, 216
The House on 92nd Street 67
Hoveyda, Amir-Abbas 129
How to Marry a Millionaire 1, 78, 82–87, 89, 91, 120, 164–166, 213
Howard, Leslie 37
Hudson, Rock 88, 136
Hughes, Howard 70, 87
Humoresque 1, 39–42, 112, 140–14, 212
Hunchback of Notre Dame 101
Hunter, Ian 37
Hunter, Jeffrey 68, 74, 75, 86
Hurok, Sol 76, 215
Hurst, Fanny 39
The Husband's Queen 43
Huston, John 27, 29, 30, 36, 58, 69, 215
Hutton, Betty 64
Hyer, Martha 113, 115

I Hear America Singing 29, 215
I Wasn't Born Yesterday 35
The Spirit of West Point 26, 194–195
Ice Frolics 215
I'd Climb the Highest Mountain 215

Igiroşanu, Horia 7
Illingworth, Sir Gordon 78
Impulse see *The Forbidden Street*
Ingram, Rex 9, 10
The Invincible Six 125–126, 129, 184–185
It Happened One Night 21
Iturbi, Joseph 44
Ivano Paul 16

Jacks, Robert 73
Jacobs, W. W. 215
Jaffe, Mildred 20, 23
Jaffe, Rona 112
Jaffe, Sam 23
Jamois, Marguerite 112
Jan Garber and His Orchestra 25, 187
Jean-Christophe 215
Jerome, Moe 215
Jessica 117–119, 181–182, 212, 213
Joan of Arc 42
Jobert, Marlene 129
Joe Reichman and His Orchestra 25, 187, 197, 200–201
Johnny Belinda 1, 39, 47–51, 61, 112, 120, 143–145, 213
Johns, Glynis 66
Johnson, Nora 58–59, 65
Johnson, Nunnally 58–59, 63, 65, 71, 72, 73, 82, 85, 86, 87, 119, 155, 166
Jones, Edward 63
Jones, Jennifer 149
Jourdan, Louis 87, 89, 90, 112, 113, 115
Joyce, Brenda 98
Judith and the Holophernes 86, 215
Jurgens, Curt 125, 127, 128, 177

Keane, Margaret 113
Keith, Agnes Newtown 58, 59
Keith, Brian 121, 122
Keith, Slim 44
Kemp, Hal 29, 189, 200
Kent, Rockwell 12, 13, 14
Kerr, Deborah 110, 111
Keuning, Mark 59
Kiki 8
Kilgallen, Dorothy 87
The Killer Heroes see *The Invincible Six*
Kimble, Laurence 22
Kiss and Make Up 19, 28, 29, 203–204
Klein, Wally 22
Knight, Eric 18–19, 214
Knotter, Isabella 22
Knowles, Patric 59
Koach, Howard 36
Korda, Alexander 110

Koster, Henry 75, 95, 96, 100
Krasner, Milton 109, 167
Kwan, Nancy 116

Ladd, Alan 101–102, 103
Laemmle, Edward 20, 206
Lake, Veronica 32
Lamarr, Hedy 32, 33–34, 35
Lamas, Fernando 93
The Land of the Trembling Earth see *Lure of the Wilderness*
Landi, Elissa 18
Landis, Carol 29
Lange, Hope 110, 112, 113, 114
Lasker, Ed 120
Lassie Come Home 18
The Last Leaf see *O'Henry's Full House*
Laura 94
Laurel, Stan 21
Laurents, Pierre 8
Lauro, Achille 216
Lautrec, Toulouse 26, 132
Lawrence, Andre 121
Lean, David 120
Lederer, Charles 20
Le Gallienne, Richard 12, 13
Leicester, James 42
Leigh, Vivien 116
Leighton, Buddy 23
Leighton, Isabel 21
Leighton, Margaret 112
Leisen, Mitchell 76, 215
Lenin 8
Leo Reisman and His Orchestra 192
Léontovich, Eugénie 99, 172
Leslie, Joan 25
Lesson in Love 19, 214
The Letter 29
Levant, Oscar 39, 41–42
Levathes, Peter 119
Lewis, Leopold 215
Lie Down in Darkness 215
Lindfors, Viveca 46
Lindgren, Orley 62
Listen to the Bands 200–201
Little Caesar 35
The Little Horse 105
The Little Rascals see *Our Gang*
Little Women 89
Litvak, Anatole 1, 10, 25, 30, 67, 207
Liu, Lisa 116
Lockwood, Grey 212
Lodge, John 18
Loggia, Robert 120
Lollobrigida, Gina 101
Long Day's Journey into Night 107
Lord, Robert 35
Loren, Sophia 101, 102–103, 104, 116, 131, 175, 212

Lorre, Peter 30, 31, 32, 34, 35, 36, 37–38, 130, 137, 217
Lorring, Joan 37
Love, Marilyn 213
Loy, Myrna 98
Lubin, Arthur 22
Lubitsch, Ernst 20, 52
Lund, John 96
Lupino, Ida 28, 44, 45–46, 53, 54, 55, 58
Lure of the Wilderness 73–75, 157–159, 212
Lust for Life 98, 216
Lydia Bailey 69–71, 155–157
Lynley, Carol 121, 123
Lynn, Jeffrey 28
Lyon, Ben 64
Lysistrata 117, 118
Lytess, Natasha 83, 85

MacArthur, James 178
MacMurray, Fred 93, 99
Madame Curie 76
Magloire 71
The Maltese Falcon 27, 29–30, 215
Mammoulian, Robert 18
The Man Who Broke His Heart 18, 214
Mangano, Silvana 86
Mankiewicz, Joseph L. 69
Margaret, Princess 98
Marie Green and Her Merrie Men 188–189
Marie of Edinburgh, Princess see Marie of Romania, Princess
Marie of Romania, Princess 11
Marin, Edwin L. 207
Marshall, Brenda 28, 29
Marshall, Roger 127
Marshall, William 62, 70
Martha 217
Martin, Dean 119
Martin, Freddy 188, 197
Martin, Tony 120, 216
Marton, Andrew 217
Marx, Samuel 129, 216
Mascagni, Pietro 18, 214
The Mask of Dimitrios 1, 2, 29–33, 130, 134–136, 212, 217
Mason, Richard 115
Massine, Léonide 26
Mastroianni, Marcello 119, 216
Mathieu, Charles 43
Mathis, Johnny 108
Matthews, A.E. 57
Mature, Victor 53, 70
Maugham, Somerset 215
May the Best Wife Win see *Woman's World*
McCarey, Leo 119
McCarthy, Frank 67
McCarthy, Nobu 116

McCord, Todd 50
McGuiness, James K. 20
McGuire, Dorothy 47, 89, 90, 120
McIntyre, Harry 129
McKay, Gardner 121, 123
McNally, Stephen 49
McNamara, Maggie 89, 90
McSherry Mary 78
Merrill, Dina 122
Merrill, Gary 71, 72, 73
Michelangelo 8
Michelle, Donna 122
Midnight Alibi 26
The Midwife of Point Clery see *Jessica*
Mildred Pierce 39
Milland, Ray 66, 96
Miller, Anne 32
Miller, Arthur 116
Minnelli, Vincent 89, 98, 216
Mirea, George Demetrescu 6
Mitchell, Cameron 85
Mitchum, Jim 125
Mitchum, Robert 92, 101
Mitford, Nancy 110
Modigliani, Amedeo 7, 8, 132
Moffat, Ivan 100, 102
Mojica, José 18, 214
The Monkey's Paw 215
Monroe, Marilyn 82–84, 85, 86, 87, 89, 92, 94, 116, 119–120, 165, 213
Montgomery, Robert 119, 216
Moorehead, Agnes 49, 50, 51, 76, 116, 117
Moreno, Rita 116
Morison, Patricia 29
Moross, Jerome 136
Morris, Wayne 44
Mrs. Miniver 76
The Mudlark 63–66, 67, 84, 151–154, 212
Mussolini, Benito 19
Mussolini, Vittorio 22
My Favorite Wife 119
My Mother and Mr. McChesney see *Scandal at Scourie*
My Old Man see *Under My Skin*

Napier, Alan 23
Neame, Richard 127
Near My God to Thee see *Titanic*
Negri, Pola 136
Negulesco, Christina "Tina" 119, 213
Negulesco, Dusty 42–44, 48, 51, 54–55, 56, 57, 62, 63, 69, 71, 86, 87–88, 89, 90–91, 93, 94, 97, 102, 104, 105, 113, 115, 117, 119, 120, 124, 125, 129, 131, 132, 213
Negulesco, Gabrielle "Gaby" 119, 213

Negulescu, Aneta 3
Negulescu, Athena 3
Negulescu, Costea 6, 7
Negulescu, Gabriela 3
Negulescu, Georghe "Ghiţă" 3, 4, 6, 7, 8, 9
Negulescu, Sabina 3, 6, 36, 126
Negulescu, Virginia 3
Negulescu. Georgeta 3, 36
Nelson, Ozzie 27, 196
Nelson, Ruth 39
Nestor, John 129
New Orleans 19, 214; see also *To-Night We Live*
Newman, Alfred 115, 171
Newman, Lionel 184
Niven, David 37, 63, 96
Nobody Lives Forever 35–36, 41, 139–140, 212
Noël-Noël 117
Norman, Barry 213
Nureyev, Rudolph 125
Nuyen, Francis 116
Nye, Ben 64

O'Brien, Marianne 32
Odets, Clifford 39
Offenbach 26
O'Hara, Maureen 56, 57, 105
O. Henry's Bagdad on the Subway see *O. Henry's Full House*
O. Henry's Full House 75, 76, 159–161
Olivier, Laurence 63, 120, 216
O'Neill, Eugene 107
Ophuls, Max 110
Oppenheim, E. Phillips 119, 120, 216
Orsatti, Frank 30, 63
Osborn, Paul 115
Other Winters, Other Springs 129, 216
Our Gang 42
Our Love see *The Gift of Love*
Over the Wall 199
Ozzie Nelson and His Orchestra 196

Paget, Debra 159
Palmer, Adele 115, 181
Papa's Delicate Condition 98
Paris Calling 29, 206–207
Paris, Texas 120
Parker, Eleanor 36, 40, 47, 93
Parker, Suzy 112, 113, 115
Parrish, Robert 69
Passage Between Two Seas 217
Passage to Marseille 33
Passenger List see *Titanic*
Passion Flower Hotel 216–217
Patrick, John 115
Patton, Virginia 199
Payne, John 105
Pearlberg, William 56

Peck, Gregory 88, 96, 216
Peluso, Adelina 90
Perry, Joan 44
Peters, Jean 69, 70, 74–75, 76, 89, 90, 93
Petit, Pascale 116
Petit, Roland 97, 98
Petrescu, Constin 8
The Phantom President 16, 211
Philipe, Gérard 62
Philips, Duncan 13, 14, 132
Phone Call from a Stranger 71–72, 154–155, 212, 213
Picasso, Pablo 8, 97, 132
Pickford, Mary 29, 96
Pickles, Vivien 128
Pidgeon, Walter 76, 77, 78
The Playgirls 191
The Pleasure Is All Mine 86, 215
The Pleasure Seekers 121–123, 182–184
Ponti, Carlo 101, 216
Portrait of a Star 212
Powell, William 85
Power, Tyrone 66, 70, 87, 98
Prelle, Micheline see Presle, Micheline
Preminger, Otto 92, 207
Prentiss, Paula 122
Presle, Micheline 61–62, 70
Presley, Elvis 196
The Pride and the Passion 101
The Pride of the Marines 36
Private Lives 119
Prokosch, Frederic 32, 34
Prosperi, Franco 125, 126
Puccini, Giacomo 29, 215, 217
Purdom, Edmund 79

Qahremanan see *The Invincible Six*
Quine, Richard 116, 207
Quinn, Anthony 101
Quirk, Lawrence 59

Radji, Parviz C. 129
The Rage of Paris 23
Rain 41
Rainer, Louise 21
Rains, Claude 37
The Rains of Ranchipur 98–100, 171–173
Ransford, Maurice 78
The Rape of the White Dove 129, 216
Rapsody in Blue 39
Rathbone, Basil 23
Ratoff, Gregory 75, 76 117
Ray, Andrew 64
Ray, Nicholas 69
Ray, Ted 64
Reagan, Ronald 25
The Reality Trip 213
Reinhardt, Wolfgang 37–38

Index

Reisch, Walter 78, 163
Reisman, Leo 27, 192
Remick, Lee 112
Rennie, Michael 71, 99
Renoir, Jean 73
Renoir, Pierre-August 9
Reynolds, Debbie 86, 112
Riber, Willy 79
Richard Himber and Orchestra 192
Richards, Stephens 189
Richardson, Ralph 63
Ridgely, John 44
Riesling 8
Rinehart, Mary Roberts 26
Rio 23, 210–211
Ritt, Martin 112
Ritter, Thelma 78–79, 97
River of No Return 92, 207
Roach, Hal 21–221
Road House 1, 53–56, 145–146
Roaring Guns 199
The Robe 82, 83, 98
Roberts, Kenneth 69
Roberts, Stephen 17, 18
Robertson, Dale 68, 69, 70, 71
Robinson, Casey 20, 61
Roche, France 213
Rockefeller, David 124
Roeca, Sam 126, 216
Rogell, Sid 89
Rogers, Charles 21
Rogers, Ginger 97
Rolland, Romain 215
Roman Holiday 87
Romero, Cesar 70
Room at the Top 115
Rose, Helen 99
Rosher, Charles 27
Ross, Frank 98, 99
Ross Wyle, Alexa 71
Rossellini, Roberto 89
Rotha, Paul 18
Rox, John 15
Rubin, Mann 112
Rudie, Evelyn 106
Runyon, Damon 26
Rush, Barbara 74, 86

Sagan, Françoise 105, 107–108
St. John, Jill 122
Sand Against the Wind 119, 216
Sanders, George 87, 115
Sandstrom, Flora 116, 216
Satan Met a Lady 27
Saul, Oscar 53
Scandal at Scourie 76–78, 163–164
Schary, Dore 76, 78
Scholl, Jack 215
Scott, Zachary 31
The Sea Hawk 29
Seaton, George 69
Secondari, John H 89

Sellers, Peter 129, 216
Selznick, David 32
Sentimental Journey 105
Sergava, Katya 15
Seventh Heaven 17
Sex in the City 115
Shadburne, Sherry 29
Sharp, Margery 56
Shayne, Robert 199
She Hired a Husband see *Expensive Husbands*
Shearer, Norma 28, 119, 216
Sheridan, Ann 19, 29, 32, 35, 44
Sheridan, Clara Lou *see* Sheridan, Ann
Sherman, Vincent 47
A Ship Is Born 26, 201
Sidney, Bob 122
Siegel, Don 216
Siegel, Sol C. 69, 88–89, 91
Simmons, Jean 70
Sinatra, Frank 89, 101
Singapore Woman 1–2, 28–29, 133–134
Sirk, Douglas 1, 105
Six Hits and Miss 194
Skinnay Ennis and His Orchestra 25–26, 187–188, 197
Skouras, Spiros 64, 67, 91, 95, 101, 104, 105, 212
Smith, Alexis 25, 28
Smith, Constance 65
Smithee, Allen 216
Snody, Robert 58, 59
So Zwei Pechvogel 22
Soliz, Charita 116
Something's Got to Give 119
Sommer, Elke 125
Sommers, Edith 112, 117, 120, 121
A Son Comes Home 214
The Songs of the Songs 18, 211
South American Sway 200
Soutine, Chaïm 15
Spanish Fiesta 26, 191
Sperling, Milton 128
The Spiral Staircase 47
The Spirit of Annapolis 26, 193–194
Stanwyck, Barbara 29, 40, 79–80, 89
Stark, Ray 115, 116, 207
State Fair 122
Steele, Alfred 113
Steele, Anthony 64
Steiner, Max 50, 145
Stephens, Martin 110
Stevens, George 120
Stevens, Rose Ann 196
Stewart, James 66
Stewart, James K Reverend 44
Stokowski, Leopold 62
Storm in Haiti see *Lydia Bailey*
The Story Temple Drake 16–17, 50, 211

Strâmbu, Ipolit 6
Stratou, Dora 101
A Streetcar Named Desire 47
Streisand, Barbra 124
Stutsman, Judge Carl A. 23
Sullivan, Ed 25, 187, 214
Sullivan, Jack 31
Swamp Girl see *Lure of the Wilderness*
Swamp Water 73
Swanson, Gloria 66
Swarhout, Gladys 62
Sweetheart Serenade 198–199
Swigart, Franklin J. 22
Swiss Cheese see *Swiss Miss*
Swiss Miss 21–22, 209–210

Take Care of My Little Girl 67–69, 70, 152–154, 212
Taurog, Norman 16, 18, 121
Tedford, Charles L. 25
Temple, Shirley 96
Thank Your Lucky Stars 198
That Forsyte Woman 77
There Is No Place Like Rome see *Three Coins in the Fountain*
This Is the Night see *Tonight We Sing*
This Is Your Life 212
Thomas, Bob 41
Thompson, Harlan 19, 29, 204
Thorndyke, Sybil 57
Those Endearing Young Charms 31
Those Good Old Days 189
A Thousand and One Nights 43
Three and a Day 15–16, 133
Three Came Home 59–61, 148–149
Three Cheers for the Girls 196–197
Three Coins in the Fountain 78, 88–92, 93, 96, 98, 104, 107, 109, 120, 121, 123, 166–167, 169, 212, 213–214
Three for the Show 86, 215
Three Men and a Girl 139
Three Strangers 36–38, 138–139
Tierney, Gene 89, 94, 122
Tiffin, Pamela 121, 122, 123
Titanic 213
To-Night We Live 19, 214; see also *New Orleans*
Tobin, Genevieve 19
Todd, Richard 66
Tonight We Sing 76, 211, 215
Too Much of Everything see *The Beloved Brat*
Tosca 18, 204
Totheroh, Dan 44
Totten, Robert 216
Touvanova, Tamara 26
Travilla 68

Index

The Treasure House of Martin Hews 119, 120, 216
Trilling, Steve 47
Trotsky, Leon 8
Il Trovatore 18
Trundle, Steffie 52
Tunberg, Karl 110
Turner, Cheryl 99
Turner, Lana 98, 99
Tuttle, Frank 16, 19, 211
Twain, Mark 96
Twelve O'Clock High 67
Two Weeks in Another Town 89

Under My Skin 61–62, 149–151
The United States Army Air Force Band 194
The United States Marine Band 195
The United States Merchant Marine Cadet Corps Band 186
The United States Navy Band 195
The United States Service Bands 197–198
The University of Southern California Band and Glee Club 190
Utrillo, Maurice 8

Valdez, Luz 116
Valentino, Albert 62
Valentino, Rudolph 62
Van Gogh see *Lust for Life*
Vanderbilt, Cornelius 78
Varsi, Diane 112
Vicki see *Scandal at Scourie*
Vidor, Charles 69
Viertel, Salka 44
The Village of the Damned 110
Villaverde, Marquesa de 123

Vincenot, Louis 29
Vincent, Allen 47, 145
Vladova, Milada 26
The Voice That Thrilled the World 201
Von Cube, Irmgard "Irma" 47, 145
von Flotow, Friedrich 217
Von Frisch, Gunther 16

Wagner, Richard 193
Wagner, Robert 79, 80
Wald, Jerry 39–40, 41, 46, 47, 48, 50, 51, 88, 11–112, 113, 115, 215
Wallis, Hal 32–33
Walsh, Raoul 46, 215
Ward, Clayton 59
Warner, Jack 27, 30, 31, 32, 33, 34, 37, 39, 46, 47, 48, 50, 51, 56, 214
The Wave Dark 104, 202
Way Out West 22
The Way to Love 18, 211
Wayne, David 85
Wayne, John 101
We Believe in Love see *Three Coins in the Fountain*
Webb, Clifton 79, 87, 89–90, 93, 94, 95, 96, 100–101
Webster, Jean 96
Weisbart, David 120
Welles, Orson 129, 130, 217 102, 103
Westmore, Perc 41
Wheeler, Lyle 78
White Gardner, Neila 105
Whitman, Stuart 125
Whitman, Walt 29, 215
Widmark, Richard 53, 54, 55
Wilde, Cornel 53, 54–55, 93, 94

Wilder, Billy 48, 69
Wilder, Gene 213
William, Warren 27
Williams, Tennessee 47
Willoughby, Bob 114–115
Winchell, Walter 32
Winters, Shelley 71, 72, 86, 89
Wise, Robert 69
Woman from Singapore see *Singapore Woman*
Woman of My Life 216
Woman's World 93–95, 168–169
Women at War 26, 198
Wood, Natalie 116
The Wooden Horse 64
The World of Suzie Wong 115, 116, 119, 207
Wright, Joseph 68
Wright, T. C. 48
Wright, Teresa 47
Written on the Wind 105
Wyler Wiliam 69
Wyman, Jane 25, 48–50, 51, 144, 145
Wynn, Keenan 72

Yannidaki, Chryssoula 104
The Yearling 48
Young, Loretta 47
Young Man with a Horn 215

Zanuck, Darryl Francis 53–54, 55, 56, 58, 63, 65, 67, 70, 73, 75, 76, 78, 79, 82, 83, 84, 86, 87, 88–89, 91, 92, 93, 95–96, 98, 99, 101, 126–127, 128, 129, 25, 216, 217
Zanuck, Darrylin 73
Zanuck, Richard D. 87, 124
Zanuck, Virginia 95, 130
Zimablist, Efram, Jr. 121

www.ingramcontent.com/pod-product-compliance
Ingram Content Group UK Ltd.
Pitfield, Milton Keynes, MK11 3LW, UK
UKHW050532150426
5217IPUK00026B/1897